Awaken Healing Light

of the Tao

**Mantak Chia
and
Maneewan Chia**

AWAKEN HEALING LIGHT

HEALING TAO BOOKS/Huntington, New York

Editor: Judith Stein
Contributing Writers: Chuck Soupios, Michael Winn,
                    Mackenzie Stewart, Valerie Meszaros
Illustrator: Juan Li
Cartoonist: Don Wilson
Cover Illustrator: Ivan Salgado
Graphics: Max Chia
Designers and Desktop Publishing: Maneewan Chia,
                    Valerie Meszaros

First Published in 1993 by
Healing Tao Books
P.O. Box 1194
Huntington, NY 11743

ISBN: 0-935621-46-6
Library of Congress Catalog Card Number:

Manufactured in the United States of America

02 03 04 05 / 10 9 8

Dedicated to Healers Everywhere

Table of Contents

     The Goal of the Taoist Practice
     International Healing Tao Course Offerings
     Outline of the Complete System of the Healing Tao
     Course Descriptions:
          Introductory Level I: Awaken Healing Light
          Introductory Level II: Development of Internal Power
          Introductory Level III: The Way of Radiant Health
          Intermediate Level:Foundations of Spiritual Practice
          Advance Level:The Realm of Soul and spirit

THE GOAL OF THIS BOOK

All Healing Tao books are based on the real experiences of the many people who practice the system diligently. This book is for both beginning and advanced students. It reflects the many refinements and improvements in the Healing Tao system developed over 20 years of teaching, hundreds of workshops, and feedback from thousands of students. I present this book to you to introduce the foundations of the Healing Tao System. You will find simple and easy-to-follow instructions on how to awaken the Healing Light, Chi, or life-force within. May the Chi be with you!

WORDS OF CAUTION

The meditations, practices, and techniques described herein are NOT to be used as an alternative to professional medical treatment. This book does not attempt to give any medical diagnosis, treatment, prescription, or suggestion for medication in relation to any human disease, pain, injury, deformity, or physical condition. Also if there are illnesses based on mental disorders, a medical doctor or psychologist should be consulted. Such problems should be corrected before you start training.

The practices described in this book have been used successfully for thousands of years by Taoists trained by individual instruction. Readers must not undertake the practice of Chi Nei Tsang without personal training by the Healing Tao since certain of these practices, if improperly done, may cause injury or result in health problems. This book is intended to supplement individual training by the Healing Tao and to serve as a reference guide for these practices. Anyone who undertakes these practices on the basis of this book alone does so entirely at his or her own risk.

Chinese medicine emphasizes balancing and strengthening the body so that it can heal itself. The meditations, internal exercises, and martial arts of the Healing Tao are basic approaches to this end. Follow the instructions for each exercise carefully, and do not neglect the supplemental exercises, particularly the Microcosmic Orbit Meditation. Also pay special attention to the warnings and suggestions in each chapter. People who have high blood pressure, heart disease, or a generally weak condition should proceed cautiously. Pregnant women should not practice Chi Nei Tsang. Those people with venereal disease should not attempt any practices involving sexual energy until they are free of the disease.

The Healing Tao is not and cannot be responsible for the consequences of any practice or misuse of the information in this book. If the reader undertakes any exercise without strictly following the instructions, notes, and warnings, the responsibility must lie solely with the reader.

MASTER MANTAK CHIA AND MANEEWAN CHIA

MASTER MANTAK CHIA

Master Mantak Chia is the creator of the Healing Tao System and the director of the Healing Tao Center in New York. Since childhood he has been studying the Taoist approach to life as well as other approaches. His mastery of this ancient knowledge, enhanced by his study of other disciplines, has resulted in the development of the Healing Tao System which is now being taught in the United States, Canada, Europe, Australia, and Thailand.

Master Chia was born in Thailand to Chinese parents in 1944. When he was six years old, Buddhist monks taught him how to sit and "still the mind." While he was a grammar school student, he first learned traditional Thai boxing. He then was taught Tai Chi Chuan by Master Lu, who soon introduced him to Aikido, Yoga, and more Tai Chi.

Later, when he was a student in Hong Kong excelling in track and field events, a senior classmate named Cheng Sue-Sue introduced him to his first esoteric teacher and Taoist Master, Master Yi Eng. At this point, he began his studies of the Taoist way of life. He learned how to circulate energy through the Microcosmic Orbit, and, through the practice of Fusion of the Five Elements, how to open the other Six Special Channels. As he further studied Inner Alchemy, he learned the Enlightenment of the Kan and Li, Sealing of the Five Sense Organs, Congress of Heaven and Earth, and Reunion of Man and Heaven. It was Master Yi Eng who authorized Master Chia to teach and heal.

In his early twenties Mantak Chia studied with Master Meugi in Singapore, who taught him Kundalini, Taoist Yoga, and the Buddhist Palm. He was soon able to clear blockages to the flow of energy within his own body. He also learned to pass life-force energy through his hands to heal the patients of Master Meugi. He then learned Chi Nei Tsang from Dr. Mui Yimwattana in Thailand.

Later, he studied with Master Cheng Yao-Lun who taught him the Shao-Lin Method of Internal Power. He also learned from Master Yao-

Photo: Julian Goble

Mantak Chia and Maneewan Chia

Lun the closely guarded secret of the organs, glands, and bone marrow exercise known as *Bone Marrow Nei Kung* and the exercise known as *Strengthening and Renewal of the Tendons*. Master Cheng Yao-Lun's system combined Thai boxing and Kung Fu. At this time he also studied with Master Pan Yu, whose system combined Taoist, Buddhist, and Zen teachings. From Master Pan Yu he learned about the exchange of the Yin and Yang power between men and women, and also learned how to develop the *Steel Body*.

To understand the mechanisms behind healing energy better, Master Chia studied Western medical science and anatomy for two years. While pursuing his studies, he managed the Gestetner Company, a manufacturer of office equipment, and became well-acquainted with the technology of offset printing and copying machines.

Using his knowledge of Taoism combined with the other disciplines, Master Chia began teaching the Healing Tao System. He eventually trained other teachers to communicate this knowledge, and he established the Natural Healing Center in Thailand. Five years later, he decided to move to New York where, in 1979, he opened the Healing Tao Center.

Since then, centers have opened in many other locations including Boston, Philadelphia, Denver, Seattle, San Francisco, Los Angeles, San Diego, Tucson, and Toronto. Groups have also formed throughout Europe in England, Germany, the Netherlands, Switzerland, Austria, Australia, and Thailand.

Master Chia leads a peaceful life with his wife, Maneewan, and their young son, Max. (In 1990 Max, at age 11, became the youngest certified instructor in the Healing Tao System.) Master Chia is a warm, friendly, and helpful man who views himself primarily as a teacher. He presents the Healing Tao in a simple, practical manner while always expanding his knowledge and approach to teaching. He uses a word processor for writing and is very much at ease with the latest in computer technology. He and has written and published eight Healing Tao Books: in 1983, *Awaken Healing Energy through the Tao*; in 1984, *Taoist Secrets of Love: Cultivating Male Sexual Energy*; in 1985, *Taoist Ways to Transform Stress into Vitality*; in 1986, *Chi Self-Massage: The Tao Way of Rejuvenation, Iron Shirt Chi Kung I*, and *Healing Love through the Tao: Cultivating Female Sexual Energy*; in 1989, *Bone Marrow Nei Kung*; in 1990, *Fusion of the Five Elements I* and *Chi Nei Tsang: Internal Organ Chi Massage. Awaken Healing Light of the Tao* is his tenth book.

Master Chia estimates that it will take twenty books to convey the full Healing Tao System. In June, 1990 at a dinner in San Francisco, Master Chia was honored by the International Congress of Chinese Medicine and Qi Gong [Chi Kung] who named him the Qi Gong Master of the Year. He is the first recipient of this annual award.

MANEEWAN CHIA

Born in China, Maneewan Chia was raised in Hong Kong and eventually moved with her parents to Thailand where she grew up to attend the University and earn a B.S. Degree in Medical Technology. Since childhood, Mrs. Chia has been very interested in nutrition and Chinese health food cooking. This she learned by assisting her mother, a very fine cook. Since her marriage to Mantak Chia, she has studied the Healing Tao System and currently assists him in teaching classes, including Taoist Five Element Nutrition, co-authoring most of his books, and managing the Healing Tao Center.

Acknowledgements

We extend our gratitude to the many generations of Taoist masters who have passed on their special lineage as an unbroken oral transmission over thousands of years. We particularly thank Taoist Master I Yun (Yi Eng) for his openness in transmitting the formulas of Taoist Inner Alchemy.

We offer our eternal gratitude to our parents and teachers for their many gifts to us. Remembering them brings joy and satisfaction to our continued efforts in presenting the Healing Tao System. Special thanks to Maneewan and our son, Max, for their desktop publishing skills.

We express our deep appreciation to Michael Winn for his overall help in planning the structure of this book and his firm guidance and editorial comments throughout its preparation.

We express our special thanks Juan Li for his fine illustrations; as always, he has played an integral role in presenting the Healing Tao concepts and techniques. Thank you also to Don Wilson for his wonderful cartoons.

We also thank Jampa Mackenzie Stewart for his writing and editorial contributions.

We thank Judith Stein, Mark R. Lipsman, Kimberly Baldt, Marcia Kerwit, and Chuck Soupios for their assistance in preparing, editing, and proofreading the manuscript, and to Linda Hoffer and Cecilia Caldas for their proofreading assistance.

Our thanks to Valerie Meszaros for her help in design and desktop publishing.

We thank Kenneth S. Cohen, Stuart S. Mauro, O.M.D., and John P. Painter, Ph.D., for their constructive comments on the Three Pure Ones and for sharing their insights on various other areas of esoteric Taoist yoga; and Steven Post for his Feng Shui insights.

Special thanks to Dr. Lawrence Young for clarifying the relationships between anatomy and energetic pathways.

Thank you to Susan Aaron, Esq. and Gary Oshinsky, Esq. for their legal advice and comments. Thanks to Carson Tsang and Jeeraporn Sae-Heng for scanning the many illustrations into the book.

Finally, we wish to thank our certified instructors, students, and sponsors throughout the world for their ongoing contributions to the system and for preserving the vitality of the Healing Tao practices.

Preface

What Is the Tao of Cultivating Inner Light?

by Michael Winn

Ten years ago, I was among a handful of curious Westerners sitting in a tiny office in New York's Chinatown, listening to a boyish-looking 38-year-old Chinese immigrant from Thailand named Mantak Chia. He was teaching us ancient Taoist methods of self-transformation, which he had received by oral transmission. His teacher, the Hermit White Cloud, lived in the mountains of China and had attained the rarefied state of "breatharian." This meant he was living on subtle "airs" and no solid food. White Cloud's story might have ended there, as has been the case with similar teachers for several millennia, were it not for the drive of this young Taoist master to clarify for modern minds the Tao of regulating the human bioenergetic system.

I was eager for a spiritual path with practical application for all areas of life. At the time, I was working as a war correspondent in Africa, and the Six Healing Sounds were very effective in relieving high levels of stress. I found Taoist "energy medicine," closely allied with noninvasive medicine like acupuncture and herbs, to be an extremely portable self-health system. Taoism had a fresh psychology that was spirit-based, yet was successful in helping me deal with chronic anger and other emotional imbalances.

Most important, Taoism taught sexual vitality as an essential aspect of spiritual development. I used the sexual practices to cure myself of chronic sexual frustration and to "get clear" enough to attract a wonderful wife. On a deeper level, my soul was seeking a mystical expression in which the uniqueness of my individuality was recognized, and in which all the separate strands of my fragmented self were woven together in a meditational process of spiritual tranquility. I wanted a silent inner path that didn't require joining a new religion or bowing at someone else's feet—in short, the Tao.

Inspired by how quick and effective the Taoist methods were, Master Chia's small group of students joined him in forming the Healing Tao Center. Over the next decade, this organization succeeded in making many of the most arcane secrets of Chinese internal alchemy accessible to Westerners. This is evidenced by a worldwide network of 200 instructors and tens of thousands of practitioners from all walks of life and religions happily cultivating their Chi, or life-force.

The Microcosmic Orbit is the key to balancing energies in the body. The book that launched this wave of interest was Chia's *Awaken Healing Energy Through the Tao* (Aurora Press, 1983), a classic in its field that offers the essentials on how to guide the life-force so it flows in a loop, known as the basic Microcosmic Orbit, up the spine and down the front acupuncture channels of the body. Its impact has been widespread, as it provided the piece of the puzzle missing from many of the partial teachings arriving in the West from India. These only showed the energy ascending up the spine, a practice that can lead to spaciness and which ultimately weakens the body if the aroused bioenergy is transferred to the head center prematurely.

Happily, some yoga manuals are now beginning to show the descending, or Yin, channel, which may also reflect a growing respect for the spiritual power of the feminine/goddess energy. Taoism is one of the oldest spiritual paths to openly advocate cultivating the feminine to gain balance and wholeness. Taoism is rooted in an underlying deep ecology of the body that affirms the importance of the body in the spiritual process. It teaches that one can reach heaven only by first harmonizing one's soul with the earth.

Awaken Healing Light of the Tao is a sequel that expands on the basic methods of cultivating Chi in the Microcosmic Orbit. It offers a deeper glimpse of Taoist spiritual theory and more advanced meditational methods for absorbing higher frequencies of energy into the basic Orbit. Following the classical Chinese model of the "three treasures," these frequencies are identified as the Earth Force, the Higher Self or Cosmic Force, and the Universal Force. This teaching is neither religion nor philosophy, but a spiritual science that emphasizes practical benefits to health, sexual vitality, and emotional and mental balance, and which promises--like a shining carrot at the end of a very long stick--physical immortality.

Cultivating "inner breath" is a science. There are many excellent yoga and martial arts teachers with effective methods of cultivating Chi (or prana, as it is known in India). Most of these teachings rely on "outer breath" methods. They use special postures, gentle circular movements such as Tai Chi Chuan, and physical breathing to stimulate and regulate the flow of Chi. These methods are known as pranayama in India and Wai Dan Chi Kung in China.

The Healing Tao also uses many Chi Kung methods, and this book includes a new section on spinal Chi Kung. But its primary emphasis is on Nei Kung or "inner breath" methods, which directly focus the mind within the physical body and awaken subtle body energies using pure awareness. This method may seem more difficult to beginners, but after some concentration power is developed it is truly effortless, and far more profound. I found it simple and satisfying to integrate these internal Taoist practices into yoga, Tai Chi, and other kinds of meditation.

The energy body is the key to manifesting spirit. The Healing Tao system offers an inner map and a series of practical methods that help one more quickly experience the energetic system which links the physical body with the emotions, thoughts, individual soul, and universal spirit. This internal map we simply refer to as "the energy body," a term that lumps together the whole spectrum of intermediate levels between the physical body and the pure spirit.

Exercising these intermediate levels of life-force is essential in Taoism to bridge the gap between God as spirit and what the Chinese sages called the "Great Clod," the mundane material level of earth life. Knowing the connection between the body and spirit keeps one focused in the present moment and balances whatever aspect of oneself is crying for attention. Chi, the life-force, is not worshipped like some abstract or distant deity; it is seen as the power of God or divine love (to use Western terms), stepped down into the everyday world.

Chi is the process of the Tao functioning at many different levels simultaneously within us. It is the key to healing and the practical means of manifesting love and harmony. The highest power one can manifest in this dimension is physical immortality. I found this idea hard to swallow at first. But it stands to reason: If in each moment one can stay aware of the Tao, the eternal source of life, one's biological cells will constantly be rejuvenated by its pure vitality. The Bible mentions elders living 900 years, and stories from Atlantis talk of people living thousands of years. Modern human beings have degenerated, but I accept the Taoist teaching that it is never too late to change oneself.

Awakening the "healing light" refers to a more subtle level of the life-force, sometimes referred to in Western esoteric traditions as the higher "astral light" of the soul. This inner light is also experienced along a whole rainbow spectrum of color as the Original Chi, the clear light or pure neutral light of the soul, shines through the more dense or material subtle body, which is polarized into Yin and Yang energy patterns.

Each frequency or vibrational density is associated by the Taoists with specific kinds of subtle energy: the earth's water and plant energy emits a blue-green color, spinal/bone marrow energy is white, Higher Self (Cosmic Force) energy is golden, and Universal energy is violet as it is stepped down through the polestar. The generative force of the earth (reflected in the seven stars of the Big Dipper) is red, and sexual energy in humans is pink, the mixing of blood and semen. Black is the color of the unborn Tao, the absolute void of the Wu Chi from which all spirit emanates. It is important to note that some people are not at all visually oriented and may never see any colors with their inner eye. They are more apt to "feel" the quality of these different frequencies, with the same end effect.

Chakras and the Microcosmic Orbit. How are the seven chakras related to the Microcosmic Orbit? As a longtime student of hatha yoga, kundalini yoga, and kriya yoga, I feel qualified to answer that the Microcosmic Orbit balances and integrates all the chakras into a single unified chakra. The term chakra means "wheel," which implies energy in motion. Contrary to popular New Age conception, the chakras have no individual power and are only minor nodal points through which larger forces flow.

You cannot "open" or "close" a single chakra. To step up the energy level of one chakra requires more energy flowing through the entire system. The Chinese call the two most primordial forces Yin (the receptive) and Yang (the radiant). Rotating Chi in the Orbit up the spine and down the front channel regulates the positively and negatively charged points opposite the chakras. I believe these polarities create the minor vortices called chakras, causing them to spin like wheels. By increasing Chi flow in the Orbit, the energies flowing through all the chakras are amplified and balanced simultaneously. Eventually these polarized energy currents link together to open a neutral channel in the center of the body, called the Thrusting Channel, which is the birth canal for spiritual rebirth as an immortal.

The Orbit around the body is like an empty vessel that reflects whatever energies one allows to flow in it. The quality of the energy changes in the Orbit as one expands one's consciousness to include more frequencies of inner light. As the simple loop of the Orbit fills with Chi and overflows into the other acupuncture meridians and vital organs, it becomes the "energy egg" of a radiant human aura. One "cracks" this egg by pulsing into and opening the five gates in the feet, perineum, heart/palms of the hands, Third Eye, and crown that connect the Microcosmic Orbit to the three macrocosmic energies of the Earth, Higher Self, and Universe.

In this book, different Taoist practices are described that help amplify and refine reception of these energies: Iron Shirt Chi Kung for rooting the Earth Force, Fusion of the Five Elements for transmuting emotional energy, Healing Love for harnessing sexual impulses for spiritual purposes, and Kan and Li ("water and fire") meditations for stabilizing the Higher Self and dissolving all boundaries so as to receive guidance and love from the Universal Force.

To a beginner, these many different practices and energies can be a bit overwhelming. For this reason, beginners may find it easier to first read *Awaken Healing Energy Through the Tao* (Aurora Press, 1983) to get a simple and firm grounding in the basic orbit and inner smile, without worrying about absorbing higher frequencies from Earth or Heaven. It is a major shift for most people to even examine the existing vibrational patterns in their own body. *Awaken Healing Light of the Tao* will provide a more sophisticated overview of spiritual practices that range from beginning to advanced. It is best to proceed slowly, starting with the basic Orbit, and eventually all the practices will become familiar and simple variations on one theme: how to play with your life-force. It will speed your growth if you can connect with a Taoist instructor or community, or come to a week-long Healing Tao summer retreat.

More advanced cultivators will soon find themselves in the opposite position—recognizing that energy-cultivation methods are only tools, meant to be dropped when they are no longer needed. Once you have stabilized changes in your energy body, you can focus more on the Yin or receptive phase: sitting in stillness and growing your Shen, your immortal body, which is nothing more than your spirit descended into and stabilized within this physical dimension.

Your life is your own unique spiritual path, and if you cultivate your inner light, it will always shine on the Great Way or Great Tao. May the life-force be with you as you explore these precious methods!

Winter Solstice 1992

Michael Winn is a general editor of Healing Tao Books, a senior Healing Tao instructor, and chairman of the Healing Tao Instructor's Association. He is co-author with Mantak Chia of *Taoist Secrets of Love: Cultivating Male Sexual Energy* (Aurora Press, 1984). He lives on a mountaintop in Cold Spring, N.Y., with his wife, Joyce Gayheart, where they grow younger each year. He teaches Taoist meditation, sexology, and self-healing privately in New York City.

CHI AND
THE MEDICINE

by Lawrence Young, M.D.

It is a widespread belief that we have some kind of energy inside our bodies called life-force. Those who have strong and abundant life-force enjoy perfect health and vitality. In old age and sickness, this life-force gets weaker. When it becomes totally dissipated, the flesh-and-blood body dies.

Unfortunately, most people have only a vague notion of life-force; medical doctors and scientists are just beginning to investigate this energy. Serious study of the life-force was, however, a closely guarded secret in most esoteric schools throughout history in such diverse parts of the world as Egypt, the Himalayas, and Tibet, and among various traditions of shamanic and psychic healers. Secrecy was thought necessary because exploiting such knowledge for selfish purposes could lead to great harm to others and eventually backfire on oneself as well. The destruction of the legendary Atlantis was frequently cited as the foremost example of such misuse.

China was an exception to this rule of secrecy. Over the last five thousand years, tens of millions of Chinese have practiced Chi Kung, healing their own illnesses and in many cases actually saving their own lives. Millions more have benefited from acupuncture, which has cured many diseases and relieved much suffering.

Acupuncture employs mechanical means, such as needles, to manipulate the body's life-force for treating various illnesses. The theory and practice of traditional Chinese medicine is based on restoring the normal physiological flow of Chi energy in the body and correcting abnormal flow with herbs, needles, focused heat application (moxibustion), focal point massage, and other means. This knowledge was not limited to monks and hermits, nor were royalty and the rich the only people helped by such knowledge; peasants and scholars, merchants and officials alike have practiced Chi-Kung and benefited from acupuncture.

Why is it that in China the study of life-force energy was not secretly guarded, as in other parts of the world? Acupuncture and Chi-Kung are like the many nuclear reactors all over the world operated by the civilian sector to generate electric power. Such facilities are carefully regulated, but the secrecy and security is in no way comparable to the security at military installations or at companies manufacturing nuclear weaponry. Acupuncture and Chi-Kung are benign forms of life-force study proven to be safe and effective for wide dissemination and practical application, as borne out by their track records over the past five thousand years in China.

Since it took over 40 years ago, the Communist regime has sought to destroy all religious and esoteric teachings in China. But it has recently encouraged extensive research into the Chi phenomena of acupuncture and Chi Kung. Although scientists under the Communist regime do not view Chi in the same context as the esoteric schools, they have nevertheless validated the phenomena of Chi during the application of acupuncture needles. Through cooperative efforts, they have mapped out the routes of Chi flow sensation during acupuncture, and the map so recorded agrees exactly with the meridians of energy flow used by acupuncturists for the last five thousand years.

These modern Chinese scientists have also tabulated the reported Chi flow experienced by people practicing Chi Kung, and the energy routes agree exactly with the acupuncture and Chi Kung texts passed down through the centuries. The scientists had an unlimited source of data to work with, because Communist China under the old leadership pursued a policy of isolation, independence, and self-dependence. Western drugs and medical technology were accepted and honored by the Communist regime but were in scarce supply. The Communist state therefore made an all-out effort to encourage the use of acupuncture, Chi Kung, and herbs for treating illness and in preventive medicine.

In so doing, Communist China has inadvertently helped validate the phenomenon of life-force energy in the human body and disseminate this esoteric knowledge far and wide. There is an extensive list of illnesses and conditions for which Communist China officially sanctions the use of Chi Kung. The list spans the gamut of disease, from hypertension to cancer, functional organ disorders to postoperative convalescence. Numerous magazines reporting anecdotal cures as well as serious scientific journals on Chi Kung are published regularly. Even energies radiated from the palms of Chi Kung practitioners have been documented. That radiated Chi is reported to have the properties of wave forms as well as of particles of matter. It has been observed to alter the molecular structure of water and other chemicals.

Although Communist China is not the only place in the world expounding the benefits of Chi Kung in recent years, in terms of sheer numbers, it has made the greatest contribution. The same holds true for scientific research on Chi; no other country or institution to date has done as much as China. However, when the Communists took over China 40 years ago, countless numbers of Chi Kung practitioners fled to other countries. Although few claimed to be master teachers, nevertheless, having benefited personally from activating their Chi, even to the extent of saving their own lives, these otherwise quite ordinary citizens frequently had an urge to show others how to do it as well. This grassroots approach has kept Chi Kung alive and flourishing for thousands of years in China, despite the lack of official sponsorship. There were no organized schools or universities for Chi Kung until the Communists took over in China. But because Chi-Kung had stayed alive at the grassroots level, the mass exodus of Chinese from Communist China has also inadvertently helped spread Chi Kung all over the World.

I have had a general internist medical practice in the Chinese community in New York City since 1976. I employ only conventional Western medical methods. I have a license to use acupuncture on my patients, but I usually refer them to more skillful practitioners. Whenever my patients have had all the appropriate tests and conventional Western treatments and are still not feeling better, I suggest they add Chi Kung to their regimen.

The word got around that I was the Chi Kung doctor in the community. As a result, people who had previously benefited from Chi Kung came to me to tell their stories. Gradually, I collected enough anecdotal cases to write a book about the medical effects of Chi Kung. One version of the book was in Chinese, and since its publication, many more people have come forward unsolicited to tell me their experiences with Chi Kung. Their stories have confirmed my lifelong conviction that the Chi described in Chi Kung and acupuncture is a universal phenomenon, a normal component of physiology universally present in everyone, irrespective of age, color, sex, race, or creed.

In Communist China, people learn Chi Kung primarily from state-sponsored schools or classes. In the rest of the world, most Chinese people learn Chi Kung from an uncle, a neighbor, a friend at work, or just about anyone who has benefited from Chi Kung. Close to a quarter of these teachers are self-taught; they read written accounts of other people's experience, follow the suggested procedures. activate their life-force energy, and achieve the healing they need. The best-known book on Chi Kung healing in China is *Meditation According to Master Yun*, written by Master Yun in 1914 when he was 42 years old.

Master Yun wrote of suffering from a full-blown case of pulmonary tuberculosis at the age of 28; death seemed just around the corner. He had no formal instruction in Chi Kung, just a book. He had enough time to hurriedly ask for some pointers on Chi Kung just after his brother died of tuberculosis, like so many others in his village, across China, and around the world at the time. Yun then withdrew to the country, where he devoted himself to intensive practice of Chi Kung. He completely cured himself in only 85 days, activating a classical sensation of acupuncture energy flow in the front and back acupuncture meridians. He was surprised by that sensation, which was both intense and alarming. In 1954 he wrote his final book, drawn from his wealth of firsthand experience in Chi Kung healing and meditation. Master Yun eventually passed on in his 90s without sickness.

Many self-taught practitioners followed Master Yun's instructions written almost 80 years ago, activating their life-force and healing without much difficulty. I am not saying everyone can or should learn Chi Kung by reading an antique text; I simply observe that this life-force is universal, and that making use of Chi is everyone's birthright.

In 1980, I gave a lecture at the annual convention of the American Holistic Medical Association on the healing power of Chi Kung. At this same convention, Master Mantak Chia conducted a practical Chi Kung workshop. Before the workshop, Master Chia gave a brief demonstration of Chi Kung methodology. One medical doctor and two nurses instantly experienced the acupuncture energy flow during these brief 10-minute sessions. One of the trio felt the Chi energy spinning around the front and back meridians nonstop all that day and night until the next afternoon, when Master Chia showed her how to cool it down during the formal workshop.

There is one additional observation worth mention in the 1980 AHMA experience. The doctors and nurses who instantly activated their

Chi energy flow vividly and intensely all had 5 to 15 years of experience in regular meditation of various types (mostly Transcendental Meditation). But for most of Master Chia's students, prior experience with meditation is not necessary; among my Chinese patients in New York, neither the word meditation nor the principles of meditation were even mentioned, yet they all benefited from Chi Kung. Since then, Master Chia has helped tens of thousands of non-Chinese, spanning the whole spectrum of socioeconomic strata in many major nations around the world, activate their Chi energy.

Quite independently of talking to Master Chia's students, my own contacts from my medical practice in New York's Chinatown have brought me other medical doctors, pharmacists, nurses, artists, writers, bankers, businesspeople, Catholic and Protestant clergy, and laypersons; all these people have told me of the great benefits Chi Kung practice has brought to their lives.

Although Communist China has contributed greatly in the last 40 years to the scientific validation of Chi Kung and has recently caused the practice to become extremely popular in Communist China, through its atheistic fervor the Communist hierarchy has practically destroyed the root source of Chi Kung--the Taoist monasteries and adepts. Nearly all Taoist monasteries were torn down, and the adepts and novices were burned alive unless they were willing to forsake their faith and return to the production line of the Communist Party. All the esoteric texts the Communists found were burned. The only adepts left were those who managed to flee the country, go underground, or outwardly go along with the Communists while inwardly waiting for the sun to come out again.

So, essentially, the Chinese Communists took the golden egg out of Mother Goose and then did away with her. While the Communists have promoted and validated Chi Kung for health maintenance, disease prevention, and the treatment of certain sicknesses, advanced studies for qualified students in China are no longer possible because the high teachers have been killed and the high-level texts destroyed.

Fortunately, with the exodus of people into Hong Kong, Taiwan, and Southeast Asia in the late 1940s and early 1950s, some of these high-level texts were somehow smuggled out. Some fairly advanced Taoist adepts also managed to escape into Southeast Asia and Taiwan. When President Nixon opened up dialogue and travel restrictions with China, more Taoist texts that had been hidden underground were able to be smuggled out. So not every high teaching on Chi is forever lost. But who can understand these archaic texts? Who is scholarly enough to be able to expound on these ancient writings, and yet has had enough personal experience with life-force energies to really make any sense out of these texts and impart their essence to their students?

Master Mantak Chia is such a teacher, if not the only such uniquely qualified Taoist teacher in the Western world. He studied with several high teachers who were lucky enough to have escaped from China to reside in Southeast Asia. Master Chia has had access to many Taoist texts saved from Communist destruction. After China opened up somewhat, a number of Taoists who had safely kept the high teaching and ancient texts underground imparted all they had to Master Chia. His mastery of the Chinese language, both spoken and written, enabled him to read all these ancient texts, while his high-level personal experience with the life-force, both in himself and in his students, enabled him to understand and impart the ancient teachings. His fluency in English and knowledge of medical science further enables him to communicate fully in a form that is both intelligible and sensible to Westerners.

Lawrence Young, M.D.
December 25, 1992
New York City

Lawrence Young, M.D., is an internist in private practice in New York City. He is a member of the American Medical Association and a licensed acupuncturist. He has studied and practiced Chi Kung since he was 12. He is widely read in Taoist texts and takes every opportunity to talk to Chi Kung practitioners. He has authored a book in Chinese, *Chi Kung and Healing*, and one in English, *Report of the National Clearing House on Meditation and Relaxation*.

Introduction

WHAT IS THE TAO?

THE GOALS OF THE HEALING TAO

The word *Tao* means *the way*, the way of nature and the universe, or the path of natural reality. It also refers to a way in which we can open our minds to learn more about the world, our spiritual paths, and ourselves.

A practical system. Taoism is a practice of body, mind, and spirit, not just a philosophy of mind. When we have the true sense of the Tao, of the real knowledge and wisdom, we will be able to make the right decisions in our lives.

Taoism involves many practical disciplines that can restore our lost youth, energy, and virtues while awakening our deepest spiritual potentials. Taoists regard these practices as a technology that can help us learn universal truths if we are willing to open our minds.

The final destiny. The ancient masters recognized that these potentials can include the possibility of attaining conscious freedom in the after-death state. Through specific exercises, one can avoid suffering the experience of death by expanding the consciousness beyond the physical body before its demise. This makes it possible to determine one's future existence before leaving this life.

Universal Spiritual Independence

All spiritual paths ultimately lead to the truth. The Tao is both a philosophy and a technology for seeking and finding the truths of the universe, nature, and humanity. Its focus goes beyond one single path or viewpoint. The Tao is not a religion, as it requires no initiations or ceremonies, but it is the outcome of all religions, departing from dogma at the point of truth. It leaves behind all religious beliefs, just like the clothing of past seasons. The Tao is also the goal of science, but it leaves

1

behind all scientific theories as partial and temporal descriptions of the integral truth. Taoism includes all matters of religion and science, yet its breadth goes far beyond the limits of devotion or intellect.

The Master Keys. Taoist teachings are like master keys unlocking all doors. They assist people in their lives, as do all religious teachings. Yet the teachings of the Tao transcend religion while retaining the essence of spirituality. They explain and demonstrate the truths of the universe directly, rather than on the level of emotions, thoughts, or beliefs. For this reason, students of the Tao have little cause for skepticism or endless searching.

The Ultimate Truth. Philosophy, science, and religions all contain some aspects of truth that reflect the Tao. The teachings of the Tao reflect the center of the ultimate truth (ourselves and the universe) and help us reach it on our own. We can believe in any religion or spiritual path and still benefit from these teachings, because the Tao serves only to promote universal spiritual independence. There are no ultimate masters or gurus in Taoism because we become our own masters, capable of controlling our own destinies and knowing who we really are as we explore the marvelous powers hidden within the Tao of humanity. All the great gods, immortals, sages, saints, and holy men and women are our teachers and advisers.

Cultivating Body, Mind, and Spirit

We need food to nourish our bodies, minds, and spirits. Religions try to fulfill us with spiritual food when we don't know how to fulfill ourselves. Taoism suggests that everything in life can provide nourishment for some aspect of our being if we know how to access that nourishment. Taoist practices can help us determine our goals and receive physical, mental, and spiritual food in a natural way. They also teach us how to return to our source, the *Wu Chi* (the Godhead), and thereby attain spiritual independence as we learn to live harmoniously with nature and the universe.

The practices of Taoism have three main goals:
- Learning to heal, love, and be kind to ourselves as we develop compassionate hearts and a wholeness of being;
- Learning to help, heal, and love others from the abundance of healing and loving energies we receive from the forces of nature, heaven, and earth;

- Learning about our *Original Source* and helping it unfold within ourselves.

THE THREE BODIES

The ancient Taoists saw the importance of working on all three levels of our being: the physical body, the energy body, and the spirit. All three are important in forming a ladder with which we may climb consciously into the spiritual worlds and, just as important, back into the physical world to be creatively active here. This ladder enables Taoists to learn about the inner worlds and to return to the physical world with knowledge and increased energy. An *Immortal Body*, which is developed in the practice of Internal Alchemy, enables one to establish a constant link between life and the after-death (or pre-birth) state.

Ancient Taoist sages believed we were born to be immortal. We become mortal by draining ourselves of Chi through engaging in excessive sexual activity, indulging in negative emotions, and depending only on material sources to supply our life-force. The masters recognized that different levels of immortality can be achieved through Internal Alchemy, and they devised many practices for this purpose. The ability to transcend even death through the transmutation of one's physicality into the *immortal spirit body* is the highest goal of Taoism. This level, known as physical immortality, takes the longest to achieve.

Healing the Physical Body:
Becoming Like a Child to Return to the
Original Source

The basic foundation of Taoist practice is learning to conserve the physical energy within our bodies so that it will no longer scatter and weaken as a result of our worldly interactions. Full spiritual independence requires that we avoid being drained of this energy through the eyes, ears, nose, and mouth, or through excessive sex. The novice in the Taoist System begins with a wide range of exercises that develop the physical body into an efficient and healthy organism, able to live in the world and yet stay free of the tensions and stresses of daily life. One aspires to return to a childlike state of innocence and vitality, to regain the *Original Force* that is our birthright. Specific goals of this level are to learn how to heal oneself, how to love oneself, and how to love others.

3

The Foundation Practices:
Conserving Energy to Follow the Light

The first level of practice is to develop a healthy body, which can take up to 12 months of diligent training. During this process we learn how to condense and conserve our life-force through the *Microcosmic Orbit* meditation, *Healing Love* practice, *Inner Smile*, *Six Healing Sounds*, and *Iron Shirt Chi Kung*. We learn to gather and refine our life-force into a *Chi ball* (energy sphere) so it will not dissipate when we are ready to leave this world. As people grow older, their life-force weakens, often resulting in illness and suffering. Using drugs to combat illness drains so much of the body's life-force that there may not enough energy left to follow the primordial light (clear light) to the Wu Chi (our Original Source—God) at the moment of death. The basic practices of the Healing Tao ensure that we retain enough vital energy to make that journey.

Stopping energy leakage through conservation and recycling. The Microcosmic Orbit is the body's major energy pathway. Along this path there are nine openings. If we learn how to seal them when we are not using them, by that simple act of conservation we will immediately have more energy. This basic Orbit is taught in great detail in my first book *Awaken Healing Energy Through the Tao* (Aurora Press, 1983).

The Microcosmic Orbit meditation is the first step toward attaining these goals, as it develops the power of the mind to control, conserve, recycle, transform, and direct *Chi* (the Chinese term for energy, or life-force) through the body's primary acupuncture channels. By managing our Chi effectively, we gain better control over our lives; by using our energy wisely, we discover we already have plentiful Chi.

With the advanced Orbit, one learns to connect with and draw from the unlimited source of Universal Love, a Cosmic Orgasm formed by the union of the three main sources of Chi accessible to humans: the *Universal Force*, the *Earth Force*, and the *Higher Self (Cosmic) Force*. This process is both energizing and balancing. It prepares one for working with greater amounts of Chi in the higher levels of meditative practice, particularly in developing the energy body.

Transforming negative energy into virtues: Opening the heart. The *Inner Smile* and *Six Healing Sounds* are simple yet powerful practices that teach us how to relax and heal the vital organs and to transform negative emotions back into a rich source of energy. They help open the heart center and connect us with unlimited Universal Love, improving daily interactions and providing a vehicle for the virtues, which derive

4

from the internal organs. Taoists perceive the heart as the seat of love, joy, and happiness, which can connect with Universal Love. It is also a cauldron in which the energies of our virtues are combined and strengthened. Through the Inner Smile, you will feel these virtuous energies generated from their respective organs. You will then gather these into the heart to be refined and blended into compassion, the highest of all virtues. This is a most effective way to enhance one's best qualities.

Conserving, recycling, and transforming the sexual energy. A Taoist gains strength through the conservation and recycling of sexual energy, as described in my two books, *Taoist Secrets of Love* (for men) and *Healing Love Through the Tao* (for women). When collected, sexual energy *(Ching Chi)* becomes an incredible source of power that can be used by the individual or shared with a sexual partner via the Microcosmic Orbit pathway during sexual intercourse. With practice, singles and couples can learn to increase and intensify sexual pleasure. The collected and transformed sexual energy is an important alchemical catalyst used in higher meditations. Once you have an abundant sexual energy, you can connect to the unlimited Cosmic Orgasm experienced every moment by your Higher Self, which is the most basic energy in every cell of your body.

Managing the Life-force. In the practices of *Iron Shirt Chi Kung* and *Tai Chi Chi Kung*, one learns to align the skeletal structure with gravity to allow a smooth, strong flow of energy. With strong fasciae, tendons, and bone marrow and good mechanical structure, we can manage our life-force more efficiently. The body also gains a sense of being rooted deeply in the earth, so one can tap into the Mother Earth healing force.

Chi Nei Tsang. Chi Nei Tsang is the best technique for healing both yourself and other people without draining your own energies. Chi Nei Tsang is a Taoist abdominal massage system; it releases blockages that can prevent the smooth flow of energy in any of the bodily systems. These include the lymphatic, organ, meridian, circulatory, and nervous systems of the body.

Five Element Nutrition. The Taoist approach to diet is based on determining the body's needs and then fulfilling them according to the five elements of nature, which support the five major organs of the body. This system reveals and strengthens any weak organs by balancing one's food intake to enhance any deficient elements. It does not condemn most foods that people enjoy (including sweets), but instead creates a better program in which these foods can support the body's internal balance rather than disrupt it. Choosing and combining foods in this way can help us avoid the cravings we sometimes fall prey to.

Developing the Energy Body

Our Vehicle to Travel in Inner and Outer Space

The next level of the Healing Tao system consists of the *Fusion of Five Elements I, II,* and *III*. These practices can take up to one or two years to learn well. They use the extra energy saved through the foundation practices, including recycled negative energies, to build a strong energy body that will not dissipate. Developing this energy body awakens a part of oneself that perceives and acts free of environmental, educational, and karmic conditioning. Once the energy body is strong, it becomes a vehicle (like the space shuttle) to help the untrained soul and spirit for the long journey home, back to the Wu Chi.

At this stage of development, the energy body serves only as a vehicle, not yet having been given life through spiritual rebirth, but the energy body can still be trained to function in the heavenly realms.

If we do not have a chance to practice awakening or to give birth to the soul and immortal spirit during life, the primordial light will awaken us at the moment of death. Unfortunately, we may be too untrained and inexperienced to follow this light. To prepare for the journey, the energy body is a vehicle of great importance. We can train and educate the energy body so it can help the untrained soul and spirit recognize and follow the primordial light back to our original source.

It is also important during our lifetimes to develop an "internal compass," which is associated with the pineal gland, to help us focus on the light when it comes to us.

When we are ready to give birth to the real soul, the energy body will act like a booster rocket to help boost the soul into its higher dimension of the immortal spirit. At the highest level, all three of these bodies merge into one.

Each level of development gives us a chance to go further in the journey back to the Wu Chi. Taoist methods of absorbing stellar energies help rejuvenate the physical body and strengthen the soul and spirit bodies for their interdimensional travels.

Recycling Our Negative Emotions

Our emotional life, filled with constant vicissitudes, drains our vital energy. Through the Fusion of Five Elements meditations, one learns to transform into usable energy the sick energy of negative emotions that has become locked in the vital organs. Taoists understand morality and good deeds as the most direct path to self-healing and balance. To be good to others is good for oneself as well. All the good energies we create are stored in the energy body like deposits in a bank account. By helping others and giving them love, kindness, and gentleness, we receive more positive energy back in return. When we open our hearts, we are filled with love, joy, and happiness. We can actually transform the essence of our hearts from the material into the immaterial to gather supplies of this positive energy for use in the heavens as well as on earth.

From Taoist experience, we know that when we leave this world we can go directly to heaven, depending on how much energy we have been able to transform into the energy body prior to death. Just like money in the bank, the more we transform our physical being to our spiritual being, the more we have in heaven. The more good we do here, the more positive energy we have up there.

Forming the Spirit Body

Planting the Seed of Immortality

The Inner Alchemy meditation of the Lesser Enlightenment of *Kan and Li* (water and fire, sex and love) reunites the male and female within each of us. It involves the practice of self- intercourse, which by internal sexual coupling of the sexual energies enables one to give birth to the soul body. The soul body then acts as a "baby sitter" to help nurture the spirit body. The soul is the seed, but it can also be matured into the immortal body if one has not had the chance to raise the spirit body in this life. Practitioners of Taoist Alchemy believe that if we give birth to the spirit body and develop the immortal body in this life, we can overcome the cycle of reincarnation.

Once the "baby sitter" or soul body is formed, it is in the *Yin* stage, or infancy (soul embryo). We need to feed, raise, educate, and train the young soul to become fully grown.

Once the soul body is developed, we can give birth to the spirit body. To cultivate the young spirit body until it is fully mature can take 14 to 18 years. We also use the energies of nature (trees, sun, moon, and stars);

7

virtually all sensory experiences of a positive nature become nourishment for the growth of the spirit within the physical body.

Many masters who attained this level of the immortal body were able to transform the material into the immaterial and transfer it into the spirit body. At the moment of death, they were able to transfer their consciousness, their energy, and the physical elements of their bodies up with them into the spirit body, although even this level is not yet the true immortal body. In this process their physical bodies actually shrank in size; they may have weighed two-thirds of their usual weight after their physical deaths occurred. This meant they had successfully transformed much of their material being into an immaterial state while retaining full consciousness.

Cultivating the Yang Stage of the Immortal Body: Marrying the Light

We cannot breed a dog with a snake; to merge with the light of the Tao, we must awaken and nourish the awareness that we are in truth children of the light. Once we have fully grown the spirit body, it will be the same frequency as the light of the Tao and can become one with that light. Other traditions refer to this light by such names as the Holy Spirit or Great Spirit; we also refer to it as the "outer light."

The Greater Kan and Li meditation teaches us how to recognize the inner light of our own spirits and shows us how to merge with or "marry" it to the outer light. Once we capture and "marry the light," we give birth to the second stage of the true immortal spirit. Taoists refer to this as the *Yang* body. One continues to transform the physical body energy to feed the immortal spirit so it can mature.

At this stage of practice, we learn to digest increasingly higher-grade energies of the Higher Self and Universal Forces from the sun, moon, planets, stars, and galaxies, and from the mind of the Tao itself. An awakening to that which is eternal and enduring occurs through this practice. Cognizant of our true nature as spirits, we experience the ability to leave the physical body and travel in the immortal spirit body, which leads to experience of the inner worlds of spirit. Fear of death is vanquished as we become familiar with life beyond physicality.

Greatest Enlightenment of Kan and Li

At this level one transfers all physical essence into the immortal body. When all the body's material elements are transformed into subtle Chi, what remains is known as the "rainbow body." When a master of this level leaves this world, there is nothing left of the physical body but nails and hair. Death is still necessary to speed up the process.

Sealing of the Five Senses, Union of the Kun and Kan, Reunion of Heaven and Man

At this level death is transcended entirely. One can simply transform the physical body into the immortal body and leave this world or return to it at will. This is the state of complete physical immortality. It takes from 80 to few hundred years to complete these practices and transform all the material elements of our body into the immaterial. The final goal of ascending to heaven in broad daylight is reached.

There are records in Chinese history of many thousands of Taoist immortals who reached the level of daylight ascension in the presence of many witnesses. In the Bible, Elijah and Moses also accomplished this feat. In the final stage of this practice, the adept can unite the immortal spirit body, the energy body, and the physical body, or separate them at will. It is then that the human being knows full and complete freedom as an immortal, where no world is a boundary.

Chapter 1

AN OVERVIEW OF
TAOIST INNER ALCHEMY

THE FOUNDATIONS FOR
TRANSFORMATION:
External and Internal Alchemy

For more than five thousand years, the Taoist masters researched and developed various practices to attain happiness and immortality. Many of these were methods of *External Alchemy*, which included the Immortal Pill (Figure 1-1) and potions that used mercury, crystals, crystal essences,

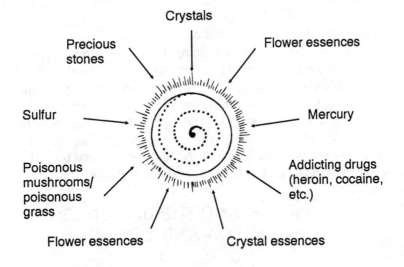

Crystals

Precious
stones

Flower essences

Sulfur

Mercury

Poisonous
mushrooms/
poisonous
grass

Addicting drugs
(heroin, cocaine,
etc.)

Flower essences

Crystal essences

Figure 1-1. Immortal Pill

flower essences, herbs, precious stones, and so forth. The wisest of the masters realized that external methods were a limited approach and that certain ingredients were often hard to find. Their solution was to develop methods of *Internal Alchemy*, in which the body's energies could be combined with those of the earth and the cosmos and transformed to serve as the ingredients for immortality and happiness. After many centuries of testing, these internal methods have proven far more effective in enhancing health and developing the spirit.

In their constant search for an unlimited source of energy, the Taoists turned their attention inward to uncover the mysteries surrounding their life-force. They discovered a universe within and found that it perfectly reflected the outer universe. The masters reasoned that to become connected to the outer universe, one must first gain control of this inner universe, which they experienced as a flow of energy, or *Chi*, through their bodies.

Scientific studies corroborate the Taoist findings, indicating many parallels between the inner and outer worlds. In their book *Powers of Ten*, Phillip and Phyllis Morrison reflect this research as they explore the relationships between the microcosm of the human body and the macrocosm of the universe. The authors note that a telescopic view of one thousand light-years into space appears almost identical with a microscopic view of human cells enlarged to one angstrom. Although the ancient Taoists could feel this relationship internally, they had no means of providing any tangible evidence.

By meditating and practicing internal exercises, the masters developed their inner senses so they could learn more about the inner universe. They eventually discovered the *Microcosmic Orbit*, the pathway through which the distilled essence of internal energy runs up the spine and down the front of the body (Figure 1-2). They perceived that this circuit connects our physical, energy, and spiritual bodies, and that it can ultimately be used to fuse these into one immortal body. The study of Internal Alchemy was born out of this perception.

WU CHI AND THE UNIVERSE: RELIGION AND SCIENCE

Ancient Taoism is rooted in profound observation of naturally occurring universal processes and their effects on human nature. The West's

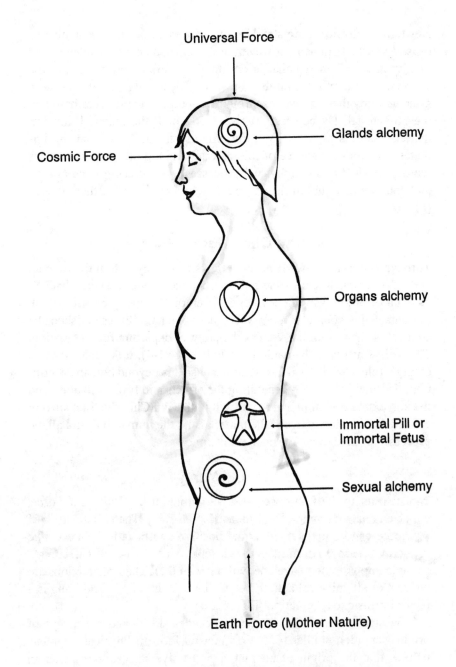

Figure 1-2. Inner Alchemy: Combination forming the Immortal Pill or the Immortal Fetus

Newtonian physics understands these processes as the mechanics of cause and effect. Taoism, however, understands them as the interactions of a vast sea of energy that is constantly creating and recreating the universe in an infinite number of ways. Most religions and esoteric systems study these processes through scriptures and practices based on the immaterial. By contrast, Taoists study both the material and immaterial aspects of nature and the universe in the belief that the immaterial is both the source of the material and a product of it. In other words, physical and nonphysical processes are sources for each other, and both are essential in the co- creation and evolution of the universe (Figure 1-3).

Wu Chi: Our Original Source

Through observing nature and the effects of energy within the human body, the ancient Taoists were able to trace the universal energy back to its point of origin. Having developed an empirical approach with which to contact this source of observable phenomena, they established the concept of the primordial void as the point of departure for all creation. This void was given the name *Wu Chi* (Figure 1-4). It is depicted as an empty circle in traditional Taoist art because it is beyond human description. For energy to begin generating the effects and forms of nature and the universe, something had to stir within the Wu Chi. This first stirring created the division between the material and the immaterial, and all the processes of the universe began at this time.

Yin and Yang

Taoists refer to the first observable variations of the *Universal Force*, which emanates from the Wu Chi, as *Yin* and *Yang*. The two qualities of this force can be understood as the positive and negative poles of the primordial energy. Yin and Yang are inseparable tendencies of all energy, and it is impossible to have one without the other. Their interactions are the root of all universal action; hence, the polarity of Yin and Yang is a factor intrinsic to all creation (Figure 1-5).

Western science has in recent decades developed a concept of original creation similar to that of ancient Taoism. Physical scientists believe that the origin of all matter and universal processes was an explosion referred to as the *Big Bang*. This original event resulted in the creation of elemental particles arrayed in increasingly complex con-

14

Immaterial aspects
God
↑
Spirit energy
↑
Soul energy
↑
Compassionate heart
(next level of energy of the heart)
↑
The heart opens, transforming all negative energies
into positive energies and combining all virtues into love
↑
Love, joy, and happiness come from
the heart and emanate outward
↑
Religion; esoteric studies; nonphysical energy of the heart

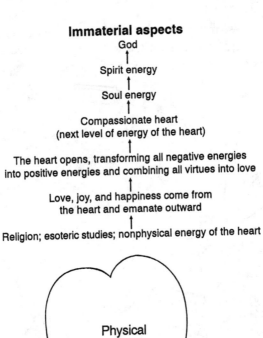

Physical
Heart

Material aspects
Medicine
↓
Science
↓
Science studies how the heart works on a physical level
↓
Understanding the heart's function
can help to heal most heart diseases
↓
Heart operation
↓
Altering heart (pacemakers, bypass surgery, etc.)
↓
Very extreme physical changes (artificial heart, etc.)

Figure 1-3. Physical and nonphysical processes are sources for each other, and both are essential in the co-creation and evolution of the universe.

figurations. These particles eventually became the building blocks of all matter. The Big Bang is estimated to have taken place some 15 to 20 billion years ago, initiating the process of time and shaping the known universe.

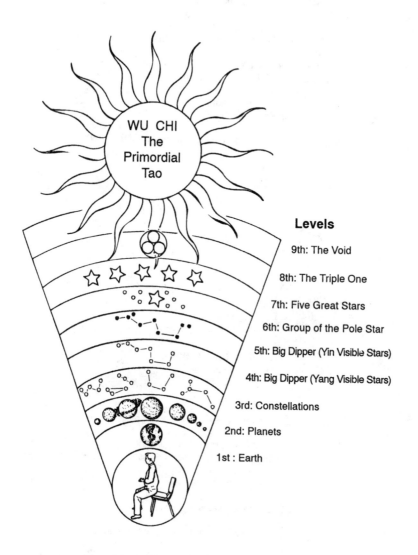

Figure 1-4. Wu Chi—the Primordial Tao

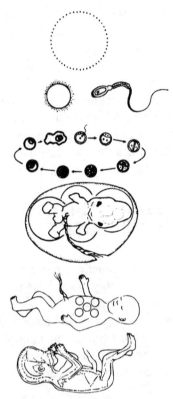

WU CHI

Yin=egg
Yang=sperm

Fertilization to implantation
in the uterus

Triple Warmer

Five Organ Systems

Twelve meridians; 365
acupuncture points

**Figure 1-5. The formation of a child mirrors
the formation of the universe.**

The Five Major Processes of Energy

The Taoists observed that Yin and Yang interactions universally follow five basic patterns, which came to be known as the Five Processes of Energy (or *Five Phases* or *Five Forces*). Such interactions have been erroneously translated as *five elements*, thereby confusing the process with the actual physical elements. In Taoism the physical elements found in nature symbolically express the motion of the Five Processes of Energy. Thus fire represents energy rising; water represents energy sinking; wood represents energy expanding; metal represents energy solidifying; and earth represents stable or centered energy. Each of the Five Processes of Energy depends on the interactions of Yin and Yang emanating from the primordial void.

These five elemental processes are expressions of energy that can be observed in nature and throughout the universe. In space they regulate the motions of all the planets, stars, and cosmic phenomena. In nature they promote interactions between the five elements of fire, water, wood, metal, and earth. Within the human body they affect the five major organs: the heart, kidneys, liver, lungs, and spleen. Just as Western science understands atoms and subatomic particles to be the fundamental units of all matter, the Five Processes of Energy are understood in Taoism to be the essence of all processes. The forces that regulate the cosmos are identical with those that physically affect our planet and our bodies.

THE INFLUENCE OF STARS AND LIGHT ON OUR INNER UNIVERSE

Another example of the parallels between the inner and outer universes is the way star energies affect our lives. The energy of stars can manifest as different colors of light, various sound frequencies, or as cosmic dust. The Taoist masters discovered that each human life is developed, structured, and influenced by various groups of stars (including their planets and the cosmic particles they produce), and that these influences control the birth, death, life-force, and good or bad fortunes of each individual (Figure 1-6).

To explore the patterns of these stellar energies in detail, the Taoists developed the science of astrology to a very high level. They also learned about another important form of energy they called the *Earth Force*, which derives from the stars, but is accessed through the earth. Chinese astrology differs from Western astrology in that it places more emphasis on the earth, which is closest to us and has a disproportionately greater influence on us than other planets. The Taoist masters saw the earth as a great, intelligent being whose elemental changes and seasons dominated the changes in human life.

Although astrology is only one esoteric aspect of cosmic study, the effects of stellar energies on humans are real, just as the radiation from the sun (which is also a star) is real. Each day of a person's life reflects a continuing need to absorb energy from the planets, stars, and cosmic particles. The absorption of these energies from the earth and stars nourishes the organs, glands, senses, soul, and spirit of a human being.

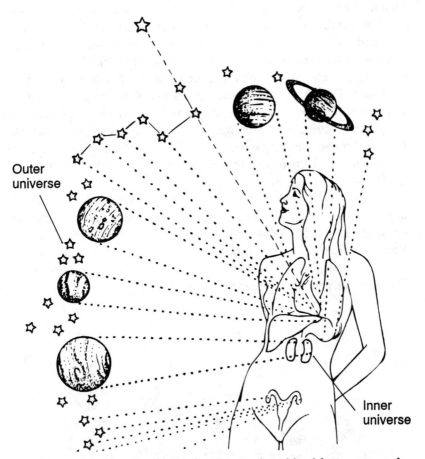

Figure 1-6. Human life, birth, death, good and bad fortunes are influenced by light, sound, and frequency.

THE THREE MAIN SOURCES
OF EXTERNAL CHI

What Are the Three Forces?

The first force is called the *Universal Force*, or *Heavenly Chi*. It includes the energies of all planets, stars, and galaxies and the presence of Universal Love. This vast, all-pervading force nourishes soul, spirit, and Chi within each individual and in every living thing. Taoists say that the moon, which can be considered a planet, has a strong magnetic field that combines with the earth's field to draw Chi from hundreds of billions of stars and planets within our galaxy (Figure 1-7). In meditation, we access this energy through the crown point at the top of the skull.

The energy of the *Higher Self*, or *Cosmic, Chi* is the second force of nature. Cosmic wave/particles (particles of light) are part of the Original Chi that spirals into matter to form the stars and planets. The magnetic powers of the earth, moon, and universe cause these particles to drift through our atmosphere like dust. It is the Taoists' belief that human flesh is formed from the fallen cosmic dust of the universe, just as is suggested in the Bible.

These particles nourish the mind and the essences of all the internal organs, glands, and senses within this physical dimension. Humans are considered to be the highest manifestation of the Cosmic or Higher Self Force, capable of gathering this energy into their bodies through meditation and returning it to its primordial source. Our main doorway for absorbing this energy is the mid-eyebrow point.

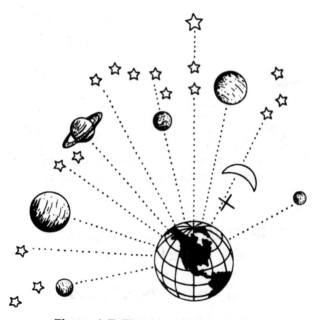

**Figure 1-7. The earth and moon form
a unique combination which has the power to draw Chi
from billions of stars within our galaxy.**

The *Earth Force* is the third force of nature, which includes the energies of Mother Earth: all plants, animals, water, minerals, and natural formations (oceans, mountains, etc.) on our planet. The earth's gravitational force, the electromagnetic field that surrounds the earth, and the earthly Five Elements are some of the major aspects of this energy. We access the Earth Force through the soles of the feet and bring it into the torso at the perineum and sexual organ. These energies nourish the physical body, supplying our daily life-force and giving us the power to heal ourselves. They also nourish the soul and spirit within us as the Yin force balances the Yang force from above.

The Three Forces Sustain All Life Forms

The Universal Force, the Higher Self Force of human beings, and the Earth Force work together in harmony to sustain all life forms (Figure 1-8). The ancient Taoists referred to these ruling forces as the *Three Pure Ones*, for they were the first energies to emerge from the Wu Chi, the Great Emptiness. Traditionally they were visualized as three emperors residing in the three *Tan Tiens*, the upper, middle, and lower palaces of the body. Through the cultivation of these three forces, which manifest in the human body as *Ching, Chi*, and *Shen*, we enhance the development of the physical, energy, and spiritual bodies respectively.

The *upper Tan Tien* connects to the brain, the glands, and the universal and cosmic energies through the force of Shen or spirit. This includes the Third Eye, the crown, and the entire head.

The *middle Tan Tien* connects to the heart and all other organs through the natural force of our soul, known as Chi.

The *lower Tan Tien* connects the physical body, the sexual energy, and Mother Earth through the force known as Ching (sometimes spelled Jing). It is centered between the navel and the kidneys.

Vegetables, Animals, and Minerals: Our Secondary Sources of the Universal Force

The Taoists observed that plants and trees are always extending themselves upward to absorb the Universal Force in the form of light and invisible cosmic waves from the sun, moon, and stars. The animals, in turn, consume the vegetation to absorb this force indirectly, and humans receive it from both plant and animal life. Plants, animals, and minerals predigest the Universal Force and provide us with food which, together

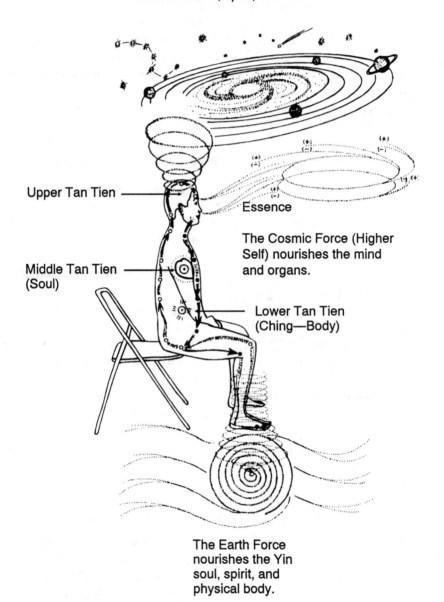

The Universal Force
nourishes soul, spirit, and Chi

Upper Tan Tien

Essence

The Cosmic Force (Higher
Self) nourishes the mind
and organs.

Middle Tan Tien
(Soul)

Lower Tan Tien
(Ching—Body)

The Earth Force
nourishes the Yin
soul, spirit, and
physical body.

Figure 1-8. The Three Forces sustain all life forms.

with the breath, has become our only means of absorbing energy, because we have gradually forgotten how to receive it directly.

Digesting food is an inefficient method of absorbing Chi from secondary sources. Because we have become so dependent on these sources, the vibratory rates of our energy body have been lowered to receive these minute amounts of energy, which are all they can supply. This is why the Inner Smile and Microcosmic Orbit meditations are so important, as they are the means by which we can absorb these forces directly once again.

Humans as Channels for the Universal and Earth Forces

In a limited way, we naturally receive some of the life-giving forces directly, although meditative practices are necessary to store them in the body. The Taoists noted that, unlike other animals, humans stand in an erect position, which directs the head toward the heavens and the tailbone toward the earth, creating a direct channel for the Universal and Earth Forces. In this erect posture, the coccyx directs the Earth Force upward as the head's position directs the Universal Force downward. Both forces combine in the brain and spread out to the whole body, which is thereby nourished and strengthened (Figure 1-9).

This channel is the source of our mental development, which, according to Taoism, has surpassed that of the known animal kingdom because these forces naturally enhance the powers of the mind. Animals, particularly quadrupeds, tend to raise their tails up to the heavens to channel the Universal Force downward while drawing the Earth Force up through the four feet (Figure 1- 9). This type of channeling enhances the body before the energy reaches the brain (although both forces eventually circulate to the head), thereby giving the animals increased physical strength instead of the superior mental capacity that humans receive.

In humans, the Universal Force flows downward in a clockwise spiral to the crown, where it penetrates and nourishes all the glands within the head before continuing down through the palate. The Earth Force ascends through the soles of the feet and up through the genitals, perineum, and coccyx, passing the heart's center, until it reaches the salivary glands of the tongue. Another path draws the Earth Force up the spine and into the brain. In this way humans have the ability to channel the essences of the Universal and Earth Forces to balance and strengthen

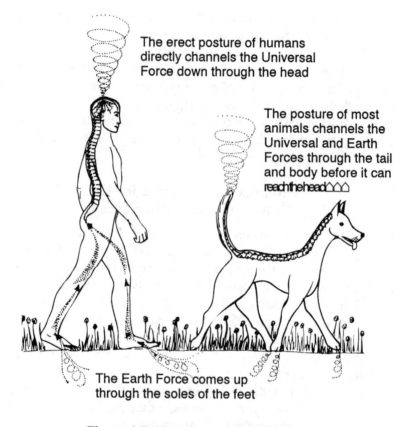

The erect posture of humans directly channels the Universal Force down through the head

The posture of most animals channels the Universal and Earth Forces through the tail and body before it can reach the head ^^^

The Earth Force comes up through the soles of the feet

Figure 1-9. Humans as channels for Universal and Earth Forces

body, mind, and spirit (Figure 1- 10). Pushing the tongue up against the palate connects the two channels of the Microcosmic Orbit and activates the forces in the saliva, which becomes sweeter and refreshed with energy. (Taoists regard the saliva as a mixture of the Universal and Earth Forces.)

The Greater Heavenly Cycle and the Smaller Heavenly Cycle

All living creatures absorb the three main forces in accordance with the earth's orbit around the sun. The earth's motion through the universe, making a full orbit every 365.25 days, is part of the Macrocosmic Orbit of the Universal Force, which causes the four seasons and associated

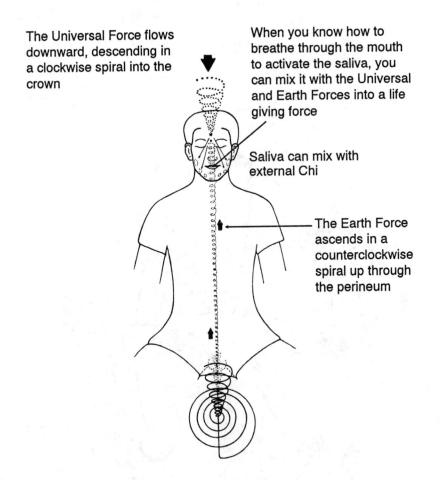

The Universal Force flows downward, descending in a clockwise spiral into the crown

When you know how to breathe through the mouth to activate the saliva, you can mix it with the Universal and Earth Forces into a life giving force

Saliva can mix with external Chi

The Earth Force ascends in a counterclockwise spiral up through the perineum

Figure 1-10. Humans have the ability to channel the essences of the Universal and Earth Forces to balance and strengthen body, mind, and spirit.

changes in the earth's energy (Figure 1-11). If our principal force (Original Chi) is not abundant enough to draw and absorb the Universal Force, we receive less energy than we expend in our daily lives, thereby depleting our bodies and promoting the onset of old age, sickness, and death. This is similar to how battery cells, when we forget to recharge them, become drained and lose their ability to hold a new charge.

By opening the Microcosmic Orbit (Smaller Heavenly Cycle) within our bodies, we can develop a connecting link to the Macrocosmic Orbit (Greater Heavenly Cycle) of the universe, through which we can

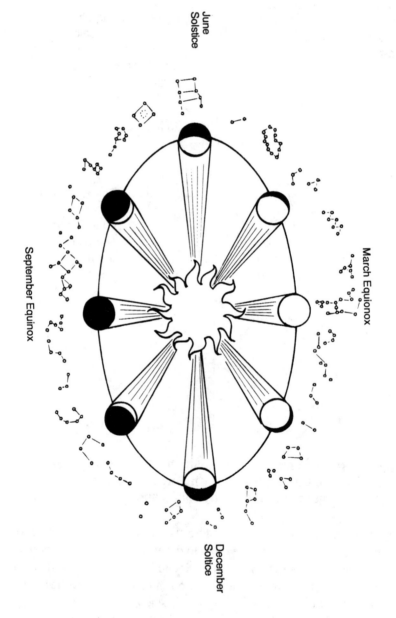

Figure 1-11. Each orbit of the earth around the sun is analogous to one round of the Macrocosmic Orbit.

tap into and absorb the original source of all power (Figure 1-12). Taoists learn to absorb and transform this force directly, rather than depending entirely on plants, animals, and motions of the earth to provide energy. After developing the *Energy Body* and extending it into space, they learn to access energies that are purer and more highly refined (Figure 1-13). This means that humans are not necessarily restricted by the earth's orbit.

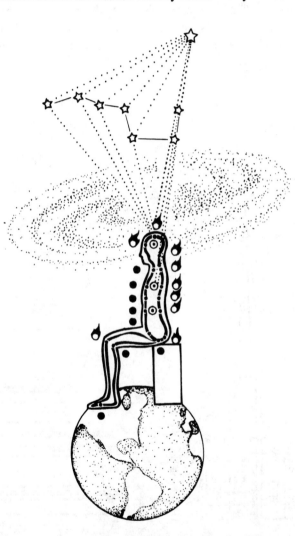

Figure 1-12. By opening the Microcosmic Orbit and connecting to the cycle of the Universal Macrocosm, we can draw in more of the Universal Force.

We can extend ourselves into the universe to draw the forces we need to replenish our life-force (Figures 1-13 and 1-14).

The Three Pure Ones are the sources of our Prenatal or Original Chi. In turn, it is our Original Chi that helps us draw and absorb the Universal, Higher Self, and Earth Forces. By understanding how to absorb and digest more energy from the these three forces, we can eventually replace any lost Original Chi that has been depleted during the course of our lives (Figure 1-15). An abundance of this Original Chi makes all other forms of energy much more assimilable. Combining the external forces with

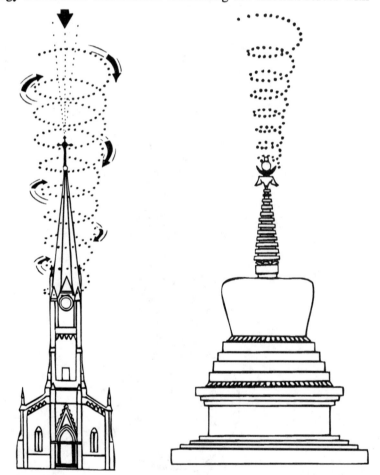

Figure 1-13. Churches and temples extend into the sky to capture the Universal Force and channel it down to people who do not know how to access it by themselves.

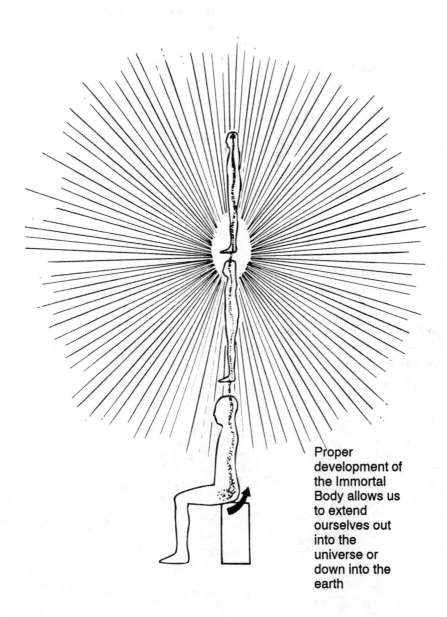

Proper development of the Immortal Body allows us to extend ourselves out into the universe or down into the earth

Figure 1-14. If we develop spirit and soul bodies, we can extend ourselves out further into the universe without having to depend on others.

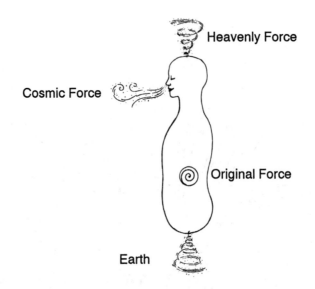

Figure 1-15. The Original Force is like a battery in our bodies because it can be recharged with practice.

our internal energies produces a healthy body and a stronger life-force. With meditative practices, such as the Microcosmic Orbit, this process is enhanced tenfold.

Chapter 2

CHI

Chi

Figure 2-1. Chi is the movement in the universe, but not the intelligence.

WHAT IS CHI?

Perhaps the most basic and general principle of Taoist thought is the concept of Chi. Its status in Chinese philosophy is developed in the popular works of Lao Tzu (604-511 B.C.) and Chuang Tzu (399-295 B.C.), but its origins go back much further. The word Chi has many translations, such as *energy, air, breath, wind, vital breath, vital essence,* and so forth. Although difficult to define, it can be thought of as the activating energy of the universe.

Chi condenses and disperses in alternating cycles of negative and positive (Yin and Yang) energy, materializing in different ways, forms, and shapes. It can be neither created nor destroyed. Instead, Chi transforms itself and reappears in new states of existence. All states of existence, therefore, are temporary manifestations of Chi, especially those of physical matter.

Chi is the source of all movement in the universe (Figure 2-1). The motions of the stars and planets, the radiation from the sun, and the

31

patterns of our thoughts and emotions occur because of Chi. It is considered to be the source of our life-force and the animating factor in all living beings.

Chi also binds things together. It is what keeps the constituents of our bodies from separating and dissipating. When the human body loses its breath of life, the original energy (life-force) leaves it, allowing the body to decompose.

Chi holds the organs, glands, blood vessels, and other bodily parts in place. When the body's Chi becomes weak, a loosening of the organs can occur in which they drop from their normal positions, leading to poor functioning and ill health. Chi also warms the body; any increase or decrease in bodily heat indicates the strength of its flow. We think of warmth in mammals as a "vital sign," showing that Chi is present.

The Chi that forms the heavens and earth is essentially the same as the Chi that forms living beings. This was expressed by the ancient Chinese philosophers as follows:

> Wu Chi (The Great Void) consists of Chi. Chi condenses to become the myriad things. Things of necessity disintegrate and return to the Wu Chi. If Chi condenses, its visibility becomes effective and physical form appears. Chi in dispersion is substance, and so is it in condensation. Every birth is a condensation, every death a dispersal. Birth is not a gain, death not a loss.... When condensed, Chi becomes a living being; when dispersed, it is the substratum of change.— Zhang Tsai (1020-1077 A.D.)

> A human being results from the Chi of Heaven and Earth. The union of the Chi of Heaven and Earth is called human being.—*Simple Questions,* Chapter 25 (Figure 2-2)

In *The Foundations of Chinese Medicine*, Giovanni Maciocia explains:

> According to the Chinese, there are many different "types" of human Chi, ranging from the tenuous and rarefied, to the very dense and coarse. All the various types of Chi, however, are ultimately one Chi, merely manifesting in different forms.

The Bible's Book of Genesis says, "God created man in His image." Similarly, in Chinese thought, human beings are a microcosm of the universe. Thus, Chi flows throughout the universe, and it also flows through humans. Through studying how our own Chi works, we can also understand the workings of the universe. In Taoist Inner Alchemy, we

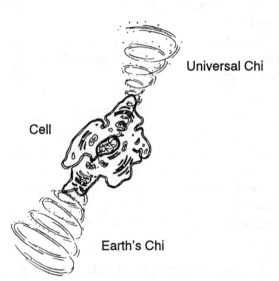

Universal Chi

Cell

Earth's Chi

Figure 2-2. Living cells are capable of using external Chi to develop intelligence, contracting and creating as they build on themselves with more energy.

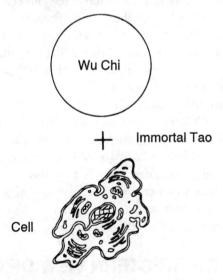

Wu Chi

+ Immortal Tao

Cell

Figure 2-3. The highest goal of Taoist Inner Alchemy is to transform our cells to unite with and become the cosmic cells of the universe. These cells are capable of living forever.

begin the process of spiritual exploration within the laboratory of our own body and mind.

The highest goal of Taoist Inner Alchemy is to transform our cells to unite with Cosmic (Higher Self) Energy and become immortal cosmic cells of the universe (Figure 2-3).

CHI IN OTHER CULTURES

The idea of Chi is not unique to the Chinese. Nearly every culture in the world has a word to express this concept. Dr. John Mann and Larry Short, authors of *The Body of Light*, count 49 cultures around the world that articulate the concept of Chi in one form or another.

In Hebrew, the word is *Ruach*, and it appears in the first chapter of the Book of Genesis:

> In the beginning God created the heavens and the earth. The world was without form and void, and darkness was upon the face of the deep; and the Ruach [spirit, wind, or breath] of God was moving over the face of the waters.--Genesis I:1-2

Ruach was present at the creation of the universe, even before light. The term means Breath of God or Divine Breath.

In Japanese, the term *Ki* expands the concept of Chi to include the Chinese idea of *Yi* or *intention*, indicating that our mind or will is a major influence governing the movement of Chi, which is very important in meditation and in the martial arts.

In Sanskrit, the word for Chi is *Prana*. The Tibetan word is *Lung*. In Lakota Sioux it is known as *Neyatoneyah*. The Bush People of the Kalahari speak of it as *Num*, which means Boiling Energy. In the Islamic world Chi is referred to as *Barraka*. Although many cultures possess an awareness of Chi, the Chinese have refined this concept and integrated it into their culture to an unparalleled degree. Chi is a pivotal factor in Chinese medicine, martial arts, meditation, science, painting, calligraphy, architecture, interior design, and poetry.

THE WESTERN VIEW OF CHI

In contrast to most world cultures, the concept of Chi appears to be generally absent from contemporary Western medicine and the more conservative establishment scientific circles. Not surprisingly, however, the idea of life-force energy and its relationship to healing has been embraced and explored by many Western researchers.

F.A. Mesmer (1734-1815), the famous Austrian physician, was a pioneer in Western research involving energetic principles. He conducted many experiments and public demonstrations of the phenomenon he called "animal magnetism." Mesmer believed he could harness a universal magnetic power and direct it with his hands to heal people. He had many successes, especially with cases of hysteria, but his ideas were not accepted by conventional physicians. Because Mesmer never proved the existence of animal magnetism in a laboratory, they viewed him as a fraud. Eventually the local medical establishment pressured him to leave Vienna.

Mesmer was confronted with similar attitudes when, after he moved to Paris, the Parisian medical community appointed a commission to investigate his practices. The commission had to admit Mesmer's methods worked, but they refused to accept his explanation of animal magnetism and chose not to attribute his successes to any known scientific principles. Originally called mesmerism, his methods later became known as hypnosis.

More recently, Wilhelm Reich, an early disciple of Sigmund Freud, became intrigued with something he called "orgone," a form of primordial cosmic energy (Chi), which he related to sexual energy. He received much criticism and was persecuted for his theories, despite his many clinical successes. The U.S. Food and Drug Administration won an uncontested injunction against him, which prohibited him from selling orgone-accumulating devices on the grounds that the existence of orgone could not be proven. Reich refused to defend his scientific ideas in court and ignored the injunction. He was tried for contempt of court, convicted, and sentenced to two years in a federal penitentiary. He died in Lewisburg Prison in 1957.

Attitudes began to change in the West after President Richard Nixon reestablished diplomatic relations with China in 1972. In Beijing, Chinese doctors performed emergency surgery on *New York Times* correspondent James Reston, using only acupuncture for anesthesia. Since then many delegations of Western physicians to China have witnessed similar events. Eventually, Western medicine had to admit that Chinese doctors have practical applications of Chi that can indeed heal the human body. In a few short years, many Chinese medical schools

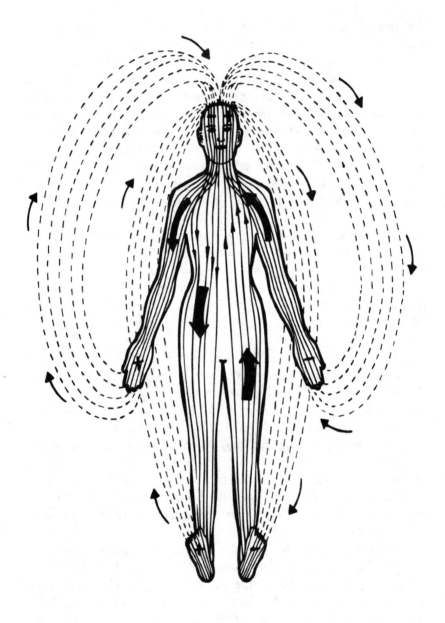

Figure 2-4. The Body Electric

were established throughout the United States and Europe, and most Western cities now have many acupuncturists to serve the ailing.

Because the concept of Chi is not limited to any single area of current Western science, it is difficult for Westerners to understand. It is not easily pigeonholed into either physics, electrical engineering, biochemistry, medicine, or psychology, and yet it is clearly related to all of them. Now a few scientific synthesizers are emerging who have broad enough training and sufficient curiosity to research Chi. Interestingly, the discovery of endorphins, the body's natural painkillers, resulted from an investigation into how acupuncture anesthesia works. This is only the first of many scientific breakthroughs that will occur as scientists continue their research into Chi.

Currently, several reputable scientists are exploring the phenomena of Chi. Dr. Herbert Benson, physician and author of *The Relaxation Response*, is currently conducting a research project on Chi Kung. Dr. David Eisenberg, a Harvard Medical School graduate, wrote *Encounters with Chi*, a book about his experiences with acupuncture and Chi Kung masters while a student at an acupuncture college in China. Dr. Robert Becker, a Syracuse University orthopedist and author of *The Body Electric* (Figure 2-4), is seeking to explain Chi in light of his research into bioelectricity and its relationship to the mind and healing. It was Dr. Becker's research into electricity and its role in regeneration that led to the current method of using low-level electrical currents to stimulate mending of fractures.

CHI AND SELF-HEALING

From the Taoist perspective, health and healing depend on the quantity and quality of Chi in the body. Acupuncture, acupressure, herbology, and many other healing arts work directly to balance internal energy. Chi is a causal factor in a wide range of bodily phenomena. For example, a deficiency of Chi in the kidneys may result in a physical and psychological illness characterized by nervousness, sexual inhibition, or impotence. (Either an excess or deficiency of Chi can cause illness.)

Exercise fortifies the muscles with the body's energy, enhancing our ability to consume more Chi. The Taoists discovered that opening the major energy channels can increase the Chi circulation more effectively, amplifying it with energy absorbed from external sources. They assert

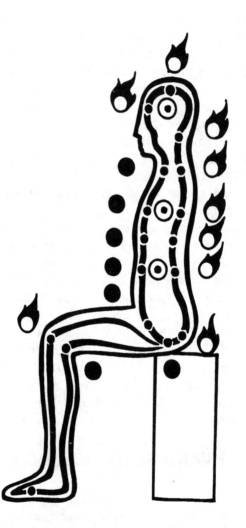

**Figure 2-5. Practice with the Microcosmic Orbit
will increase the bioelectric flow (Chi).**

that meditation, a proper diet, and exercise are very important to one's life and spiritual growth.

Most illnesses and pain result from blockages of Chi, as too many protons condense in the wrong places. This impedes the flow of electrons through major channels of the body. By releasing such blockages and increasing the Chi flow, we can often heal ourselves without resorting to medical treatments. Working with Chi to heal the body is a form of "needle-less" acupuncture. By using the inner senses to circulate Chi through the Microcosmic Orbit, we establish a clear and open channel, so our internal health can maintain itself. Not only are blockages removed as the body's natural Chi flow is enhanced, but practice also helps the body absorb more Chi from other sources (Figure 2-5).

External Chi received from the earth, sun, and stars can be transformed and refined into enhanced life-force for self-healing and spiritual growth. The centers of the Microcosmic Orbit receive surplus Chi from these sources as well as from the organs and glands. The circulation of this energy feeds any points that are deficient and balances the body's Chi in general, lessening the need for acupuncture and other healing arts. Internal work provides the best form of health maintenance and preventive medicine.

Taoist masters of modern times can see the energetic deficiencies that cause illnesses in people. They also know how difficult it can be to teach people to heal themselves, especially those who are very sick. Still, the masters realize that teaching self-healing is better than allowing others to become dependent on them for healing. But there are times when self-healing techniques may be beyond someone's capabilities. For this reason the Taoists developed various forms of Chi meditation, Internal Alchemy, and acupuncture, which can use mind power, certain Chi Kung exercises, or needles to open any blockages that cause pain and sickness.

THE TWO TYPES OF INTERNAL CHI: HEREDITARY AND ACQUIRED

Although there are many different types of Chi, they all fall under two basic categories: Hereditary Chi and Acquired Chi .

Hereditary Chi

Hereditary Chi is the Chi that is with us from conception to death. It nourishes us in the womb and is the foundation of our life-force until we die. The Chinese call this type of Chi *Pre-Heavenly Force*, *Early Heavenly Chi*, *Pre-Birth Breath*, or *Prenatal Energy*. Although there are several types of Hereditary Chi, the most important form for our purposes at this time is the *Original Chi* or *Original Force* (Yuan Chi) (Figure 2-6).

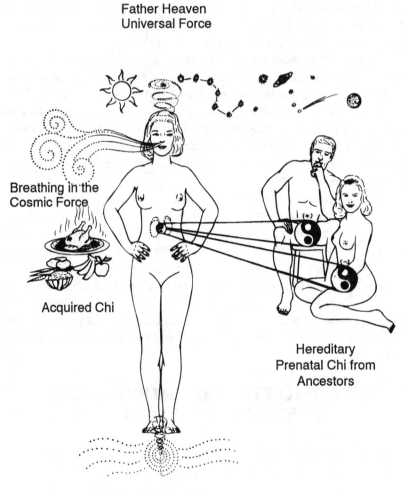

Father Heaven
Universal Force

Breathing in the
Cosmic Force

Acquired Chi

Hereditary
Prenatal Chi from
Ancestors

Mother Earth's Force

Figure 2-6. There are many different types of Chi, in two basic categories: Hereditary Chi and Acquired Chi.

Acquired Chi

Acquired Chi includes all the types of Chi that are produced after birth. The Chinese call this type of Chi *Post-Heavenly Breath*, *Later Heavenly Force*, *Post-Birth Chi*, or *Postnatal Energy*. (It is important to understand that these colorful terms are all just different translations of the same words in Chinese.)

The primary sources of this Chi are the food we eat, the water we drink, and the air we breathe. In addition, whether we are conscious of it or not, we are constantly receiving energy from the Three Forces: Universal or Heavenly Energy, Higher Self or Cosmic Energy, and Earth Energy. Many Taoist practices are directed toward teaching us to better attune to, absorb, and digest the energies of these Three Forces.

THE ORIGINAL CHI IN HUMANS

Original Chi: Our Source of Life-Force

Although it derives from the forces of Heaven and Earth, Original Chi is instilled in our bodies through the love and sexual union of our parents. Taoists believe that during the act of love and sex, all bodily essences of man and woman condense into orgasmic Chi, which draws in and reunites the Universal, Higher Self, and Earth Forces. Yin and Yang orgasmic energies combine with these external forces as the sperm and egg unite, establishing our Original Chi at conception (Figure 2-7). Taoists refer to this as the Reunion of Heaven and Earth.

Once these forces are united, they draw in even higher forces from the Wu Chi. The act of love and sexual union draws in so much of these powerful forces that it can create a new human life (Figure 2-8). During pregnancy and after birth, an infant is continuously nourished by these forces through the nutrients supplied by its mother (first through the umbilical cord, later through breast-feeding).

Original Chi: The Body's Battery

When the umbilical cord is cut and we start to breathe, Original Chi is stored within our bodies, just like the charge of a battery. In Taoist physiology, the Original Chi is stored in the space between the navel, the kidneys, and the sexual center, slightly above the pelvic area (Figure 2-9). During every moment of every day we draw on this Chi for combustion

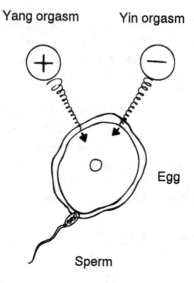

Figure 2-7. Reunion of Yin and Yang,
the Original Chi in humans

Figure 2-8. The first complete cells have the power to draw
and unite the Heaven, Earth, and Cosmic Forces.

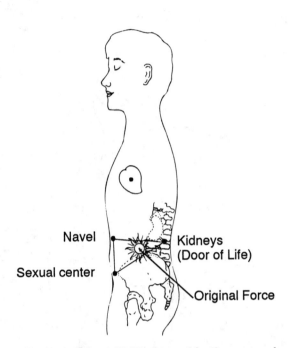

Navel

Kidneys
(Door of Life)

Sexual center

Original Force

**Figure 2-9. The Original Chi is stored in the space between
the navel and the sexual center.**

of energy from external sources, such as food, air, and energies from the earth, moon, sun, and stars.

The process is similar to the electrical system in a car, which depends on the battery to initiate its operation (Figure 2-10). The spark from the battery, combined with air and fuel, produces internal combustion. The force of the internal combustion powers the engine, which, in turn, runs the car. After ignition has been achieved and the engine is running, the battery is no longer required to produce the spark because the generator or alternator takes over to maintain the current. The generator then restores any lost charge back to the battery. When the battery is in good condition it can be recharged continually, just as Original Chi can be replenished with energy indirectly with Chi taken from the vital organs, food, and air, or directly through any of the Three Major Forces.

Original Chi can escape the body in many ways, such as excess talking, working, reading, daydreaming, or sexual activity. In other words, we deplete our Original Chi when we don't use our senses and

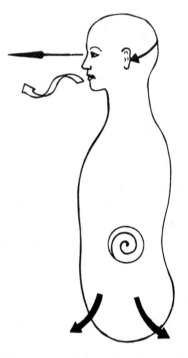

**Figure 2-10. Original Chi is like a battery powering the body.
We use this energy in our daily lives.**

sexual energy in the proper way. Taoists regard sexual energy as a major part of the Original Force.

   Today we are tempted to dissipate our life-force in many directions. Many magazine advertisements and television commercials, for instance, are designed to activate our sexual desires. Once sexual desire is activated, it stimulates sensual desires as well. These desires drain our Original Force out to combine with the message of the advertisement. Our senses become charged with craving for every sort of stimulation and product, just as the advertisers intend (Figure 2-11). We are convinced to buy and consume many things we do not need. This overconsumption saps the life-force and prevents us from using it for more productive healing and spiritual purposes.

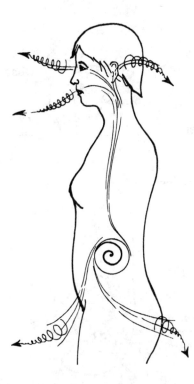

Figure 2-11. Once our sexual desires activate and leak out, our senses become charged with cravings for many kinds of stimulation. This further drains our energies.

Many other factors in daily life drain our Original Force and sexual energy reserves. When too much sexual energy is lost through ejaculation or menstruation, both the will (which is related to the kidneys and sexual energy) and the body begin to grow weak. When the will is weak, unhealthy eating habits develop. Bad diet, criticizing other people, sexual harassment, and foul language cause more loss of sexual energy through the mouth. Focusing on the shortcomings of others and viewing pornography drain sexual energy through the eyes and weaken the liver. Listening to gossip and criticism hurts the ears and kidneys and directly drains the sexual energy. Negative thinking, obscene thoughts, daydreams, and excessive sexual fantasies drain the brain, marrow, and sexual energy (Figure 2-12).

The ancient Taoist masters warned, "Guard your senses and sexual energy!" We have become accustomed to the constant onslaught on our

45

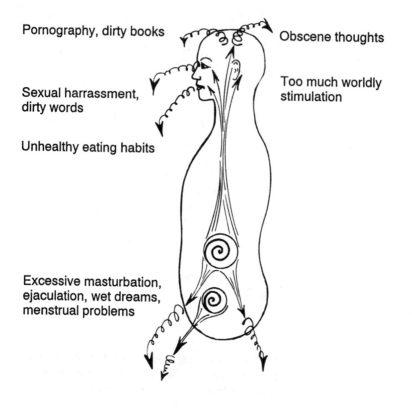

Pornography, dirty books

Obscene thoughts

Too much worldly
stimulation

Sexual harrassment,
dirty words

Unhealthy eating habits

Excessive masturbation,
ejaculation, wet dreams,
menstrual problems

Figure 2-12. Sexual energy leaks out in many ways.

senses and accept it as part of our culture, but we must recognize the dangers of advertising and break free from its mind-numbing effects. If we want to be in control of our lives, we must guard and conserve our life-force and sexual energy.

By maintaining the Original Chi, we can increase endurance and longevity. But if we neglect to recharge ourselves, our "internal batteries" will become weak.

Every time we inhale, the Original Breath from the lower abdomen rises to the mouth and mixes with externally drawn air. We can learn how to draw the Earth Force through the sexual organ, perineum, and sacrum; the Cosmic Force through the mid-eyebrow; and the Universal Force through the crown. The advanced breathing techniques enable one to breathe through the whole body (Figure 2-13).

Proper inhalation and exhalation of air move internal energy up, then down through the Functional Channel at the mouth. If we do not know how to bring this energy down to the navel, or if we neglect to do so, it will flow out the nose or mouth with each exhalation. We can lose even more Original Chi if we overexert ourselves and become short of breath.

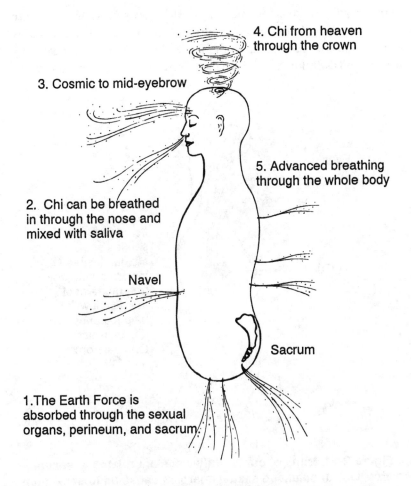

4. Chi from heaven through the crown

3. Cosmic to mid-eyebrow

5. Advanced breathing through the whole body

2. Chi can be breathed in through the nose and mixed with saliva

Navel

Sacrum

1.The Earth Force is absorbed through the sexual organs, perineum, and sacrum

Figure 2-13. Each time we inhale, we draw in energy.

How to Increase and Restore the Original Chi

Focusing your vital Chi until it is supremely soft, can you be like a baby?—Lao Tsu

If we have a free moment during the day, it is helpful to turn the senses and sexual desires inward and fix the mind, eyes, and heart on the Original Force. This will help conserve and increase the Force (Figure 2-14).

Proper Breathing and the Microcosmic Orbit

One of the major reasons for practicing the Microcosmic Orbit is to return the body to a state of innocence and virtue, as in infancy when our energy was pure and full. According to the Bible, Jesus said that we can only return to God as children. Through the Microcosmic Orbit meditation we

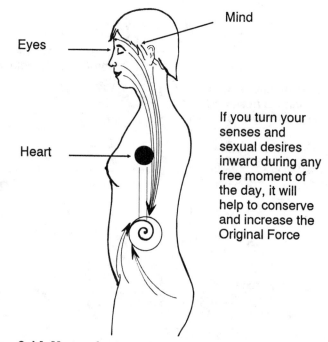

Eyes

Mind

Heart

If you turn your senses and sexual desires inward during any free moment of the day, it will help to conserve and increase the Original Force

Figure 2-14. Many of our worldly vices are related to sexual desires. Our unbalanced sexual energies cause us to seek many forms of gratification in material things we don't really need.

can give birth to a new self, restore our lost Original Force, and return to a childlike energy.

As stated earlier, the Original Breath moves upward to the mouth where it mixes with the food we eat and the air we breathe. We can learn to consciously take in the Universal, Higher Self, and Earth Forces to mix them with our Original Chi, and then bring these down through the Functional Channel to the navel, where they can be refined to increase and restore our Original Chi.

Learning and practicing the Microcosmic Orbit meditation is the best way to maintain the Original Chi. By keeping the channels open and flowing and by drawing external energy into the body, we conserve our Original Chi and increase our ability to digest and use the energies we take in from outside, which we call external Chi or Acquired Chi. As in making investments, it is better to spend the interest we collect from what we have saved and inherited than to deplete our principal by spending more than we take in or earn.

Breathing In Cosmic Energy

Taoists say there is life-force in the air, but it is separate from the major elements of oxygen, nitrogen, and carbon dioxide. The air is also made up of ions (charged protons and electrons), which are often depleted by pollution, overcrowded conditions in our cities, air conditioning, concrete buildings, and other features of modern society. Without these energy particles, people become weak and tired. Science is studying ways to replace these particles in areas depleted by human tampering, but to absorb their energies, we must separate them from the air, just as fish separate oxygen from the water. Taoist masters use the mind, the inner eye, and the heart to distinguish and categorize the various forms of Chi in nature and the universe (Figure 2-15).

Breathing is one of the most important functions that sustains our lives. What most of us don't realize, however, is that the cosmic particles of energy in our atmosphere are just as important to our survival as oxygen. (These ionized particles are also referred to as the *Later Heavenly Force*.) Charged electrons supply the electrical current within our cells. If these are depleted, we can become weak, tired, and depressed, or we might suffer from negative emotional states and even physical illness.

The Taoists realized that breathing external energies into the lungs does not make the best use of them for the body. They also discovered that Chi can be separated from the air as it is being inhaled and mixed

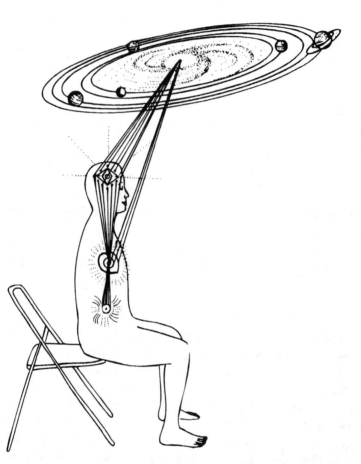

Figure 2-15. Taoist masters use the mind, the inner eye, and the heart to distinguish and categorize the various forms of Chi in nature and the universe.

with the Original Force in our saliva. We can then swallow this energy with the saliva so that it can be used immediately and more efficiently by the body. We can also use the mid-eyebrow point, the palms, and the skin to absorb energies for the body's use. Taoist masters created many exercises to help us take in external forces, such as Chi Kung, Tai Chi, and various forms of meditation. Meditations, such as the Microcosmic Orbit, are the most direct way to take in these energies.

Conserving Sexual Energy Maintains and Rebuilds Our Original Force

We must also maintain our sexual energy, which is referred to as *Ching Chi* by Taoists. It is part of our Original Force, and it can be increased, provided the Ching Chi is conserved. When supplemented by the energies of the air we breathe and the food we eat, our Original Force helps the body produce sexual energy. People unknowingly deplete themselves of this energy, however, through excessive ejaculation and menstruation, wasting an incredible source of potential life-force. By redirecting sexual energy into the internal organs and glands (Figure 2-16), people can have wonderful sex and an abundance of energy to heal and rejuvenate their bodies. Sexual energy, or Ching Chi, was discovered to be the most powerful force within the body when it is recycled internally. This process heals and strengthens the other organs and glands, increasing their production of Chi.

Sperm and ovum are the condensed essences of the Universal and Earth Forces, and their power, Ching Chi, compounds itself regularly if it is recycled. Drawing on these sources of energy increases the life-force tremendously, and an enhanced life-force translates into nourishment for body, mind, and spirit. The first step in transforming sexual energy into

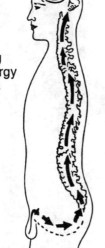

Redirecting
sexual energy
into organs
and glands

**Figure 2-16. Sexual energy
(Ching Chi)—part of the Original Force**

51

life-force is to open the channels of the Microcosmic Orbit so that positive Chi can be circulated up into the higher centers and transformed to fulfill the body's needs.

CHI AND MEDITATION

Thousands of years ago, Taoist masters discovered the body's Chi centers through internal observation. This involved removing the body from external stimuli and meditating, so that the inner senses could be activated. By quieting the mental and physical processes and using their inner senses, the masters discovered that some parts of the body have more Chi than others. They serve as gathering points of nourishment for particular organs and glands. These centers can receive Chi from outside sources such as electromagnetic power, the earth's vibration, light, and frequency or sound from the moon, sun, and stars. The Universal Force,

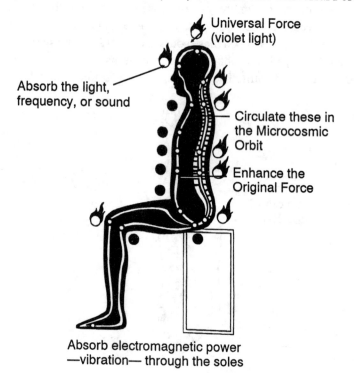

Universal Force
(violet light)

Absorb the light,
frequency, or sound

Circulate these in
the Microcosmic
Orbit

Enhance the
Original Force

Absorb electromagnetic power
—vibration— through the soles

Figure 2-17. The Microcosmic Orbit

in the form of the red and violet light of unconditional love, adds to this nourishment (Figure 2-17).

The masters learned that these centers connect to form a pathway, which they called the Microcosmic Orbit. At that time, they had no concept of electricity as we know it today. Nonetheless, they were able to access the body's electromagnetic energy flow (Chi).

The masters learned to use the mind and the inner eye to guide Chi through this pathway. They used it to heal themselves, thus creating a foundation for spiritual work. As they developed their inner senses to distinguish and categorize Chi according to its various sources (sun, moon, stars, etc.), they also learned how to absorb more Chi from each source into their bodies.

The Microcosmic Orbit pathway is composed of two major channels, referred to as the Governor and Functional Channels. The Governor Channel runs from the perineum up the spine and over the head, ending at the palate of the mouth. The Functional Channel runs from the perineum up the front of the body, ending at the tip of the tongue. Touching the tip of the tongue to the palate connects both channels.

The Microcosmic Orbit is like a large reservoir of Chi that supplies nourishing Chi to the rest of the body. First, it fills the Extraordinary or Ancestral Channels. (There are eight Extraordinary Channels in total. The Governor and Functional Channels—the channels of the Microcosmic Orbit—are the first two. These feed the remaining six Extraordinary Channels.) Then it fills the twelve Ordinary Channels: the six Yin channels and the six Yang channels. The Yin and Yang channels are each connected to one of the vital organs. This is how the Microcosmic Orbit meditation sends nourishing Chi throughout the entire body.

All people are born with the Microcosmic Orbit route open and flowing. Even in the mother's womb, the Chi of a fetus flows through its own Microcosmic Orbit (Figure 2-18). After birth, this route usually stays clear and open until the onset of puberty, when the body experiences the stress of hormonal change and rapid growth and the emotions run strong during the awkward phase of adolescence. Stress is one of the major factors behind the Chi blockages that occur in the channels of the body during adulthood. By consciously reopening the Microcosmic Orbit, we can increase the efficiency of our energy consumption and begin to replenish any losses of Chi.

Because the spiritual qualities, or virtues, are linked with our vital organs, Taoists practice restoring and keeping the physical body in robust

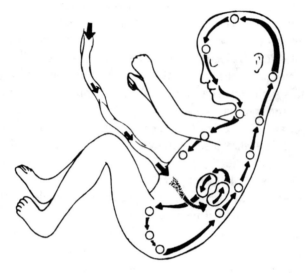

**Figure 2-18. The Microcosmic Orbit circulates Chi
in the fetus while it is still in the mother's womb.**

health as the foundation for spiritual work. When an organ is not receiving enough Chi, the physical health of the organ may become impaired; at the same time, it will be more difficult for the virtue linked with that organ to manifest.

Chi acts as a link between the physical body, the energy (soul) body, and the spirit body (Figure 2-19), in the same way that fuel in a boat's engine creates the force that pushes it across water. Chi is the fuel for each of these bodies. Just as a boat can be stranded without gas, so too can the body, soul, and spirit be hindered by low energy.

This does not mean that people who are sick are incapable of spiritual growth. It is more difficult to concentrate on spirituality when the need for healing is great, but the healing process itself can be a spiritual experience if one embraces it wholeheartedly.

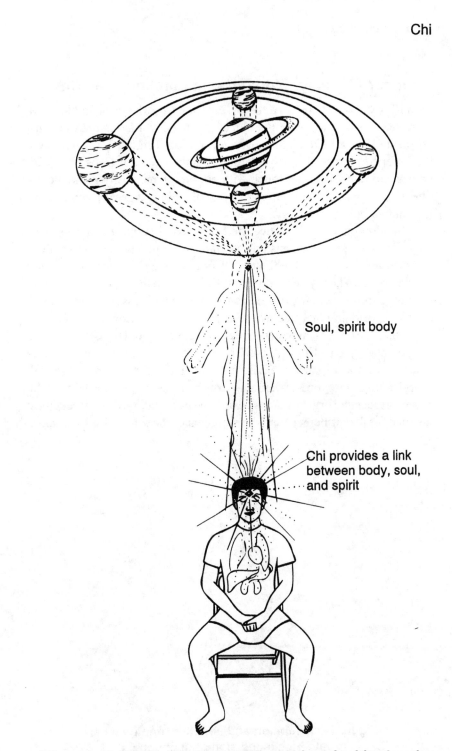

Soul, spirit body

Chi provides a link
between body, soul,
and spirit

Figure 2-19. Physical health is the foundation of spiritual work.

Inner Alchemy: Working with Emotions and Chi

In the Taoist way of Inner Alchemy, emotional work goes hand in hand with energy work. Many of the blockages that occur along the channels are created by, or linked with, negative emotions (Figure 2-20). Through the Inner Smile and the Six Healing Sounds, we learn to listen to our bodies and to get in better touch with our emotions, positive and negative. Developing virtuous energies helps clear blockages, promote healing, and gather more energy.

In addition, as we practice the Microcosmic Orbit meditation, we may discover physical tensions at various important energy points. Physical tensions are often the results of negative emotions that we are holding onto. When we can move our Chi through these points, we learn to release those tensions; this helps us process their associated negative emotions, bringing that trapped energy back into the flow of life.

Once we have cleared away negative emotions and transformed that trapped energy back into usable Chi, we can then enhance the natural qualities of the organs: the virtues, which are the organs' essential energies. In other words, when the virtues are being expressed, the Chi of their associated organs is at its peak. This pure, natural energy becomes the food for the refinement and development of the soul and spirit bodies.

**Figure 2-20. Tension and negative emotions can
create blockages along the channels.**

If we neglect to nurture our good emotions and just work on bringing more energy into the body, we may energize our negative emotions, making them more powerful and thus more difficult to control and transform. This is why some spiritual leaders become corrupt; they become entranced with power but neglect the daily practice of refining their Chi and nourishing their virtuous energies. Development of the virtues must continue until it becomes an automatic process. Only then can one truly understand what it means to be called a master.

Developing the Power of the Mind

All systems of meditation aim to quiet the mind and nurture the spirit. When the mind is agitated, it overflows with thoughts and feelings, reacts to everything, and often overreacts, causing the life-force to become scattered. Because the mind is so occupied with this flow, it cannot give its full power to any one thought or feeling; lacking incisive power, it becomes scattered and diffuse. It is like the rays of the sun: when the sun's rays are diffused, they have some warmth. But if they are focused through a magnifying glass or lens, they have enough heat to burn paper. In the same way, when we quiet the mind through meditation, it becomes focused and strong. This is what we mean by "mind power."

To quiet the mind, the mind must first become focused on something. We call that something "the object of meditation." Other systems use many different things as the object of meditation: mantras, koans, the breath, visualizations, analytical subjects to ponder, and so forth. In the Healing Tao, the object of meditation is Chi.

Chi is our life-force. This makes it unique as an object of meditation. When you use your mind power (thought), eye power (senses), and heart power (organs) to focus on your life-force itself, you not only gain control of your mind, you learn to control your life as well. All these powers combine to become the highest state of consciousness, which Taoists call Yi (Figure 2-21).

Taoist meditations help still the mind and body so we can absorb, recycle, refine, and conserve higher energies. Most of the common meditation techniques have similar goals but are less direct in their approaches. The differences are especially obvious between *passive* meditations, which are commonly taught to Westerners for relaxation purposes, and the *active* methods practiced in Taoism.

Passive meditations usually consist of "silent sitting," which involves facing a blank wall and observing thoughts to silence the mind.

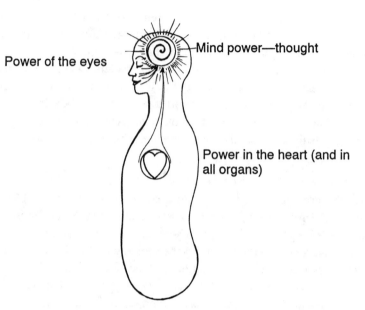

Power of the eyes

Mind power—thought

Power in the heart (and in all organs)

Figure 2-21. All these powers combine to become the highest state of awareness, which Taoists call Yi.

This often includes mantras or chanting to lull the mind into deeper states of consciousness where thought processes are minimal. Active meditations focus the mind to open channels for the circulation of energy, which nourishes body, mind, and spirit.

The energy transformations of the Healing Tao are active processes in that we consciously transform negative emotions into positive virtues, and sexual energy into life-force and spiritual energy. Passive techniques may attain some of these benefits inadvertently, but the Taoist methods help us consciously achieve our goals by working actively and directly with our internal energies. Taoists use the passive state after practice to just sit quietly with the effects of the practice, letting things happen as they need to. This is called *Wu Chi*, sitting still and doing nothing. Yang is active, and Yin is passive. The main practice of the Taoist is training the mind, eyes, and heart to tap the Universal, Cosmic, and Earth Forces to help increase our Original Force (Figure 2-22).

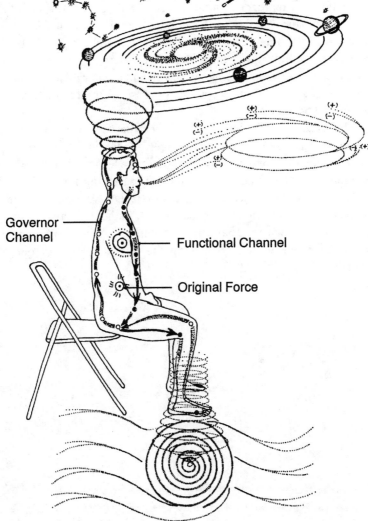

Figure 2-22. Training the mind, eyes, and heart to tap the Universal and Cosmic Forces increases our Original Force.

Taoist Meditations: A Practical Approach

The true goal of all meditations is pure awareness or enlightenment, which produces a higher vibration, light, or frequency in our life-force. The Healing Tao approach accumulates, circulates, and refines life-force energy to enhance all bodily functions, including the production of spiritual energies that derive from our organs and glands. Instead of silencing the mind, this system uses it to increase the flow of Chi throughout the body, enhancing our health and our spiritual growth. The *Healing Light* meditation serves this purpose as the foundation of all Healing Tao practices.

The secrets of Chi circulation have been passed down for thousands of years through several Taoist lineages. Those in China who were fortunate enough to receive this essential knowledge experienced great improvements in the quality of their lives. The Healing Tao teaches these secrets to help us become responsible for our lives. We can become our own masters by focusing on spiritual growth, rather than awaiting death and judgment for what we have neglected in life. As we learn to control our life-force, we gradually develop the means to control our own destinies.

Chapter 3

THE VIRTUES

OPENING THE MIND AND THE HEART

There are two major approaches to spiritual disciplines. One may embrace concepts related to faith, good deeds, prayer, right action, confession of sins, and so forth. This approach gradually changes a person's negativity into virtuous energy, which is close to the Original Force, or Wu Chi. Taoism offers another approach, involving the creation of a vehicle in the form of the *energy body* and eventually the *spirit body*. These subtle bodies act as space shuttles, allowing consciousness to travel back to its source (Figure 3-1). Some systems describe the heavenly realms but offer only faith as a means of returning to them. Faith is helpful, but other preparations during life can provide a more direct

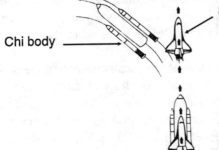

Chi body

Spirit body

(3) The shuttle flies free (the spirit body)

(2) Booster rockets lift off with the shuttle (the soul body or Chi body)

(1) Central tower and launching pad (the physical body)

Figure 3-1. The booster rocket separates from the shuttle (The soul body completes the lifting of the spirit body.)

means of accessing a desired heavenly place before physical death occurs.

Taoism recognizes both the development of virtuous energies and the cultivation of life-force to create the soul and spirit bodies as important aspects of spiritual growth. Both approaches are related, because retaining and recycling internal energy into life-force can help open and pacify our minds and hearts, bringing forth love, joy, happiness, respect, and honor. These virtues then bring forth other virtuous energies, such as kindness, gentleness, courage, openness, and fairness.

The heart is like a cauldron (Figure 3-2) that can be used to combine all the virtues into the energy of compassion, the ultimate virtue and a necessary attribute for our spiritual being. At the same time, our spiritual essence and life essence can be combined into one force, giving birth to the energy body (the vehicle) and the spirit body (the captain). We can train these subtle bodies to connect our consciousness to our source before we must depart from this world.

THE VIRTUES:
The Heart of the Healing Tao Practices

The quality of our internal energy is just as important to our health and spiritual development as the quantity. As we increase our internal energy flow and accumulate a surplus of Chi, we must also emphasize spiritual development to maintain balance in our daily lives. In essence, our spiritual qualities are our positive attributes, or what the Taoists call *virtues.*

We need food to sustain our lives. Physically we need material food, but we must also nourish other, subtler bodies within us, known as the soul and spirit bodies. The energies of our virtues, the universe, the stars, and the planets provide a source of spiritual food. Although we are trained to depend on our religious beliefs (Figure 3-3) to provide this nourishment, spiritual food is actually all around us. We just need to be taught how to absorb and digest it. Taoism offers the means by which we can access these energies to cultivate the soul and spirit and enhance our total being.

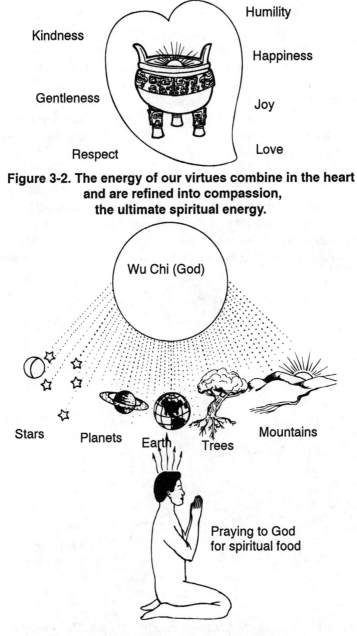

Humility

Kindness

Happiness

Gentleness

Joy

Respect

Love

Figure 3-2. The energy of our virtues combine in the heart and are refined into compassion, the ultimate spiritual energy.

Wu Chi (God)

Stars

Planets

Earth

Trees

Mountains

Praying to God for spiritual food

Figure 3-3. Spiritual leaders train us to absorb these forces in the form of God.

Understanding Our Virtues

Taoists believe that we are all born with the virtues of love, gentleness, kindness, respect, honesty, fairness, justice, and righteousness. These are actually higher aspects of our emotions, which are derived from the positive energies of our organs. When we are abundant with virtues, our life-force flows smoothly and efficiently. If we neglect to cultivate the virtues, however, we run the risk of channeling our accumulated energies directly into our negative emotions, exacerbating any negative or neurotic tendencies we may have. (Keep in mind that we usually exude the emotional energies that are most prevalent within us.)

Unfortunately, as we mature and encounter more stress in our daily lives, negative emotions such as fear, anger, cruelty, impatience, worry, sadness, and grief often predominate. These have deleterious effects on the internal organs and glands and can drain our life-force, causing our bodies to function on less energy and at a lower vibratory rate. Medical science acknowledges that the presence of negative emotions can wear

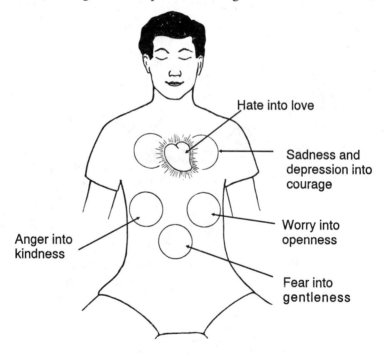

Hate into love

Sadness and depression into courage

Worry into openness

Anger into kindness

Fear into gentleness

Figure 3-4. Transform negative energy into positive energy through the Inner Smile practice.

down the body's resistance to disease before any clinical evidence of disease exists.

Transforming negative emotions into virtuous energies is a much better option, because it enhances our life-force (Figure 3-4). The Healing Tao system emphasizes this through recycling, transforming, and refining internal and external Chi to accentuate our positive traits (rather than our negative ones). When we learn to detoxify the organs through Taoist practices, we can reestablish our virtues and become self-regulating individuals, able to make decisions and control our destinies. Transforming internal energy also promotes a higher vibratory rate and enhances our spiritual growth.

Compassion: Combining the Virtues

Compassion is the highest expression of human emotion and virtuous energy. It is a level of development that takes hard work and serious meditation before it can blossom in one's life. It is not a single virtue, but the distillation and culmination of all virtues, expressed at any given moment as a blend of fairness, kindness, gentleness, honesty and respect, courage and love (Figure 3-5). The power to express any or all of these

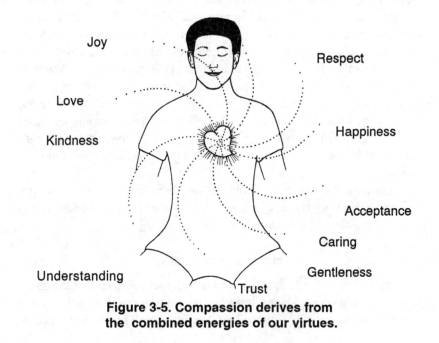

Figure 3-5. Compassion derives from the combined energies of our virtues.

virtues at the appropriate moment indicates that a person has internally unified himself or herself into a state of compassion.

Compassion is often misunderstood to be based on sympathy, which is actually a weakness individuals show when they are easily affected by the emotions of others. In fact, the combined strengths of the virtues produce an energy more closely related to empathy, which is a superior state that can acknowledge the emotional outpourings of others without being thrown off balance by them. The difference between empathy and compassion, however, is that compassion is not an emotion or a feeling, but a higher state of consciousness that naturally radiates the best human qualities.

Taoists regard compassion as the finest form of Chi; it is very easy to refine and transform into life-force.

Developing a Foundation for
Higher Emotional States

In the early stages of the Healing Tao system, students begin absorbing and transforming energy for the development of the physical, energy, and soul bodies. Cultivating the virtues and compassion is the other half of the practice, which refines the relationship among these bodies. The more virtuous energy you develop, the more easily you will be able to clear your channels of any blockages to your energy flow as you transform and refine your energy by circulating it in the Microcosmic Orbit.

You can't grow a healthy garden in a place full of weeds. Many of us strive to live virtuous lives and conscientiously try to be loving in our dealings with others. But if we open our hearts prematurely, before we have weeded our "internal gardens" by first cleansing our energy channels, we can end up polluting even the most loving intentions with emotional debris. To have a healthy garden, you must first clear away the weeds.

Furthermore, we must build up an abundance of loving energy before we can truly share it. Otherwise, how can we give good energy to others if we haven't got enough for ourselves?

Born to Be Equal

We are all created equal; kings and commoners alike share the same human experiences of being born and growing through childhood and adolescence to maturity (Figure 3-6). Yet if we don't know how to access higher forms of energetic nourishment, we have to depend on others who do know how. Many religions and spiritual teachers have the highest ethics and are willing to share their wisdom openly, while others keep their knowledge secret in order to hold on to their wealth, power, and position.

Taoists observe that one's energy is unprotected when one has not learned to open and clear the Microcosmic Orbit and develop the virtues. Such an individual is highly vulnerable to unethical people who may try to drain his or her life-force to build their own immortality.

In many religions and spiritual organizations, people are taught to surrender themselves, drop their egotism, practice self-sacrifice, and love others before they have accumulated enough energy and virtue to love themselves, much less the people close to them (Figure 3-7). Sometimes they are influenced to surrender themselves and their energy in subtle ways they don't consciously recognize. This is a form of energy vampirism. They gradually become weaker and poorer, eventually losing

Figure 3-6. In the beginning, we are all born equal.

Surrender
No egotism
Self-sacrifice
Give, give, and give more

Figure 3-7. When we don't know how to cultivate love and Chi within, the more energy we give out, the smaller we become.

Too much power
Too much Chi
Too much money

We give up more immortality and become smaller and smaller

Figure 3-8. Some systems or religions demand that we give up more Chi.

their life-force to others who are in turn becoming stronger, wealthier, and more powerful (Figure 3-8).

Our spiritual ignorance is reflected in the habits of our society. Not knowing how to nurture true spiritual growth, millions of people are slipping further away from their spiritual essence as they search for fulfillment through material gain.

UNDERSTANDING THE ENERGY OF LOVE

When studying the virtues, we must examine love as a category unto itself to better understand its energetic influences. The Taoists view love as an internal energy of the heart rather than a product of the mind. Although we generally think of love as a positive force, what we commonly call love can actually evoke more negativity in our lives than all the other negative energies combined. For example, we know that extreme love can often quickly turn to hatred of the most bitter and violent kind (Figure 3-9).

The misunderstanding of love can also create a vehicle that allows our negative emotions to drain our life-force away in the form of self-sacrifice. True compassion, which controls sexual desire, comes from a combination of compassion energy in the heart and sexual energy (Figure 3- 10). While our personal supply of energy is limited, the loving energy

Figure 3-9. Love alone can change to extreme hate.

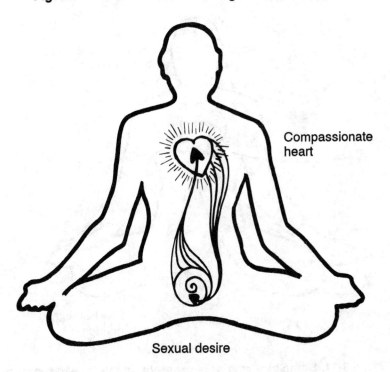

Figure 3-10. True compassion, which controls sexual desire, comes from a combination of compassion energy (in the heart) and sexual energy.

of the universe is inexhaustible. When we know how to connect to this wellspring, we will always have enough love for ourselves and for others. Yet if we are not taught how to tap into the higher forces to enhance and replenish our supply, we often end up giving away more than we can afford. Eventually this can cause us to drain out our sexual energy and burn out the love in our hearts (Figure 3-11).

We assume love exists at all levels of life, but because it is promoted so much, we often become desensitized to what it is and what it really feels like. We expect love in a personal way from those who are close to us, and in a spiritual way from those who become our role models. Yet our needs are almost never fulfilled by the words and actions of others. Even in dreams we seek love, which indicates our inner needs for acceptance and companionship from others. The question of what love is has puzzled men and women for centuries. The answer can only be found within ourselves.

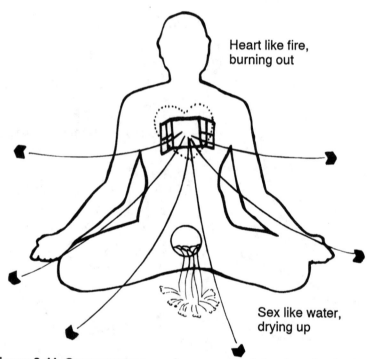

Heart like fire, burning out

Sex like water, drying up

Figure 3-11. Some systems only promote giving love in the form of self-sacrifice, giving more than we have to give. Eventually this can cause us to burn out. Many worldly endeavors also drain our sexual energy, causing it to dry up.

The Inner Source of Love

A major problem in our modern world is that we always look outside ourselves to fulfill our needs without realizing that others seek fulfillment in the same way. It is our nature to assume, for one reason or another, that everyone else has what we need, just as others make the same assumption about us. Out of habit, we all seek love externally without nurturing our own source of that energy from within (Figure 3-12). This leaves us with very little to share.

Logically, if others are also seeking love, they expect us to have enough loving energy to fulfill them in some way. If we do not cultivate love within ourselves, however, we can only drain their energies until the relationship comes to an end. Success in any relationship depends on the ability of two parties to share in an abundance of love that derives from both sources. The key word here is *abundance*. Once we are full of love within, we can connect to the unlimited love in the universe and share it abundantly with others.

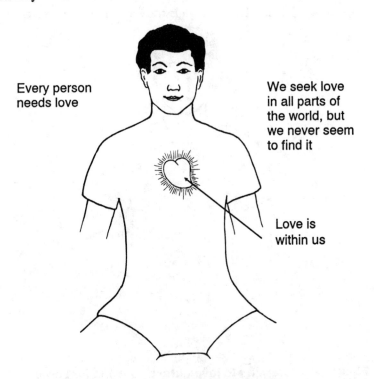

Every person needs love

We seek love in all parts of the world, but we never seem to find it

Love is within us

Figure 3-12. Love is within our heart.

Some people believe love has value only if it comes from others, but they fail to realize love can turn against them if they do not have enough of that energy to reciprocate. The point is, without judging the ability of others to love, we must turn our attention inward to nurture and develop our own sources of loving energy and establish a state of abundance within ourselves. This could reduce some of the problems causing the high divorce rate in our society.

Learning Self-Love

Taoists say we can't really love others until we can love ourselves. This a crucial step in learning to love others (Figure 3-13), because we can extend the energy of love only when it overflows beyond the needs of our bodies.

The stress of trying to give away too freely what you don't have enough of can create blockages in the Microcosmic Orbit and can also block the unconditional love from Heaven and from Mother Earth (Figure 3-14). Taoists also say love is truly an energy that resides in the

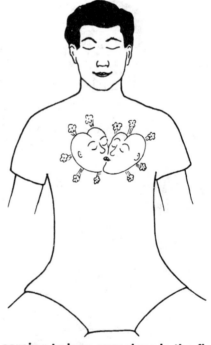

Figure 3-13. Learning to love ourselves is the first crucial step in learning to love others.

heart. It can be activated by external stimuli, but we can also awaken it from within. Because loving energy is accessible from within, we can resolve our primary need for love by using this energy first to replenish the internal organs and glands. Practices such as the Inner Smile help us achieve this.

While learning self-love, one should remember that even the loving energy within us derives from the Original Force of the Wu Chi. This means the heart's energy provides a connection to our divine source, Universal Love. Many people have problems comprehending their relationship with this source and thereby feel abandoned. This is often because they are so out of touch with their inner selves that they have forgotten how to reach the love within and have consequently lost their sense of this connection. Although divine love is unlimited, its manifestation within us occurs in the much smaller vessel of our bodies, and the connection between these inner and outer sources requires constant attention and alignment. We must cultivate love within ourselves first to

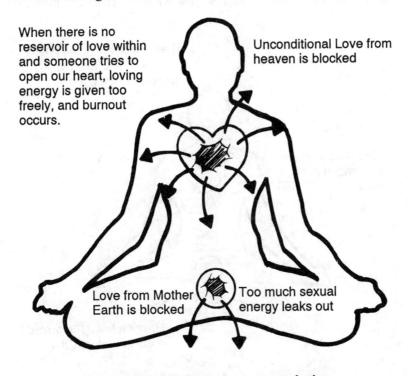

When there is no reservoir of love within and someone tries to open our heart, loving energy is given too freely, and burnout occurs.

Unconditional Love from heaven is blocked

Love from Mother Earth is blocked

Too much sexual energy leaks out

Figure 3-14. Blockages are created when we let love and sex drain out.

have the power to draw in unconditional love from Heaven and gentleness and kindness from Mother Earth (Figures 3-15).

In Taoism, each internal organ is believed to have its own individual soul, spirit, and courageous energy. By practicing love and respect to cultivate these aspects of the organs, the whole body improves, and one learns to love the body as a whole. Gradually, changes become noticeable in the character and attitudes displayed in one's daily life, which indicate that the loving effect is expanding to all parts of body, mind, and spirit. After learning self-love—which is not to be confused with egotism or narcissism—and connnecting with Universal Love, one becomes abundant with loving energy to share with others. Practice is the key.

Unconditional Love Reflects Compassion

Nature and the universe seem cruel. Only the strong can survive, and only humans have sympathy for weakness, because we ourselves are weak. It is through human weakness that we try to place conditions on

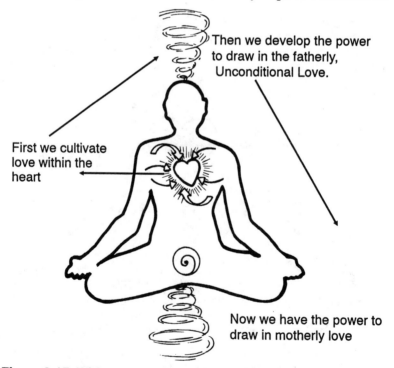

Then we develop the power to draw in the fatherly, Unconditional Love.

First we cultivate love within the heart

Now we have the power to draw in motherly love

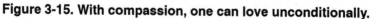

Figure 3-15. With compassion, one can love unconditionally.

74

love, which, in truth, has no conditions. Taoists revere compassion as the highest form of virtue because its basis is empathy, not sympathy, and it elevates the consciousness beyond human weakness. With compassion, one can love unconditionally and thereby accept the world on its own terms without suffering.

A SYSTEM BASED ON VIRTUES:
The Highest Chi

The system I learned from my master is based on the positive energies of love, kindness, gentleness, respect, and honesty; this is the highest Chi Kung practice. With these energies an adept can counteract all kinds of evil (Figure 3-16). It is said that even fire cannot hurt one who has perfected their use. My master's teacher, the grand master, had studied under Taoist masters in the temples for 40 years. When this grand master understood enough, he retired to a cave to practice in solitude. He could not duplicate the environment of the temple in a cave, however. There were no statues, and no one else was around to appreciate such things as rituals or ceremonies.

After about 10 years of studying in the Taoist temples, my master decided to apprentice himself to the grand master in the cave. But like many adepts of his time, this highly advanced teacher lived a secluded life in a very inaccessible place. It was difficult even to carry enough food for the journey. Eventually my teacher made his way to this master's cave, but after a short period of introduction, the grand master left his

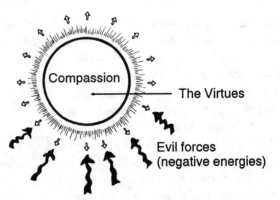

Figure 3-16. Virtue can counteract all negative forces.

body during meditation and did not return to it for weeks. My master ran out of food and had to leave.

The next time, he was smarter. When he went to the cave, he took more food and a brush. He dusted off the grand master's body, which was in a state of suspended animation, and protected it from predatory animals. The grand master would occasionally come back, open his eyes, and see that he was being taken care of before he would leave his body again.

Finally, when the grand master came back and realized he would soon be leaving his body for good, he began to teach the system to my master, who stayed with him for about three years. My master practiced the system and thought about many others he had learned during his travels. He realized that there are many paths to choose from in this world, and some work better for some people than others.

Today, it is not necessary to study in temples or search for masters in the wilderness. There is no need to depend on statues, temples, ceremonies, and rituals to aid in your spiritual growth. With the Healing Tao system, you learn to depend completely on your senses, glands, and organs—the inner universe, by which you can make the connection to the outer universe (Figure 3-17). You can also maintain your family, career, and lifestyle while learning the same practices that the masters had to struggle for.

TRANSFORMING NEGATIVE EMOTIONAL ENERGIES

Our society is known for its fast pace, its stressful conditions, and its inability to handle the tons of garbage it produces daily. This includes not only trash from our homes, but also the emotional garbage produced within our bodies. Both are expensive to remove from the environment. One requires sanitation services; the other is sometimes relieved by medical or psychological methods.

According to an article in *Newsweek* magazine (November 1989), a family of three throws out approximately 7 bags, or 87.5 gallons, of garbage per week. Average disposal per month amounts to about 29 bags, or 379 gallons; and every year the same family of three disposes of approximately 350 bags, or 4,550 gallons of garbage. The accumulation of stress and negative emotions is likewise enormous.

The Problem of Dumping Emotional Garbage

No community likes to have trash dumped near it, and garbage disposal becomes more expensive as trash must be hauled farther away. People often try to solve this problem by illegally dumping their garbage across state lines near someone else's home, but this is a short-term solution, as lawsuits are brought and fines must be paid. Efforts to build new landfills or expand old ones are hampered by the communities that want them built elsewhere. Unable to stop creating garbage in our homes or inside our bodies, we continue to dump it in some other state (Figure 3-18) or on someone else's shoulders (Figure 3-19).

Americans collect over 160 million tons of garbage each year, and the cost for its removal is enormous. With the figures mentioned for

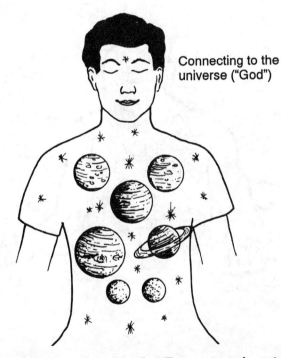

Connecting to the universe ("God")

Figure 3-17. Students of the Healing Tao system do not depend on temples, churches, stories, ceremonies, or rituals, but on inner and outer Universal Forces.

Figure 3-18. We have no problems dumping garbage in other states.

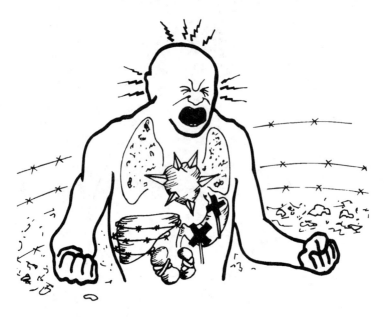

Figure 3-19. We don't want our own garbage, but we have no problem dumping it on someone else.

external waste, one can only imagine the cost to our health of trying to relieve the emotional stresses that accumulate during the same period. Just as new landfills are hard to find where we can dump our garbage, new storage space for our negative emotional energies is also scarce when our bodily systems become clogged with internal trash. The only alternative to disposing of garbage from internal or external sources is to recycle it.

Recycling Negative Emotional Energies

Recycling is the most important practice in energetic and ecological conservation. Consider that the expense of turning bauxite into new aluminum is 10 times that of reprocessing used cans, yet every three months we throw out enough aluminum to rebuild the nation's entire airline fleet (Figure 3-20). Glass, paper, and certain plastics can all be

Figure 3-20. There is enough wasted aluminum in our garbage to rebuild every airline fleet in the nation.

recycled. Kitchen wastes, dead leaves, and grass clippings from the lawn can all be turned into compost, but people prefer to spend money on expensive fertilizers, allowing useful byproducts to become garbage. Because our society is uneducated about how to take care of these problems, the suffering they cause is exacerbated year by year. We can, however, learn from Taoism about personal conservation: just as garbage can be turned into compost, we can recycle negative emotional energies such as hatred into positive ones like love (Figures 3-21 and 3-22).

Dumping negative emotions on our fellow human beings has become as common as taking out the garbage. In fact, when we harbor hate, anger, and fear inside, we tend to be obsessed with our own problems and less concerned for others; as a result, we also produce more external garbage (Figure 3-23). None of us wants other people to dump on him or her, but most of us can't prevent our own negative wastes from pouring out when circumstances force our bodies and minds to overload. Although we have psychological methods to help release built-up emotional stress, these solutions are costly, slow, and not always applicable to new

Figure 3-21. Recyle garbage into compost.

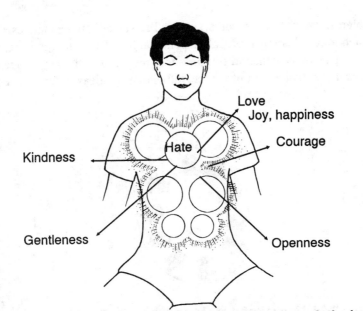

Figure 3-22. Recyling our emotional energies through the Inner Smile and Six Healing Sounds

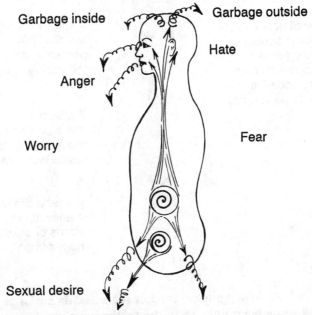

Figure 3-23. The more garbage we have inside, the more garbage we produce outside.

problems. Preventive measures, such as Taoist meditative practices, offer a much longer-lasting approach to personal health and energetic conservation. The focus of these disciplines is to recycle emotional garbage into energy that enhances our life-force, rather than to release it from the body.

Figure 3-24. Many useful energies are suppressed because most of us have not learned how to recycle them properly.

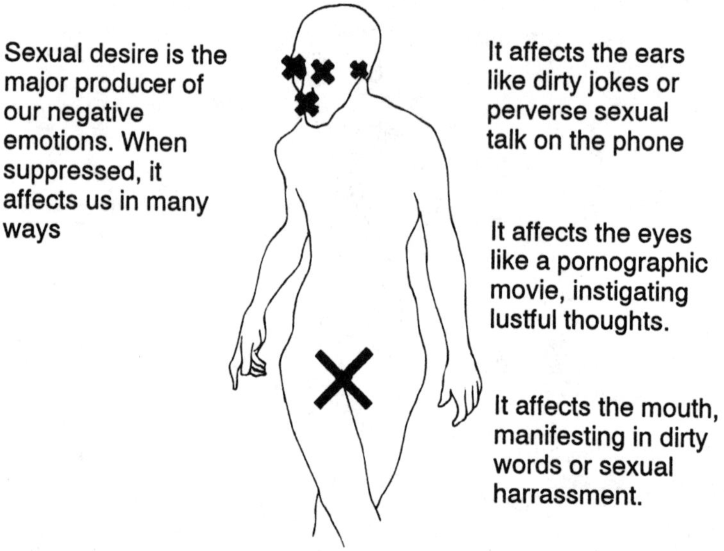

Sexual desire is the major producer of our negative emotions. When suppressed, it affects us in many ways

It affects the ears like dirty jokes or perverse sexual talk on the phone

It affects the eyes like a pornographic movie, instigating lustful thoughts.

It affects the mouth, manifesting in dirty words or sexual harrassment.

Figure 3-25. When suppressed or regarded as sinful or dirty sexual energy becomes like garbage. We have nowhere to dump it, and no knowledge of how to recycled it.

This principle is related to our sexual energy as well. In our society, we have been taught that sexuality is sinful or dirty like garbage, and should therefore be supressed. It is true that sexual desire is a major producer of negative emotions, but instead of repressing it, we can recycle and transform that same sexual energy into pure life-force energy. The holy sages of many traditions know how to do this and have attained spiritual mastery as a result.

Although religion and society often try to suppress our sexual energy, the problem is that they offer no positive alternatives. They have not taught us how to recycle and tranform this powerful force. When sexual energy is suppressed, it may end up expressing itself in other sense desires (Figure 3-24). Sexual desire may affect the ear as a desire to hear dirty jokes or perverse sexual conversations. It may go out to the eye as a need to see pornographic movies. It can affect the mouth and manifest in foul language or sexual harrassment (Figure 3-25). Suppressed sexual desire can also create other negative emotions such as hate, anger, cruelty, and violence (Figure 3-26). All these things pollute our society.

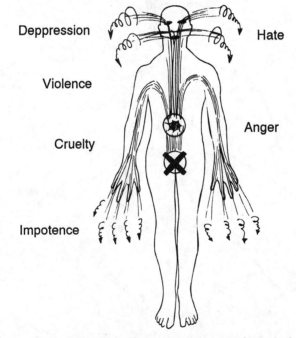

Figure 3-26. Sexual desires also create a foundation for other problems and more emotional garbage.

Enhancing Our Life-Force with Recycled Energy

Taoist theory regards all positive and negative internal energies as parts of our life-force. When we become angry, it means that some of our life-force has been stored with a negative charge, empowering the reaction of anger (Figure 3-27). To prevent future responses of anger, we can locate the source of that energy and transform it, so that whenever we are confronted by upsets in our lives, we can apply more effective emotional responses, such as patience. If someone or something triggers in us a response of anger, frustration, sadness, or depression, it is simply because we have not prepared ourselves by transforming our negative energies into positive life-force. Tremendous amounts of life-force can become negative emotional energies if we allow this to happen, just like a disease spreading throughout the body.

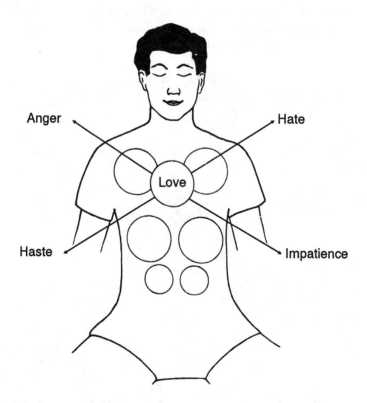

Figure 3-27. Negative energies and emotions are not necessarily sinful, but they indicate that our life-force has been changed.

TAOIST WAYS TO TRANSFORM STRESS INTO VITALITY

There are a few basic Healing Tao practices that people can easily learn to transform any stressful energies. Many other approaches also work. Some emphasize positive thinking (without actually transforming the negative energy), others simply try to release the negative emotion (as stated earlier). Taoists do not judge these methods; instead, they offer a time-proven approach that begins with energy transformation through the basic exercises of the Inner Smile and the Six Healing Sounds.

The Inner Smile

Understanding the Body

One should begin by studying the internal organs and glands. When problems exist within the organs, certain emotions may arise. When someone is sick or weak in the lungs, the emotions of sadness or depression may occur. Overheating or congestion of the liver can cause anger or moodiness. Weakness in the liver can cause a drop in productivity and a lack of control or balance. When the heart overheats, it can cause impatience, hate, and cruelty to arise. Weakness in the heart can result in a lack of warmth and vitality. Weakness in the spleen, stomach, or pancreas can produce worry, anxiety, and a lack of stability. Weakness in the kidneys can cause fear and a lack of willpower and ambition (Figure 3-28).

The Basic Inner Smile

Once you know the general locations of the organs and glands, close your eyes and smile to them, beginning with the pituitary and pineal glands in the head. Smile down to the thyroid, parathyroid, thymus, and heart. Feel love and happiness grow from the heart center. As you smile to the lungs, feel courage arise. As you smile to the spleen, stomach, and pancreas, feel openness and fairness. As you smile to the liver and gall bladder, feel kindness. As you smile to the kidneys and the bladder, feel gentleness. As you smile to the sexual organs, feel creativity. When you smile to the organs, negative energies will gradually change into positive life-force.

Eventually, you will learn how to use the inner eye to get in touch with every part of your body. You will also learn how to sense good

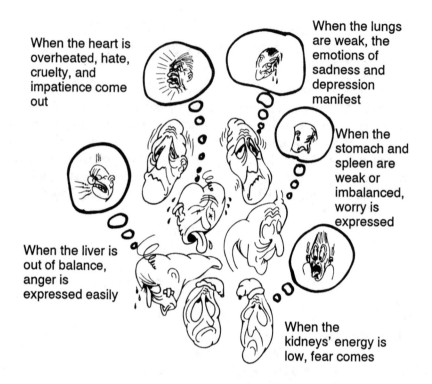

When the heart is overheated, hate, cruelty, and impatience come out

When the lungs are weak, the emotions of sadness and depression manifest

When the stomach and spleen are weak or imbalanced, worry is expressed

When the liver is out of balance, anger is expressed easily

When the kidneys' energy is low, fear comes

Figure 3-28. Weak organs can produce negative emotional state.

feeling and to enhance energies within the organs by practicing the Inner Smile as you transform any negative energies you feel. In time these sensations will become programmed into your mind, and you will be able to simply recall the feeling of moving energy to help speed up your practice.

The Inner Smile and the Practice of Forgiveness

The Taoist way of forgiveness is to practice the Inner Smile. When you sense negative feeling (emotions) arising, practice no judgment of people or events. Simply get in touch with your inner self, and use the Inner Smile meditation to transform your negative feeling into the positive energy of the virtues (Figures 3-29 and 3-30). This requires daily practice to master, but the effects will eventually influence people around you, who will appreciate your higher vibration.

Once you learn to love yourself and connect to the unlimited reservoir of Universal Love, you will have such an abundance of love

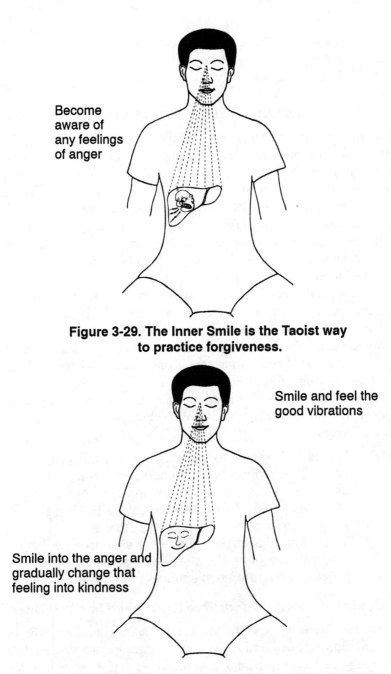

Figure 3-29. The Inner Smile is the Taoist way to practice forgiveness.

Become aware of any feelings of anger

Smile and feel the good vibrations

Smile into the anger and gradually change that feeling into kindness

Figure 3-30. Tranform negative into positive energy.

that you will overflow with it. You can send love to your loved ones and to people who are suffering. You can open your heart still further by learning to love your enemy.

The Inner Smile Meditation

The Inner Smile is used to begin every meditation in the Healing Tao system, and it is presented here in complete detail. Once you have mastered it, you can decide where in your body you wish to send smiling energy and for how long it is needed. In the beginning, it may be necessary to spend up to 20 minutes to complete this exercise as described. Daily practice will shorten this period, however, and you will feel the Inner Smile take effect on your body and consciousness more rapidly. After you learn the steps here, you can use abridged version as a guideline for practice.

You can do the Inner Smile any time and place that are convenient. Some students spend more time on the Inner Smile if their bodies need it, but most use it to energize their bodies quickly before they go on to the Microcosmic Orbit meditation, which is the major part of their beginning practice. Even during the advanced meditations, students should always maintain an awareness of the Inner Smile. Whenever there is trouble in an organ, or if you are particularly tense, you can use the inner eye to smile inwardly, healing your body and relieving your state of being (Figure 3- 31).

NOTE: *This is a good time to make use of your anatomy book. Check the location of each organ and gland before you meditate, and keep the book open in front of you as you practice. Note the color and shape of each organ and learn to feel the texture and disposition of each with your internal senses. Getting to know your internal system takes some time, and a good, colorful reference source will prove invaluable.*

The Eyes: The Source of Your True Smiling and Healing Power

A smile is an incredibly powerful tool of communication. If we arrive in a foreign land, or are in a group of strangers, a sincere smile from another person helps us feel at ease immediately, almost as if we were with old friends instead of in a sea of unfamiliar faces. For a smile is familiar; it gives us the message of acceptance, love and understanding, appreciation

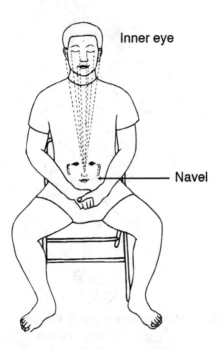

Figure 3-31. Smile inwardly.

and safety. As a result, when we receive a truly warm and loving smile, we relax and let down our defenses. It activates our parasympathetic nervous system's "relaxation response," producing distinct physiological changes in our endrocine glands, our nervous system, our musculature, our circulatory system, our respiration, and our digestive tract; in fact, nearly every system in the body can be dramatically affected by the simple fact of receiving a smile.

Just as a smile is effective in communicating with other people, it is also an amazingly powerful healing tool in communicating with ourselves. For we are always communicating with ourselves, consciously or subconsciously, but unfortunately the message is not always positive. Self-loathing and low self-esteem are all too common in modern society, and, aside from the psychological and sociological effects of a negative self-image, our own health may suffer as a result. Many serious illnesses, such as cancer, heart disease, and diabetes, are often preceded by long periods of chronic negative emotions.

In contrast, smiling inward helps us feel a sense of self-respect and gratitude for our organs and glands (Figure 3-32). As we contemplate our anatomy and physiology, we can marvel and feel joy that our bodily parts

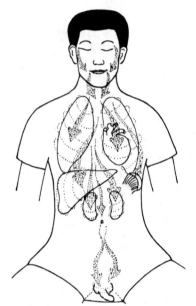

Figure 3-32. Smile inwardly and feel gratitude for your glands and organs.

are doing their jobs to keep us alive and healthy. It is hard not feel a sense of awe and wonder when we pay attention to the marvelous design of our bodies, to the intricate network of systems working together to keep us in balance. When we turn our awareness inward and smile to our organs with love and appreciation, it sets into motion the same chain of positive physiological changes associated with the relaxation response that is activated when we smile.

Smiling to the Glands and Organs

1. Sit comfortably near the edge of your chair with your feet flat on the floor. Keep your back straight, but not stiff. Stay relaxed, and clasp your palms together in your lap, left palm on bottom, right palm on top.

2. Close your eyes and become aware of the soles of your feet. Feel their connection to the ground and the energy of the earth (Figure 3-33).

3. Become aware of yourself sitting on the chair with the hands together and the tongue pressed against the palate. Create a source of smiling energy up to three feet in front of you. This can be an image of your own smiling face, or of someone or something you love and respect, or any memory of a time in which you felt deeply at peace, perhaps feeling sunshine, being by the ocean, or walking in a forest.

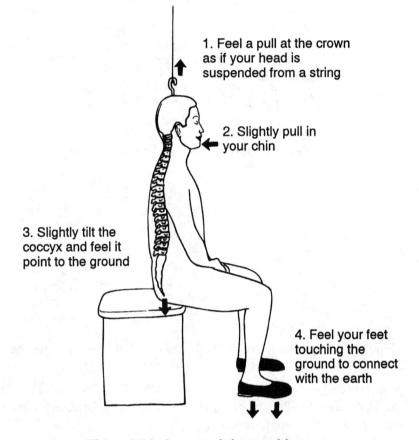

1. Feel a pull at the crown as if your head is suspended from a string

2. Slightly pull in your chin

3. Slightly tilt the coccyx and feel it point to the ground

4. Feel your feet touching the ground to connect with the earth

Figure 3-33. Correct sitting position

4. Become aware of the midpoint between your eyebrows through which you will draw this abundant smiling energy in front of and around you. Let your forehead relax, and allow the Third Eye to open. As the smiling energy accumulates at the mid-eyebrow, it will eventually overflow into your body.

5. Allow the smiling energy to flow down from the mid-eyebrow through your face, relaxing the cheeks, nose, mouth, and all the facial muscles. Let it flow down through your neck. You can roll your head slowly and gently from side to side as you do this.

6. The Thymus Gland. Let the smiling energy continue to flow down to your thymus gland, which is located behind the upper part of

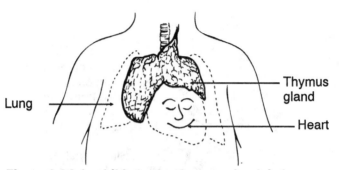

Figure 3-34. In children, the thymus gland is larger.

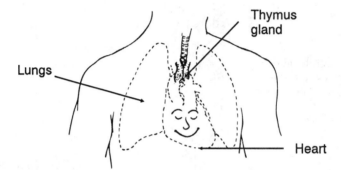

Figure 3-35. Let the thymus gland smile to the heart, and let the heart smile back.

your sternum, and picture it glowing with vibrant health (Figures 3-34 and 3-35). Feel the thymus gland become warm as it begins to vibrate and expand like a flower blossoming.

7. The Heart. To help activate the heart energy, you can raise the clasped palms and place both thumbs lightly against the heart center. Let the warm, smiling energy spread from the thymus gland into the heart. Draw more smiling energy from the source you created through the mid-eyebrow, and let it flow like a waterfall down into the heart. When you smile inwardly to the heart, it will generate the virtues of joy and happiness. Spend as much time here as you need to feel the heart relax and expand with loving energy. This expansion will feel like a flower blossoming. Try to remember your best experience of love, whether it was emotionally or divinely inspired, and fill your heart with that same feeling again. Love your heart.

The heart is associated with the negative emotional energies of hastiness, arrogance, and cruelty. When you smile into the heart, these energies will dissipate, creating the space for the virtuous energies of love

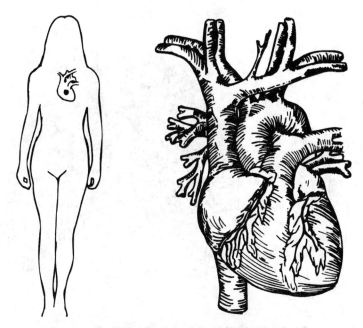

**Figure 3-36. Picture the heart and smile to it.
Feel it smile back to you.**

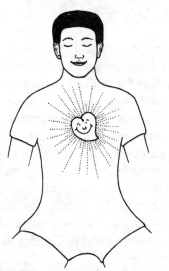

Figure 3-37. Feel the heart smiling back to you.

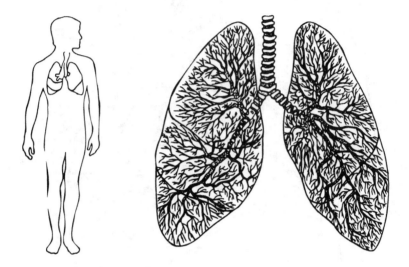

Figure 3-38. Smile to the lungs, and let the lungs smile back to you.

and joy to expand. Smile to the heart until it smiles back to you (Figures 3-36 and 3-37).

8. The Lungs. Let the joy and happiness generated in the heart expand outward to your lungs (Figure 3-38). Feel the lungs open as the happy, smiling energy flows into them. If you are a visually oriented person, look into the lungs with your inner sight, or if you are more feeling oriented, feel the lungs expand with positive energy. The lungs may appear to be pink and spongy, or they may feel abundantly full. If there is anything you see or feel in the lungs that is unpleasant to you, get rid of it. You can clear the lungs of energetic, emotional, and physical pollution by smiling into them as you mentally increase the amount of Chi absorbed with each breath. Feel the air flow from the tip of the nose down into the lungs, following it all the way out to the tiny air sacs where oxygen is exchanged for carbon dioxide. Thank your lungs for breathing and helping sustain your life.

You should feel your entire chest cavity filling with smiling, loving energy. The lungs are associated with the negative emotional energies of sadness and depression and the virtuous energies of courage and righteousness. When you smile into the lungs, you will dissolve any sadness or negative feelings, creating space for courage and righteousness to expand.

NOTE: *Remember you can go back to the source of smiling energy in front of you—your vision or memory of a happy moment—to get more energy any time during the meditation. If you feel your attention wandering, or if you feel the effect of the Inner Smile becoming weak or diluted, just gather more smiling energy from the source. The Chinese say, "If you want water, you should go to the well."*

9. The Liver. Let the smiling, loving energy continue to build up in the heart and flow out to the lungs. Next you will direct it to the liver (Figure 3-39), which is the largest internal organ, located just below the right lung within the lower rib cage. Feel the liver become immersed in smiling, loving, joyous energy. The liver is associated with the sense of sight, as it controls the energy of the eyes. Use your inner vision to see the liver and determine its condition. Its surface should be smooth and glossy, and it should feel relaxed and uncongested. You can use your eyes to smooth out any part of its surface or to relax any area that seems tense.

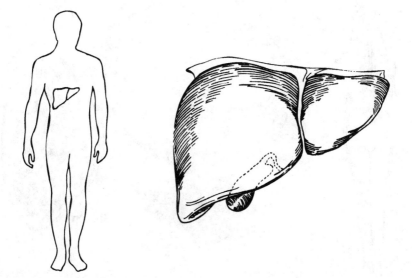

Figure 3-39. Smile to the liver, and let the liver smile back to you.

Feel gratitude for the liver's work in detoxifying the body, helping to store blood, and producing bile.

The liver is associated with the emotion of anger and the virtue of kindness. When you smile to the liver, you will dissolve any anger and allow the kindness energy more space to expand. The Chinese suggest this also helps strengthen your decision-making power.

10. The Pancreas. Let the smiling energy now flow from the liver across the abdomen into the pancreas, which is located within the left lower rib cage, extending from the solar plexus area under the liver and directly beneath the left lung. Thank the pancreas for making digestive enzymes, producing insulin, and regulating blood sugar. As you smile into the pancreas, see that it is healthy and functioning smoothly.

11. The Spleen. Continuing around to the left, smile into the spleen (Figure 3-40), which is just next to the left kidney. Don't worry if you don't know exactly where it is. If you smile in that direction, you will gradually get in touch with it. If you need to, return to the source of smiling energy in front of you, and let the smiling energy flow in through the mid-eyebrow and down to the area of the spleen. As smiling, loving energy builds up in the spleen, let it flow into the kidneys.

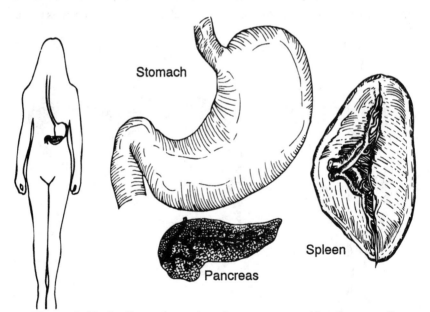

Stomach

Spleen

Pancreas

Figure 3-40. Smile to the spleen/pancreas, and let them smile back to you.

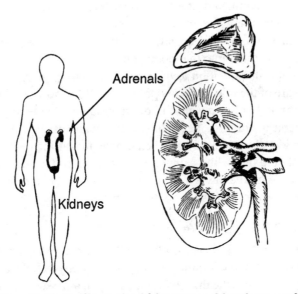

Adrenals

Kidneys

Figure 3-41. Smile to the kidneys, and let them smile back to you.

12. The Kidneys. Smile down to the kidneys and feel them begin to expand with radiant energy (Figure 3-41). You can use your inner vision to inspect the kidneys to be sure their surface is smooth and glossy and that they are filtering properly without any congestion. The kidneys are associated with the emotion of fear. As you smile into them, fear melts away, and the virtue of gentleness can grow. Keep smiling into the kidneys, and let the smiling energy build up until they are full.

13. Next, send the smiling energy down into the urinary bladder, urethra, genitals, and perineum.

Women: The collection point for female sexual energy is known as the Ovarian Palace, located about three inches below the navel, midway between the ovaries. Smile the accumulated energies into the ovaries, uterus, and vagina. Thank the ovaries for making hormones and giving you sexual energy. Bring the combined sexual, smiling, and virtue energies up to the navel, and visualize the energies spiraling into that point.

Men: The collection point for male sexual energy is known as the Sperm Palace, located one-and-a-half inches above the base of the penis in the area of the prostate gland and seminal vesicles. Smile, and visualize spiraling the accumulated energies down into the prostate gland and testicles. Thank them for making hormones and giving you sexual energy. Bring the combined sexual, smiling, and virtue energies up to the navel, and spiral them into that point (Figure 3-42).

14. Return the attention to the source of smiling energy in front of you. Be aware of the mid-eyebrow point, and allow more smiling energy to flow in through it like a waterfall pouring down into the organs. Once again immerse the thymus, heart, lungs, liver, pancreas, spleen, kidneys, urinary bladder (Figure 3-43), and sex organs in smiling energy. At this point you should be feeling calm and peaceful. If you wish to stop now, you can smile into the navel and collect the energy by spiraling it to the center as you cover the navel with the palms.

Smiling into the Digestive Tract

Again, after you have finished smiling to the organs, you can return your attention to the source of smiling energy in front of you before directing this energy down into the digestive tract. As you amass an abundance of Chi, let it overflow down behind the nose and into the mouth. You will

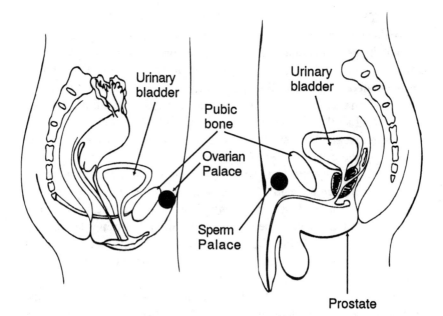

Figure 3-42. Sexual center

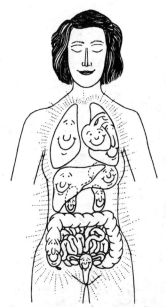

Figure 3-43. Feel all the organs smile back at you.

then use the saliva as a vehicle for this energy to permeate the digestive system (Figure 3-44).

Activating the saliva. The saliva is considered a precious fluid in Taoism. It has been called the Long Life Wine or Jade Fluid. There are many special techniques involving the saliva and the act of swallowing. Moving your tongue around inside your mouth generates more saliva. There is a Taoist method to enhance this process.

Slide the tongue around the outside of the teeth, with the tip running along the gums. Start from the upper back teeth on the left side, and slide the tongue over to the upper right side. Then continue to circle back from the lower teeth on the right side, pointing the tip of the tongue down to the lower gums, and slide over to the lower left side again. Return again to the upper teeth on the left side. You can continue going around the mouth this way a few times (the Taoists recommend 36 times), then do the same thing on the inside surface of the teeth and gums. This helps generate an abundance of saliva.

Swallowing the Chi. Now imagine your saliva is imbued with all the smiling energy flowing from the mid-eyebrow point. Gather the saliva into a ball resting on the middle of the tongue. Put the tongue up to the roof of the mouth, and swallow the saliva quickly with a big gulp

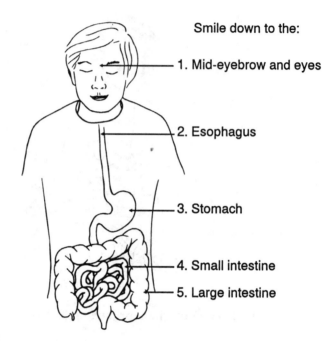

Smile down to the:

1. Mid-eyebrow and eyes

2. Esophagus

3. Stomach

4. Small intestine

5. Large intestine

Figure 3-44. Smile into the digestive tract.

into the stomach, thereby swallowing the Chi into the digestive tract. As you do this, you will bring smiling energy down through the esophagus, stomach, small intestine, large intestine, rectum, and anus.

The digestive system is very sensitive to emotions, and many people experience digestive problems when they are under stress. When the body is on alert, as in the fight-or-flight response, digestion stops and the stomach's digestive juices stop flowing. So pay particular attention to relaxing the stomach and intestines, and be sure to notice if the inner surfaces of these organs are irritated. Spend as much time as you need to bring smiling energy to any places where you feel discomfort.

Smiling to the Glands, Nervous System, and Bone Marrow

After you finish smiling to the organs and the digestive tract, once again bring your attention back to the source of smiling energy, which is located up to three feet in front of you.

1. Draw the smiling energy in through the mid-eyebrow point directly into the left and right brain. Move the eyes around clockwise and

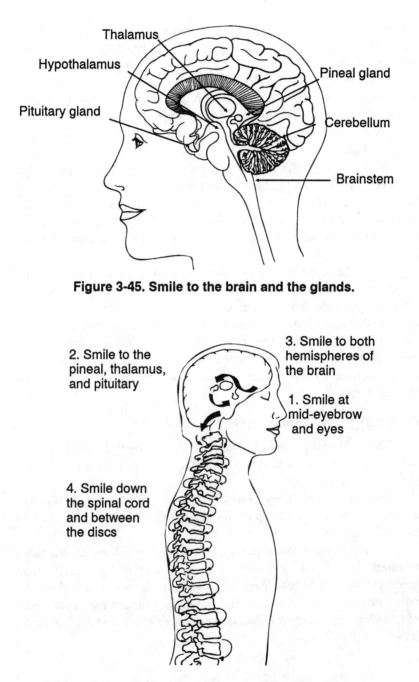

Figure 3-45. Smile to the brain and the glands.

Thalamus

Hypothalamus

Pituitary gland

Pineal gland

Cerebellum

Brainstem

2. Smile to the pineal, thalamus, and pituitary

3. Smile to both hemispheres of the brain

1. Smile at mid-eyebrow and eyes

4. Smile down the spinal cord and between the discs

Figure 3-46. Smile to the spinal cord and bone marrow.

counterclockwise 9 to 18 times to balance the left and right brain hemispheres. As you do this, feel the Chi in the brain spiraling with the eye motions as it amasses. Let the smiling energy accumulate here.

2. Locate the pituitary, thalamus, and pineal glands (Figure 3-45). Smile into the pituitary gland, three or four inches behind the Third Eye, and feel it blossom. Smile into the thalamus gland, located directly above the spinal cord, slightly behind and above the pituitary gland. Smile into the pineal gland at the crown.

3. Now project the smiling energy, using the power of your mind and eyes, like a flashlight beam onto the vault of the skull. Let it shine through the left brain, then sweep across the skull, shining through the right brain, and then back again. You can let the smiling energy spiral around inside the brain, and then concentrate it once again in the brain's center.

4. Let the smiling energy continue to flow to the back of the skull. Feel the skull breathing; absorb the Chi into the skull and into the marrow. Then let it flow down the spinal column, vertebra by vertebra. As stated earlier, you have 24 separate vertebrae: 7 cervical vertebrae, 12 thoracic vertebrae, and 5 lumbar vertebrae. Bring your smiling energy around each vertebra and disc, one by one. Then continue smiling down to the 5 fused vertebrae of the sacrum and the 4 fused vertebrae of the coccyx (Figure 3-46).

Collecting and Storing Energy at the Navel

Men: Cover the navel with both palms, left over right. Massage with a spiraling motion down toward the right side (clockwise) 36 times (Figures 3- 47 and 3-48).

Women: Cover the navel with both palms, right over left. Massage with a spiraling motion down toward the left side (counterclockwise) 36 times (Figure 3-49).

Men and women: Reverse directions, and spiral back into the navel 24 times (Figures 3-48 and 3-49). (Men spiral counterclockwise; women spiral clockwise.) Move closer to the navel with each cycle. You have now completed the Inner Smile and should feel an increase in your flow of Chi. Practice this exercise as soon as you wake up. It is the best stress reducer in the world.

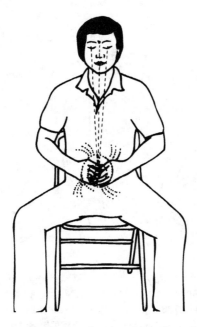

Figure 3-47. Collecting and storing the energy

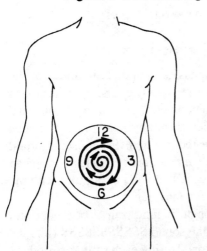

Men collect the energy by spiraling outwardly from the navel 36 times clockwise

Then they spiral inwardly 24 times counterclockwise, ending at the navel

Figure 3-48. How men collect energy

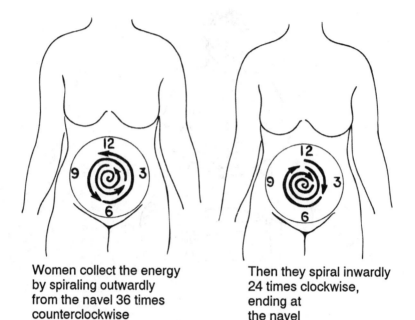

Women collect the energy
by spiraling outwardly
from the navel 36 times
counterclockwise

Then they spiral inwardly
24 times clockwise,
ending at
the navel

Figure 3-49. How women collect energy

The Six Healing Sounds

The Six Healing Sounds help us emphasize the good vibrations of the organs by strengthening their positive energies. They also heal the organs while balancing their individual functions with the rest of the internal system. Each sound can be performed from any position, but serious practice is usually initiated from a seated position. The most important aspect of practice is to feel any negative emotional energies so you can transform them into positive life-force. Once you are familiar with the organs and their correlating sounds, you may begin.

The Lung Sound. Place your tongue behind your closed teeth, and with a long, slow exhalation, create the sound SSSSSSSSSSS (like the sound of steam coming from a radiator). During each resting period (as you slowly inhale), smile to the lungs. Picture them surrounded by white light, and concentrate on feeling the virtue of courage, which is directly related to the lungs' energy. (This will help enhance the positive energy of the lungs.)

The Kidney Sound. Form an O with the lips, as if preparing to blow out a candle, and with a long, slow exhalation, produce the sound

WOOOOOOO. During each resting period, smile to the kidneys as you picture them surrounded by a bright blue color. Feel the virtue of gentleness, which will enhance the positive energy of the kidneys.

The Liver Sound. Place the tongue near the palate, and with long, slow exhalation, produce the sound SHHHHHHHHHH. During each resting period, smile to the liver. Picture it surrounded by a bright green color, and feel the virtue of kindness. This will enhance the positive energy of the liver.

The Heart Sound. With the mouth wide open, exhale a deep breath slowly, and produce the sound HAWWWWWWWWW. During each resting period, smile to the heart, and picture it surrounded by the color red. Feel love, joy, and happiness to enhance the positive energy in the heart.

The Spleen Sound. Again place the tongue near the palate, and with a long, slow exhalation, produce the sound WHOOOOOO from the throat, like the sound of an owl. (This is more guttural than the Kidney Sound.) During each resting period, smile to the spleen, and picture it surrounded by a bright yellow color. Feel the virtue of fairness, which will enhance the positive energy of the spleen.

The Triple Warmer sound. *(Practice this while lying down, if possible.)* With your mouth open, exhale slowly as you produce the sound HEEEEEEEE. During each resting period, try to imagine a huge rolling pin flattening out your body from the forehead down to the toes. This will balance all the energies activated by the other sounds and help relax the body thoroughly.

With daily practice, you will find negative emotional energies have little or no room to grow. It always helps to spend some time sorting out emotional trash. See what can be recycled internally, just as paper, glass, and plastic from your home can be recycled. You will feel much better as you learn to transform negative energies into positive life-force, rather than dumping them on others.

Chapter 4

ENERGETIC PREPARATIONS FOR THE HEALING LIGHT MEDITATIONS

We will begin by learning a few techniques to loosen the body, open channels, and activate the Chi flow. This will enable you to draw the Universal, Higher Self, and Earth Forces into the bone to "wash the marrow" and to absorb these energies so the bone marrow will regenerate and grow. This also establishes a good foundation for the Microcosmic Orbit meditation by making it easier for you to feel the energy you will be working with. Descriptions of these preparations require many words, but the movements are simple. Once you understand these movements, they can be performed within minutes.

Creating bodily awareness. From a comfortable posture, you will relax and smile inwardly, focusing your attention on the mid-eyebrow to open and expand it. Then you will concentrate on loosening the muscles of the perineum.

Spinal Cord Breathing and Spinal Cord Rocking. Although Spinal Cord Breathing and Spinal Cord Rocking are not included in this chapter, we mention them here because these two methods for loosening the spinal cord are extremely important and should be practiced before every meditation session. For a detailed description of Spinal Cord Breathing and Spinal Cord Rocking, please refer to the Appendix in the back of this book.

Techniques for enhancing the sensation of Chi. You will learn several effective ways of feeling Chi. Then you will explore various methods for guiding your Chi and increasing the Chi flow to specific places, including the use of the mind and eyes, touching the points of the Microcosmic Orbit, and breathing techniques.

Preparing for the Microcosmic Orbit meditation. Preparations for the Microcosmic Orbit meditation include finding a quiet and pleasant environment conducive to practice and precise procedures for establishing a good meditation posture.

Activating the Original Chi in the Lower Tan Tien: Warming the Stove. The Lower Tan Tien (located between the navel, kidneys, and sexual center) is the foundation of Taoist meditation, the place where we begin and end each round of practice. You will be guided through the ways of awakening the Original Chi stored in the Lower Tan Tien. This aroused Original Chi will later be used to start the flow of Chi through the Microcosmic Orbit.

CREATING BODILY AWARENESS

You can do this exercise standing, sitting, or lying down. Try to keep the spine straight and aligned with the hips, shoulders, and head.

If you choose to stand, keep the feet at shoulders' width, maintaining 70 percent of the weight on the heels and 30 percent on the balls of the feet. Also keep the toes slightly apart.

Getting Started

1. Relax all the joints by lightly shaking the body, the hands, and the spine (Figure 4-1). Rest, be aware of the spinal cord, and keep the joints very loose. Straighten the mid-back (T-11 area) and maintain the alignment of the spine.

2. Relax the shoulders, keeping the neck straight. The head should feel as if it is suspended. The most important thing is to relax.

3. Keep the knees loose and flexible without bending them. They should be comfortably straight, but not locked.

4. Breathe normally. Don't try to control the breath, but gradually forget about breathing. The breath should be naturally gentle and soft.

5. If you choose to sit or lie down, the same rules apply: relax and stay comfortable while gently maintaining the alignment of the spine. Breathe normally without trying to control the breath. If you are sitting, the feet should be flat on the floor at the same width as the shoulders. In

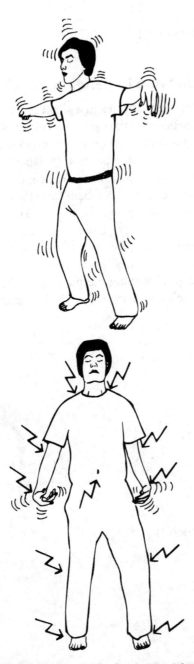

Figure 4-1. Shake all the joints loose and feel them open.

a lying position, you may put a pillow beneath the knees to keep them slightly bent.

Opening and Expanding the Third Eye

The *Third Eye* (mid-eyebrow) lies in a slight depression of the forehead located above and in between the eyebrows (Figure 4-2). When this point is opened through meditation, it opens the consciousness to truth, wisdom, benevolence, and psychic powers. It also enhances latent powers of healing and the body's vibrations. This center can be used to send energies out to others, or to receive them from the universe. Frequencies emanating from the Third Eye can be used to explore unknown realms for higher sources of energy. By amplifying and transmitting the vibratory rates of our virtues, we can attract higher frequencies and light to be absorbed and used internally.

1. The first step in opening the point at the Third Eye is to smile inwardly as you relax the muscles of the forehead (between the

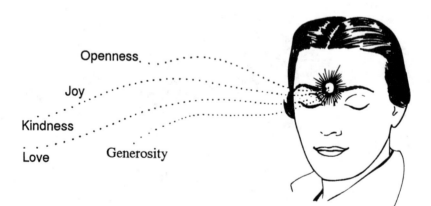

Openness

Joy

Kindness

Love   Generosity

Figure 4-2. Focus the smiling energy on the mid-eyebrow point. Feel the virtues of openness, love, kindness, and generosity.

**Figure 4-3. You can use the fingers to massage
the muscles of the forehead (between the eyebrows)
in a spiraling motion to loosen the area.**

eyebrows). You can use the fingers to massage in a spiraling motion
around the area to loosen it (Figure 4-3). You may also bend the index
fingers and gently press both knuckles (second joints) together on the
Third Eye, then maintain the pressure of the knuckles against each other
as you slowly pull them away from the point.

2. Focus the energy of your smile on this point, then feel the smiling
energy radiate out through it. Also try to feel the virtues of openness,
kindness, love, and generosity expanding within you. Smiling energy will
gradually arise from the heart and radiate out from the Third Eye.

3. Relax the body, smile from the heart, and radiate the smiling
energy out through the mid-eyebrow point (Figure 4-4). Internal energies
will calm down, and the Yin and Yang qualities will start to come into
balance.

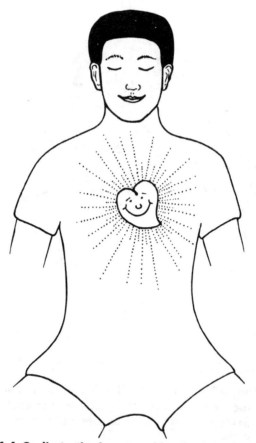

**Figure 4-4. Smile to the heart and let the heart smile back
to your mid-eyebrow.**

Relaxing the Muscles of the Perineum

The perineum's center (also known as the *Gate of Life and Death*) lies
between the genitals and the anus. The specific point you will focus on
is a depression located directly beneath the anus (Figure 4-5). This gate
is extremely important because it controls the flow of sexual energy,
guiding it upward to the higher centers, and prevents the organs' energies
from leaking out through the base of the body (Figure 4-6). The perineum
is also considered the "floor" of the internal organs because it must
withstand the pressure of their combined weight. When it is kept healthy
and strong, the perineum holds the organs in place, preventing them from
sagging down and losing their energy through its gate.

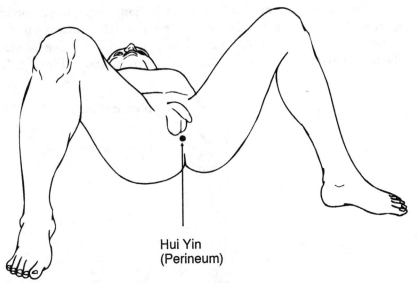

Hui Yin
(Perineum)

Figure 4-5. The Gate of Life and Death for men

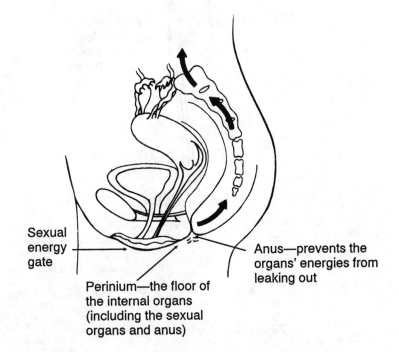

Sexual
energy
gate

Anus—prevents the
organs' energies from
leaking out

Perinium—the floor of
the internal organs
(including the sexual
organs and anus)

Figure 4-6. The Gate of Life and Death for women

This center also connects the body to the Earth Force, which can be used to cleanse and rejuvenate the bone marrow. (Bone marrow is one of the major sources of Chi.) This will help open channels and balance the Higher Self and Universal Forces absorbed from above (Figure 4-7).

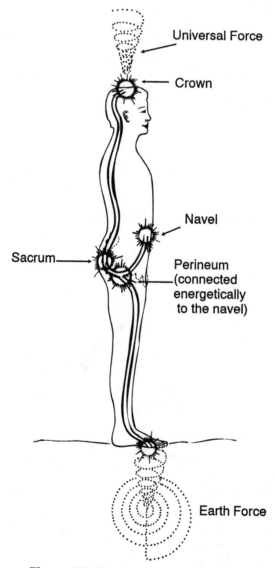

Universal Force

Crown

Navel

Sacrum

Perineum
(connected
energetically
to the navel)

Earth Force

Figure 4-7. Perineum connection

When sexual energy is activated, passing through the perineum, it helps establish the connection between these forces. It reunites the *Pre-Heaven Force* (the original life-force we receive from our parents) with the *Post-Heaven Forces* absorbed from food, air, sun, and stars. All energies absorbed after birth help us maintain the life-force. Such interactions depend on the strength of the perineum and its energetic connections.

The muscles of the perineum (Figure 4-8) can be difficult to relax, which is one reason we often lose the feeling of their connection to the coccyx and the spine. When they become weak and consistently loose, we become more susceptible to illness.

The following steps help develop more sensitivity in this center:

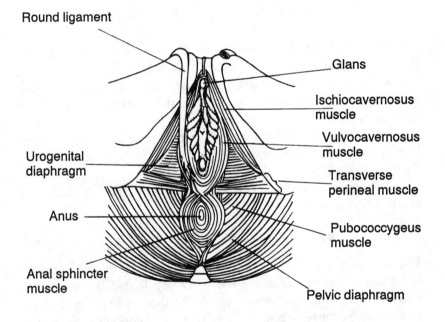

Round ligament

Glans

Ischiocavernosus muscle

Vulvocavernosus muscle

Urogenital diaphragm

Transverse perineal muscle

Anus

Pubococcygeus muscle

Anal sphincter muscle

Pelvic diaphragm

Figure 4-8. Muscles of the perineum

Figure 4-9. Massaging the perineal point

1. Use the fingers to massage the perineal point until you feel it relax (Figure 4-9), then contract the muscles around it.

2. Men. Relax and contract the point three, six, or nine times, holding each contraction tightly for about five seconds as one set. Do three to six sets.

Women. Relax and contract this point two, four, or six times, holding each contraction for about five seconds (Figure 4-10) as one set. Do three to six sets.

3. Rest, and smile to the center of the perineum. Feel its connection to the coccyx and spine.

Feeling Your Energetic Centers

You will learn to feel the energy of your body and its individual organs and glands. This will make it possible for you to distinguish between negative and positive influences and to use the mind and inner eye to change bad feelings into good feelings. Once you know your own internal energies, it will be easier for you to feel the Universal, Higher Self, and Earth Forces. The feeling can be different for each person.

Some may feel the naval area expanding or swelling. Some may feel the insides of the legs become warm as a line of warm energy extends down to the feet. If you feel this sensation, you can absorb it deep into the bones to help regenerate the bone marrow.

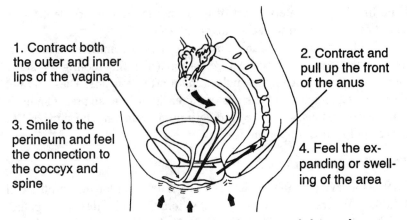

1. Contract both the outer and inner lips of the vagina

2. Contract and pull up the front of the anus

3. Smile to the perineum and feel the connection to the coccyx and spine

4. Feel the expanding or swelling of the area

Figure 4-10. Contracting the muscles around the perineum

The sexual organs may feel an electric numbness or some form of arousal. Later this feeling can spread up through the body, and you may experience the balance of the inner and outer energies. The whole body may feel a pleasant tingling sensation. To finish the exercise, smile as you relax the mid-eyebrow and focus smiling energy from the heart to the perineal area. You can practice smiling and relaxing the Third Eye and the perineum any time you have a few moments to sit or lie down quietly.

Once you have mastered these exercises, they need not be repeated before each meditation session as a warm-up. Instead, you will find them incorporated within the main practice of the Microcosmic Orbit.

TECHNIQUES FOR ENHANCING THE SENSATION OF CHI IN MEDITATION

Circulating Chi in the Microcosmic Orbit

What Does Chi Feel Like?

The essence of the Microcosmic Orbit meditation is to use the mind to move Chi in a loop through the body, beginning and ending at the navel. You will naturally want to ask at this point, "What does Chi feel like?" and "When I feel the Chi, how do I get it to move where I want it to go?"

The fact is that you already have Chi moving through every part of your body. It is the life-force that animates your body. Without it, there is no life! Unfortunately, most of us do not know how to identify the sensations associated with the movement of Chi.

Chi has many sensations. Some of the most common are tingling, heat, expansion, an electrical sensation (like the feeling of static electricity), magnetic energy, pulsation, or effervescence. These are not the actual Chi itself, but the signs of increasing Chi in an area. Chi itself is more mysterious, subtle beyond definition. Detecting the signs of Chi movement is most important for now.

The Mind Leads the Chi

There is a saying in the Taoist classics, "The mind moves and the Chi follows." Wherever we focus our attention, the Chi will tend to gather and increase. Because Chi is the force behind all movement, simply focusing the attention on an area of the body will cause increased activity in the nerves in that area. Muscular activity, lymphatic flow, and blood circulation may also be affected. All these systems are moved by Chi, so the Chi circulation to an area must increase when these other systems increase their activity. This means we are automatically affecting the Chi

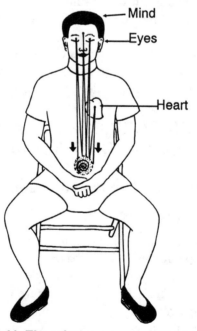

Figure 4-11. The mind moves and Chi follows.

flow to an area merely by focusing the attention on that area (Figure 4-11).

As we learn the Microcosmic Orbit practice, we will also learn a variety of related techniques, such as spiraling, touching the points, applying hand positions (mudras), and breathing, to activate the points. All these methods help us use more of our mental powers to enhance our concentration on each point. The stronger the focus, the greater the movement of Chi. Understanding this is crucial to developing an effective practice of the Microcosmic Orbit meditation.

When your energy flows effortlessly through the pathways and you no longer need to use your hands, breath, or spiraling to activate the points, you will have reached a higher level of skill. If you then feel your mental concentration is strong enough to gather and direct Chi without these additional techniques, you may use them at your own discretion, or forego using them altogether. Keep in mind that they are simply auxiliary techniques to enhance the essential practice when necessary.

The Methods

1. Spiraling: The Mind/Eye Connection

From whirlpools, tornadoes, and the spiraling electrons of our cells to the spiraling formations of galaxies and nebulae, nature moves in spirals. Spirals initiate vortex-like force-fields of energy that gather, draw in, and condense other energies. Just as nature uses spirals throughout the universe, we can use them to improve the functions of our bodies through meditation.

In this method we use the power of the mind, the eyes, and the heart to draw energy into the centers of the Microcosmic Orbit, spiraling and condensing the Chi into each point. You will turn the mind, eyes, and awareness inward to feel the centers, focusing on each one individually until a sensation of energy occurs. Then you will continue using the mind and the eyes to guide the energy of each center to the next successive center along the Microcosmic route, activating them in turn and connecting them energetically, which produces a kinesthetic (bodily) sensation that outlines the Orbit's pathway.

You can practice in stages to learn inner-eye power training, as you would practice the alphabet before learning how to write. In the Microcosmic Orbit meditation, we use all these techniques to enhance our Chi. The energy at this beginning level may feel as if it is just under the skin or flowing through the more superficial layers of the body.

In the beginning, you will learn to feel the Chi through the physical stimulus you create by moving the eyes as you develop the ability to mentally control the spiraling process. If you cannot feel the Chi after using the mind and eye movements alone, try touching each point lightly with your hands during practice, and focus behind the point of contact. (Eventually you won't need any eye movements or physical assistance.) The exercises that follow will help you learn to feel the Chi as you spiral it at each station.

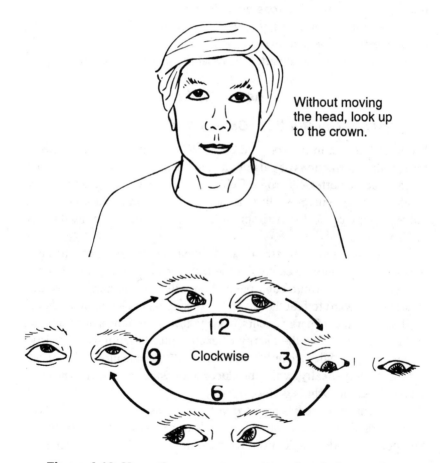

Without moving the head, look up to the crown.

12
9 Clockwise 3
6

Figure 4-12. Move the eyes one quarter of a circle at a time.

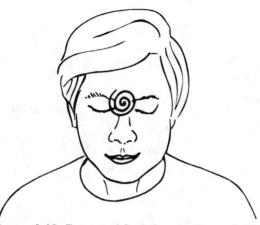

**Figure 4-13. Rest and feel the energy spiraling.
at the mid-eyebrow**

A. Spiraling power with eyes open (Figures 4-12, 4-13, and 4-14). Spiraling clockwise from the center has the power to condense the Chi at the center.

1. Open the eyes, and without moving the head, look up to the crown of the head, then to the right, then straight down, and then left.

2. Look up again.

3. Repeat these steps from 9 to 36 times.

4. Close the eyes, inhale, and feel the energy or Chi ball produced by the spiraling. Exhale and feel the energy condense between your eyebrows. When the condensing power is great enough, it will reverse and expand like a mini-orgasm or explosion, releasing the pressure.

5. Reverse spiraling in a counterclockwise direction outward from the center has the power to expand the inner Chi to connect with the external Chi outside the body. At the point of maximum expansion, the flow will reverse itself and pulse back toward you.

Repeat the same steps as for spiraling clockwise, but move the eyes counterclockwise instead.

6. This exercise can also be performed on a horizontal plane: look front, look right, look behind you (suck the eyes in lightly), and look left. Then reverse. This is the pattern you will use to gather Chi at your navel. Imagine you have a ball at the navel, and practice rotating it to the left (counterclockwise as you look down) and then reversing and spinning it to the right. You can coordinate the eye movement with the rotations. Some Taoists visualize a spinning Tai Chi symbol.

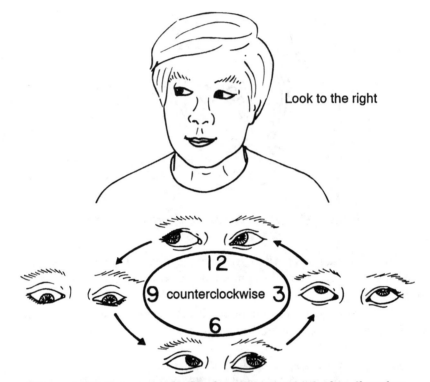

Figure 4-14. Reverse spiraling in a counterclockwise direction.

B. Mind/eye spiraling power with eyes closed. This is the same as the previous exercise, except it is done with eyes closed. Repeat the steps from 9 to 36 times spiraling clockwise, then repeat spiraling counterclockwise (Figure 4-15).

C. Advanced mind/eye spiraling power with no physical eye movement. This practice truly involves mind/eye power and will help you learn to use your inner vision. You will feel a certain kind of energy, and your mind will form an image of the crown of the head through the "inner eye."

You can use the inner eye to check yourself internally and to help heal parts of your body whenever necessary.

1. Close the eyes, and without physically moving them (or the head), use the mind to look up to the crown, then to the right, then straight down, and then left.

Figure 4-15. Close the eyes, and without moving the head, move the eyes clockwise and counterclockwise.

2. Look up again.

3. Repeat these steps from 9 to 36 times.

4. Rest, and feel the energy produced by the spiraling.

5. Repeat the same procedures in a counterclockwise spiral.

6. Repeat the exercise, using the inner eye to move horizontally: front, right, back, and left, then reverse.

NOTE: *From this point on, you can use the power of the mind to work with the inner eye (if you are visually inclined), or you can continue to move the physical eyes to help spiral the energy.*

D. Most advanced mind/eye training: Contracting and relaxing to condense in and pulse out Chi. We can use the unique muscle power of our eyes both to activate our own Chi and to draw in and condense the unlimited Chi of nature.

The eyes are an outer extension of the brain. They have a close connection to both the parasympathetic and sympathetic nervous systems. In fact, the eyes are so important that 4 out of 12 of the cranial nerves are involved solely with vision and eye muscle movement (Figure 4-16).

The muscles in the iris are classified as Yin or Yang according to their functions. The circular muscle (sphincter pupillae muscles) of the

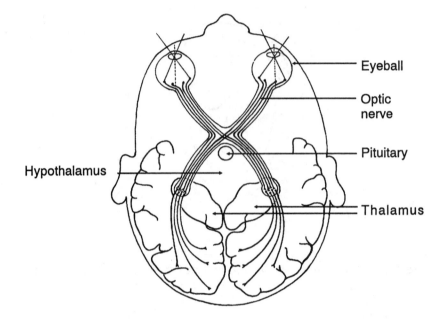

Figure 4-16. The eyes are the outer extensions of the brain.

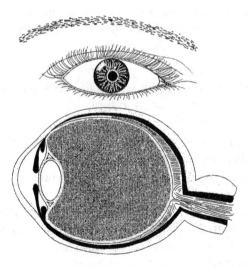

Figure 4-17. Contract the iris with the circular muscle.

iris decreases pupil size when there is too much light, so it is regarded as Yin. It is activated by the parasympathetic nervous system, the Yin branch of the nervous system associated with rest and repose, the "relaxation response," slowing the heart rate, and other Yin functions.

The circular muscle of the iris (Figure 4-17) is related to the other sphincter muscles in the body, such as the sphincter muscles around the eyes and the mouth, the anal sphincter muscles (please see Figure 4-8), the urogenital diaphragm, the muscles around the vagina, and the penis. The heart also has the same type of circular muscle. Contracting and releasing the iris and the other muscles around the eye will help create and activate a pulsing reflexive resonance with all the other circular muscles. When all these muscles are activated, they have the power to gather and condense the mind/eye power (Figure 4-18).

The radial muscle of the iris (dilator pupillae muscle) dilates the pupil; it is regarded as Yang. It is activated by the sympathetic nervous system, the Yang branch of the nervous system associated with the "fight or flight" response, increased heart rate, rapid breathing, and other stress or danger reactions. The radial muscles have the power to extend energy

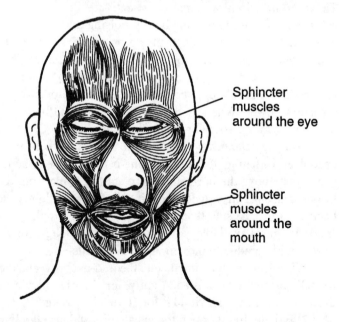

Sphincter muscles around the eye

Sphincter muscles around the mouth

Figure 4-18. When all these muscles are activated, they have the power to gather and condense mind/eye power.

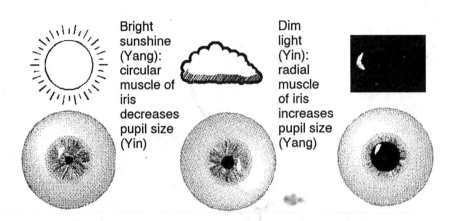

Bright sunshine (Yang): circular muscle of iris decreases pupil size (Yin)

Dim light (Yin): radial muscle of iris increases pupil size (Yang)

Figure 4-19. Condensing light into the body

out and connect to distant energies. The circular muscles of the iris have the power to draw in and condense those distant energies.

When you use advanced mind/eye power, you lightly contract and relax the circular muscles of the iris and the muscles surrounding the eye. These contractions automatically activate the anus and the sexual sphincter muscles. Once this bodily pulsing and pumping is activated, you will find it very easy to inhale as you draw in energy and then condense it within you as you exhale by focusing inwardly.

The iris is very responsive to light, especially sunlight. When there is bright sunshine (Yang), the iris decreases the pupil size (Yin), creating a suction power. When there is little light (Yin), the iris increases the pupil size (Yang), allowing your Chi to expand.

Practice condensing light into the body (Figure 4-19). Use a candle or look at the sunlight; the safest time is the sunrise or sunset, when the sun is just above the horizon. To protect the retina from damage in the bright or strong sun, you need to blink the eyes and lightly move the head back and forth. At sunset and sunrise, the eye can look without blinking. If no sunlight is available, you also can use candlelight, or a 60-watt bulb to start with, gradually moving up to 100 watts.

1. Look at the light, inhale into the mid-eyebrow and the mouth, and partially close the eyelids and lightly dim the irises down. Feel yourself drawing in the light and hold it for 10 or 15 seconds.

2. Exhale, lightly open the eyes, and condense the light Chi in the mouth. Relax and let the Chi expand in the mouth. Gradually you will feel the essence of the sun, known as the solar essence, get thicker and thicker.

If you are looking at bright sunlight, start by blinking the eyes 20 to 30 times. Lightly close the eyes and see the light in front of you. Inhale lightly, dim the eyes, and draw the light into you. You can gather the moon essence in the same manner, only you don't have to blink the eyes and move the head (Figure 4-20). Please see Chapter 11, "Chi of the Sun and Moon."

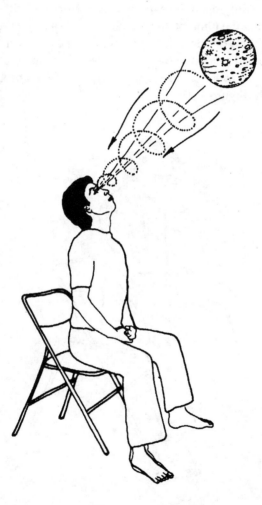

Figure 4-20. Looking at the sun/moon to gather the light essence

Next, we will add to the exercise the sphincter muscles of the eyes, mouth, anus, and perineum. Smiling will help activate the sphincter muscles in the eyes and mouth.

3. Smile, inhale lightly, dim the eyes, and lightly contract the muscles around the eyes and the mouth. At the same time, also feel the anus, perineum, and sexual organ lightly contract.

4. Feel these as you draw the light energy into the mid-eyebrow and the mouth, charging the saliva with it.

5. Exhale, lightly open the eyes, and condense the light Chi in the mouth by focusing the mind on the mouth and saliva as you exhale.

Don't use force, or you will feel a cramp in the stomach. If you get a cramp, exhale and relax into the cramp a few times to help release it. You may also swallow the saliva (charged with Chi from absorbed light) into the stomach (Figure 4-21).

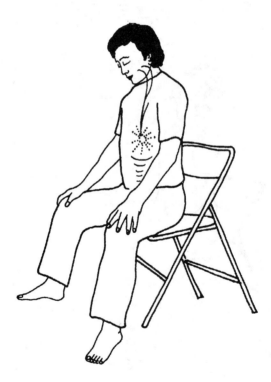

Figure 4-21. Swallow saliva to the stomach (Original Force).

6. Add the tongue. Inhale, press the tongue up to the palate, dim the eyes, and contract all the muscles as above.

7. Exhale and relax the tongue but continue to touch it to the palate. Follow the entire procedure (steps 1 through 7) six to nine times and rest. Feel the Chi ball in the mouth increase and the tongue start to vibrate as if electricity is flowing.

2. Using the Hands to Help Guide the Chi

NOTE: *This section includes explanations of the different methods you will use in later chapters. You may want to refer back to these explanations as you progress in your practice.*

A. Touching the points. Another very effective method of enhancing the sensation of Chi at each center is to touch that point with your hand and focus behind the point of contact as you go through the

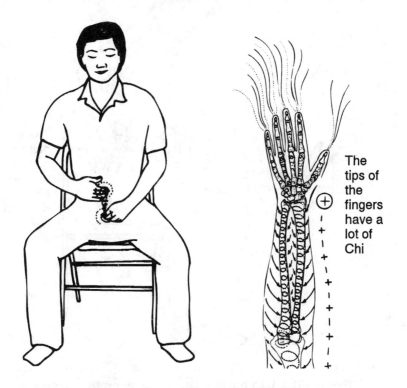

The tips of the fingers have a lot of Chi

Figure 4-22. Touching the navel and sexual center

Microcosmic Orbit meditation. To use this method, keep the right palm over your navel and move the left hand or fingers to touch whatever point or energy center you are focusing on. You can either place the palm so that the Lao Gung point on the center of your palm is directly over that point, or you may simply touch the point with the three middle fingers (Figure 4-22). (This is useful in places where it is too awkward to use the palm.)

The hands have abundant Chi flowing into them, and they can help guide additional Chi into the energy centers to activate them. Touching the points will also help you focus more attention on those areas. The more you focus the mind/eye on each point, the more Chi gathers there. Eventually, with practice, you will become more sensitive to the subtle

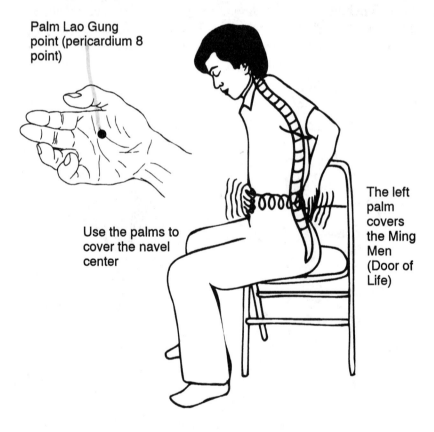

Palm Lao Gung point (pericardium 8 point)

Use the palms to cover the navel center

The left palm covers the Ming Men (Door of Life)

Figure 4-23. Use the Lao Gung points on the palms to cover the navel and the Ming Men point.

sensations of Chi at each center, and you will no longer need to touch each point. In the beginning stages, however, touching the energy centers will help your practice of the Microcosmic Orbit meditation immensely.

B. Holding the palms above each point. In this technique, the emphasis is on healing. It can help enhance your concentration and increase your inner sensitivity to the organs, glands, and nervous system. By holding the palms over each center and adding their external focus to your mental concentration, you can help guide and condense the energy into each center (Figure 4-23).

Hold the hands about two or three inches away from each station until you feel the energy radiating from the palms into each center. This method can also be used for self-healing on any part of the body that needs it, including the internal organs and glands. Just use the mind to channel the Universal Force (or light) through the palms to any painful areas.

Using the hands this way also helps focus the attention so the mind doesn't wander during meditation. At this level of your practice, you may feel the energy has started to move deeper inside you. As you learn through practice to see and feel deeply into the organs, your ability to sense the connecting energy channels will improve greatly.

3. Using Breath to Regulate Chi Flow

A. Small Sip Breathing to stimulate Chi flow. Small Sip Breathing stimulates Chi flow into the olfactory nerve. Long Sip Breathing stimulates the thalamus, hypothalamus, and pituitary gland, which activates the center of the brain and stimulates the nerves (Figures 4-24 and 4-25).

Small Sip Breathing combines the powers of the mind, the eyes, the heart, and the breath to open any energy point (Figure 4-26). For this technique, you will need to hold the breath, as this condenses more Chi into each point. With each inhalation you will take three, six, or more shallow sips of air. (Those who cannot comfortably hold their breath for long periods should practice using the other methods until their capacity improves.) Small Sip Breathing is especially useful for people with low energy, or for people with normal energy levels who nevertheless cannot feel any Chi flow.

CAUTION SHOULD BE USED WITH THIS AND ANY OTHER CHI KUNG PRACTICE THAT ALTERS THE NATURAL PATTERN OF BREATHING. IN SOME CASES, WHEN THE CHEST

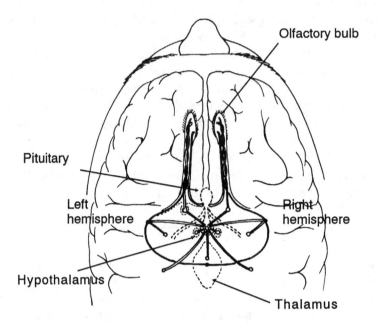

Olfactory bulb

Pituitary

Left hemisphere

Right hemisphere

Hypothalamus

Thalamus

Figure 4-24. The olfactory nerve has a connection to the thalamus, hypothalamus, and pituitary glands. The olfactory bulb connects the hypothalamus to all the other glands.

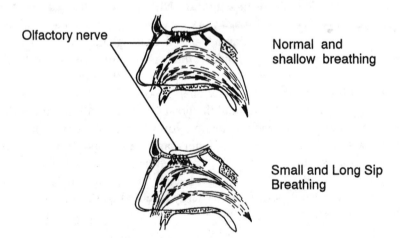

Olfactory nerve

Normal and shallow breathing

Small and Long Sip Breathing

Figure 4-25. Normal and shallow breathing will not stimulate the olfactory nerve. Small and Long Sip Breathing will stimulate the olfactory bulb and thereby all the other glands.

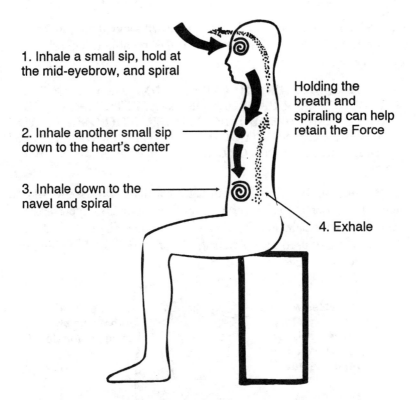

1. Inhale a small sip, hold at the mid-eyebrow, and spiral

Holding the breath and spiraling can help retain the Force

2. Inhale another small sip down to the heart's center

3. Inhale down to the navel and spiral

4. Exhale

Figure 4-26. Small Sip Breathing combines the powers of the mind, the eyes, the heart, and the breath to open any energy point.

IS TOO TIGHT OR THE ABDOMEN FEELS TOO FULL, HOLD-ING THE BREATH CAN CAUSE CHEST PAIN. PEOPLE WITH LUNG AND HEART PROBLEMS, GLAUCOMA, HIGH BLOOD PRESSURE, HEMOPHILIA, ATHEROSCLEROSIS, OR OTHER SERIOUS PROBLEMS SHOULD NOT USE THIS METHOD.

1. Inhale several small sips of air without exhaling, then hold the breath for five seconds as you spiral the energy at any given center. Then exhale, rest, and repeat.

2. Now focus the attention at the navel. Inhale three to six small sips toward the navel without exhaling. Exhale, condense, and retain the energy of the breath at the navel with mind/eye power.

3. You take three to six short sips into each point at first. After a while, you may need to sip only one to three times into each point to activate it, and then go on to the next point without exhaling if you are still comfortable. As you progress, you may be able to cover several points in one inhalation.

CAUTION: BE SURE TO EXHALE ANYTIME YOU FEEL UN-COMFORTABLE OR SHORT OF BREATH! THE PRACTICE IS NOT ENHANCED BY HOLDING THE BREATH LONGER IF YOU ARE STRAINING TO DO IT. DO NOT STRAIN! REMAIN RELAXED AND COMFORTABLE.

B. Long Sip Breathing to calm and condense the essence of Chi (Figure 4-27). Long Sip Breathing is useful for anxious or hypersensitive persons, for acute pain, and for emotionally or mentally disturbed states of mind. It is also used for the transition from Small Sip Breathing to a deeper meditative state.

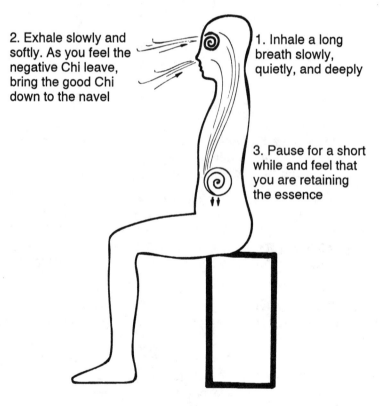

2. Exhale slowly and softly. As you feel the negative Chi leave, bring the good Chi down to the navel

1. Inhale a long breath slowly, quietly, and deeply

3. Pause for a short while and feel that you are retaining the essence

Figure 4-27. Long Sip Breathing

1. Be aware of the iris and sphincter muscles of the eyes, mouth, anus, and perineum.

2. Inhale lightly and contract the iris and sphincter muscles. Breathe slowly and gently, as if you were pulling a strand of silk through the mid-eyebrow and down into the mouth, and slowly draw the breath to any given point. Start by practicing at the navel.

3. Then exhale and relax all the muscles, exhaling slowly and softly into the point, and feel that you are retaining the essence of Chi there (even though you are breathing out). At the end of the exhalation, condense the Chi into the point. Pause for a moment at the end of the exhalation. As you pause, you will feel more energy as your breath activates that point.

Make sure to keep 95 percent of the awareness on the Original Force behind the navel and in front of the kidneys (even while you are focusing on other points along the channel).

C. Internal Breathing: Spontaneous pulsation of Chi. There are thousands of Chi Kung breathing techniques. These techniques can be very helpful in moving and directing energy in the beginning. Eventually you will want to move beyond them, to "graduate," and allow the inner breath or Chi to circulate naturally through the mind/eye/heart power.

Internal Breathing is a much gentler and safer method than Small Sip Breathing. In this method, your breath must become long, slow, soft, quiet, gentle, smooth, deep, and even. At no time should the breath be forced to be longer, slower, softer, and so forth. Instead it should be like water: if water is left alone, any sediment gradually settles to the bottom, and the water becomes clear without any effort being made to filter it. Similarly, the waves on the surface of the water gradually subside and the surface becomes calm and still like a mirror.

In Taoism we often refer to the power of *Wu Wei* or "not-doing." We say that by not doing, nothing is left undone, and things take care of themselves. That is how we achieve Internal Breathing: when we let go of trying to breathe in any special way, the body takes over, and the natural state of Inner Breathing arises by itself. At higher levels, the out breath may cease completely for short periods with no ill effect.

This induces a state of deep relaxation and heightened inner sensitivity. The flow of the Internal Breath and Chi will move at its own pace, and the Chi flow will in turn guide the pace of the breathing.

PREPARING FOR
THE MICROCOSMIC ORBIT MEDITATION

Prepare the Environment

Find a quiet place to meditate. When you are beginning the practice of meditation, it is best to find a place where there are no distractions. However, once you have mastered the Microcosmic Orbit meditation, you will be able to meditate anywhere: while you are walking, standing in line, driving your car, or lying in bed, or just about anytime.

Some places have naturally peaceful Chi, and just being there will help you get into a meditative mood. Meditators have traditionally sought out mountains, forests, caves, gardens, monasteries, or beautifully designed meditation rooms. Once you have experienced such a place, you can just recall it. Most of us live in the city or suburbs and lead active lives. You will do fine to set aside a room or corner of your room for your practice and recall your connection to the forces of nature.

Keep your meditation place clean and pleasant. Decorating it with fresh flowers or plants can also be helpful. (Cactus plants are not usually conducive to energetic meditations, however.) Some plants or flowers may not agree with your energy; some can actually drain you or make you ill. The way to find out is to stand in front of plants, trees, or flowers and extend your right hand to feel them. Train your right hand to scan them for positive energies, and train your left hand to scan them for negative energies. Try to feel any good sensations through your right hand first, then shake your left palm loose and put it over the same plant to feel any negative sensations. Whichever hand receives the sensation indicates the plant's energetic output; you should not feel good and bad sensations from the same plant. Try to feel the difference between the two hands. You should be able to distinguish a good feeling from a bad one.

After your right hand has learned to feel positive energies and your left hand can feel negative energies, comparisons will become easy. If you like a particular sensation, bring it within yourself, and feel how it affects you and your energies. If you don't like the energies you feel from a plant, move it out of the room or get rid of it. (Once you have felt a good sensation, you shouldn't feel anything negative coming from the same plant.)

A pleasant work of art or a picture of a natural setting will also help create a meditative atmosphere. It is best if the space you set aside has a feeling of privacy and is not near an area through which people may travel and interrupt your practice. When you meditate, keep all pets away from your space. Pets have their own energies, which may confuse or disturb your energies. Their odors can also distract you when you are trying to quiet down.

Avoid interruptions. You will do better in your practice if you strategically plan not to be interrupted. Plan to meditate early in the morning before other people are awake and before the phone starts ringing. The morning is usually best because the body is rested, the air is fresh, and the earth itself is energized. Late at night is also fine if you are a night owl. The major point is to select a time that works well for you with your own rhythms and schedule.

When you are preparing to meditate, turn the answering machine on and your telephone ringer off, or take the phone off the hook. If you have to meditate when other people are in the house and awake, make an agreement with them not to disturb you while you are meditating. If they are not sympathetic to meditation, tell them you are resting, which indeed you are, and that you are not taking any calls.

Every person has the right to some quiet time to recharge, and this is exactly what meditation is. When you are recharged, you have more to give others. If you do not take care of yourself, at some point others may have to take care of you!

Physical hygiene is a habit with most of us; we would not think of going a day without brushing our teeth or combing our hair. Mental hygiene is even more important, yet most of us neglect it. If you allow yourself time each day to cleanse your emotional, energetic, and physical bodies, you will soon reap the rewards in every area of your life.

Conserve Energy and Purify Your Body with an Appropriate Diet

During the beginning stages of learning the Microcosmic Orbit meditation, it is best to conserve your energy and purify yourself. If you can, abstain from sex for the first 100 days of practice to conserve sexual energy and to build up a reservoir of surplus Chi to aid in opening the Microcosmic Orbit. Intentional celibacy can be easy and quite pleasurable when practiced using Taoist methods to strengthen your sexuality. (Refer to other Healing Tao books on cultivating sexual energy to gain a clear perspective on this.)

Taoists believe in moderation, realizing that celibacy is very difficult for many people, so this is only a recommendation, not an absolute requirement. It will also help to reduce the amount of meat, fish, and poultry you eat and to increase the amount of fiber in your diet to clear your digestive tract. Unless your dietary needs are completely vegetarian, it is recommended that you eat about 80 percent grains and vegetables, 10 to 15 percent fish, and only 5 percent meat and chicken during your first 100 days of practice.

Loosen, Stretch, and Warm Up the Body Before Meditating

Once you have a quiet place and are ready to meditate, it is very helpful if you first spend a few minutes loosening up the body, particularly the spine, before you sit down to practice.

In the Healing Tao, we like to do some stretching exercises, Chi Kung, and Tai Chi before sitting down to meditate. These exercises are both invigorating and relaxing; they relieve muscle tensions, stimulate the blood circulation, get rid of stale air in the lungs, and oxygenate the blood. If you are unfamiliar with these exercises, you can take a relaxing stroll outside before meditating instead. Doing some movement before entering the stillness of meditation will add to the richness of your sessions. It can help you shake off the sluggishness that comes from being too sedentary and can also ease the tensions that might build up during a hectic day. Then when you sit down, you are ready to begin. Use the exercises in the Appendix at the back of the book to loosen your spine first, such as:

Spinal Cord Breathing
Spinal Cord Rocking
Crane-Neck Rocking
Combined Movement Rocking
Shaking the spine up and down to loosen it

Wear Loose and Comfortable Clothing

The clothing you wear for meditation should be loose and comfortable. It is very important that your clothes restrict neither the Chi flow, the blood circulation, the nervous system, nor the breathing. Tight clothes may be attractive and fashionable, but they are usually not suitable for practice. Warmup outfits or sweat clothes are excellent for practice, and long skirts are fine for women. Shorts are also fine in warm weather. Elastic waistbands are best, as they do not impede breathing. If your outfit does not have an elastic waistband, it is often a good idea to loosen the belt and perhaps the top button of your lower garment so that the lower abdomen is not restricted.

Many people are more comfortable meditating with their shoes off; it helps create a more relaxed feeling. However, if your shoes are comfortable, it is all right to leave your shoes on while practicing. Because you will be sitting still for a while, it is often a good idea to dress a little more warmly than you might think necessary if the weather is on the cool side, especially since your body may tend to cool down. This is not always the case, however; some people become quite warm during the practice, so use your own judgment.

It is preferable to wear clothing of natural fibers so your body can breathe. Synthetic materials tend to close the pores of the skin, impeding its ability to absorb energy. People who cover most of their bodies with synthetic socks, pants, and shirts often become closed to external energies. Because the head is the only area exposed to external Chi, all interactions between the body's energies and the external Chi must occur there. This causes too much heat to rush up to the brain. This is especially problematic for people who are mentally oriented. When most of the body's parts are sealed off, more internal energy rises to the head, causing overheating and even hair loss. During meditation, all the pores open wider, and breathing in energy through them requires looser clothing. When you have learned to breathe through the skin, your body will need to contact more fresh air.

Establish a Stable Sitting Position

The body must be stable for the mind to be stable. It has been said, "An anxious mind cannot exist in a relaxed body." The mind and body are clearly connected, and when the body and breath become peaceful, the mind easily follows.

If your posture is firm and balanced, it will be easy for you to relax, and you will already be halfway toward achieving a tranquil and focused mind. Conversely, if your posture lacks balance and stability, your muscles will soon tire and become tense. You will find it difficult to relax, and your attention will waver like a candle in the wind. Thus it is well worth taking a few minutes to adjust your posture.

There are seven points to consider in preparing a good meditation posture: base, hands, spine, shoulders, chin, eyes, and tongue.

1. The Base. Your base is the foundation of a good meditation posture, so it is the first point on which to focus. Many styles of meditation advocate sitting on the floor in cross-legged or lotus position. The advantage of these postures is that they help gather the Chi of the extremities in toward the center of the body, which can be beneficial. These postures can also be very stable if one can sit in them comfortably. The full lotus posture (also called the full-locked position) enables one to sit in deep samadhi-like meditation for hours, days, or weeks, and to go out of the body without falling over (Figure 4-28).

Figure 4-28. The advantage of the lotus position is that it helps gather the Chi of the extremities in toward the center of the body.

The disadvantage of these postures is that they do not always accommodate the movement of internal and external forces tapped in the Taoist practices. In all energy-oriented disciplines, including the Microcosmic Orbit meditation, one needs to establish a good connection with the earth's energy to stay grounded. The more Chi one moves through the body, the more important grounding becomes to prevent overheating of the organs and other negative side effects. The soles of the feet provide an ideal connection to the earth through the Yung Chuan (Bubbling Spring) points. These are specifically designed to absorb the earth's energy and conduct it up into the body. The legs also help filter the raw energy to make it more readily digestible; crossed legs cannot do this.

Most people who are used to sitting in chairs are neither comfortable nor stable sitting on the ground for long periods of time. For this reason, being required to sit on the ground to meditate can present a real obstacle. To facilitate practice and properly absorb the earth's energy, it is recommended that you sit on a chair to practice the Microcosmic Orbit meditation. A dining room chair or a padded folding chair would be the best choice.

Your weight should be evenly divided over four points, just as the weight of a table is distributed between its four legs. For us, the four points are the two feet and the ischial tuberosities, or the two points of the ischium (sitting bones) (Figure 4-29). The feet should be placed flat on the floor at about the same distance apart as the hips. They should neither be drawn in too close to the chair nor extended too far away, and the calves of the legs should be vertical, like pillars. If possible, try to have the knees and hips at the same level, or keep the knees slightly higher.

The part of the pelvis known as the ischium is structurally designed to hold a tremendous amount of weight. Architects have copied its design to use as a base for skyscrapers. Many people have the bad habit of leaning back and sitting on the coccyx and sacrum instead of the ischium. This puts pressure on the sacrum, which is one of the major pumps in the spine for cerebrospinal fluid, a vital cushion for the nervous system. It is therefore wise to honor Mother Nature's design by sitting on the ischium and not on the tailbone. Once you have found an appropriate base position, check to make sure your weight is evenly distributed over the four points. Then you will have established a solid base to support the body during meditation.

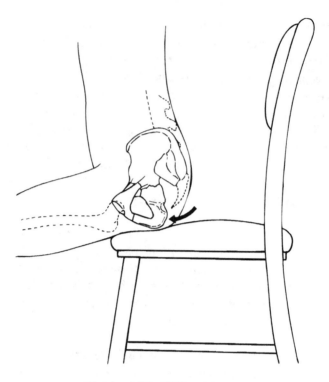

Figure 4-29. Sitting bones

2. The Hands. Let your hands rest in your lap, clasped together with the right palm over the left palm and the right thumb and forefinger wrapped around the base of the left thumb. If it feels more comfortable, it is also fine to place a pillow on your lap and rest the hands on the pillow in the clasped position (Figure 4-30). We use different hand positions for different forces, and these will be discussed later on.

There are probably as many different hand positions (often called mudras) as there are different systems of meditation. Those who have learned other systems of meditation may be attached to the mudra they have previously learned. We recommend that you use the hand position described above. It works especially well to consolidate and balance the energies generated during the Microcosmic Orbit meditation. Also, if you use another hand position, it may trigger old associations, and you may discover in the middle of your session that you are unconsciously doing your old meditation practice instead of the Microcosmic Orbit.

Figure 4-30. Using a small pillow helps release shoulder stress.

3. The Spine. The spine should be straight but not stiff, and in good vertical alignment with gravity. You may find it helpful to imagine your head is being pulled up by a string. As the head rises, allow the spine to elongate, increasing the space between each vertebra (Figure 4-31).

Some people find their backs become tired during long rounds of meditation. Good alignment is very helpful in preventing this, because it takes some of the stress off the muscles and puts it instead on the skeletal structure where it belongs. The skeletal structure can support hundreds of pounds without effort when properly aligned. Practicing Iron Shirt Chi Kung and Tai Chi can also be very helpful for strengthening the muscles you use in sitting and for learning the body mechanics of good alignment.

The spinal column houses many nerves, and it is also a major part of the Microcosmic Orbit pathway. If the spine feels relaxed, clear, and

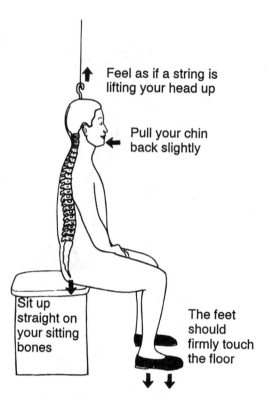

Feel as if a string is lifting your head up

Pull your chin back slightly

Sit up straight on your sitting bones

The feet should firmly touch the floor

Figure 4-31. Correct sitting position

open, the mind will feel more awake and alert too. (See the Appendix for Spinal Cord Exercises.)

4. The Shoulders. The shoulders should be relaxed and balanced over the hips. The armpits should be slightly open, allowing enough space to hold a Ping Pong ball (Figure 4-32). This permits free circulation of blood and Chi into the arms and also keeps the nerves flowing into the arms from being impinged.

5. The Chin. The chin should be drawn back slightly so that the ears are over the shoulders. This should be done with as little strain as possible; if you strain too much to bring the head back, your muscles will soon tire and you will not be able to hold still in your position through the entire round of meditation.

6. The Eyes. Your eyes should generally be closed during the practice. This eliminates visual distractions and helps you turn the attention inward. It is also more relaxing to have the eyes closed. If you

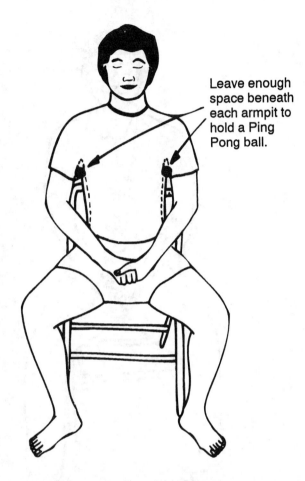

Leave enough space beneath each armpit to hold a Ping Pong ball.

Figure 4-32. Arms' position

are not comfortable having the eyes closed, or if you become sleepy or start to lose your equilibrium, it is all right to have the eyes slightly open with the gaze directed downward, or focus on the nose, and from the nose focus into the heart. You can open the eyes for a while if you feel sleepy or distracted, and then close them as you turn your focus inward (Figure 4-33).

7. The Tongue. The tip of the tongue should be touching the upper palate (Figure 4-34). This connection acts like a switch in that it connects the Tu Mo and Ren Mo, the Governor and Functional Channels. The exact location of the connection point may vary. Traditionally there are

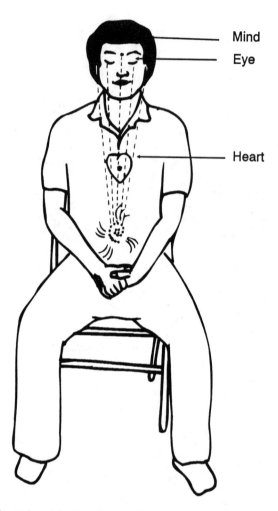

Mind

Eye

Heart

Figure 4-33. Turn the mind and eyes inward. Focus into the heart and then down into the navel.

three possible locations: the *Wind Point*, the *Fire Point*, and the *Water Point* (Figure 4-35).

The Wind Point. The Wind Point is on the hard palate about one-half to one inch from where the teeth and gums meet. This point of contact is recommended by most Tai Chi and Zen masters; however, the Taoist classics warn that if the tongue is held in this position, one may develop "internal wind" and become sleepy. In some Taoist systems, the tongue is held in this position to aid the energy flow in the Wind Pathway.

146

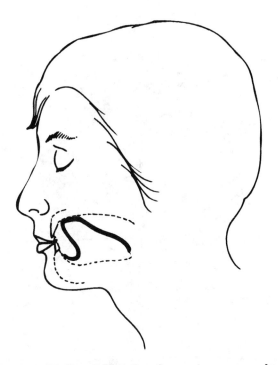

Figure 4-34. Touch the tip of your tongue against the upper palate.

The Fire Point. The Fire Point is on the middle of the palate. The Taoist classics caution that if the tongue is held in this position, the mouth may become too dry. In some Taoist systems, the tongue is held here to facilitate the energy flow through the Fire Pathway.

The Water Point. The Water Point is toward the back of the mouth where the hard and soft areas of the palate meet. It is also called the Heavenly Pool point, because when the tongue is held in this position, the saliva tends to flow copiously. Taoists traditionally favor this point because saliva is highly valued as an expression of Original Chi, which blends with the Chi absorbed from food and drink while helping us absorb external Chi from the universe. The Water Point is also used in some Taoist systems to help the energy flow through the Water Pathway.

Even though the Water Point has some positive benefits, stretching the tongue to this point and holding it there for a long time is a strain for many people. Yogis in India and China sometimes cut the small piece of flesh under the tongue, the frenulum, to make it easier for the tongue to

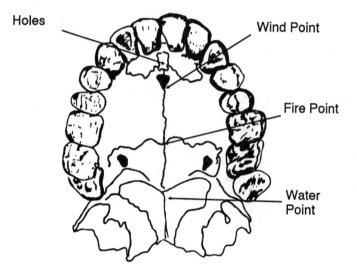

Figure 4-35. The palate

reach back to this point. It is neither necessary nor desirable to go to this extreme; the points closer to the front of the mouth can be just as effective in making the connection. If you are using the Wind or Fire Point and find yourself growing sleepy or dry in the mouth, simply bring your tongue back to the Water Point for a short time until the problem goes away. Then you can return your tongue to a more comfortable position.

The best point for you to use is the one where you feel the strongest sensation of Chi. To determine this:

1. Rub the tip of the tongue vigorously from the front to the back of the palate 9 to 18 times.

2. Then, starting at the front, slowly move the tip of the tongue from the front (Wind Point) toward the back (Water Point).

3. Eventually, you will experience one or more of the following sensations on the tongue: tingling, metallic taste, electrical sensation, heat, or a general feeling of increased sensation in the tongue. This will indicate the place that is the optimal connection point for you. Your optimal connection point may vary from day to day, and it may not be in the exact location of any of the points described above. The most important factor is that a good connection is made each time you practice.

ACTIVATING THE ORIGINAL FORCE: WARMING THE STOVE

We start the process of activating the Original Chi by focusing the attention in the area between the navel, the Door of Life, and the sexual center to "warm the stove" as a preparation for stimulating the Original Chi that flows into the body through this point. One manifestation of successfully stimulating the Original Chi is heat or warmth. Original Chi is like a battery. It provides the spark to start the energy flowing strongly through the Microcosmic Orbit.

There are five processes underlying all the practices.

1. Generating the Force to activate the movement of energy.
2. Gathering the Chi that has been generated into a Chi ball.
3. Condensing the Chi ball into a Chi dot or pearl.
4. Expanding or pulsating the Chi inside you.
5. Storing the Chi in the Tan Tien center or at any point you are working on. Rest and do nothing; allow the Chi to move itself.

1. Bellows Breathing: Generating the Force

Sit on a chair with the back straight and the feet touching the floor about as far apart as the hips. Place the hands over the navel. Start with the Inner Smile practice described in Chapter 3. Notice the sensations of energy as you smile to the area about one and a half inches behind the navel. At this time, some people may already feel a strong sensation of heat or warmth in the navel region. If not, just continue to be aware of the sensations at the navel with your smiling awareness (Figure 4- 36).

When you inhale, expand the lower abdomen at the navel area (below and around it) so that it bulges outward. Feel the diaphragm descend. Then, keeping your chest relaxed, exhale with some force to pull the lower abdomen back in, as if you were pulling the navel back toward the spine. Feel the sexual organs pull up also. Repeat 18 to 36 times (Figure 4-37).

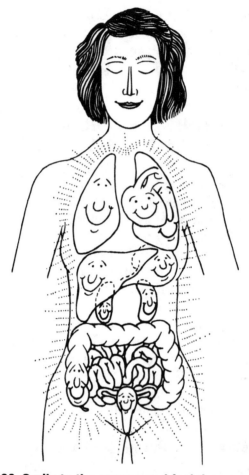

Figure 4-36. Smile to the organs and feel the organs smile back to you.

This massages the organs, especially the kidneys and the aorta and the vena cava pathways to and from the heart, emptying them of trapped energy and toxins.

2. Rest and Gather the Chi at the Navel

Rest, and keep the hands covering the navel. Lightly close the eyes and use the mind/eye power to help gather and condense the energy you have been generating. (For details, see the instructions for Most Advanced Mind/Eye Training above.) Inhale, lightly contract the iris and sphincter

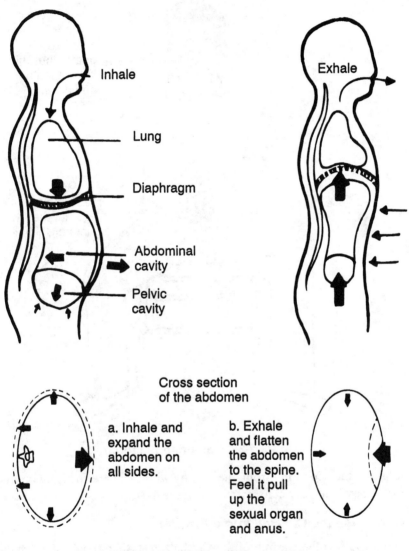

Inhale

Lung

Diaphragm

Abdominal
cavity

Pelvic
cavity

Exhale

Cross section
of the abdomen

a. Inhale and
expand the
abdomen on
all sides.

b. Exhale
and flatten
the abdomen
to the spine.
Feel it pull
up the
sexual organ
and anus.

Figure 4-37. Inhalation and exhalation

muscles into the mid-eyebrow and mouth, and gather the energy into a Chi ball.

Exhale very slowly down to the navel and relax all the muscles. Try to really feel the warmth. Use the mind/eye power to gather it into a Chi ball just behind the navel. For some people this is very easy, and for others

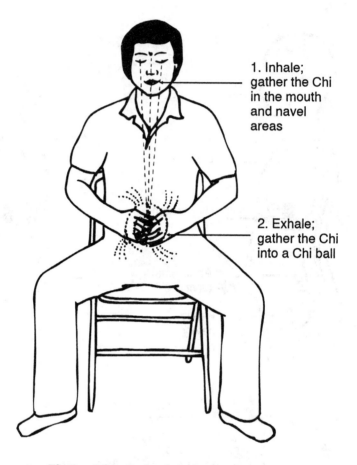

1. Inhale; gather the Chi in the mouth and navel areas

2. Exhale; gather the Chi into a Chi ball

Figure 4-38. Gathering the force

it takes time. Counting from one to nine while you are focusing on the navel may help your concentration (Figure 4-38).

Condense the Chi Ball into a Chi Dot

Once you feel the warmth of the Chi ball, rest, then inhale and exhale normally. Use just the mind/eye power, not the muscles, to gather and condense the Chi.

When you exhale, feel the navel slowly begin to grow warm. Use the mind/eye power to condense the Chi ball into a Chi dot from the heat retained there (Figure 4-39).

For some people, using a sound helps. Repeat the word "Chi" in your mind, or count nine to one and one to nine, as you exhale and breathe

Figure 4-39. Exhale and condense the Chi ball into a Chi dot.

down into the dot. Feel the energy in that area. When you use the word "Chi," it may help you concentrate, and you can increase the warm feeling more effectively. Feel the pulse of the aorta and vena cava in this area.

NOTE: *Just after you exhale, you will feel something in the navel. In the beginning, the sensation may be just in the skin layer. At this time, you can increase the sensation of warmth by condensing the Chi dot up to nine times.*

Expansion or Pulsation of the Chi

When you exhale very slowly and condense the energy at one point, you will feel the Chi pack into that point. When you relax the mind/eye power, you will feel a sudden pulsation, like a mini-orgasm or explosion in the mind and the point or center you are working on. The Chi pressure moves the Chi with great force. Sometimes the Chi suddenly goes to the crown, to the feet, to the hands, or to the back. The condensing and pulsation happen automatically (Figure 4-40).

Storing the Force

Once you can feel the Chi condensing and expanding, keep the mind/eye power easily focused at any given point. The Chi will feel stronger and more stable and will not scatter or weaken. We call this stage Storing the Force. Once you have achieved this relaxed state of concentration, the

Figure 4-40. Relax and feel an expansion or pulsation.

Chi may move on its own power to heal or balance you in any part of your body-mind.

Radiance practice. Now move the hand about two or three inches in front of the navel and see if you can still feel the sensation of warmth radiating around you and protecting your energy field. This practice trains the mind, eyes, and heart to cultivate the energy. In the beginning you will just feel the warmth in the skin layers. That is enough for now. Later you will feel it radiate into your entire aura.

Rest, and relax the body and mind for a moment. Feel the energy around the navel area. If you have digestive problems, the abdomen may be cold at first. As you progress in your practice, it will feel warm, and the problems may improve.

3. Loosening the Intestines with Spiraling Movements

1. Cover the navel with the hands. Lightly massage the abdomen and intestines by moving the hands in a clockwise direction, from the bottom to the right to the top to the left (Figure 4-41).

2. Pay close attention to what you are doing as you begin to slowly circle your hands around your abdomen and simultaneously use the stomach muscles to move your body in a spiraling motion. This is very important, because it activates the intestines. When the Chi is stuck in the intestines, the Chi does not move well throughout the whole body. Do this 36 times.

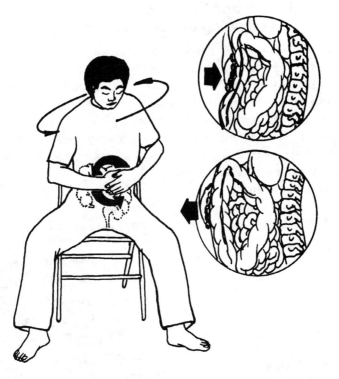

Figure 4-41. Massage the abdomen.

3. Then rest. Close the eyes, keep the hands over the navel, relax, and feel the navel's warmth. Exhale into the navel, sending the essence of the breath to the navel.

Although you will exhale, you will feel something going down into the navel. When you feel the energy, gather it into the Chi ball you have previously formed at the navel.

4. Rest. Just sit back quietly, but still feel the pleasant, warm sensation inside you. These two exercises will help you warm up the navel.

4. Warming Up the Kidneys and Activating the Door of Life

Moving the Chi between the two kidneys is very important in Taoism. We believe the kidneys store part of the Original Chi. They also store sexual energy, activate the Chi in the two kidneys, and balance them in the Door of Life. To do this practice, close the eyes, and see the kidneys with the mind's eye. Taoist practice depends heavily on this mode of internal sensing, because all the organs are connected with the universe. If you want to access the universe, you must access it through the subtle energies of your organs (Figure 4-42).

Generating the force

1. Put the right hand over the right kidney and place the fingertips of the left hand just above and to the right of the navel. Inhale and exhale

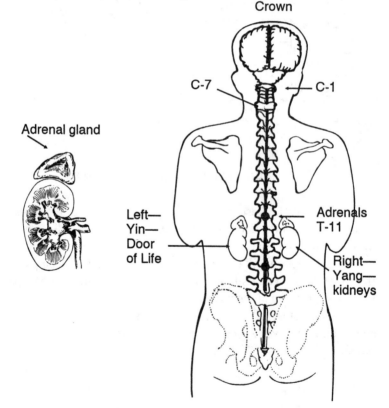

Figure 4-42. Warm up the kidneys and activate the Door of Life.

to the right kidney as you make a spiraling movement with the waist and pull the right side of the stomach in toward the right kidney. When you pull the stomach in toward the back, you will feel something in the back; that is your right kidney. Repeat 9 to 18 times.

2. Rest. Keep the hand on the back over the right kidney. Now compare your right side and your left side. You may feel the right side is more open, warmer, and lighter. When you do the exercise with awareness, you are starting to direct energy into the area of the kidneys.

3. Put the left hand on the left kidney and place the fingertips of the right hand just above and to the left of the navel. Repeat the steps for Bellows Breathing and Loosening the Intestines described above, but spiral at the waist to the left side (Figure 4-43).

Gathering the Force

4. Rest. Now put the right hand on the navel and the left hand over the Door of Life (located on the spine opposite the navel and between

Figure 4-43. Massage the kidneys and spiral the lumbar region to help open the Door of Life.

the two kidneys). Close the eyes and just be aware of the warm feeling at the Door of Life. Relax, inhale, and very slowly exhale to the Door of Life. Use mind/eye/muscle power to form a Chi ball at the Door of Life. Repeat 9 times. Feel nice and comfortable (Figure 4-44).

Condensing the Force

5. The exhalation is very important. The energy of the out-breath is gathered by the mind. Condense it and relax; let the energy pulse or expand into the kidneys. When you feel a lot of energy generated, gather the energy into one dot or pearl of light between the kidneys at the Door of Life, using the word "Chi" to help you concentrate.

6. Next, store the Chi between the kidneys. Relax the breath and let the energy flow, but keep the mind focused between the kidneys.

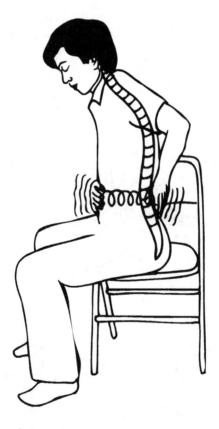

Figure 4-44. The right palm covers the navel; the left palm covers the Door of Life.

5. Activating the Original Force

1. Place one hand over the Door of Life and the other hand over the navel. Feel the navel become warm. When you feel both hands become warm, they will activate together. When you feel the navel and the Door of Life are warm, picture in between them, in the center, a single yellow ball of fire or red flame of energy about the size of a Ping Pong ball. We call this "the Original Energy in the center."

2. Direct the mind's eye to look inward down into the center, and focus 95 percent of the awareness on the warm Chi ball there. Use the other 5 percent to gather the energy from the front (navel) and back (Door of Life) into one ball in the center (Lower Tan Tien). As the fire in the Tan Tien grows warm, the navel and Door of Life will also grow warm. All you have to do is warm the navel and Door of Life, let the warmth condense into the two Chi balls, and draw these two Chi balls or dots together; the space in between will start getting warmer by itself (Figure 4-45). We call this "Training the mind to gather and condense the Force."

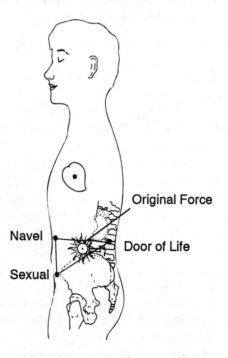

Figure 4-45. The Original Force

3. Now bring the hands back to the front and cover the navel, but still be aware of the center. When you feel the center become warm, continue to exhale into it, and say the word "Chi." Even though you are exhaling, feel that you are still retaining the energetic essence of each breath at the center. Exhale, pause, and just use the mind and the word "Chi" to concentrate on that dot. The dot will feel warmer. Rest.

4. Gather some saliva (which the Taoists traditionally refer to as the Jade Nectar or the Water of Life) by rolling the tongue around in the mouth. When you have accumulated a good amount, swallow the saliva and direct it with the mind down toward the Tan Tien. At the same time, use the mind power to warm the Tan Tien region. Be aware of the pulse at the Tan Tien and focus the mind on it. As the region starts to heat up, let the warmth radiate out, extending back toward the kidneys and pulsing down toward the sexual organs. Enjoy this pulsing feeling as the red dot or Chi ball at the Tan Tien expands and contracts rhythmically.

6. Activating the Sexual Energy Center and Amplifying the Original Chi

1. Men. Gently massage the kidneys, the testicles, and the navel area.

Women. Gently massage the breasts, kidneys, ovaries, and waist (for more detail, see Chapter 10).

When you feel the energy begin to expand at the sexual center, move the palms to cover the sexual center. Using mind/eye power, lightly contract and relax the muscles around the eyes. Also lightly contract and relax the circular testicle/vaginal and anus muscles several times. This will help gather the sexual energy you have activated.

2. Pause for a while. Feel the energy expand at the sexual center.

3. Cover the sexual center with the left hand and the navel with the right hand. Feel the navel, sexual center, and the Door of Life become warm. Suddenly you will feel the Original Chi activate in the Lower Tan Tien.

4. Now it is very important to rest. Lightly, effortlessly, using only the power of the mind, eyes, and heart, feel the sexual organs and anus close and lightly pull up toward the Original Chi in the Lower Tan Tien. Draw the sexual energy up to activate and join with the Original Chi, as if you were sipping it up through a long straw.

5. Inhale, and then exhale down to the center spot of the Original Force. Feel a pressure there. Gradually feel the Original Force start a light

160

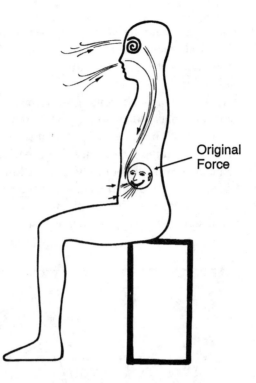

Figure 4-46. Feel the Original Force breathing.

suction to pull up the sexual organ and the anus toward the force. You can also imagine that the Original Force has a mouth and nose and is breathing and pulsing inside. Do not strain (Figure 4-46).

6. Use the mind and gentle breathing to amplify the pulse at the spot of the Original Chi. The aorta and vena cava pass through this area; they are the biggest circulatory pumps outside of the heart. The pulse is like a step-up transformer. When this pulse is activated and amplified, the heart does not have to work as hard, and the whole body benefits. Gathering the energy there also increases the flow of Chi and lymph. Gently press the fingers into the abdomen about an inch to the left and slightly above the navel; you will feel the pulsing of the aorta and vena cava. If you can actually feel the pulsing there, it will be very helpful (Figure 4-47).

7. After you inhale with a feeling of gentle expansion, exhale with a slight natural contraction. Place the hands on the sides just below the ribs to feel yourself breathing from the lower abdomen. Relax the whole body, allowing the rib cage to hang gently. When you inhale, feel the sides of the lower abdomen and the lower back gently expanding in all directions simultaneously. Exhale naturally and observe the breath moving in and out of the Tan Tien.

Gradually feel the breath becoming slow, long, deep, fine, and even as it moves in and out with the Original Force (the "metaphysical womb"). Feel the breath become so fine that it seems as though you are not breathing at all: holding the essence, but not actually moving air. It may feel like pulsing, warmth, or tingling in the Tan Tien. Mentally say the word "Chi" as you inhale and exhale into the Original Force at the Tan Tien. Spend five to ten minutes with this feeling.

Collect and store the energy at the navel (see details in Chapter 3).

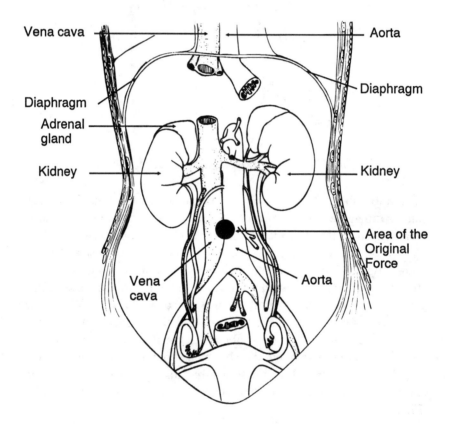

Figure 4-47. The aortic pulse is just above the navel and slightly off the center line.

THE DAILY PRACTICE OF CHI

A daily routine of Taoist meditation will help you feel happiness, joy, love, kindness, gentleness, and courage, and the Chi you generate will help you heal and maintain your body. When you are abundant with virtuous energies, they will automatically expand and radiate out to those around you. People will wonder why being near you changes their sadness into happiness and their depression into pleasure. By practicing the Cosmic Inner Smile and the Smaller Heavenly Cycle, you will receive healing light from the universe. Others will feel your energy and enjoy your presence.

When you sit down to practice these meditations, you will very quickly learn how to move energy into the Microcosmic Orbit and how to absorb the Universal and Earth Forces into the body. The more Chi you feel within yourself, the more easily you will be able to enhance your virtuous energies. If you have a lot of anger, you will also learn how to transform that negativity into positive energy. The more you practice, the sooner the healing forces will come to you.

The easiest way to feel your Chi and virtues at work is to interact with others, helping them feel the same good energies. Remember, however, that you should never interfere with another person's life just to gratify your own ego. People who truly want you to help them will always let you know it; otherwise, the best way to be of service is to exemplify the virtues in your own life. Practice with love in your heart, and others will learn from your example.

IMPORTANT POINTS TO REMEMBER

1. *The more you relax and allow the Chi to flow, the more quickly you will master these techniques. Relaxation also helps harmonize the body's energies to achieve the best results in healing. If you are too stiff when you try to meditate, you cannot get in touch with your own healing abilities. Also, if you relax too much without enough physical movement, your body will feel like it is falling apart, and your Chi will drain out.*

2. *Relaxing the Third Eye (mid-eyebrow) will help you relax the whole body and absorb cosmic energies into the organs and bone structure.*

3. *When practicing, smile down the length of the spine as you look inward. Try to see your spine surrounded with Chi. You may feel warmth, numbness, or an electric current flowing through your body.*

4. *Feeling is the beginning of mastery. The inner senses must be developed so they can lead you to the awareness of internal energy. Taoist meditations are the most direct way to develop one's ability to feel energy and the mind/body connection.*

5. *The nerves in the spine serve as conductors of internal sensation. They will help you feel your internal energy flow because they are connected to all the organs, glands, and limbs of the body. Rocking the spine activates the organs and glands through the nerves. The more you remain loose, the better your nerves will conduct the impulses that sharpen your inner senses.*

6. *By smiling inwardly as you practice rocking, you will develop an inner balance of the energies flowing through the spine, thereby strengthening the spine and its connections to the organs and glands. This will enhance your ability to feel the organs and their energies.*

SUMMARY

Creating Bodily Awareness

1. *Lightly shake the whole body.*

2. *Open and expand the Third Eye.*

3. *Relax the muscles of the perineum.*

Spinal Cord Breathing and Rocking

(See Appendix for details on the Spinal Cord Warm-ups.)

1. *Start by sitting or standing erect with the back comfortably straight.*

2. *Do spinal cord breathing 18 to 36 times.*

3. *Hold the palms together (right over left) and rock the upper body back and forth from the waist. Relax and concentrate on releasing tensions and loosening the spine. Breathe into the spine and absorb Chi into the marrow. Keep the head and neck loose and maintain the clasped-hand position.*

4. *Rock the body from side to side.*

5. *Practice Crane-Neck Rocking.*

6. *Next, rotate the upper body from the waist in a circular motion. Lean forward slightly as you move to the right, then lean backward as you move to the left. The head motions should loosely follow the directions of the body.*

7. *Practice Circular Rocking of the upper body. First pull the right shoulder back, then pull the left shoulder back as you push the right shoulder forward. Keep alternating these motions steadily with a constant flow. Move back and forth as you twist the body and keep the hands clasped.*

8. *Finally, combine all the previous motions while clasping the hands. You should be able to emulate a silkworm by moving the upper body in circular motions while twisting it from the shoulders. Stay relaxed and loose.*

9. *Rest, and smile to the spinal cord. Feel warm and comfortable.*

Techniques for Enhancing the Sensation of Chi

1. Mind/Eye Power Training

A. **Spiraling power with eyes open.** *Be aware of the mid-eyebrow. Lightly open the eyes and look to the front, then the right, then the back, then the left. Do this from 9 to 36 times, rest, and feel the mid-eyebrow open. Then repeat in the counterclockwise direction from 9 to 36 times.*

B. **Mind/eye spiraling power with eyes closed.** *Close the eyes, and without moving the head look up to the crown. Move the eyes one quarter of a circle and look right, down, left, and up. Do this from 9 to 36 times, rest, and feel the mid-eyebrow open. Then reverse. Repeat at the navel, but rotate it front-right-back-left and vice-versa, using a small Chi ball or visualizing a spinning Tai Chi symbol.*

C. **Advanced mind/eye spiraling power with no physical eye movements.** *Close the eyes, and without physically moving them (or the head), use the mind to look up to the crown. Move the inner eye one quarter of a circle, and look right, down, left, and up. Do this from 9 to 36 times, rest, and feel the mid-eyebrow open. Reverse directions and spiral counterclockwise. Do this from 9 to 36 times, rest, and feel the mid-eyebrow open.*

D. **Most advanced mind/eye training.** *Contracting and relaxing to draw and condense. Lightly contract and relax the circular muscles of the iris and the muscles surrounding the eye. This automatically activates the anus and sexual sphincter muscles. Together these help you draw in and condense energy at the advanced stages of practice described in this book.*

2. Using Your Hands to Help Guide the Chi

A. **Touching the points.** *Use the palms or fingertips to touch each point as you focus the mind there during the Microcosmic Orbit meditation.*

B. **Holding the palms above each point.** *Hold the palms two to six inches out from the point. Focus the Lao Gong points in the center of the palms on that point and feel the Chi flowing between the point and the palms. Direct the energy into the point. This will increase the local energy at the point.*

3. Using Breath to Regulate Chi Flow

A. **Small Sip Breathing to stimulate Chi flow.** *First take a deep breath and exhale completely. Then gently breathe in three, six, or nine shallow sips without exhaling in between. Draw the energy of each breath to the point that you are concentrating on and condense it into the point. Exhale a bit and start over whenever you feel uncomfortable or short of breath. Do not strain.*

B. **Long Sip Breathing to calm and condense the essence of Chi.** *Inhale gently and direct the breath toward a given point. Then exhale slowly and softly into the point, and feel that you are retaining the essence of Chi there (even though you are breathing out). Condense the Chi into the point.*

C. **Internal Breathing: Spontaneous pulsation of Chi.** *Allow the breath to become long, slow, soft, quiet, even, gentle, smooth, and deep. Let the Chi flow at its own pace, or simply use the mind to gently guide the Chi until it moves by itself. Make no effort to coordinate the Chi flow with the breathing. Just breathe naturally and let the energy move as it will.*

Preparing to Meditate

Prepare the environment.

1. *Find a quiet place to meditate.*

2. *Keep your meditation place clean and pleasant.*

3. *Plan so that you won't be interrupted; turn off the telephone or take the receiver off the hook.*

Conserve your sexual and emotional energy and eat right.
Loosen your body before meditating.
Wear loose and comfortable clothing.
Establish a stable sitting posture.

1. *Make a solid base sitting on the edge of the chair with the feet flat on the floor a hip's width apart.*

2. *Keep the hands held together resting on the lap, with the right hand over the left.*

3. *Make sure the back is relaxed but straight and in line with gravity.*

4. *Relax the shoulders and slightly open the armpits.*

5. *Bring the chin in slightly so that the weight of the head rests on the shoulders.*

6. *Keep the eyes closed (or half open, gazing downward).*

7. *Touch the tip of the tongue to the palate and keep it there.*

Warming the Stove: Activate the Original Chi in the Lower Tan Tien

1. *Start with Bellows Breathing, 18 to 36 times.*

2. *Rest and gather Chi at the navel with the hands covering the navel.*

3. *Loosen the intestines with spiraling body movements.*

4. *Warm up the kidneys and activate the Door of Life.*

5. *Activate the Original Force by drawing the energy from the navel and Door of Life and gathering it into the Lower Tan Tien.*

6. *Activate the sexual energy to amplify the Original Chi.*

Chapter 5

POINTS OF THE MICROCOSMIC ORBIT

THE TWO MAJOR CHANNELS OF THE BODY

Through meditative practices, the ancient Taoist masters discovered a flowing current of energy in the human body. This *Chi flow* was found to follow fixed patterns through 60 major channels and approximately 365 points, or energy centers, where Chi gathers and condenses. The flow of Chi replenishes our life-force. Our body's energy points have both positive and negative poles that spiral subtle wheels of energy. These points serve as focal centers through which external forces are drawn in, absorbed, and transformed into life-force. Higher centers, such as the crown, spiral at a higher rate than lower centers. They slow down the incoming energy, like step-down transformers, regulating and refining Chi for the body's use.

Each point produces its own quality of Chi to attract or repel energy from the other centers, to direct the Chi flow in a manner that connects the points, and to supply the proper energy to the entire body. Modern science now understands that this flow of human energy is actually an electromagnetic current. The body's many acupuncture channels serve as its "wiring," which guides the life-force to nourish the organs and glands. Chi is the link between the physical body, the energy body, and the spirit body.

Knowledge of the energy flow in our bodies makes it easy to understand why the Microcosmic Orbit must be kept actively open to accommodate and enhance the movement of Chi. When we do not know how to conserve, recycle, and transform our internal force through this pathway, our energy consumption becomes as inefficient as a car that only gets five miles per gallon. By practicing the Microcosmic Orbit meditation, we can get in touch with our Chi flow and locate blockages or weak spots in its path so we can correct them. This will help us use our life-force more efficiently and achieve better internal "mileage."

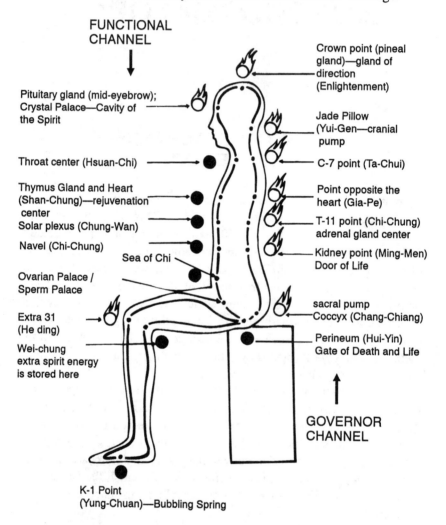

Figure 5-1. Learn to circulate your Chi in the Microcosmic Orbit. The tongue touches the roof of the palate to complete the circuit of the Governor and Functional Channels.

The Microcosmic Orbit is composed of two channels, referred to as the *Governor* and *Functional Channels* (Figure 5-1), which are like two large rivers with many tributaries. Each channel supplies Chi to 12 subsidiary routes. (Both sides together comprise 24 energy pathways.) When the body is weak or ill, it cannot generate enough energy to properly nourish these meridians, which supply Chi to the organs and glands. By drawing in external energy and circulating it in the Microcosmic Orbit, you can fill these meridians and enhance all internal functions.

Governor Channel (Du Mo or Tu Mo)

Function of the Governor Channel

The Governor Channel is the main Yang channel of the body. All the other Yang channels connect to this major pathway and are nourished by it, just as the electrical power cables leading to the individual houses on a street are fed by a main power line. Thus, if the flow through the Governor Channel is strong, the six ordinary Yang channels will have more energy flowing into them.

Exterior Location of the Governor Channel

The Governor Channel begins at the perineum and proceeds to the tip of the coccyx (tailbone). From the tip of the coccyx, it runs up the spinal column (just below the skin surface) and up the back of the neck, along the midline of the head to the crown. From the crown it travels down along the midline of the scalp, forehead, and nose and ends at the point between the base of the nose and the upper lip.

Interior Location of the Governor Channel

The interior path of the Governor Channel begins at the perineum and proceeds back to the tip of the coccyx. It runs up the outside of the sacrum and into the sacral hiatus (the eight holes), where it enters the spinal column. From there it runs up the interior of the spine and enters the skull. It flows through the back of the skull along the midline through the subarachnoid space along the fascia (connective tissue) on the surface of the brain (beneath the crown). There are also internal connections to deeper portions of the brain, such as the pineal gland, the pituitary gland, and the hypothalamus. The channel then descends about one-and-a-half inches below the skin's surface along the midline at the front of the face, ending at the upper palate.

Functional Channel (Ren Mo)

Function of the Functional Channel

The Functional Channel (also translated from the Chinese as the Conception Vessel) is the main Yin channel of the body. The six Yin Ordinary Channels connect to the Functional Channel and are nourished by it. The Functional Channel also connects with the Governor Channel at both ends; together, the two channels form the complete circular pathway known as the Microcosmic Orbit.

Exterior Location of the Functional Channel

The Functional Channel begins at the perineum or Hui Yin point (the point between the anus and the genitals). It flows up the front of the pubic region and along the midline of the front of the body to the throat. It continues upward along the midline, with its last point located just below the lower lip. For acupuncture and shiatsu purposes, the channel runs at varying depths, from one-sixteenth of an inch or less to one-and-a-half inches.

Interior Location of the Functional Channel

The interior location of the Functional Channel is more commonly used for the Microcosmic Orbit meditation. It begins at the perineum (as does the Governor Channel), and runs up the front midline at an average depth ranging from a quarter of an inch at the throat to one-and-a-half inches. It runs beneath the pubic bone and the sternum, enters the throat, and ends internally at the tip of the tongue. When you touch the tip of the tongue to your palate, this acts as a switch to connect the Functional Channel to the upper end of the Governor Channel.

When the body is healthy and abundant with Chi, many points along the Microcosmic Orbit receive surplus energy from the glands and organs. As this energy is circulated, it can feed points that are not receiving as much energy. This is how the Microcosmic Orbit balances the body's energy. When all the points are fully activated with Chi, you can proceed to open the other six "special" or "psychic" channels.

ENERGY CENTERS OF THE MICROCOSMIC ORBIT IN DETAIL

This section explains the energy centers in detail and their use in the Microcosmic Orbit meditation. There is no need to learn all the centers at one time; you can work on each center individually until you can circulate Chi through all of them. After you have become acquainted with the locations of these centers (Figure 5-1), you can learn to experience their energy by focusing on them one at a time in meditation. Eventually the energy will be felt even during other activities, as it enhances all aspects of life.

NOTE: *In the beginning stages you will feel the centers just beneath the skin and fascial layers. (Along the spine you will feel them between the skin and the spinal cord.) As you become more advanced and produce more energy, you will begin to feel the centers more deeply within the spine, organs, and glands. Eventually you will notice their sensations as deep as one-and-a-half inches inside the body.*

1. Navel: The Mind Palace (Shen Ch'ue)

Location

The Microcosmic Orbit meditation begins and ends at the navel center. The navel center is located approximately one-and-a-half inches behind the navel. (As you develop in your practice, you will eventually learn its exact location by feeling its energy.)

Properties and Relationship to Its Organs

Westerners often joke about yogis who "contemplate their navels." Most people think the navel is simply the vestigial scar of the umbilical cord, and to those who know little about meditation, the idea of focusing so much attention on that funny little hole in the middle of the belly seems a bit ridiculous. Yet the navel center is a very profound part of our energetic anatomy, the wiring of our energy body.

Our first connection to the outside world. The navel area was our first connection with the outside world. All oxygen, blood, and nutrients

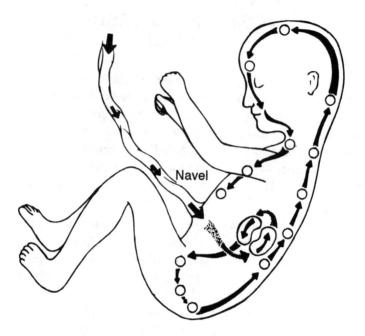

Navel

**Figure 5-2. The umbilical cord was our first
connection with the outside world.**

flowed into our fetal forms through this abdominal doorway (Figure 5-2).
As a result, the navel center has a special sensitivity that continues far
beyond the cutting of the umbilical cord at birth; it stays with us
throughout our entire lives.

The navel is the physical center of the body. In terms of the
Chinese Five Elements (Metal, Water, Wood, Fire, and Earth), the navel
area is related to Earth. Each of the Five Elements corresponds to a
direction: Metal, Water, Wood, and Fire are correlated with the qualities
of West, North, East, and South, respectively (Figure 5-3). Earth represents the center, the ground where we stand, looking out in the Four
Directions. The center point of an object is usually also its balance point.

The navel is the physical center of the body, halfway between the
upper and lower body. In martial arts, calligraphy, and other related
disciplines, one often hears of the importance of centering. The center of
the body, our center of gravity, is the most effective place from which to

Planet Venus
Autumn
Metal Force
lngs/large intestine

Planet Mars
Summer
Fire Force
Heart/small intestine

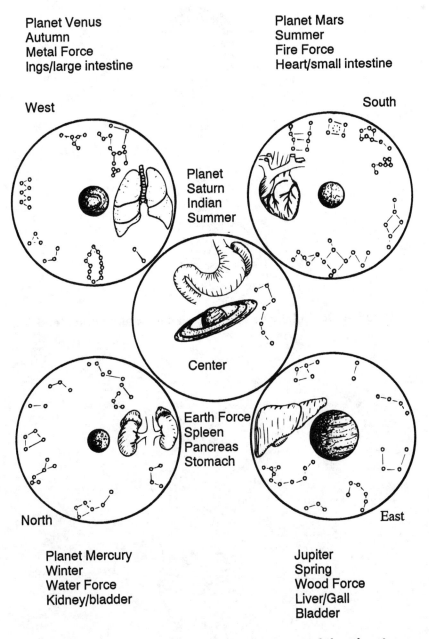

West

South

Planet
Saturn
Indian
Summer

Center

Earth Force
Spleen
Pancreas
Stomach

North

East

Planet Mercury
Winter
Water Force
Kidney/bladder

Jupiter
Spring
Wood Force
Liver/Gall
Bladder

Figure 5-3. The five elements, the organs, and the planets

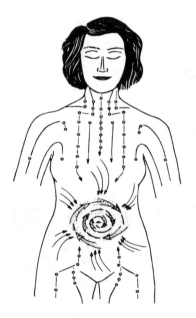

Figure 5-4. Behind the navel is the place to gather and blend Chi.

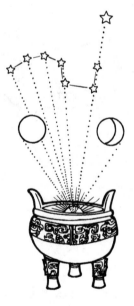

Figure 5-5. Cauldron

coordinate one's movements, and in these arts one learns to move from one's center, which is called the Lower Tan Tien in Chinese, or *Hara* in Japanese. With daily practice, you can gradually program the feeling of being centered into the navel and recall it by contacting the energy there (Figure 5-4).

The navel is the front door of the Cauldron. The external navel is actually the front door of the Lower Tan Tien, which lies deeper within the body. The exact location of the Lower Tan Tien varies somewhat from person to person, depending on physique. In some, it may be right at the level of the navel; in others, slightly below it; and in still others, slightly above the navel.

The Lower Tan Tien is also known as the Cauldron, because in the higher-level Taoist meditations, it is the place where we "gather, blend, and cook" the various energies of body, mind, and spirit for spiritual transformation (Figure 5-5). There are actually three Tan Tiens: the Lower Tan Tien at the navel, the Middle Tan Tien at the solar plexus, and the Upper Tan Tien in the brain (Figure 5-6). *Tan Tien* means "elixir

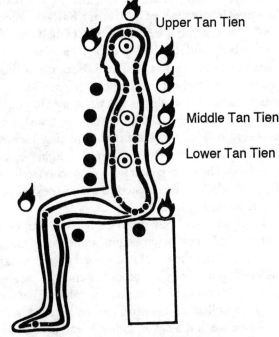

Upper Tan Tien

Middle Tan Tien

Lower Tan Tien

Figure 5-6. Three Tan Tiens

field," signifying a place where the elixir of immortality is prepared as one progresses through the stages of Taoist Inner Alchemy.

Just as the lowest part of a building, the foundation, must be made strong to support a stable structure on top of it, the elixir field needs to be cultivated to serve as a strong foundation for spiritual work. This means that working with the navel center, or "cultivating the field of the elixir," is the cornerstone for all Taoist practices.

Those who have studied Zen or Tai Chi may be familiar with the Chi Hai, or Sea of Chi point—located three finger-widths below the navel—as the traditional point of correspondence with the Cauldron. Both this point and the navel point provide access to the Cauldron, so it is technically correct to focus on either.

In the Healing Tao system, we use the actual navel point. After teaching the Microcosmic Orbit meditation for many years to tens of thousands of people, I have found that the navel is generally more sensitive and easier to feel and find, and therefore more effective as a focal point. The navel and the Sea of Chi point are two doors leading to the same place, so why not use the one that is more plainly marked?

The navel is our major Chi storage battery. Because the navel is at the center of the body, it is the point of balance of Yin and Yang energies. The body collects the Chi of both Heaven and Earth and stores, blends, and balances them at the navel. Because of this role, the navel has the capacity to safely store large charges of Chi.

Taoists regard this center as the *storage battery*. As the front door to the source of our Original Chi, it collects, transforms, and balances energies taken in from other sources, directing them to recharge the Original Chi at its source between the navel, kidneys, and sexual center (near the pelvis). The navel center has a close connection to all the energy channels, particularly those related to crown, sexual center, perineum, kidneys, and heart (Figure 5-7).

We begin and end our practice by focusing on the navel. The Microcosmic Orbit meditation begins and ends at the navel. From the very beginning of life the navel is involved in harmonizing, processing, and transforming the body's Chi as the embryo receives nourishment through the umbilical cord. In the navel, unlike other areas of the body, energy can be collected, transformed, and stored with no ill effects (specifically between the navel, kidneys, and sexual center). When we begin meditation by focusing at the navel, we access the stored Chi behind the navel at the Cauldron. This gives our practice of the Microcosmic Orbit a "jump start" by bringing out a strong energetic charge to circulate through the Governor and Functional Channels.

The navel influences the nearby organs. The navel is also important to the small and large intestines and the major lymphatic system (Figure 5-7). By concentrating on the navel, you can activate the life-force, creating warmth and expanding pressure that enhance digestion and absorption in the small intestine. Focusing on the navel also strengthens the large intestine for the elimination of waste material, while increasing the flow of the lymphatic system.

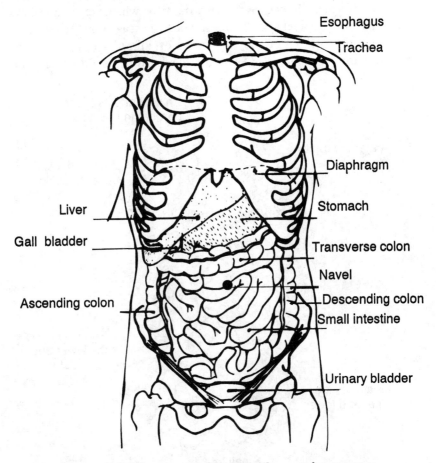

Figure 5-7. The navel influences the nearby organs.

Emotional Influences

When the navel's center is open and connected with the other centers, one feels balanced; when it is blocked or closed, it manifests in sloppy, picky, or distracted behavior (Figure 5-8).

Massaging the Navel to Release Negative Emotions

When negative emotions arise, they often get stuck in the navel area, blocking the flow of Chi and resulting in cramps. When this area becomes too congested, other maladies can also arise, and even your meditations may be affected. Massaging the area daily, or whenever such cramps arise, releases the blockages. The best time to massage is in the morning.

Lie on your back. Using one finger of either hand, apply a little pressure around the navel. (The other hand can be used to anchor the

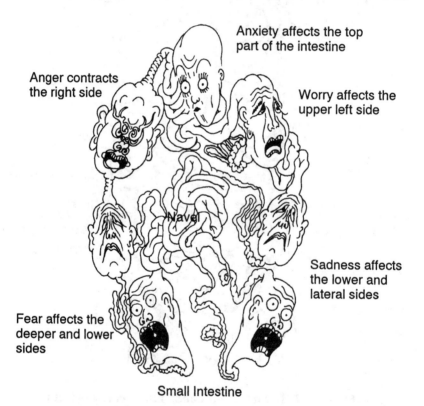

Anxiety affects the top part of the intestine

Anger contracts the right side

Worry affects the upper left side

Navel

Sadness affects the lower and lateral sides

Fear affects the deeper and lower sides

Small Intestine

Figure 5-8. When the navel area is blocked, it can cause negative emotional states in the small intestine.

area.) Do not massage the navel itself, but circle around it until you find a tender spot. Sensitive areas may feel like a lump or knot. Massage any lumps with the tip of one finger, circling on and around the spot until you feel it dissipate. Some places are tighter than others. Using minimum pressure, hold for a while, release, and repeat until the lump dissolves (Figures 5-9 and 5-10).

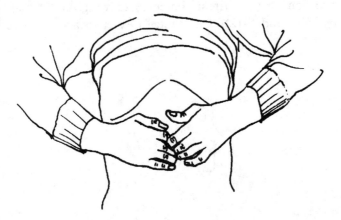

Figure 5-9. The navel connects to the other organs, and when it is blocked, it can affect these organs.

Figure 5-10. Massaging yourself

2. Lower Tan Tien, Source of Original Chi: The Internal Battery

Location

The Lower Tan Tien is located between the navel, Door of Life (kidney center), and sexual center. These three centers form a triangle with the ability to nourish the Original Force by drawing on external sources (Figures 5-11 and 5-12). This center's exact location can vary with

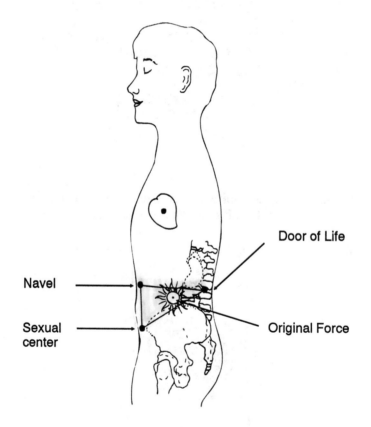

Figure 5-11. The Lower Tan Tien, Original Force

182

different people. In a man with broad shoulders and a large abdomen, the center can be one-and-a-half inches below the navel in the center of the body. In a woman of large proportions, the center may be slightly above the navel. Many martial artists feel the Tan Tien's center of gravity is between the center axis of the body and the Door of Life. Some people may feel the center's position drop slightly as their energy accumulates. The center's exact location in your body is where the sensation of its energy is strongest.

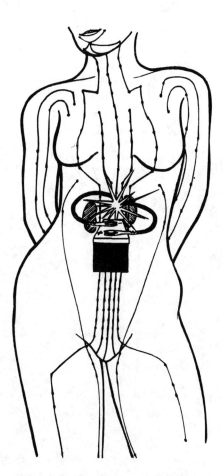

Figure 5-12. Internal battery

Properties and Relationship to Its Organs

The Lower Tan Tien, which stores the Original Chi, is also referred to as the Field of Pills or Cinnabar Field, in which Chi from all sources is blended and transformed into life-force (Figure 5-13). The Original Chi we are born with comes from the union of Yin orgasmic energy (supplied by the mother) and Yang orgasmic energy (supplied by the father).

**Figure 5-13. Original Chi can be enhanced
by all these forces and energies.**

Orgasmic energy is the combination of love energy and sexual energy. When these energies combine, they also draw on the Universal and Earth Forces to create a new energy, *Prenatal Chi*, within the forming embryo, which is made up of cells derived from both parents.

We draw on the Prenatal Chi daily along with the Universal, Earth, and Higher Self (Cosmic) Forces. How healthy we are depends on the amount of Prenatal Chi we have stored. Prenatal Chi enhances our ability to attract the greater forces of the universe to strengthen all aspects of our being. By concentrating on the area between the navel, Door of Life, and sexual center, we can gradually restore our principal energy from these external forces (Figures 5-14 and 5-15).

The Lower Tan Tien lies near the center of the body in front of the aorta and vena cava. This area contains many large lymph nodes, such as the lumbar lymph node, common iliac node, and the main draining duct in the lower abdomen. Increasing the Chi gathered here enhances

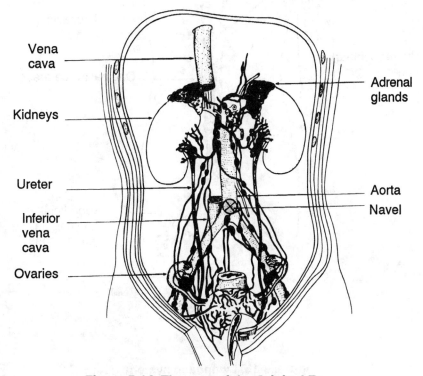

**Figure 5-14. The area of the Original Force
can affect the aorta and vena cava.**

the flow of blood, lymph, and hormones and also reduces the work of the heart. Daily cultivation of the warmth of Original Chi conserves and recycles this energy instead of allowing it to drain out.

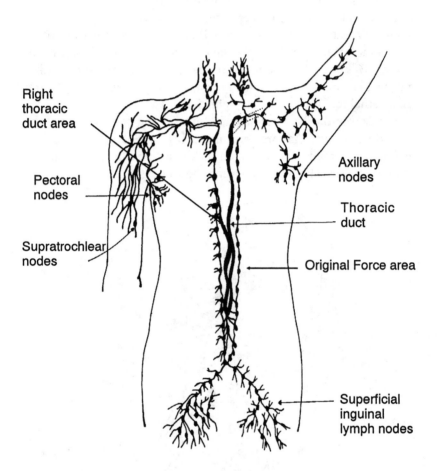

Figure. 5-15. Lymphatic system

3. Sexual Center: Sperm/Ovarian Palace (Jing Gong/Zhongji)

Location and Functions

Men. The Sperm Palace (Jing Gong) is at the base of the penis, slightly behind and below the pubic bone (about one-and-a-half inches inside the body, between the prostate gland and the pubic bone). It corresponds to the second point on the Functional Channel in Chinese medicine. This center takes its energy from the sperm made and stored in the testicles, prostate gland, and seminal vesicles. A man can use this energy by controlling the ejaculatory function, but if the orgasmic energy is not redirected into the Microcosmic Orbit, it usually passes out of the body and is lost. By concentrating on this center, you can help supply Chi to the Original Force. Techniques for retaining a man's sexual energy are described in *Taoist Secrets of Love: Cultivating Male Sexual Energy* (Aurora Press, 1984).

Closing the two gates. It is important to tonify the two main energetic gates where sexual energy tends to leak out.

The front gate is located on the glans of the penis at the urethral opening. The second gate is at the base of the penis above the urogenital diaphragm. Internally, it is at the base of the opening of the prostate gland, below where the seminal vesicles connect to the urethra.

Lightly contract these two gates in coordination with the circular muscle of the iris and the muscles around the eyes. Feel them lightly close, and feel that the Ching Chi has been retained. This conserves the life-force (Figure 5-16).

Women. The Ovarian Palace (Zhongji) is above the pubic bone, corresponding roughly to the top of the uterus (approximately one palm's width below the navel). In women, this point corresponds to the third point on the Functional Channel. To locate it, place the tips of the thumbs together at the navel and the extended index fingers together beneath them, forming an upside-down triangle. Where the index fingers meet indicates the Ovarian Palace (up to one-and-a-half inches inside the body). The areas where the little fingers naturally fall indicate the ovaries.

Energy from the ovaries accumulates in the Ovarian Palace. Each month the ovaries produce an egg from the body's finest substances and sexual energy, which is stored in the Ovarian Palace. If this egg is not fertilized, it eventually passes out of the body with all the blood and Chi reserved to nourish an embryo (Figure 5-17). When procreation is not

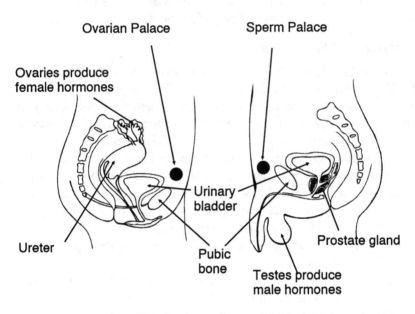

Figure 5-16. The Sperm and Ovarian Palaces

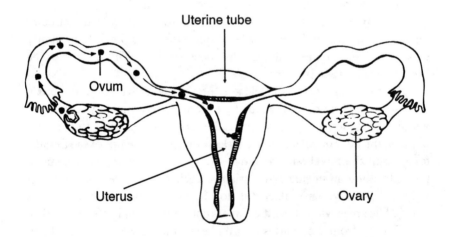

Figure 5-17. The Uterus and ovaries

intended, this loss of energy is unnecessary and unhealthy; concentrating on this center, however, supplies Chi to the Original Force. *Ovarian Breathing* permits the essence of the egg to be retained, so it can be recycled and transformed into life-force. Methods for saving this energy are detailed in the book *Healing Love Through the Tao: Cultivating Female Sexual Energy.*

Closing the two gates. In addition to practicing Ovarian Breathing, it is vital that women seal the two lower gates to prevent energy from leaking out. The front gate is at the vaginal orifice; the second is at the opening of the cervix.

Lightly close these two openings in coordination with the contraction of the iris and mind/eye muscles. This retains the sexual energy within.

Properties and Relationship to Its Organs

The sexual center includes the prostate gland, penis, and testicles in men; and the ovaries, cervix, and vagina in women. These organs contribute to the energy of the sexual center, which is regarded as the "generator," helping supply Chi to the Original Force. In men and women, the sexual center is the storage place for reproductive energy, which has creative and healing properties and is the body's most powerful Chi. When it is not being used for reproduction, this energy can be rechanneled and transformed into life-force.

Sexual energy is the only energy that can be multiplied regularly if it is stored. In practice, this involves recycling orgasmic energy through the Microcosmic Orbit, rather than allowing it to pass out of the body. This way, instead of expending one-third of the body's energy to produce sperm and ova, this third can be saved and compounded regularly through intelligent sexual activity that does not lose any of the body's essences. At higher levels of practice, sexual energy can be transformed into spiritual energy.

As stated earlier, human life begins with the sexual energies of the Yin orgasm (female) and the Yang orgasm (male) as the egg and sperm connect and fuse through the act of love and sex. The process of conception draws the Universal and Earth Forces to be combined with these orgasmic energies, and the Cosmic (Higher Self) Force supplies nourishment for the fetus to grow. When a man and a woman make love to produce offspring, Taoists refer to the act as the Reunion of Heaven and Earth.

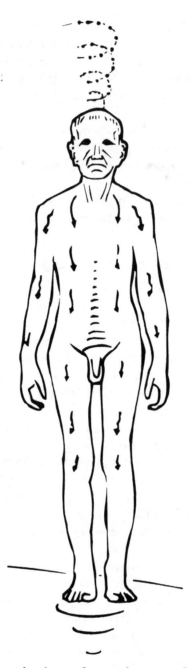

Figure 5-18. Excessive loss of sexual energy depletes the body.

Men. In men, the testes produce testosterone and other androgens, hormones that govern the development of primary and secondary sexual characteristics and sexual urges. They also inhibit follicle-stimulating hormone (FSH), which is produced by the pituitary gland to regulate the production of sperm. The strength and quality of sexual energy is directly influenced by the levels of these hormones in the body. Hormones are a major part of this Chi.

Sexual energy and hormones gradually diminish with age, causing the pituitary gland to dry out and produce an aging hormone that promotes eventual death as all bodily functions gradually weaken (Figure 5-18). If men do not maintain the vitality of the sexual center, they cannot regulate sexual energy and hormone levels to prevent aging and premature death. The practice of seminal retention not only maintains these levels but also enhances them, recycling the energy instead of allowing it to pass out of the body. This practice requires opening the Microcosmic Orbit through meditation.

Women. In women, each ovary is composed of two distinct areas, the follicles and the corpus luteum. The follicles produce estradiol and other estrogens, hormones that regulate cellular respiration, blood circulation, development of primary and secondary sexual characteristics, and sexual urges. They also inhibit follicle-stimulating hormone (FSH), which is produced by the pituitary gland to regulate the production of eggs. The corpus luteum manufactures progesterone, which stimulates secretions in the oviduct and interacts with the estrogens to regulate ovulation and menstruation. All these hormones contribute to a woman's sexual energy.

Taoists believe that for women, youth and vibrancy is maintained by increasing sexual hormone levels (thereby enhancing sexual energy) through the Healing Love practice, which gives a woman control over her menstrual cycle (Figure 5-19). By practicing the Microcosmic Orbit meditation, women can draw sexual energy up to the crown to stimulate, rebuild, and strengthen the glands.

Emotional Influences

When the Sperm or Ovarian Palace is open and connected to the other centers, one has a sense of creative and personal power; when either is blocked or closed, life is hard to enjoy.

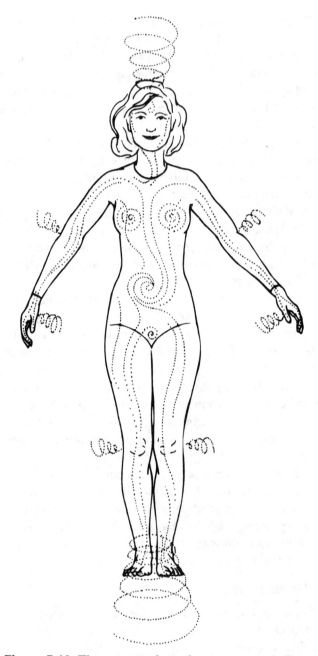

**Figure 5-19. The secret of staying young and vibrant
is to maintain and enhance sexual energy.**

4. Perineum: Gate of Life and Death
(Hui Yin)

Location

The perineal center is located between the sexual organ and the anus (Figure 5-20). This center encompasses other structures and functions in this area as well; specifically, the anus and the back part of the anus are also related to the Hui Yin point.

Four channels or "tunnels" extend from the perineum that relate to the front, back, top, and base of the body (Figure 5-21).

1. The tunnel connected to the crown channels Yang (positive) universal electromagnetic energy.

2. The tunnel connected to the soles of the feet channels Yin (negative) energy from the earth.

3. The front tunnel, which connects to the navel and sexual centers, channels the body's Original Chi.

4. The back tunnel, which connects to the coccyx and the sacrum, has eight holes and channels the electromagnetic force of nature.

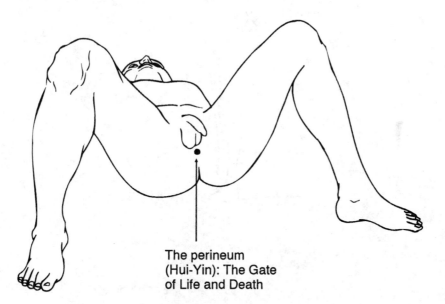

The perineum
(Hui-Yin): The Gate
of Life and Death

Figure 5-20. Perineal center

During meditation, you can lightly contract and relax the perineum a few times. This enables you to feel the electricity flowing through these connections, which can be gathered and transformed into life-force.

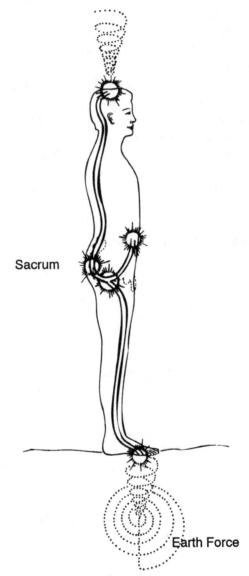

Sacrum

Earth Force

Figure 5-21. Perineal channels

Properties and Relationship to Its Organs

The Hui Yin (perineum) houses an energy pump that pushes earth, sexual, and life-force energies up the spine, enhancing the flow of Chi in the Microcosmic Orbit. This center is also known as the *Chi Bridge*, because it connects the Governor and Functional Channels (Figure 5-22). The term *Hui Yin* refers to the point where all the Yin Chi meets, connecting the Yin energy channels (especially the eight psychic channels).

Together with the anus and the back part of the anus, the perineum is known in Taoism as the "floodgate" of the organs. It is called the Gate of Death, because sexual energy and life-force can be lost through this center if it is not properly controlled. It is also called the Gate of Life, because sexual energy and the Earth Force pass up through the soles of the feet to the higher centers through this center. The perineum is considered the "seat" or "floor" of the organs because their positions within the body depend on its strength. If the perineum is strong, the organs remain in place and stay firm and healthy; if it becomes weak, the

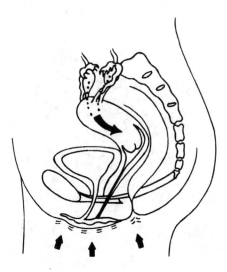

Figure 5-22. When contracted, the sexual organ and the anus act like a bridge and an energy pump for the ascending flow of Chi.

organs may lose their cohesiveness and sag (Figures 5-23 and 5-24). The perineum also works in conjunction with the coccygeal body, which plays a vital role in activating and drawing energy up the spine. When there is less Chi in this area, the blood circulates too slowly, causing hemorrhoids and back pain.

The anus (nutrition gate) is also part of the Life and Death Gate. When its connection to the perineum is strong, the life-force is secure, because the anus can increase the flow of blood, lymph, and Chi. The anus is also part of the Chi Bridge and pump that sends energy up the spine. When this connection is weak or broken, life-force can leak out, and the effectiveness of this important gate can be lost. Also, blockages

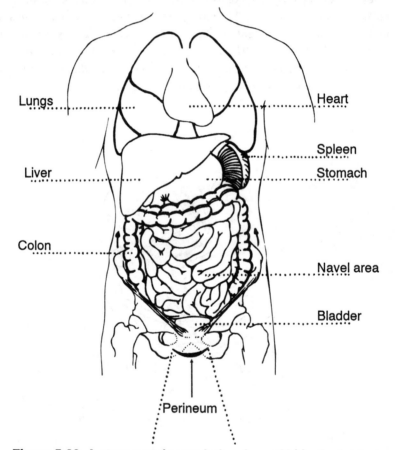

Lungs   Heart

Spleen

Liver   Stomach

Colon

Navel area

Bladder

Perineum

Figure 5-23. A strong perineum helps keep Chi in the body.

to the Chi flow at this point can produce a clogged-up feeling, like constipation, which prevents the body from releasing impurities and toxins. This is another reason to keep the energy circulating in the Microcosmic Orbit.

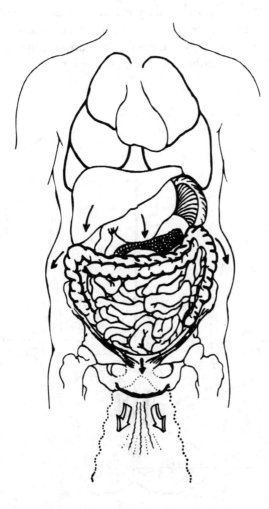

**Figure 5-24. The perineum is the floor of the organs.
If it is allowed to become weak, Chi will leak out.**

The back part of the anus is located between the anus and the coccyx, where it harmonizes Yin and Yang energies (Figure 5-25). It also helps pump sexual, earth, and life-force energies up through the spine. The back part of the anus acts like a Chi Bridge, helping energy pass from the perineum to the coccyx.

All three—the perineum, the anus, and the back part of the anus—are connected with the earth. When you contract these toward the coccyx, you can feel the earth energy rise. Taoists meditate with their feet on the ground so the earth energy can easily flow upward through them. By developing this connection, Taoists maintain a very close relationship with Mother Earth.

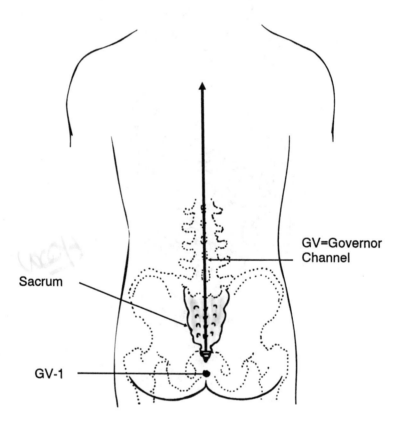

Figure 5-25. GV-1 point (Chong Giong)--Back Part of the Anus

Emotional Influences

When the perineum is open and connected, one feels grounded; when it is blocked or closed, one feels insecure.

5. Coccyx and Sacrum (Chang Qiang or Wei Lu)

In Chinese medicine, the tip of the coccyx and the sacral hiatus are considered the first two points on the Governor Channel (Figure 5-26). For purposes of meditation, although we are aware of these two points as different, we treat the coccyx and sacrum as one center. We may refer to this center as either the coccyx or the sacrum, because of the energetic interaction of the two.

Coccyx

At the coccyx, the tip of the tailbone, all forms of energy begin the journey up the spinal cord to the skull. The coccyx houses 12 branches of nerves that extend down to connect with the 12 earthly (terrestrial) branches of Yin Chi (Figure 5-27). Activating the coccyx internally (or externally with the fingers) stimulates these nerves to strengthen the organs. The coccyx also has a twist that can be tilted toward the earth to help the body

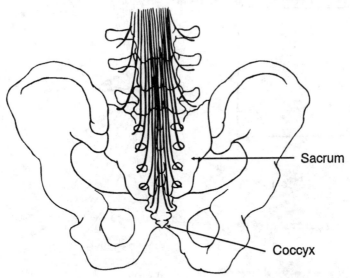

Sacrum

Coccyx

Figure 5-26. Nerves of the sacrum and coccyx

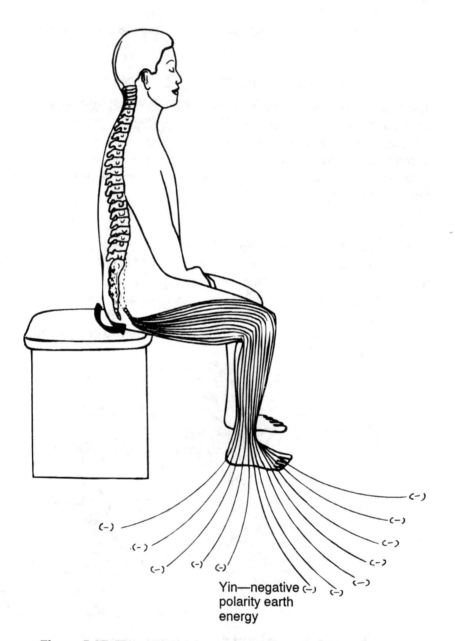

Yin—negative
polarity earth
energy

Figure 5-27. The nerves of the coccyx and sacrum connect to twelve earthly branches of energy.

connect with earth energy. (Taoists believe pointed bones are strong conductors of Chi.)

The center of Original Chi and the coccyx have a very close relationship. When you lightly contract the anus and the back part of the anus toward the coccyx, you establish a connection to the Original Force, the Earth Force, and sexual energy, which access the higher centers through the spine (Figure 5-28). These energies cannot travel beyond the lower centers if the coccygeal center is closed. Once this connection is made, it feels as if a power cable is sending electricity up the spine.

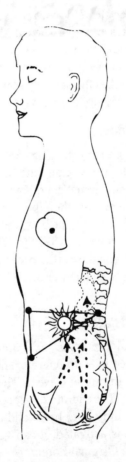

Figure 5-28. Lightly contract the anus, sexual organ, and the back part of the anus, pulling them toward the Original Force.

Our connection to the Earth Force. As stated earlier, a major difference between humans and animals is the erect position assumed by humans, with the head upward and the tailbone downward, creating a channel for the Universal and Earth Forces. The coccyx directs the Universal Force downward, the head's position directs the Earth Force upward, and the brain is nourished by both forces. Taoists acknowledge this posture as the reason for the mental development of humans. Most animals raise their tails to channel the Universal Force downward as they draw the Earth Force up through the four feet, enhancing their bodies before their brains.

The Universal Force flows downward in a clockwise spiral to the crown, where it penetrates and nourishes all the glands within the head, then continues down through the palate. The Earth Force ascends through the soles of the feet and the genitals, perineum, and coccyx, passing the heart's center, until it reaches the salivary glands of the tongue. Another path draws the earth energy up the spine and into the brain.

Properties of the Coccyx

The coccyx and sacrum are the gathering centers of all major nerves and are closely connected to the organs and glands (Figure 5-29). The tailbone also helps balance internal energy when it is open and connected to the other centers, enhancing their power and strength. When the tailbone is charged with life-force, the body feels lighter, especially when one is practicing moving arts such as Tai Chi. The coccyx also transforms and refines sexual energy and the Earth Force before they enter the higher centers. When this point is blocked or closed, the body feels heavy and unbalanced.

Center of the Sacral Hiatus

Taoists regard the sacral center as the Immortal Bone. Its center is yellowish, and its essence is earth energy. The sacrum has eight holes (referred to as the Eight Immortal Caves). The left four holes are Yang and the right four are Yin. The sacrum connects the spinal marrow to the small brain (brainstem) and upper brain and to the marrow within the brain. When the sacrum is activated, it can generate a great current of Chi and connect it to the Original Force.

Taoist practices emphasize opening and connecting both the sacrum and the coccyx to the other centers to establish a strong connection between the Universal and Earth Forces. (The eight holes reflect the eight-sided Preheavenly Pa Kua shape, which symbolizes the eight forces of the universe.) The sacrum and its holes also have a close connection to the Big Dipper, because they can absorb that constellation's energy and combine it with energy from the North Star, which are then stored at the crown.

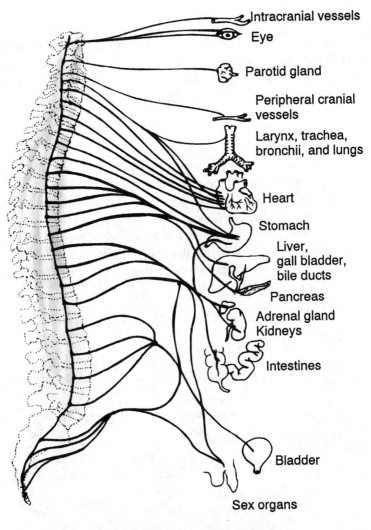

Intracranial vessels

Eye

Parotid gland

Peripheral cranial vessels

Larynx, trachea, bronchii, and lungs

Heart

Stomach

Liver, gall bladder, bile ducts

Pancreas

Adrenal gland
Kidneys

Intestines

Bladder

Sex organs

Figure 5-29. The coccyx and sacrum are connected to the organs and glands.

Location

The sacral hiatus is located about one inch up from the tip of the coccyx. This is also the location of the sacral pump, which pumps spinal fluid up the spine. (Spinal fluid supplies nutrients to the brain and spinal cord.) Using the mind to increase the activity of this pump keeps the brain young (Figure 5-30).

Properties

The coccyx and sacral hiatus centers are related to reincarnation and past lives. Taoism focuses on the present, however, holding that the cycle of reincarnation can be overcome by strengthening body, mind, and spirit and transferring the life-force to the soul and spirit bodies for the journey back to the Wu Chi, the origin of all things.

Emotional Influences

When the coccyx and sacral hiatus points are open and connected, one feels balanced; when they are closed, one feels imprisoned.

The spinal cord is the major center for the nerves and the sympathetic nervous system, through which the brain communicates with the body. By developing the powers of the mind, eyes, and heart through meditation and by practicing the Inner Smile, one can enhance and control these systems. Taoists believe these nerves are also connected to the soul or energy body.

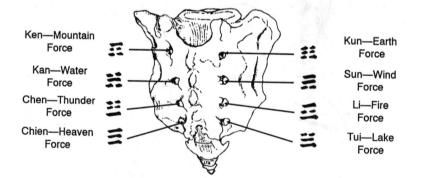

Ken—Mountain Force
Kan—Water Force
Chen—Thunder Force
Chien—Heaven Force

Kun—Earth Force
Sun—Wind Force
Li—Fire Force
Tui—Lake Force

Figure 5-30.The Eight Immortal Holes can absorb natural forces.

Bones are regarded as Yang (positive) Chi conductors; nerves conduct Yin (negative) Chi. (Bones and nerves have both Yin and Yang qualities in varying degrees.) When we combine the negative and positive charges of the bones and nerves, we can generate and conduct more Chi. Concentrating on the points along the spine enhances Chi flow and opens the spinal cord, expanding the space between the vertebral discs and creating a cushion of energy to protect them and the nerves.

6. Kidney Center: Door of Life (Ming Men)

Location

The kidney center is located between the two kidneys, directly between the second and third lumbar vertebrae on the spine (Figure 5-31). Place a finger on the spine opposite your navel and bend forward, then backward. The vertebra that protrudes and recedes most marks the kidney center.

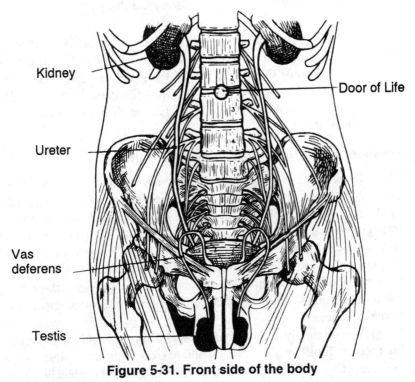

Figure 5-31. Front side of the body

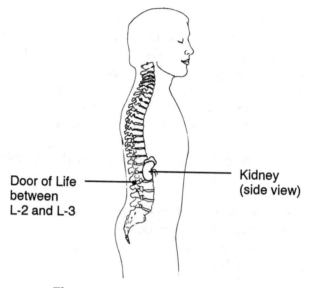

Figure 5-32. The kidney location

The kidneys are located on both sides of the spine at about waist level and are protected by the lower ribs (Figure 5-32). The left kidney generates Yin (cold) Chi; the right kidney generates Yang (hot) Chi. Together they help balance Yin and Yang qualities in the body. They also clean the blood of toxins and waste, which are then passed out of the body in the urine.

Properties and Relationship to Its Organs

The kidneys store our sexual and energetic essences and purify the blood. The kidney center is called the Door of Life because it is also the center of Prenatal Chi, our inborn vitality. When a man loses sexual energy through too much sex, or when a woman loses it through pregnancy or menstruation, the kidneys become depleted, weakening the spinal cord and causing back pain. Because the kidneys are associated with the urinary bladder, reproductive organs, bone marrow, and brain, these areas can also be drained of energy if prenatal Chi is lost through uneducated sexual practices.

It was originally thought that prenatal Chi could not be replenished, but modern Taoists say meditation and exercise can restore lost vitality and strengthen the kidneys. It is important to practice the Healing Love techniques so sexual energy is not lost during sex. If the kidneys are drained by unhealthy sexual practices, back problems may also be compounded by high blood pressure and nervousness.

The kidneys work like step-up transformers to help stimulate the body's Chi when it is low. They are the source of our ambition and willpower and serve as the crossroads of the Belt Channel, a very important area in the higher stages of practice. When the kidneys are weak, we may experience less drive and personal power in our lives. They also store part of our Original Force. When the Universal and Higher Self (Cosmic) Energies enter the navel, they pass through it to both kidneys and down to the sexual center. These forces are then stored between the navel, kidney, and sexual center.

The kidney center is a safety point that can mitigate side effects from opening channels too quickly. If you have uncomfortable sensations in your head during meditation, concentrate on the kidney center to draw excess energy from the head. Not only will the energy move out of the troubled areas, but it will also descend to the K-1 points on the soles of your feet, where you can access earth energy and recover your center. (This is especially beneficial for people with high blood pressure.)

Emotional Influences

When the kidney center is connected and open, one feels gentleness; when it is blocked, one fears being taken advantage of.

7. Adrenal Center, T-11 (Chi Chung)

Location

The adrenal center is between the adrenal glands and between the 11th and 12th thoracic vertebrae; it is often called T-11. Place a finger on the spine opposite the solar plexus. T-11 protrudes more than the other vertebrae when you bend well forward.

Properties and Relationship to Its Organs

The adrenal glands weigh about one-eighth of an ounce each and are located on top of the kidneys (Figure 5-33). They produce the hormones that keep the heart pumping and provide a powerful resource of energy to increase the heartbeat and bodily strength in emergencies. When one experiences either physical or psychological stress, the adrenals increase their metabolism to brace one for either "fight or flight." The adrenal center helps pump life-force and sexual energy up the spine to the higher centers, where they are refined. Concentrating on T-11 can also help reduce addictive tendencies related to adrenaline.

The adrenals have two functioning parts, the medulla and the cortex. The medulla manufactures adrenaline and noradrenaline. Both hormones trigger a rapid response from the sympathetic nervous system, increasing heartbeat and respiration. The adrenal cortex, the outer portion of the gland, produces a number of steroid hormones, including cortisone. These hormones regulate the body's retention and excretion of minerals, particularly sodium and potassium. Glucocorticoids, produced by the cortex, govern blood sugar levels. Dependence on stimulants, such as coffee, chocolate, nicotine, drugs, and certain herbs, gradually drains Chi from the adrenals and weakens these functions.

Adrenal power. We all experience the power of adrenaline in our bodies, although most of us don't realize it until we are confronted with a fight-or-flight situation. Substances such as coffee, nicotine, and certain drugs cause a similar response of excitement by overstimulating the

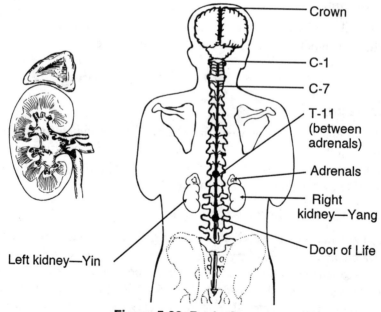

Figure 5-33. Back view

Crown
C-1
C-7
T-11 (between adrenals)
Adrenals
Right kidney—Yang
Door of Life
Left kidney—Yin

adrenal glands. As the desire for stimulation becomes habitual, one's dependence on these substances increases. Such habits deplete the adrenal glands and drain the life-force. After practicing the Microcosmic Orbit meditation for a while, you will find your natural energy level increasing and your need for stimulation from external substances decreasing.

Drugs. Ingesting drugs is the fastest way to drain adrenal energy. Ancient Taoists and other esoteric scholars explored the external forms of alchemy by making "immortality pills" for their emperors and themselves. Composed of arsenic, mercury, lead, sulfur, phosphorus, silver, precious stones, and other toxic substances, these pills shortened the lives of many emperors and Taoists alike.

Some drugs were mild poisons that did not kill the experimenters right away. Instead, the drugs tricked their bodies into becoming aroused for an immediate life-or-death struggle. Just like the drug users of today, the subjects felt alert and energetic after taking the pills, but this was just a temporary manifestation. The experimenters' adrenal glands and every cell of their bodies were forced to give up their best essences to counteract the ingested poisons. The subjects saw visions, heard heavenly music, and believed they had found God. But when the drugs lost their effect these illusions ended, and the subjects thought they needed a stronger dose to attain the supreme state permanently. All they attained was death.

From these tragic lessons the Taoists learned that the "immortality pill" must be found internally, not in external chemicals. Sexual energy can provide a veritable fountain of life, because the body keeps the reproductive system active even when we do not need to procreate. We can learn to conserve our sexual energy and tap into the Universal Force. This gives us power for self-healing, replaces lost adrenal energy, and enhances creative and spiritual work.

Emotional Influences

When the adrenal center is connected and open, one has a sensation of freedom; when it is blocked or closed, one feels weighed down.

8. Center Opposite the Heart, T-5 (Gia Pe)

Location

The Gia Pe point is between the shoulder blades and between the fifth and sixth thoracic vertebrae (T-5 and T-6), opposite the heart center (Figures 5-34 and 5-35).

Properties

The Gia Pe center has a close connection to the heart; it forms a halo of energy to protect the heart and crown centers. In higher levels of practice that involve space travel, it is known as the Wing Point, which protects the traveler (it is also called the Protecting Wing). The point also helps the heart center activate the energies of love, peace, joy, and happiness. You can activate this center by allowing the sternum to sink slightly down to the back. It acts like a pump to send energy to the higher centers.

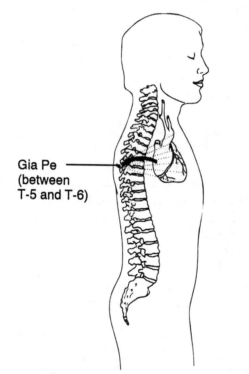

Gia Pe
(between
T-5 and T-6)

Figure 5-34. Center opposite the heart

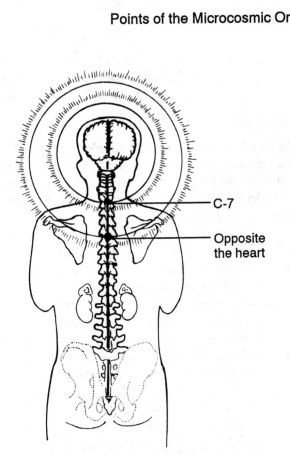

C-7

Opposite
the heart

Figure 5-35. Center opposite the heart, back view

NOTE: *The Gia Pe center is a region of hot energy. Concentration on this point by a person who is temperamentally impatient or hasty can overheat the pericardium and the heart. People with weaker hearts and cooler energy can concentrate on this point without any problems.*

Emotional Influences

The Gia Pe point is directly connected to the heart and can help activate the heart and thymus gland. When connected and open, the point gives one a feeling of freedom and a deep sense of life and its virtues; when it is blocked or closed, one has feelings of burden, hopelessness, melancholy, and chaos.

211

9. Point Opposite the Throat:
Big Vertebra, C-7 (Ta Chui)

Location

The Ta Chui or C-7 point sits just below the seventh cervical vertebra. If you lean your head forward and run your fingers down your neck, you will feel a big vertebra protruding outward at the base of the neck where the neck meets the shoulders. Just below this bone is the C-7 point (Figure 5-36).

Properties

The C-7 point is a central connection for the tendons and energies from the upper and lower regions of the body. It is also where the Yang channel of the legs connects with the Governor Channel, and it serves as a junction box for the nerves of the hands and legs. Any blockage at this point restricts the energy flow to the higher centers and redirects it to the hands and legs. This means that C-7 requires more concentration during practice so that the Chi can flow upward.

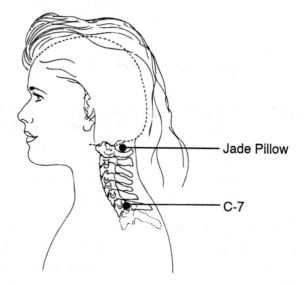

Jade Pillow

C-7

Figure 5-36. Point opposite the throat

When healers, massage therapists, and martial artists concentrate on using their hands, they draw energy away from areas of the body where it is most needed. Such people should not focus too long on C-7 before the higher centers are fully opened, because it can increase the energy flow into the arms and legs. Energy should be allowed to build up in the Microcosmic Orbit and not become sidetracked or diluted by going through other channels. The C-7 point is also used extensively in other Healing Tao practices, such as Healing Love, Tai Chi, Iron Shirt, and Bone Marrow Nei Kung, to strengthen the connections between the neck, spine, and crown while enhancing the flow of energy (Figure 5-37).

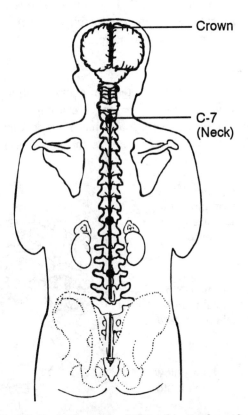

Crown

C-7
(Neck)

Figure 5-37. Use C-7 to strengthen the connections between the neck, spine, and crown while enhancing the flow of energy. Once the Chi can pass down into the body through the crown, we can direct it to the hands and legs.

Emotional Influences

The seventh cervical vertebrae (C-7) is the largest bone in the neck. When it is connected and open, C-7 enables one to embrace others with humanity; when it is blocked or closed, the result is denial, stubbornness, and feelings of inadequacy.

10. Small Brain Point: Jade Pillow (Yu Chen)

Location

The Jade Pillow lies at the opening of the base of the skull, above the first cervical vertebra. It is part of the cranial pump that draws spinal fluid and Chi upward (Figure 5-38). This area also houses the cerebellum and medulla oblongata, which are responsible for functions such as heartbeat, respiration, and muscle coordination.

Properties

The small-brain point promotes Yin energy, helping balance the Yang energy of the large brain and serving as a storage place for refined sexual energy and the Earth Force. It also has a direct connection to the crown and the Third Eye. Taoists believe the small brain has 12 energetic

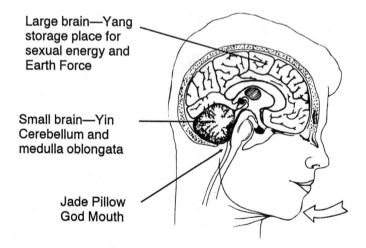

Large brain—Yang storage place for sexual energy and Earth Force

Small brain—Yin Cerebellum and medulla oblongata

Jade Pillow God Mouth

Figure 5-38. Small brain point

branches that extend down to the soles of the feet to connect to the 12 branches of earth energy.

The Jade Pillow controls the breath. The small-brain point controls breathing, and when it opens, breathing patterns can change. Sometimes it makes you breathe heavily, or slowly in long cycles. It can also cause the body to jerk uncontrollably, or it can even stop the breathing for a while. If something troublesome occurs, you can mentally tell yourself to stop at that moment and change the breathing pattern, or practice the Microcosmic Orbit, and the pattern should change.

If you're curious to see what happens with these abnormal breathing patterns, you can just let them continue for as long as you feel comfortable. After a while, your breathing should return to normal. Breathing methods are only used in the very beginning to stimulate the Microcosmic Orbit. Once you develop enough control, you will find you can use your mind alone to move the energy, which is much faster. At this point, your breathing will take care of itself naturally.

The Jade Pillow activates the back part of the cranial pump. This point is also part of the cranial pump. When you pull in the chin slightly toward the back of the neck and up toward the top of the skull, stretching the neck backward and upward, the space above the first cervical vertebra widens. This activates the Jade Pillow and stimulates the back part of the cranial pump, which sends cerebrospinal fluid, as well as Chi, into the brain (Figure 5-39).

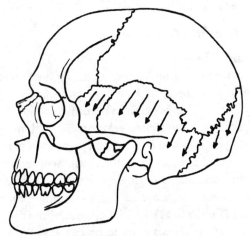

Figure 5-39. Cranial pump

The God Mouth. The God Mouth is another name for the Jade Pillow or small- brain point. By picturing the God Mouth opening wide, you expand the area's capacity while enhancing the cranial pump's action. Taoists regard this point as a storage place for extra energy and believe it receives information from above, like an antenna.

Emotional Influences

When this point is blocked and disconnected from the other points, energy can enter the upper brain, increasing the pressure in that area. This can cause illusions and hinder meditative practices. Learning the locations of the pineal, thalamus, hypothalamus, and pituitary glands enables you to guide the energy to the proper points, rather than allowing it to run wild in the brain. (The Microcosmic Orbit meditation usually relieves such problems.) Congested energy may be effectively redirected with mind/eye power. When the small-brain point is open and connected, one feels inspiration; when it is blocked or closed, one feels suffocated. When the point is congested, it also causes neck pain.

11. Crown: One Hundred Meetings (Bai Hui)

Location

The crown point is at the top of the head along the midline. An imaginary line from ear to ear connecting the highest point of the ears over the top of the head crosses the midline at Bai Hui.

Related Points of the Crown Point

The pineal gland: The back part of the crown. The back-of- the-crown point (also known as Kun Lun Mountain, the highest point of the human being and the highest peak of heaven) connects to the pineal gland approximately three inches down from the crown within the brain (Figure 5-40). The pineal gland has a close relationship with the pituitary gland behind the mid-eyebrow; when joined, they enhance personal power.

The pineal gland is considered the main receptor and "time clock" of the body. When stimulated during meditation, it controls inner vision, allows us to see auras, and provides a sense of direction by acting as an internal compass (Figure 5-41). In relation to spiritual disciplines, we can use the back part of the crown point to practice "overcoming death" by taking in external forces and combining them with sexual energy and the Original Force to form an "Immortal Body." With this body we can leave

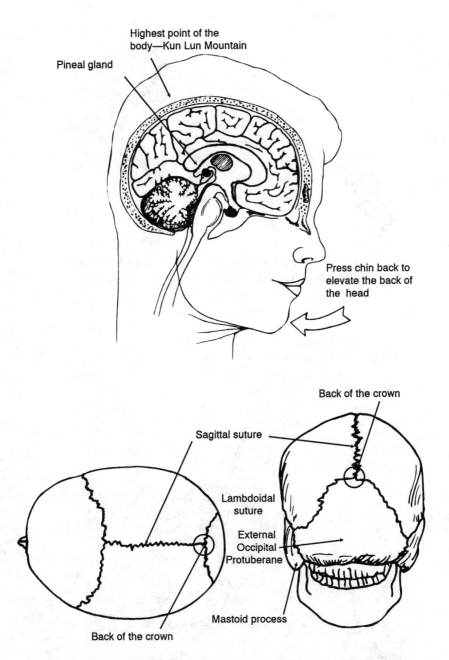

Highest point of the body—Kun Lun Mountain

Pineal gland

Press chin back to elevate the back of the head

Back of the crown

Sagittal suture

Lambdoidal suture

External Occipital Protuberane

Mastoid process

Back of the crown

Figure 5-40. The back-of-the-crown point, Kun Lun Mountain

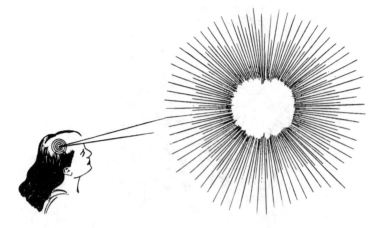

Figure 5-41. The pineal gland is our time clock and inner compass, the source of our inner vision.

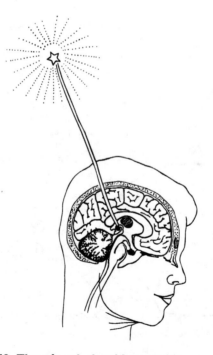

Figure 5-42. The pineal gland has a close connection to the North Pole and North Star.

the physical body before the final transition (death) occurs. The crown point provides access to other worlds; contacting them is a major goal of Taoism.

The Kun Lun Mountain point has a close connection to the North Pole and the North Star, giving us direction during out-of-body travel. (Taoists regard the North Pole as one of the Gates of Heaven.) By focusing on the tip of the Crystal Palace, the pineal gland, and the back of the crown, we can project ourselves to the North Pole or North Star as we attract its violet emanations (Figure 5-42). The pineal gland senses light and dark and influences our sexual cycles. It regulates the body's biological clock and governs body rhythms. The human pineal gland and related brain structures may be important in the cause and treatment of winter depressions. Exposure to high-intensity full-spectrum lights for several hours before daybreak gives patients significant relief from seasonal depression. By practicing the Healing Light meditation, you can receive the light of the universe even with the eyes closed.

The thalamus and hypothalamus. These points are also part of the cranial pump, and they help us access the energy of the Big Dipper constellation (Figure 5-43). (Turning the inner eye inward to the center of the Crystal Palace—also known as the Crystal Room—and the top of the crown helps activate the pump.) The points are located by tracing a line from the back of the opening of each ear to meet at the crown point of the head, then tracing another line from the mid-eyebrow to the crown (Figure 5-44). Three inches down from the point of intersection, inside the skull, is the thalamus. The hypothalamus extends about one-half to one inch beneath it. (Up to one inch further back from this point is the region of the pineal gland.)

The hypothalamus is the central processing unit for the whole hormonal system. It receives signals from the autonomic nervous system (the sympathetic and parasympathetic nervous systems) and impulses from the optic nerve, olfactory bulbs, and thalamus. Conscious and subconscious thoughts also affect the hormonal system through neuronal connections between the cerebral cortex and the hypothalamus.

Hormonal activities from the entire hormonal system (the thyroid, adrenals, ovaries, testicles, etc.) also feed back into the hypothalamus, which in turn commands the anterior pituitary gland to readjust its "master hormone" secretions. The level of "master hormones" from the anterior pituitary controls the levels of activity of the thyroid, adrenals, ovaries, testicles, and so on—the health of the whole hormonal system.

The terminal axons of other hypothalamus neurons make up the posterior pituitary. The transmitters from these axons are released from the posterior pituitary directly into the bloodstream as two additional hormones to regulate other functions of the body (Figure 5-45).

Taoists regard this point as the main switch of the Universal Force. When the spirit awakens, it resides in this place. The pineal gland acts as the male (positive) charge, and the hypothalamus acts as the female (negative) charge. When they are connected, they give out a powerful, balanced force. By focusing on this center and picturing the seven stars of the Big Dipper, you can access the constellation's energy, which emanates from the crown as a ray of red light.

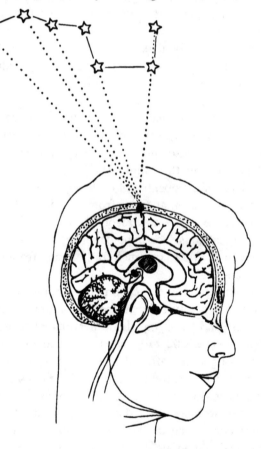

Figure 5-43. The thalamus and hypothalamus glands connect to the Big Dipper.

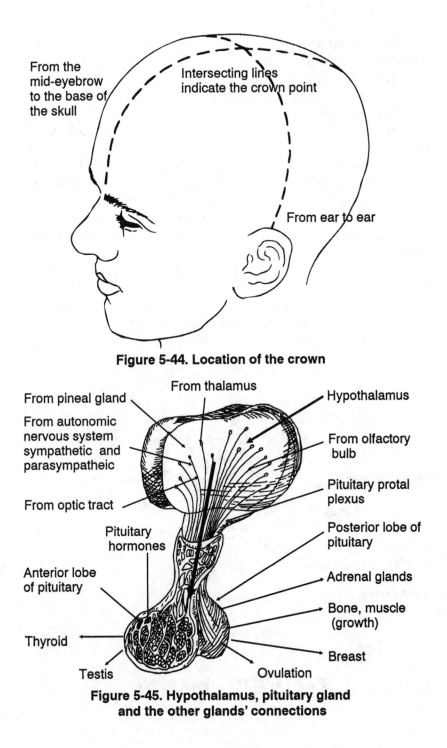

From the mid-eyebrow to the base of the skull

Intersecting lines indicate the crown point

From ear to ear

Figure 5-44. Location of the crown

From pineal gland

From thalamus

Hypothalamus

From autonomic nervous system sympathetic and parasympatheic

From olfactory bulb

Pituitary protal plexus

From optic tract

Pituitary hormones

Posterior lobe of pituitary

Anterior lobe of pituitary

Adrenal glands

Bone, muscle (growth)

Thyroid

Breast

Testis

Ovulation

Figure 5-45. Hypothalamus, pituitary gland and the other glands' connections

The Crystal Palace. The brain regulates all bodily processes, voluntary and involuntary. It records our perceptions and directs our responses to the environment. By circulating Chi from the lower points upward, increasing the Chi in the brain, we can keep the brain healthy and enhance the memory.

The Crystal Palace lies in the middle of the brain (Figure 5-46). If you imagine one line extending down from the crown, and another extending from the mid-eyebrow straight back (at the level of the tops of the ears), the intersection of the lines is the center of the Crystal Palace, which encompasses the pineal, thalamus, hypothalamus, and pituitary glands. Here the sensory and motor fibers and nerve tissues interlace in a dense network. In meditation the Crystal Palace appears like an oval crystal and shines like a mercury light.

The Crystal Palace is shaped like an egg; its tip points about 15 degrees toward the back of the crown. When we lightly pull in the chin, the small- brain point is elevated to help open the Crystal Palace and make it more accessible to the external forces we attract. The tip of the egg corresponds to the pineal gland; the center corresponds to the

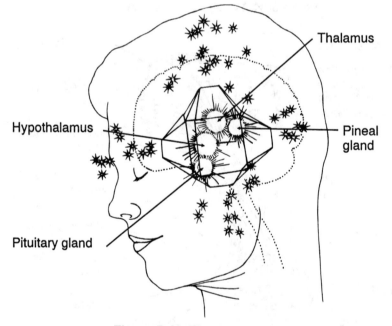

Thalamus

Hypothalamus

Pineal gland

Pituitary gland

Figure 5-46. The Crystal Palace

thalamus and hypothalamus; and the base corresponds to the pituitary gland.

Once the Crystal Palace is open, it becomes illuminated like millions of shining crystals. It can give and receive light and awaken our inner knowledge and deepest potentials. It receives light and knowledge from the universe and reflects it to the various organs and glands to enhance them (Figure 5-47). The Crystal Palace also has 10 holes connected to the 10 Celestial Stems, which in Chinese astrology regulate all heavenly energies that influence the earth.

Properties

The crown point is involved in activities of all major regions of the central nervous system and the entire sensory system.

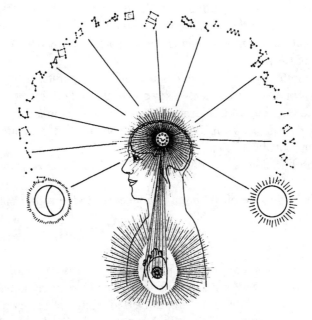

Figure 5-47. The Crystal Palace connects to the 10 Celestial Stems and the heart.

223

Emotional Influences

When the crown point is open and connected, one may feel radiant happiness and guidance from higher forces. One may also see auras and the "lead light" that guides journeys from the body (which do not only occur at death). If this point is blocked or closed, the result may be delusions, illusions, headaches, and erratic mood swings; or one may feel like a victim and slave.

12. Pituitary Point: Mid-Eyebrow or Third Eye (Ying Tang)

Location

The pituitary gland is about three inches inside the skull from the mid-eyebrow point. The pituitary point is said to be where the spirit resides (Figure 5-48).

The pituitary point is part of the Crystal Palace. It corresponds to three outer points: the midpoint of the forehead, which corresponds to the hypothalamus; the point between the eyebrows (Third Eye), which corresponds to the pituitary gland; and the point between the two eyes at the root of the nose.

The pituitary has connections to these other points:
- The pituitary is connected directly to the Jade Pillow.
- The midpoint of the forehead is connected to the crown.
- The point between the eyes is connected to the palate and the Functional Channel.
- The left side of the point is connected to the left (Yang) temple bone.
- The right side of the point is connected to the right (Yin) temple bone.

Properties

The pituitary is one of the most important endocrine (hormone-producing) glands. It receives the signals transmitted by the hypothalamus to produce many hormones that govern a wide range of bodily processes, such as thyrotropin, which stimulates thyroid functions; adrenocorticotropic hormone, which stimulates activity of the adrenal cortex; follicle-stimulating hormone (FSH), which triggers the manufacture of testosterone in males and the corpus luteum in females; prolactin, which stimulates the secretion of breast milk; and growth hormones, which govern cellular metabolism. The mid-lobe stimulates the hormone inter-medin, which regulates skin pigment cells.

The posterior pituitary influences water metabolism, blood pressure, kidney function, and the action of smooth muscle.

At more advanced levels of the Microcosmic Orbit meditation, we often start with the mid-eyebrow point, drawing Higher Self (Cosmic) Energy to activate the navel and other points along the Microcosmic route. This point activates the Higher Self Force and filters incoming

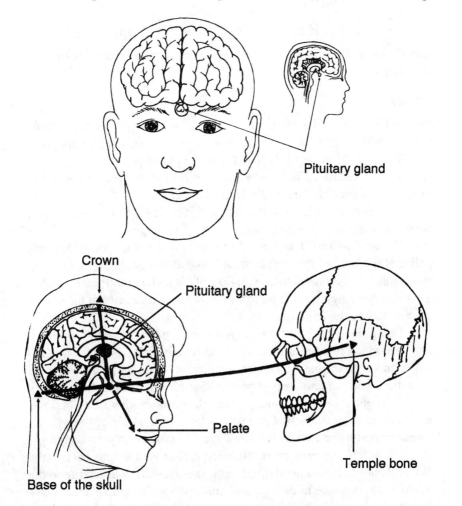

Pituitary gland

Crown

Pituitary gland

Palate

Temple bone

Base of the skull

Figure 5-48. Pituitary gland connection

food for our internal well-being. The particle forces, when taken in through the mid-eyebrow and brought down through the tongue to be mixed in the mouth with the other forces, can transformed into life-force, which Taoists know as the nectar, elixir, or water of life.

Emotional Influences

When the pituitary point is open one feels wisdom; when it is closed one feels incapable of making decisions.

13. Heavenly Pool (Hsuan Ying)

The Heavenly Pool at the palate has three aspects: the palate, the tongue, and the saliva.

Palate

Located directly behind the teeth, the palate point is a depression or hole through which Chi flows strongly down into the body (Figure 5-49).

Three positions are associated with the palate point.

Wind Position. The Wind Position is behind the teeth at the center of the palate point in the middle of the depression.

Fire Position. The Fire Position is farther back on the hard palate, where it connects to the heart and stirs up "fire energy."

Water Position. The Water Position is at the front part of the soft palate at the back of the mouth. It lies beneath the pituitary gland along the channel that connects to the Chi flow of the kidneys and sexual center. Touching the tongue to this point will draw the Yin essence of the sexual energy up into the brain.

Using the three positions. If you press the tongue behind the teeth and release it a few times, you will soon feel the Chi flow. This is often experienced as coolness, warmth, numbness, tingling, or an electrical sensation. You can find the best position for the tongue by moving it back and forth against the palate until you feel the position where the Chi flows most strongly. (Usually this is near the teeth in the hole of the palate.) Concentrate on this area as you draw the Chi down into your body.

If you feel you need more Yin energy, shift your tongue back to the Water Position. If you need more Yang energy, shift your tongue to the Wind Position at the middle palate until you feel more fire, then move back to the Water Position again. In the beginning it may be hard to keep the tongue curled for long periods, so shift its position as necessary.

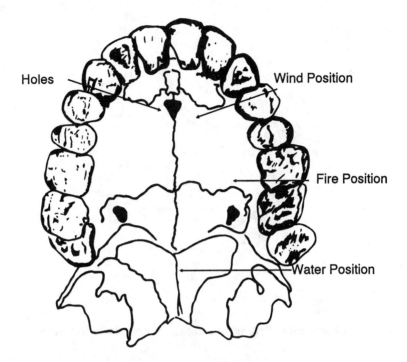

Holes
Wind Position
Fire Position
Water Position

Figure 5-49. Three positions of the palate

Tongue

The tongue has several major points (Figures 5-50, 5-51, and 5-52). When they are activated by the Chi flow, they help move Chi through the Triple Warmer meridian.

The tip of the tongue. When the tip of the tongue is placed on the lower jaw just below the teeth, the Chi flowing through it helps activate the spleen.

When the tip of tongue is held between the upper and lower teeth, the Chi flowing through it helps activate the lungs.

When the tip of the tongue is placed so it touches the upper jaw, just behind the teeth, the Chi flowing through it helps activate the heart.

When the tip of the tongue is placed on the hard palate, the Chi flowing through it helps activate the liver.

When the tip of the tongue is placed on the soft palate, the Chi flowing through it helps activate the kidneys.

The Golden Liquid point. On the left side of the tongue is a point called the Golden Liquid (or Golden Boy) point, which helps activate the

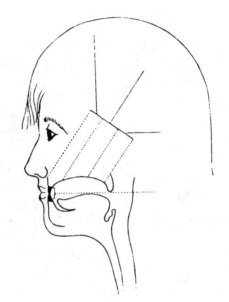

Figure 5-50. The upper palate connects to the organs

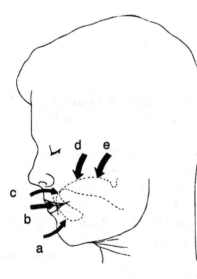

a. Lower jaw just below teeth, reflex point of the Triple Warmer

b. Front of the mouth, reflex point of the lungs and large intestine

c. Front palate, reflex point of the heart and small intestine

d. Middle palate, reflex point of liver and gall bladder

e. Back palate, reflex point of the kidneys and bladder

Figure 5-51. Relationship of the palate and tongue with the organs

228

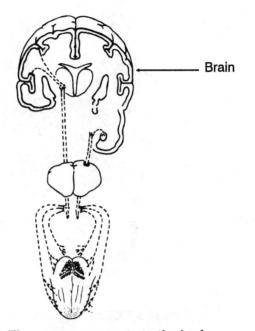

Brain

Figure 5-52. The tongue connects to the brain.

Universal Force. It connects to the Governor Channel and the Crystal Palace with a positive charge.

The Jade Liquid point. On the right side of the tongue is the Jade Liquid (or Jade Girl) point, which helps activate the Earth Force. It connects to the Functional Channel, the kidneys, and the sexual center with a negative charge.

The Gathering Spring point. The center point of the tongue is called the Gathering Spring point, and it has a neutral charge of both Yin and Yang energy (Figure 5-53). It connects to the middle Thrusting Channel, the heart, the center of the Original Force, and all the organs.

The Double Dragons. Beneath the tongue are two green tendons known as the Double Dragons, which curl or move the tongue around to help activate the three major points and increase the flow of saliva (Figure 5-54).

Saliva and the Elixir (Nectar)

When the electromagnetic life-force flows through the palate, the tongue points, and the Double Dragons, it activates the saliva (Figure 5-55),

229

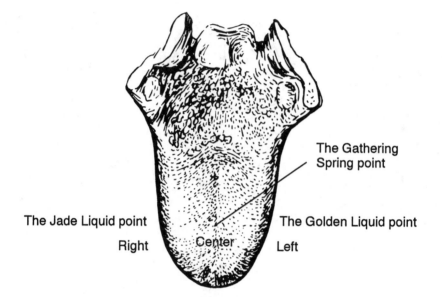

The Gathering
Spring point

The Jade Liquid point

The Golden Liquid point

Right   Center   Left

Figure 5-53. The tongue connection

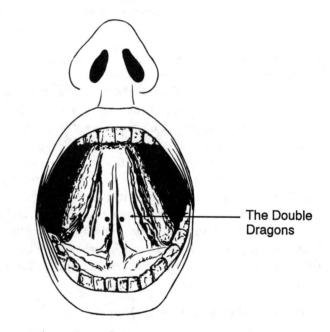

The Double
Dragons

Figure 5-54. The point below the tongue

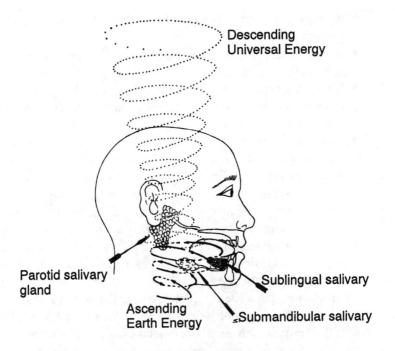

Figure 5-55. Saliva and the Elixir (Nectar)

which becomes sweet and fragrant. When you have a mouthful, you can swallow it down with a gulp to activate the points on both sides of the throat (the corresponding left and right Golden and Jade Liquid points). Taoist believe that saliva, when properly mixed with the external forces, has powerful anti-aging effects. It also cools and balances one's energy. When swallowed properly, saliva helps open the Functional Channel so energy can move down the front of body. (It is actually harder to bring energy down than to raise it.)

The saliva has several functions. It moisturizes the membranes of the mouth; it mixes with food to aid in digestion; it helps predigest carbohydrates, turning them into glucose; and it helps dissolve food before it enters the stomach. The saliva also contains some vitamins, such as B2 and K, and other digestive juices.

How to swallow the saliva. Intentionally swallowing the saliva is one of the best ways to maintain health. Mixing the saliva with the Universal, Higher Self, Earth, and Original Forces by swishing the tongue to stimulate the salivary glands has a number of benefits.

- It clears bitterness in the mouth, soothes a sore throat, and helps prevent tooth decay.
- It moisturizes the stomach and small and large intestines while helping them digest food.
- It helps moisturize the organs and joints of the body.
- It helps cool down the heart if it is overheated, and it nourishes the skin.
- Swallowing the saliva several times in succession can stop the feeling of hunger.
- When you are not feeling well and energy or mucus is stuck in your throat and chest, you can concentrate to make the navel warm, move the tongue to mix all the forces with the saliva, and swallow three to six times. This should make you feel better quickly.
- Constant mixing and refinement of saliva through higher Taoist practices helps develop the Inner Pearl, the human soul essence.
- When you cannot sleep at night, you can swallow a few times to cool down your system, which prepares the body for sleep.

Saliva as the Upper Elixir (nectar or Water of Life). I believe another fluid produced in the mouth is not the normal saliva, but a mixture of sexual energy and Original Force stored in the kidneys. When properly stimulated, these rise to the brain and activate the pineal, hypothalamus, and pituitary glands. These glands emit hormone secretions that flow down to the palate as an elixir—the "upper" water or Golden Elixir.

This occurs naturally when people make very good love together. The woman feels a moistness in her mouth that tastes like nectar, very sweet and fragrant. When properly swallowed, it is the best medicine to strengthen, heal, and enhance spiritual development.

When human love and sex combine, kidney energy is activated and rises through the Governor Channel to the crown, stimulating the glands. The fusion of human love and sexual energy also attracts Universal and Earth Forces to mix together.

14. Throat Point: Heaven's Projection (Tien Tu)

Location

The throat point is below the thyroid and parathyroid glands, just above the fossa of the suprasternal notch. If you run your finger down the midline of your neck, it will naturally fall into a V-like notch at the base

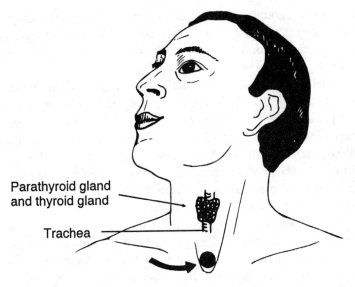

Parathyroid gland
and thyroid gland

Trachea

Figure 5-56. Throat point

of the neck and the top of the breastbone (sternum). This is the throat point (Figure 5-56).

Properties

Speech and communication. The throat point is related to speech and communication. In Taoist physiology, the tongue is the sense organ associated with the heart. The heart (Hsin) is also the natural seat of the mind. The openness of the channel between one's heart/mind and one's tongue determines one's ability to speak one's mind strongly and clearly. The throat point lies right in the middle between the heart and the tongue. If the Chi flows strongly through this point, you will find it easy to express yourself, and your speech will be clear and smooth. If the point is blocked, you will find it very hard to get the proper words out. Opening the throat point can greatly improve this situation.

Dreams. The throat point is strongly connected to dream consciousness. Over the last century, the Tibetans have become quite well known for their Dream Yoga or lucid-dreaming practice. Study of the Tibetan techniques has inspired much research into lucid dreaming and has led to many scientific discoveries about dreaming and the mind.

It is not as well known that Dream Yoga is also an important practice in many branches of Taoism. Taoists who practice Dream Yoga focus on the throat point when going to sleep so as to consciously cross the bridge between the waking state and the dream state. Being able to dream lucidly helps one gain greater control of one's Chi and also enables one to consciously bridge the gap between life and death.

Many people in the West are familiar with the famous Chinese folk novel, *Journey to the West*, which relates the story of the Monkey King and his many adventures. The Monkey King had 72 magical powers. These powers correspond to the 72,000 subtle energy channels in the body. Taoists practicing Dream Yoga seek to duplicate the Monkey King's 72 magical feats while dreaming. These include such feats as flying, becoming invisible, making duplicate images of oneself, changing into other shapes and forms, and so forth.

Being able to perform these feats in the dream state prepares the practitioner for exercising the same magical powers in the waking state. The powers are not sought for their own sake; true Taoist students are seeking wisdom and harmony with the universe, not more egotistical power. The powers are merely an indication that one has gained more subtle control of one's energy body.

Other parallel practices accomplish the same goals, such as the Kan and Li and higher-level practices. In a more mundane sense, Taoists view dream activity as a necessary function to process emotions that were not resolved or let go during the course of the day. By practicing the Inner Smile, Six Healing Sounds, and Fusion of the Five Elements meditation, we can get in touch with our emotions, process them, and clear them out. We practice forgiving and forgetting, so that we may clear and purify our Chi and spirit. As a result, we will naturally dream less. When the mind is clear during sleep, the energy body can strengthen itself while we sleep, which speeds up spiritual work.

The energy body. Because of the throat's connection to speech, the Taoists make two logical extensions. Speech is related to breath, and breath is related to Chi, so the throat point is one of the control points for the energy body.

The throat point is weak and hard to protect. If the throat point is opened before a connection is established to the other points, one's energy can be lost, or even controlled by ill-intentioned persons. Spirits or entities that wish to possess one's body are most likely to enter through the throat point. The Governor and Functional Channels should therefore be cleared and able to circulate Chi before this point is completely opened in meditation. If you are aware an attempted possession has been launched, you can counteract it by strongly circulating your Chi through the Microcosmic Orbit.

The thyroid gland. The thyroid gland, just above the throat point and surrounding the trachea, is the largest of all the endocrine glands. It controls the metabolism through production of hormones. If hormone quantities are too small, an individual can become puffy-faced, obese, sluggish, dull-witted, and in extreme cases, a semi-vegetable. If too much is produced, the results can be a tremendous appetite and a nervous disposition. The individual will gradually become thinner because of the speeded-up metabolic rate.

Iodine is the critical mineral for the thyroid, and only an extremely small amount is needed to produce the thyroid hormones. In an underactive gland, the cells multiply so they can leach the last bit of iodine out of the food consumed. In an overactive thyroid, the gland enlarges because of overproduction of the thyroid-stimulating hormone from the pituitary, or from an excess of iodine, although the latter is rare.

The thyroid hormones have several functions. They help regulate the rate of metabolism; they influence physical and mental growth; and they influence the differentiation of tissues and their development. They also help prevent a buildup of calcium in the blood by balancing the hormone from the parathyroids, which maintains blood levels of calcium by drawing calcium from the bones and teeth.

Once the Microcosmic Orbit is open and the throat point is connected to the other points, it can balance an overactive or underactive thyroid gland.

Emotional Influences

When the throat point is open and connected, one is more eloquent; when it is blocked or closed, one feels an unwillingness to change.

15. Heart Point (Shan Zhong)

There are two points of the heart to be considered. One is the actual center of the physical heart (Figures 5-57 and 5-58), which can be strengthened through meditation; the other is an energy center close to the sternum and in direct line with the points of the throat and solar plexus along Functional Channel 17 in acupuncture (Figure 5-59). Here, we discuss the energy center, which is closely connected with both the physical heart and the thymus gland.

Location

The energetic heart center is midway between the nipples in men, and one inch up from the base of the sternum in women. It connects the center

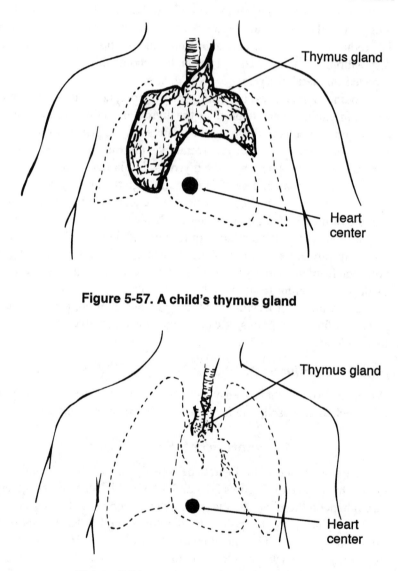

Figure 5-57. A child's thymus gland

Figure 5-58. An adult's thymus gland

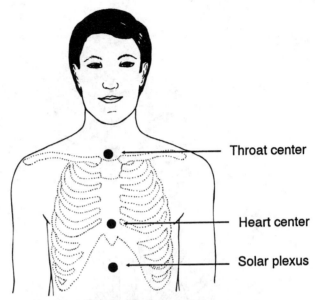

Throat center

Heart center

Solar plexus

Figure 5-59. The heart center

of the Original Force to T-5 and T-6 on the spine, as well as to the physical heart.

Properties and Emotional Influences

The opening of the heart point is very small, so it takes time to fully open during meditation (Figure 5-60). Occasionally energy congests the point and causes pain, discomfort, and shortness of breath. Massaging the sternum can relieve this. Most people also find that emotional pain is released as the associated negative energies disperse. Practicing the Heart Sound helps relieve both energetic and emotional congestion.

The virtuous emotions of love, joy, happiness, honesty, and respect are crucial properties of the heart. To help open this point, you should express these emotions, which you can cultivate through meditation, to others. After you have practiced the Inner Smile and Microcosmic Orbit meditations for a while, these virtues can be recalled very easily, because they are nourished by these disciplines. The heart point is also the gathering point of energy for the Upper Warmer meridian. When the heart is open, one feels love, joy, happiness, honesty, and respect (Figure 5-61); when it is blocked or closed, one feels paranoia, self-pity, impatience, hastiness, and hatred.

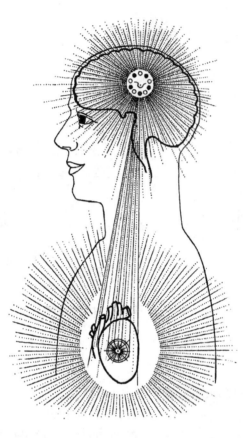

Figure 5-60. The opening of the heart is very small.

NOTE: FOR WOMEN: The heart's point and its positive emotional energies are very important for women to nurture so they can develop more control over their sexual energy, menstrual cycles, and spiritual growth. (It is also known as the Immortal Center for women.) When this point is open, its energy connects to the breasts, and it expands the virtues of the heart throughout the whole body.

In higher-level practice, women can store the energy in the heart center. Once the Orbit is open, women can start the Orbit at the navel, move up to the heart, travel up to the throat and crown, back down the spine, and then up to the navel and heart again. In women (or very Yin men), the Orbit may naturally reverse its normal route, as the front of their bodies can be more Yang and the back more Yin. In the normal route, we use the Yang fire energy rising up the spine to help clear the Yin front water channel. However, if your water energy is stronger, it can also be used to clear obstructions in the fire channel.

Seat of Love

The heart point is the seat of love and can be used to connect with the loving energies of the Universal Love. It works like a cauldron to combine all the virtues into compassion. Taoists say that the heart stores our spiritual essence in its unawakened state. When the virtues are

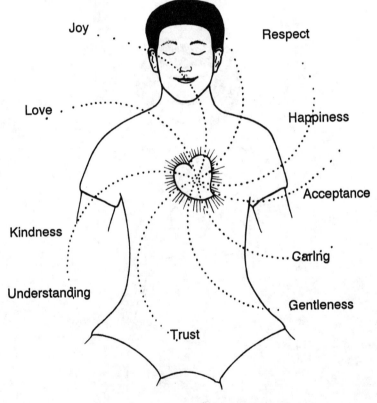

Figure 5-61. Opening of the heart

combined into compassion, the spirit awakens like a seed, which grows into a tree to bear fruit . When the heart point is opened too early, however, before the other points are opened and connected, one becomes susceptible to external influences, and loving energies can be lost.

Some religions use this center to enforce the concept of surrender, which they encourage their followers to translate into donations and charity. In these systems, people are encouraged to open their hearts, feel like flower blossom and give love before a sense of inner abundance and balance has been achieved (Figure 5-62). This is spiritually unhealthy; the concept of surrender does not require self- sacrifice to this extent. Instead, surrender simply means giving up the whims and dictates of the ego and learning to live in higher states of consciousness as we become better vehicles for our divine source: the Tao.

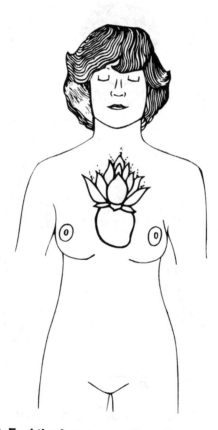

Figure 5-62. Feel the heart open like a flower blossoming.

NOTE: *Respect is one of the most important energies in a loving heart. When people feel respect, the heart opens and easily receives transmission of the Universal and Earth Forces. This principle is applied in a student's relationship to his or her teacher.*

Forgiveness and love for those one dislikes or hates are very important to help open the heart. When one has hate in the heart, it closes up and is very hard to open again. If you cannot "love your enemy," at least try to feel detached from and neutral toward them. Feel compassion for their limitations.

Relationship to the Thymus Gland

Because the heart pumps blood through the body, it contains an intricate system of blood vessels to keep the heart muscle supplied with vital nutrients. The heart point controls the heart and the thymus gland, so it is important to focus on this point during meditation to strengthen these organs.

The thymus gland, at the forward base of the neck, plays a key role in the immunological defense system, stimulating production of the white blood cells that fight disease and infection. The thymus is fairly large at birth and continues to grow until adolescence, when it begins to shrink. By middle age the thymus is much smaller, but it is still an important factor in the immune system. During the first few weeks of life, T-lymphocytes created in the thymus migrate to the bloodstream and colonize lymph nodes throughout the body. These later begin to manufacture powerful antibodies vital for immunity.

Massaging the Sternum to Open the Heart Point

Massaging the sternum between the ribs releases negative emotions, stimulates the flow of lymph, and activates the thymus gland. Use either the index or middle finger knuckle to circle continuously from the top of the sternum to the bottom, and between the ribs at the base of the sternum (Figure 5-63). When you find a painful area, spend more time on it, massaging it cautiously until the pain is released. Do not overdo the massage in the beginning, because this can cause pain afterward.

Heart

The center of the heart is red and its core pure white. The heart center produces a positive charge, corresponding to the negative charge

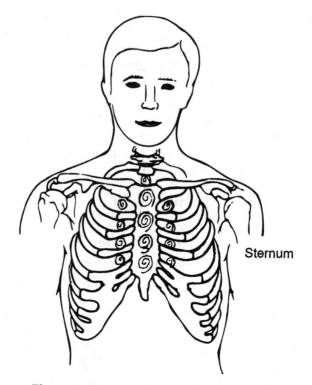

Sternum

Figure 5-63. Massaging the sternum

produced at the Door of Life and the kidneys. The two interact to harmonize the Chi flow in the whole body. Furthermore, the left side of the heart center is red and positively charged, while the right side of the heart is dark green and negatively charged. This combination produces the original spiritual energy that feeds the Shen or spirit, which is housed in the heart.

Taoists say this Original Chi splits into two parts after conception. Part of it is stored in the Crystal Palace of the brain, and part as sexual energy in the kidneys. When we combine the parts in the heart through meditation, we can restore our original spiritual essence.

16. Solar Plexus (Chung Kung) and Related Points

Location

The solar plexus point (Functional Channel 12) is slightly above the point halfway between the navel and the tip of the xiphoid process at the base of the sternum (Figure 5-64).

Properties

The solar plexus is the point for the spleen, pancreas, stomach, and liver. This point controls the aura (the body's external energy field) and determines the location of the Middle Cauldron, in which sexual and life-force energies are transformed into spiritual energy. (It is in this cauldron that the body, soul, and spirit are combined.)

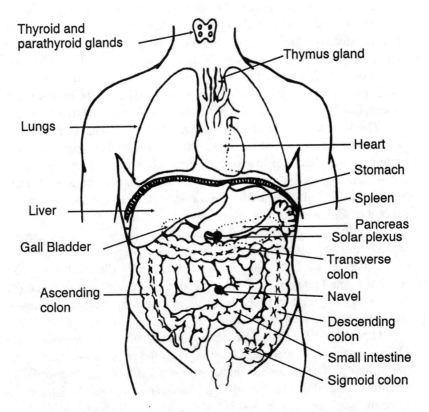

Figure 5-64. The solar plexus and the navel center

The spleen. The spleen is the largest of the lymphatic organs, the others being the thymus and tonsils. The spleen also forms blood cells, filters injurious substances from the bloodstream, stores iron for manufacturing hemoglobin, and produces the bile pigment bilirubin. Like the other lymphatic glands, the spleen is an integral part of the immune system and thus supports resistance to disease. In Chinese medicine, the spleen is responsible for transformation and transportation of Chi. The transformation occurs during digestion, in which the spleen (and the pancreas) play a major role. Blood circulation transports the nutrients (Chi) gleaned from the digestive process to all the cells in the body.

The pancreas. The pancreas, resting just below the stomach and liver, governs glucose metabolism. It is both an endocrine and exocrine gland. As an endocrine (hormone-producing) gland, the pancreas produces the hormones insulin and glucagon. Insulin is essential for the conversion of glucose (blood sugar) to energy, while glucagon converts the sugar stored by the liver back to blood sugar as needed. As an exocrine gland, the pancreas produces the digestive juices essential for the metabolism of carbohydrates, fats, and proteins, and secretes them into the small intestine. Chinese medicine does not differentiate between the pancreas and the spleen; their functions are both assigned to the spleen.

The stomach. Although we often think of the stomach as the main organ of digestion, the only foods the stomach actually breaks down are proteins. Other than aspirin and alcohol, almost no substance is absorbed in the stomach. In Chinese medicine, the stomach is responsible for the "rotting and ripening of food," the transportation of food essences, the descent of Chi, and the origination of bodily fluids.

The liver. The liver weighs about four pounds and is the largest organ in the body. It has many functions. The liver produces bile, which emulsifies the fats in the diet so they can be easily digested when they reach the small intestine. It may surprise many people to learn that the liver is as important in glucose regulation as the pancreas, because it stores and releases sugar as needed.

Often considered a detoxifying gland, the liver breaks down nitrogenous wastes, alcohol, and other ingested substances that may be harmful. It produces lecithin, another fat emulsifier, and is supported by vitamin C. In addition to storing sugar, the liver also stores the fat-soluble vitamins, such as A, D, E, and K.

The aura. The aura is the energetic field around the body (Figure 5-65). Virtually every process in the body, from digestion to muscular movement, is electrochemical. Because all functions of an electrical nature have an electromagnetic field surrounding them, many feel that the body's aura is its electromagnetic field.

Although only a few people can see auras without training, nearly everyone, consciously or subconsciously, can feel them. Electromagnetic fields interact when they overlap, and when we are around other people, our auras can influence each other. Our thoughts and feelings have electrical charges that affect our auras. It is important for the solar plexus

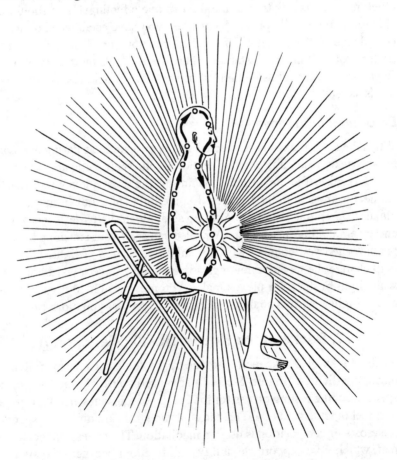

Figure 5-65. Aura from the solar plexus

point to be open, but if it is too open, one may be overly sensitive to the thoughts, feelings, and opinions of others, to the point of being unable to shut off mental and emotional static when in the company of others. This can be remedied by imagining a door or shield in front of the solar plexus point that can be raised or lowered as one wishes, depending on how intimate one chooses to be with one's present company.

Some people may criticize the idea of shielding the solar plexus, maintaining it is important for people to be open to each other all the time. I say everyone is entitled to privacy. No one is expected to keep the door to one's home, office, bedroom, or bathroom open all the time; how much more so is this true of the door to one's feelings! You should be able to open the solar plexus point when you have established trust and confidence in the presence of another, but you should also be able to protect yourself in circumstances when privacy feels more comfortable. Even the greatest saints demanded privacy. We should respect our own needs as well.

Emotional Influences

When the solar plexus is connected and open, one feels daring and able to take risks; when it is blocked or closed, one feels panic and worry.

Exercise. Picture bright sunshine in the solar plexus and feel it connect to the sun in the heavens. Let the light shine out from the solar plexus to strengthen the aura. A strong solar plexus helps deflect negative energy emanating from others. You also can send your sunshine to other people when you connect with the unlimited source of light. This will help change the negative feelings someone may have toward you. The white light of the solar plexus makes you more visible to higher forces and to higher masters so they can guide and protect you more easily.

17. Backs of the Knees, BL-40 (Wei Zhong)

At the backs of the knees is storage space for extra energy collected during meditation (Figure 5-66). In advanced spiritual practices, these spaces become resting places for the energy of the soul when it prepares to travel outside the body. The backs of the knees are difficult to access if a cross-legged position is used in meditation. The knees connect to the feet, which give support, flexibility, and freedom because of their connection to the Earth Force. When this connection is loose or weak, one feels inflexible and constricted.

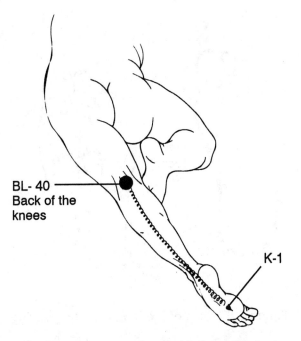

**Figure 5-66. K-1 point; the sole of the foot
(Yong-Quan)—"Bubbling Spring"**

18. Sole of the Foot: Bubbling Spring, K-1 (Yang Quan)

The K-1 point is located in the depression on the sole of each foot and is visible when either foot is flexed (Figure 5-67). This center is also known as the Bubbling Spring, from which the earth energy "springs" upward into the body. The K-1 point is directly connected to this energy and helps refine it before it enters the higher centers.

Connections of the Soles

The soles of the feet have a close connection to the palms. When used properly, this connection can help readjust the body's internal clock. By using the mind and physical touch to connect the right palm to the left sole and the left palm to the right sole, you can run the Microcosmic Orbit (especially through the coccyx, sacrum, and base of the skull) to balance these points, helping the body overcome jet lag. The soles also have important connections to the crown of the head and perineum.

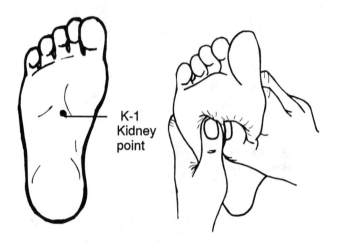

K-1
Kidney
point

Figure 5-67. Sole of the foot: Bubbling Spring

Properties

When these centers are open (on each foot), they help stabilize the body through their connection with the earth. When they are closed or blocked, one feels ungrounded or unstable because the connection with earth energy is weak.

Rubbing the Soles and Other Points of the Feet

Rubbing the soles before and after meditation helps activate the major energy channels. Massaging some of the major points of the feet also helps Chi move more easily and balances the Yin and Yang energies of the heart and kidneys (Figures 5-68 and 5-69).

    Chao Hai, the Shining Sea: The kidney point (K-6). This point is one finger's width below the inner ankle.

    Kung Sun, the Grandson: The spleen point (S-4). This point is on the inside edge of the bottom of the foot, in the hollow behind the third joint of the big toe.

    Lin Chi, Attending the Crying Child: The gall bladder point (GB-41). This point is on the top and outside of the foot at the joint in between the fourth and little toes.

Shenmai, Extending Vessel: The bladder point (BL-62). This point is on the outside of the ankle in the small depression just under and slightly behind the ankle bone.

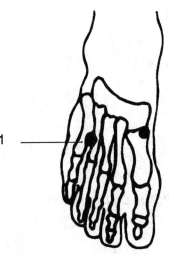

Figure 5-68. Lin Chi, attending the crying child point

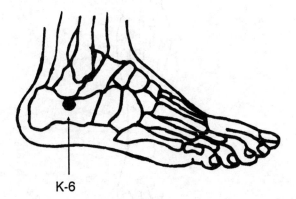

Figure 5-69. Chao Hai, the shining sea

18. Big Toe, LV-1 (Da Dun)

The Da Dun point is on the lateral side of the great toe, between the lateral corner of the toenail and the joint (Figure 5-70). It helps harmonize and cleanse the spiritual energy passing through it.

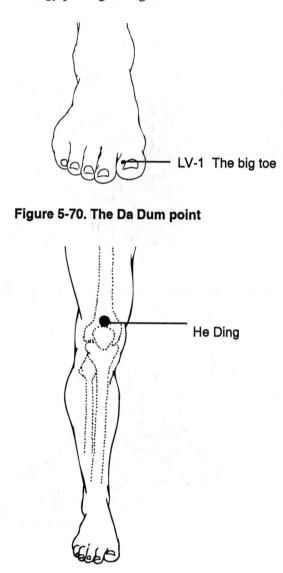

LV-1 The big toe

Figure 5-70. The Da Dum point

He Ding

Figure 5-71. Knee point

19. Kneecap (He Ding)

At the middle of the upper border of the kneecap, the He Ding point is a stopover or resting place for energy (Figure 5-71). It also helps refine the Earth Force on its way up to the perineum.

LEARNING THE POINTS

In the beginning, the most important thing to remember about the points is their locations. Take some time to find the points on your own body. If you have friends to work with, it is also helpful to find the points on them and have them locate the points on you. At your own pace, you will gradually memorize the functions of these points, but the most important thing is to practice. Once you have learned their locations, you can do the Microcosmic Orbit meditation. Eventually, depending on the strength of your practice, many functions of these points will be revealed to you, not just intellectually but through your own experience.

Chapter 6

OPENING THE BASIC MICROCOSMIC ORBIT

PROGRAM FOR MASTERING THE MICROCOSMIC ORBIT

In this chapter, we will learn some new methods to open the basic Microcosmic Orbit. In following chapters we will learn step-by-step procedures for more advanced methods of working with the Microcosmic Orbit, including techniques for amplifying the energy at each point along its path. The advanced methods are all supplementary procedures to the basic Microcosmic Orbit practice taught in this chapter.

You are advised to loosely follow the methods and time frames set forth in this book, depending on your level of experience and success. It is important to thoroughly master each step before advancing to the next level. We recommend that you practice daily for at least two weeks at each level to achieve competence. This will help you really feel the energy and will lay a strong foundation for the next level of practice. Even if you understand the principles and are learning quickly, this does not mean you will master the practice overnight. Intellectual understanding and fast learning cannot establish the mind/body connection, that comes only with regular practice. You should know each step so well that you can do it almost automatically, without any effort. Your body, brain, and nervous system will learn best through repetition of each new level of practice at regular intervals for at least two weeks.

Stages of Learning and Enhancing the Microcosmic Orbit

Chapter 6: Opening the Basic Microcosmic Orbit as taught in *Awaken Healing Energy Through the Tao* (Aurora Press, 1983). This chapter supplements the basic practice of the Microcosmic Orbit and describes various new methods for opening the Microcosmic Orbit which I have refined over the last ten years of teaching Westerners.

Chapter 7: Earth Energy and the Microcosmic Orbit. In Chapter 7, you learn how to connect with the energy of the earth, how to absorb this energy, and how to combine it with your Original Chi. You then learn how to circulate this fortified Chi through the Microcosmic Orbit to establish a "ground wire" for your Chi circulation practice.

Chapter 8: The Cosmic Force: Higher Self Energy and the Microcosmic Orbit. The methods introduced in Chapter 8 deepen your practice of the Microcosmic Orbit meditation, further opening the channels and related centers. You also learn to enhance and amplify your Chi by activating the mid-eyebrow point and drawing in energy from the Higher Self. Once you have connected to this golden energy, you learn to expand it into a golden ball of light to envelop and protect you during your practice.

Chapter 9: Opening Your Heart: Shen and the Microcosmic Orbit. In Chapter 9 you build on your practice by adding a step called Opening the Heart. Here you discover the connection between your emotions and your spirit, or Shen. After activating this important center, you use the energy of the heart to purify and balance the physical and emotional energy of the other internal organs. This practice strengthens the Microcosmic Orbit meditation and advances to the higher level of the Inner Smile.

Chapter 10: Sexual Energy and the Microcosmic Orbit. This chapter explains in detail the importance of sexual energy to Taoist practice. You focus on widening the Functional Channel, placing a special emphasis on the connection between the heart center and the sexual center. This strengthens the marriage of loving energy and sexual desire.

Chapter 11: Heavenly Chi and the Microcosmic Orbit. Chapter 11 explains the Heavenly or Universal Force (Heavenly Chi) and our links with this force through the physical, energy, and spirit bodies. It also explains the different varieties of Heavenly Chi and their significance in meditation. In the practice section you further open the Governor Channel. You learn to connect with Heavenly Chi from the

North Star and the Big Dipper, merging them with your own for strength and healing. Finally, you learn the ancient Taoist methods of circulating these external energies in the Microcosmic Orbit and combining them with your Original Chi to restore the life-force.

Chapter 12: Summary of the Microcosmic Orbit: Basic and Advanced Practices. Chapter 12 summarizes all the steps of the advanced Microcosmic Orbit meditation.

Chapter 13: Further Advanced Practices: The Macrocosmic Orbit and the Five Pulses. Chapter 13 introduces you to advanced applications of the Microcosmic Orbit, including detailed instructions on how to tap into the limitless healing power of nature. You also learn the *Macrocosmic Orbit*, or the *Greater Heavenly Cycle*, enabling you to circulate your Chi through all four limbs, in addition to the Governor and Functional Channels.

Chapter 14: Oneness with the Tao: A Daily Practice Guide. Chapter 14 provides helpful advice to assure ongoing success with your Microcosmic Orbit practice, Inner Smile, and Six Healing Sounds. Included are recommendations for practicing with the seasons.

Chapter 15: Troubleshooting Guide: Helpful Hints and Home Remedies for Simple Problems. This chapter answers commonly asked questions about the practice and addresses difficulties that may occur. Refer to this chapter first if any questions or problems arise in your practice.

Chapter 16: The Tao of Healing and Health Maintenance. This special chapter on healing presents numerous self-healing applications of the Microcosmic Orbit, Inner Smile, and Six Healing Sounds. It includes specific remedies for particular health problems and general Taoist health and healing guidelines.

OVERVIEW: OPENING THE BASIC MICROCOSMIC ORBIT

General Description

The Microcosmic Orbit meditation is a very simple practice.

1. Loosen the spine with Spinal Cord Breathing and Spine Rocking. Then sit in a stable position.

2. Relax the mind and body with the Six Healing Sounds and Inner Smile.

255

3. Use your mind to lead your energy through the loop of the Microcosmic Orbit pathway as many times as you wish.

4. When you are ready to conclude the session, collect the energy at the navel.

5. End with a little Chi Self-Massage to clear away any stiffness that you may have developed from sitting in one position during the practice.

The essence of the Microcosmic Orbit practice is to guide your Chi through a loop in your body. All other practices presented in the following chapters are merely elaborations, ways of drawing in other energies to enhance the circulation of Chi in the Microcosmic Orbit.

Techniques for Opening the Microcosmic Orbit

Opening the basic Microcosmic Orbit is different from your practice of it once you have mastered it. In the beginning, you may need to rely on the techniques in this chapter to help you feel and direct your Chi. With practice, you will depend on these methods less and less, because your Chi will move easily with the slightest direction.

A number of techniques can be used to help open the Microcosmic Orbit.

- Mind/eye spiraling or rotating a Chi ball
- Hand touching
- Breathing into each point
- Small Sip Breathing around the Orbit
- Long Sip (Deep Slow) Breathing around the Orbit
- Holding the palms above the points to stimulate the aura
- Rocking forward and back to activate the front and back channels (while standing or sitting)
- Colors and visualization
- Knocking on the sacrum with loose fists
- Knocking the teeth together and pressing the tongue to the roof of the mouth
- Inner or Womb Breathing—spontaneous pulsation of Chi

PRACTICE: PREPARATIONS FOR THE BASIC MICROCOSMIC ORBIT

NOTE: *Refer to Chapter 3, Chapter 4, or the Appendix for a more detailed description of these practices.*

Loosen the body and spine with Chi Kung warm-ups. Lightly shake the whole body. Then practice Spinal Cord Breathing, Spinal Cord Rocking, and the Crane Neck Exercise.

Clear your emotions and warm up your organs with the Six Healing Sounds. Do 2 to 3 repetitions of the sounds for each organ. This helps you tune in to your body and brings your energy to a more balanced state for healing circulation.

Establish a stable sitting posture. Check your posture: stable base, hands clasped, spine straight and in line with gravity, shoulders relaxed and balanced, chin back slightly with ears over shoulders, eyes gently closed, and tongue touching the roof of the mouth.

Once you are in a good sitting position, take a few minutes to focus and prepare yourself.

Prepare yourself to focus inward. Become aware of your surroundings. Feel the sensation of your feet touching the floor, of your hands clasping each other, of the chair beneath you.

Be aware of the sounds inside the room, outside the room, and within your body.

Be aware of your breath. Feel the body naturally expand as you inhale and contract as you exhale. This helps exercise the veins and arteries. Breathe in and out with awareness in this way at least 18 to 36 times.

Relax with the Inner Smile. Always relax first with the Inner Smile before beginning the Microcosmic Orbit meditation. The Inner Smile is a very effective way to deeply calm all parts of the body and mind and to get in touch with our positive aspects. Relaxation is important to health and well- being as an antidote to stress, but it is only the beginning of Taoist meditation, not the final goal. There is a saying, "Amateurs meditate to relax; professionals relax to meditate." It is hard to reach a deep state of meditation if the body and mind are not relaxed; always be sure to allow enough time for the Inner Smile before beginning the Microcosmic Orbit meditation.

It is always best to smile to the whole body before you begin practice of the Microcosmic Orbit, but if time is short, you may do only part of the Inner Smile. In the early stages, you can focus on any of the front, middle, or back lines of the Inner Smile, as outlined in chapter 3. In advanced practice of the Microcosmic Orbit meditation, however, it is vital to smile down to the organs of the front line first to activate the virtuous energies you will connect to the Universal, Cosmic, and Earth

257

Forces. Bringing in too much raw energy without first tuning in to the frequencies of the virtues can give you "Chi indigestion"!

See "The Virtues" in Chapter 3 for detailed instructions on the Inner Smile (Figure 6-1).

Warming the Stove: Activate the Original Chi in the Lower Tan Tien

1. Start with Bellows Breathing 18 to 36 times.

2. Rest and gather Chi at the navel, with your hands covering the navel.

3. Loosen the intestines with spiraling body movements.

4. Warm up the kidneys and activate the Door of Life.

5. Activate the Original Force by drawing energy from the navel and Door of Life and gathering it into the Lower Tan Tien.

6. Activate the sexual energy to amplify the Original Chi.

7. When you have completed the previous steps and can feel the pressure, pulsing, and suction, lightly pull up the sexual organ and the

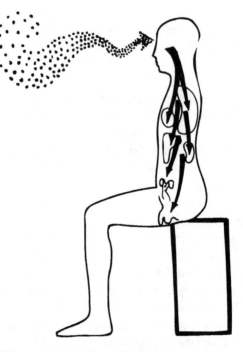

**Figure 6-1. Smile to help activate the
virtuous energies in the organs.**

anus toward the area of the Original Force. Continue to breathe into this area and feel pressure build there.

8. As the pressure increases, you will feel the energy run strongly to you. Let the Original Chi radiate to wherever it wants. The Microcosmic Orbit may open for you spontaneously and effortlessly at this point; the energy may flow down to the coccyx, up the spine to the crown, and back down the Functional Channel in the front. The Chi may also rush to sick places anywhere in the body, places that need healing. Your Original Chi knows where it needs to go; it is the very best medicine for self-healing. You need not feel you have to direct it if it starts flowing and radiating by itself. Just relax and let it go wherever it wants.

It is important to have a strong feeling of the Original Chi at the navel center to complete the Microcosmic Orbit. It is the major source of Chi in the body, and if this reservoir is low, the Chi in the channels will also be low. For this reason, you should not be in a hurry. If you take some time to nurture Chi and bring your awareness to this spot, the Microcosmic Orbit will open more easily and naturally.

PRACTICE: OPENING THE MICROCOSMIC ORBIT

In this first practice section, we recommend three techniques for enhancing the sensation of Chi: the mind/eye power method, the hand-touching method, and the natural breathing method. You use them in combination to draw energy into the centers of the Microcosmic Orbit.

Use mind/eye power to spiral and condense the Chi into each point. Use the hand-touching method to focus your awareness and move the Chi. **Always use the right hand to send energy and the left to receive it.** Finally, use deep, slow breathing to expand and open the centers. Breathe naturally into each point. Let your breath be long, deep, quiet, calm, smooth, soft, and even.

Awaken Healing Light: Transport the Force Through the Microcosmic Orbit

NOTE: *If you need practice with the mind/eye power method, refer to Chapter 4.*

Move Energy from the Navel to the Perineum

1. Place the fingers of the right hand on the navel center, and the fingers of the left on the sexual center (Figure 6-2). Let the energy radiate from the Original Force and run down to the sexual center. Spiral at the sexual center with your mind and eyes 36 times counterclockwise to expand the energy at the center, then 36 times clockwise to condense the energy into the sexual center. Send energy from the right hand to the left and imagine the channel between these two points opening wide with the increased flow of Chi. Feel that you have made the connection.

As you inhale, breathe as if you were inhaling into the sexual center, filling it with fresh energy. As you exhale, again feel as if the breath is flowing into the sexual center, strengthening and energizing it. Mentally say the word "Chi" as you exhale and focus the mind on the sexual center to increase the energy there. Repeat the inhalation and exhalation 9 to 18 times. Concentrate on the sexual center until you can feel the Chi accumulate. Feel the line of energy extending from the navel down to the sexual center.

2. Move the left hand to the perineum and touch the perineum with three fingers. Let the energy radiate from the navel and sexual center

Figure 6-2. Touch the navel with the right hand and touch the sexual center with the left.

down to the perineum. Send energy from the right hand to the left, and imagine the channel between these points opening wide with the increased flow of Chi. Spiral your energy or rotate a Chi ball there with mind and eyes 36 times counterclockwise and 36 times clockwise.

Inhale and exhale into the perineum, using the word "Chi" to increase the energy there. Repeat 9 to 18 times.

3. Gather energy into a Chi ball at the Lower Tan Tien. Rotate this Chi ball (3 to 5 inches in diameter) top to front to bottom to back, as if rotating the ball in the same direction as the Orbit. Let it spin as fast or slowly as it wants. By resonance, this spinning ball helps stimulate the flow of the Orbit. Lower the Chi ball to the perineum.

B. Raising Energy Up the Spine

1. Move the left hand to the sacrum and coccyx. Place the palm over the sacrum and touch the tip of the coccyx with the tip of the middle finger. Place the right fingertips over the sexual center (Figure 6-3).

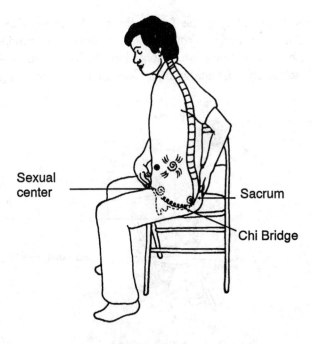

Sexual center

Sacrum

Chi Bridge

Figure 6-3. Chi Bridge

261

2. To make a Chi Bridge, very slightly pull up on the perineum, using the mind more than muscle to close the sexual organs (men feel as if they are gently raising the testicles and retracting the penis; women lightly squeeze the vaginal muscles). Then gently tighten the anus, pulling it toward the coccyx. Finally, gently tighten the back part of the sphincter muscle between the anus and coccyx, and feel as if you were sipping energy into the coccyx and sacrum through a straw. Send energy from the right hand to the left, and imagine the channel between these points opening wide with the increased flow of Chi. Let the energy radiate from the navel, sexual center, and perineum into the coccyx and sacrum. Spiral or rotate there with the mind and eyes 36 times each way. Inhale and exhale into the coccyx and sacrum, using the word "Chi" to increase the energy there. Repeat 3 to 9 times.

3. Move the left hand to the Door of Life. Let the energy radiate up into the Door of Life. Spiral the energy or rotate a Chi ball there using mind/eye power 36 times each way. Inhale and exhale into the Door of Life, using the word "Chi" to increase the energy there. Repeat 9 to 18 times.

4. Move the left hand up to the T-11 point. Let the energy flow to the T-11 point. Spiral the energy or rotate a Chi ball there using mind/eye power 36 times each way. Inhale and exhale into the T-11 point, using the word "Chi" to increase the energy there. Repeat 3 to 9 times (Figure 6-4).

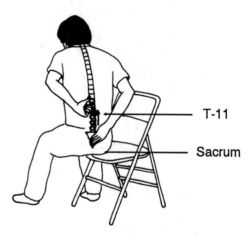

T-11

Sacrum

Figure 6-4. Sacrum and T-11 points

5. Let the energy radiate up to the Wing Point opposite the heart (between T-5 and T-6). Spiral the energy or rotate a Chi ball there using mind/eye power 36 times each way. Inhale and exhale into this point, using the word "Chi" to increase the energy there. Repeat 3 to 9 times.

6. Move the left hand up to the C-7 point. Let the energy radiate to the C-7 point. Spiral the energy or rotate a Chi ball there using mind/eye power 36 times each way. Inhale and exhale into the C-7 point, using the word "Chi" to increase the energy there. Repeat 3 to 9 times (Figure 6-5).

7. Move the left hand up to the Jade Pillow point. Let the energy radiate up into the Jade Pillow. Spiral the energy or rotate a Chi ball there using mind/eye power 36 times each way. Inhale and exhale into the Jade Pillow, using the word "Chi" to increase the energy there. Repeat 3 to 9 times (Figure 6-6).

8. Move the left hand up to the back of the crown point. Let the energy radiate to the back of the crown. Spiral the energy or rotate a Chi ball there using mind/eye power 36 times each way. Inhale and exhale into the back of the crown, using the word "Chi" to increase the energy there. Repeat 3 to 9 times.

9. Move the left hand up to the top of the crown point. Let the energy radiate to the top of the crown. Spiral the energy or rotate a Chi ball there

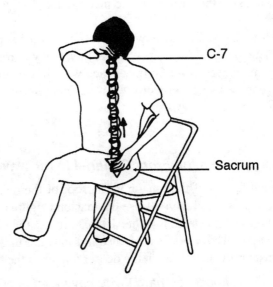

C-7

Sacrum

Figure 6-5. Sacrum and C-7 points

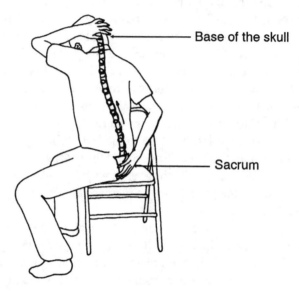

Base of the skull

Sacrum

Figure 6-6. Sacrum and base of skull

using mind/eye power 36 times each way. Inhale and exhale into the top of the crown, using the word "Chi" to increase the energy there. Repeat 3 to 9 times.

10. Move the left hand down to the mid-eyebrow point. Let the energy radiate to the mid-eyebrow. Spiral the energy or rotate a Chi ball there using mind/eye power 36 times each way. Inhale and exhale into the mid-eyebrow, using the word "Chi" to increase the energy there. Repeat 3 to 9 times.

Send Energy Down the Front Channel to the Navel

1. Touch the tip of the tongue to the roof of the mouth. Press the tongue to the palate and then release the tension (Figure 6-7). Do this 9 to 18 times. Knock the teeth together 18 to 36 times, then lightly clench and release them. This vibrates the bones and activates the bone marrow, to help transport the Chi through the denser matter of the bones.

NOTE: *Don't knock too hard if you have a lot of fillings in your teeth!*

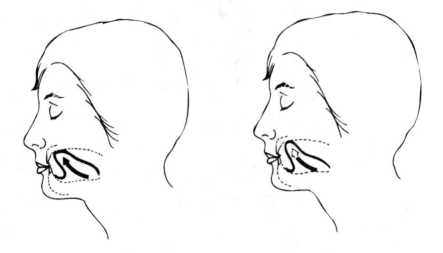

Figure 6-7. Press the tongue, then release it.

Let the energy radiate to the palate. Spiral the energy or rotate a Chi ball there using mind/eye power 36 times each way. Inhale and exhale into the palate 3 to 9 times, using the word "Chi" to increase the energy there.

2. Move the left hand down to the throat center point and touch the point with three fingertips. Gather some saliva in the mouth and swallow down. Let the energy radiate down to the throat center. Spiral the energy or rotate a Chi ball there using mind/eye power 36 times each way. Inhale and exhale into the throat center, using the word "Chi" to increase the energy there. Repeat 3 to 9 times.

3. Move the left hand down to the heart center point and touch the point with three fingertips. Let the energy flow down to the heart point. Spiral the energy or rotate a Chi ball there using mind/eye power 36 times each way. Inhale and exhale into the heart point, using the word "Chi" to increase the energy there. Repeat 3 to 9 times (Figure 6-8).

4. Move the left hand down to the solar plexus point and touch the point with three fingertips. Let the energy flow down to the solar plexus point. Spiral the energy or rotate a Chi ball there using mind/eye power 36 times each way. Inhale and exhale into the solar plexus point, using the word "Chi" to increase the energy there. Repeat 3 to 9 times.

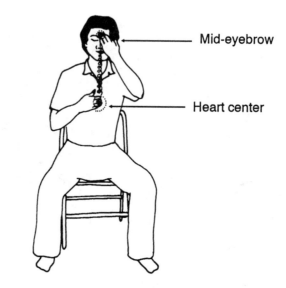

Figure 6-8. Mid-eyebrow and the heart center

5. Let the energy return to the navel. Spiral the energy or rotate a Chi ball there using mind/eye power 36 times each way. Inhale and exhale into the navel point, using the word "Chi" to increase the energy there (Figure 6-9). Repeat 3 to 9 times or more if you need it, feeling the pulsing behind the navel. If you have any trouble bringing the energy down from the crown to the navel, use the hands to gently stroke the energy down. Repeat the stroking movements until you feel you have successfully brought any excess energy from the head, throat, or chest, or any stuck energy, down to the navel.

6. You can either end the active or Yang stage of your meditation here, or you can continue to guide the energy flow through the Microcosmic Orbit as many times as you like (Figure 6-10).

Yin Stage: Rest in the Original Chi

1. Rest. Just relax your mind and body. Find the neutral point in the center of your body. It could be at the navel, the heart, or the head, whatever feels most neutral to you. Simply be there. Do nothing but absorb the fruits of having circulated the energy through the Microcosmic Orbit and balanced your Chi flow.

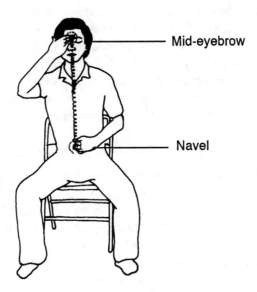

Figure 6-9. Mid-eyebrow and the navel

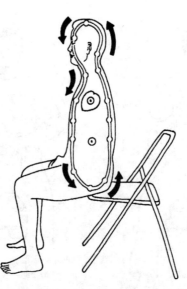

Figure 6-10. Use mind/eye/heart power to guide the Chi flow into the Microcosmic Orbit.

2. Allow the energy to do whatever it wants to do. It may reverse direction; it may flow to other areas of the body; the body may shake and vibrate; you may hear high-pitched sounds. Spend five or ten minutes at this stage, giving yourself the chance to reap the fruit of your Microcosmic Orbit circulation: a sense of inner peace, calmness, and clarity. Let the physical body dissolve into your Original Chi, resting in the state of emptiness, making no effort whatsoever.

End the Meditation

1. When you are ready to conclude the session, bring the energy to the navel and collect the energy, letting it return to the area behind the navel and in front of the kidneys to recharge your Original Force. Spiral the energy or rotate a Tai Chi symbol around the navel 36 times outward and 24 times inward (men, clockwise out and counterclockwise in; women, counterclockwise out and clockwise in) (Figure 6-11).

2. Rest for a moment and enjoy the comfortable peaceful feeling you have created in your meditation. Feel the spaciousness inside your body and mind now that you have cleared out physical and mental tensions.

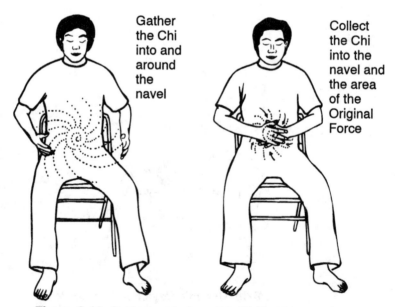

Gather the Chi into and around the navel

Collect the Chi into the navel and the area of the Original Force

Figure 6-11. Gather and store the Chi in the navel.

3. Finish with Chi Self-Massage.

4. Get up slowly and carry this feeling with you into activity. Whenever you are starting to feel sick or stressed, return the mind and the breath to the center. With regular practice, you will be able to recapture this pleasant feeling at any time.

ALTERNATIVE WAYS TO OPEN THE MICROCOSMIC ORBIT

If you prefer, you may use any of these other methods, either in addition to or instead of the mind/eye power and the hand-touching methods, to enhance the sensation or movement of Chi through the Orbit. The Preparation and Conclusion steps are the same as for the previous meditation.

Small Sip or Long Sip Breathing

Small Sip Breathing combines the powers of the mind/eyes/heart and the breath to open the centers. Those who cannot comfortably hold their breath for a series of short inhalations should practice the other methods until their capacity improves. It is a good method if you feel low energy or simply want more stimulation of your Chi flow. Do not use small sips when in an anxious or overactive emotional state.

If you are anxious, use the Long Sip method to calm the energy while guiding it through the Orbit. Long Sip Breathing has inhalations and exhalations of equal length. If you are very anxious or need to release pent-up emotion, you can lengthen the exhalation.

> **CAUTION: PEOPLE WITH LUNG AND HEART PROBLEMS, GLAUCOMA, HIGH BLOOD PRESSURE, HEMOPHILIA, ATHEROSCLEROSIS, INSOMNIA, HEADACHE, OR OTHER SERIOUS PROBLEMS SHOULD NOT USE THE SMALL SIP METHOD, AND THEY SHOULD TEST THE LONG SIP METHOD FOR SHORT PERIODS OF VERY GENTLE BREATHING TO MAKE SURE IT IS NOT TOO STIMULATING.**

Preparations. Follow the same preparatory steps as in the previous meditation: Chi Kung Warm-Ups, Six Healing Sounds, stable sitting posture, Inner Smile, and Warming the Stove.

Microcosmic Orbit

1. Focus the mind at the navel. Gently inhale six small sips of air without exhaling, and feel that you are drawing Chi from the Lower Tan Tien to charge up the navel. Hold your breath as you spiral or rotate the energy at the navel using mind/eye power. Then exhale, rest, and retain the energy of the breath at the navel. Repeat 3 to 9 times. (You may sip up to 6 times into each point at first. After a while, you may need to sip only 1 to 3 times into each point to activate it and go on to the next point without exhaling if you are still comfortable. As you improve, you may be able to cover several points in one inhalation.)

CAUTION: BE SURE TO EXHALE ANYTIME YOU FEEL UN-COMFORTABLE OR SHORT OF BREATH. THE PRACTICE IS NOT ENHANCED BY HOLDING YOUR BREATH LONGER IF YOU ARE STRAINING TO DO IT! DO NOT STRAIN; REMAIN RELAXED AND COMFORTABLE.

2. Move the awareness to the sexual center. Inhale six small sips to draw energy from the navel to the sexual center, spiraling at the sexual center with each sip.

Exhale, rest, and repeat 3 to 9 times.

3. Continue in the same way to the perineum, sacrum, Door of Life, T-11 (T-5 and C-7 optional), Jade Pillow, and crown. Each time you will sip energy into the point of focus, drawing Chi from the previous point (Figure 6-12).

4. Bring the energy down by exhaling in short sips from the crown to the Third Eye, palate, throat center, heart center, solar plexus, and back to the navel. When you bring the energy down, Small Sip Breathing is optional. You can use the mind/eye spiraling technique alone if you wish, or you may use one or more exhalations at each point on the front descending channel (Figure 6-13).

5. Long Sip Breathing can be used immediately after a few rounds of Small Sip Breathing, or it can be used separately. It is very simple: inhale from the perineum up the spine to the crown in one long, slow, deep breath. Then exhale from the crown down the front to the navel and perineum. Repeat 6 to 9 cycles, then rest, and watch your Chi circulate in the orbit.

6. Repeat steps 2 through 5 as many times as you like. After a few cycles around the Orbit, you may find that you no longer need to rely on

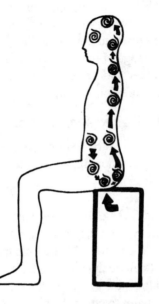

**Figure 6-12. Small Sip Breathing guides the Chi
flow from the navel down to the perineum and up to the crown.**

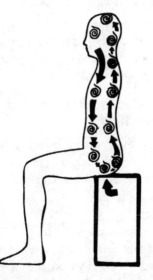

**Figure 6-13. Small Sip or Long Sip Breathing guides
the Chi flow into the Microcomic Orbit.**

either Small or Long Sip Breathing, spiraling, or rotating a Chi ball; your energy will flow on its own or with gentle guidance by the mind.

7. When you are ready to conclude, bring your energy back to the navel. Rest in the Yin stage of meditation, as in the previous meditation.

Conclusion. Gather and collect energy at the navel, and use Chi Self-Massage as in the previous meditation.

Hold the Palms Above the Microcosmic Orbit Points

This method works on the aura level of your energy field. In all other respects, it is the same as touching the points.

Preparations. As before.

Microcosmic Orbit

1. Bring the hands above the navel, with the palms facing inward about 2 to 6 inches away from the navel. Hold them there until you feel energy radiating from the center of the palms into the navel. The center of the palm is energetically connected to the heart (Figure 6-14).

2. Move both palms down to cover the sexual center (Figure 6-15).

3. Move the left palm to cover the sacrum. The right palm remains at the sexual center (Figure 6-16).

4. Move both palms along the Microcosmic Orbit pathway, stopping above the Door of Life, Jade Pillow, crown, Third Eye, palate, throat center, heart, solar plexus, and navel. Stop long enough at each point to feel pulsing and vibration (Figures 6-17 through 6-20).

5. Repeat steps 1 through 4 as many times as you like.

Conclusion. Gather and collect energy at the navel, and use Chi Self-Massage as in the previous meditation.

Rock Forward and Back to Activate the Front and Back Channels

This method involves moving the body as if you were in a rocking chair. You rock back as the energy ascends the Governor Channel and rock forward as it descends the Functional Channel.

Preparations. As before.

Microcosmic Orbit

1. Be aware of the navel as you inhale.

2. Exhale slowly and deeply, and at the same time rock the upper body forward and direct the energy from the navel down to the perineum.

3. As you inhale slowly and deeply, rock back and gently draw the energy up the spine all the way to the crown.

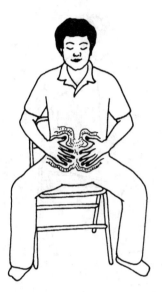

Figure 6-14. Palms above the navel center

Figure 6-15. Palms above the sexual center

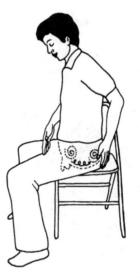

Figure 6-16. Right palm above the sexual center and left palm over the sacrum

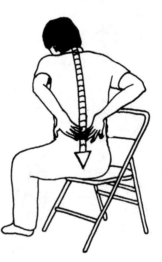

Figure 6-17. Palms over the Door of Life

Figure 6-18. Right palm over the base of the skull and left palm above the mid-eyebrow

Figure 6-19. Palms over the crown

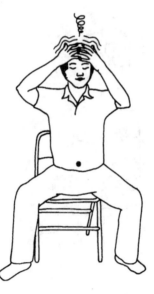

Figure 6-20. Palms over the mid-eyebrow

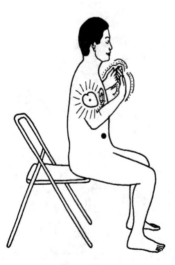

Figure 6-21. Palms over the heart

4. Exhale slowly, rock forward and guide the energy down the front channel to the perineum.

5. Repeat steps 3 and 4 as many times as you like.

6. When you are ready to finish your meditation, exhale, rock forward, and bring the energy back to the navel.

Conclusion. Gather and collect energy at the navel, and use Chi Self-Massage as in the previous meditation.

Circulate the Microcosmic Orbit with Internal Breathing

Chi, the Chinese word for energy, also means breath. Chi can refer to external breathing (through the lungs) or the internal breath that flows through the energy channels, and indeed they are connected in many subtle ways.

Practicing the Microcosmic Orbit using Internal Breathing means that you guide the Chi with the mind and intention alone. You breathe naturally and let the Chi move at its own pace. You do not need to coordinate the movement of Chi with your breath.

Practicing the Microcosmic Orbit using Internal Breathing is a more advanced way of practice. You will probably find that this method works easily after you have practiced the previous methods for a while. In fact, you may find that you evolve to the Internal Breathing method spontaneously and naturally after practicing the other methods.

Knock the teeth together and press the tongue to the roof of the mouth

We have already used this method in the first meditation, and we mention it here to emphasize that this is a special technique to help connect the upper Magpie Bridge at the palate, the place where the Governor Channel and the Functional Channel meet. Once you have learned to connect these two channels, you can dispense with this method.

1. If you are having difficulty bringing the Chi down from the Third Eye to the palate, touch the tip of the tongue to the roof of the mouth. Press the tongue to the palate and then release the tension. Do this 9 to 36 times and feel the electric charge pass from the palate to the tongue.

2. Lightly knock the teeth together 18 to 36 times, and then clench and release them. This vibrates the bones and activates the bone marrow to help transport the Chi through the denser matter of the bones. Let the energy radiate into the palate.

Remember, don't knock too hard if you have a lot of fillings in your teeth!

Colors and visualization

With this method we are truly awakening the healing light. It is not generally used in the basic Microcosmic Orbit meditation, but will be used extensively in the following chapters. You will connect with the light frequencies of Heaven Chi, Earth Chi, and the Cosmic Force to amplify, energize, and widen your Microcosmic Orbit.

SUMMARY

Stay at this level of opening and circulating in the basic Microcosmic Orbit for at least two to four weeks before proceeding to the advanced practices in the following chapters. Remember: all the proceeding practices are variations on the basic practice presented in this chapter. Spend as much time as you need to fully awaken and really *feel* the healing energy of your Original Chi, and to learn to feel its circulation through your Governor and Functional Channels. Do not be in a hurry to go further. You must get your basic energy wiring in place before working with practices that boost your fundamental energy.

Although the meditation is simple, the benefits are amazing. With regular practice, your mind will become calmer and clearer and your body will feel wonderful and healthy. Chronic aches and pains often disappear, and many people experience healing at a variety of levels.

These claims may seem extravagant, but no leap of faith is needed to determine whether the benefits are real or not. The proof is in your own experience; the results speak for themselves. As you learn to control your life-force, you will gradually improve your entire physical being. As you open yourself to the energies of the universe, circulating them through your body, you will eventually experience a universal connection with all things.

Chapter 7

EARTH ENERGY AND THE MICROCOSMIC ORBIT

WORKING WITH EARTH ENERGY

Chi is like electricity. In fact, recent Western research suggests Chi may actually be the bioelectric force governing all life and movement in the body. As one begins to practice redirecting the Chi by means of the mind/eyes/heart, yoga, Chi Kung postures, or special movements, the Chi current can become very powerful. The mind/eyes/heart can gather and focus the Chi just as a magnifying glass can gather and focus the rays of the sun, making the energy more concentrated and intense. If you "wire" the energy of the body, the need for grounding arises, otherwise serious problems may occur. Drawing in the earth's energy is stabilizing and Yin. We can send excess Yang and sick energy into the earth. We can also absorb cool Yin healing earth energy directly into the body.

How Grounding Works

Electrical energy is powerful and must be treated with caution and respect. Electricity activates nearly every convenience in the modern world, from the spark plugs and batteries in cars, to computers, lights, stoves, refrigerators, and air conditioners. Electricity is extraordinarily helpful, but it can also harm or even kill us if we disregard its safety rules and precautions.

One of the most important rules is: the higher the voltage, the greater the need for grounding. Not all lower-voltage appliances require a ground wire, but higher-voltage equipment such as washers, dryers, power tools, and heavy machinery invariably have ground wires (Figure 7-1).

Figure 7-1. The galaxy supplies the energies that the earth needs to recharge itself, but when we drain our planet's resources, the earth loses the ability to recharge itself.

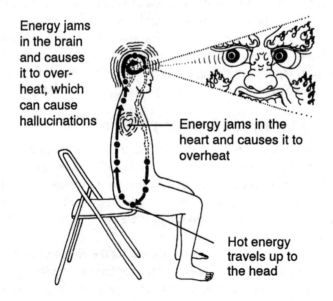

Energy jams in the brain and causes it to overheat, which can cause hallucinations

Energy jams in the heart and causes it to overheat

Hot energy travels up to the head

Figure 7-2. Kundalini syndrome

Our Chi works in a similar way. In the normal day-to-day life of most people, "grounding the Chi" is beneficial but not essential. When one undertakes practices that focus, direct, and increase the flow of Chi, grounding is a critical factor in maintaining a safe and balanced practice.

Chi, like electricity, tends to become hotter, or more Yang, as it increases in intensity. By contrast, earth energy is cool and Yin. When we connect our energy flow to that of the earth, we can discharge excess Yang energy into the earth. We can also absorb the cool Yin energy of the earth directly into our bodies to tonify the kidneys' Yin and blend it with our hot Chi to cool or balance it. It is much like adjusting the water temperature in the bathtub: if the water is too hot, add more cold; if too cold, add more hot.

By keeping our energy balanced in this way, we are able to effectively and safely manage and circulate greater amounts of Chi.

Just as larger and more powerful engines have more cylinders and consume more energy, we can become more productive and increase our spiritual potentials as we develop the ability and capacity to handle greater amounts of Chi.

In the higher-level practices of the Healing Tao, you can learn to draw Chi from outside sources: the sun, moon, earth, stars, Five Elements or Five Major Forces of heaven and earth, trees, plants, and animals. Drawing in, absorbing, and digesting this outer Chi greatly strengthens the energy body and is very beneficial in this life and the next. All these practices require one to learn to ground oneself and to conserve, balance, and transform the various types of Chi inherent in the body, including emotional and sexual energy, before trying to manage large amounts of Chi from outside sources.

Side Effects of Ungrounded Energy Practices

Kundalini Psychosis

Without grounding, the practitioner may experience many negative side effects from energy practices. Among the many possible side effects, "Kundalini psychosis" (also known as "Kundalini syndrome" Figure 7-2.) is one of the most common. Kundalini psychosis occurs when too much hot or Yang Chi rushes up the spine (or right or left psychic channel) to the brain and gets stuck there. Symptoms include intense heat and/or pressure in the head or heart, visual and auditory hallucinations, paranoia, disorientation, obsessive thinking, and insomnia. These symptoms can persist for days, weeks, or even longer.

Some people have experienced Kundalini psychosis spontaneously, without having done any energy practices at all. Others have activated it accidentally through recreational drug use. There are also some who have triggered Kundalini psychosis as a result of doing meditation practices that do not emphasize balanced energy circulation. Hakuin Zenji, the father of the Japanese Rinzai school of Zen Buddhism, wrote in his famous book *The Embossed Tea Kettle* about the "Zen illness" that frequently afflicted his monks and nearly killed him. Hakuin finally went to a Taoist hermit for a cure.

In modern times, people who experience Kundalini psychosis usually do not know what is causing the problem and are often diagnosed as psychotic. Many have been institutionalized in psychiatric hospitals and treated, usually unsuccessfully, with strong medication and psychotherapy. Because the root of this disorder is actually energetic, the most effective cure for Kundalini psychosis is to lead the energy back down from the head to the navel or soles of the feet. This is accomplished by opening the Microcosmic Orbit.

Bringing the energy down is much easier if one learns grounding techniques. Earth energy, Yin and magnetic, helps attract the energy downward. One can also draw the Yin earth energy upward; this cools the heat in the head and increases the kidneys' Yin power. The rapidity and effectiveness of this cure can be dramatic; often symptoms are reduced almost immediately, and total cures can be brought about within two or three weeks, if not days.

Other Side Effects

Other problems that can occur from lack of grounding include overheating, high blood pressure, headaches, heart palpitation or arrhythmia, lack of focus on the details of life, distractedness, or a general sense of "spiciness." All these symptoms can usually be effectively prevented through the simple technique of opening the Microcosmic Orbit and learning to connect to the energy of Mother Earth (Figure 7-3).

You may need to practice more to vent any excess energies (or negative emotional energies) that tend to stick in the heart or in the head when the Microcosmic Orbit is first opened.

Figure 7-3. Rooting to Mother Earth's energy

Connecting with Earth Energy: Grounding Training

Taoist adepts have traditionally emphasized a holistic approach to achieving harmony in life. A Taoist would not simply practice meditation alone; his or her practice would be reinforced with Chi Kung and/or martial arts exercise, proper diet, a peaceful life-style, and a healthy environment. To the Taoists, skill in meditation was enhanced and reinforced by martial arts training such as Tai Chi, Hsing I, and Pa Kua Chuan, and martial arts training was improved and supplemented by Chi Kung practice. These are all important cornerstones in building a good foundation for long life and spiritual growth.

Grounding and the Microcosmic Orbit Meditation

In the Healing Tao System, we begin to learn how to connect with earth energy in the Microcosmic Orbit meditation. The first stage in opening the Microcosmic Orbit is to open the basic loop of the Governor Channel and Functional Channel. In all subsequent practices, we bring more Chi into the Microcosmic Orbit by means of either the Inner Elixir or the Outer Elixir. For all the reasons previously mentioned, it is extremely important that the first connection made is the one to Mother Earth. You should avoid opening your connections to Heavenly Energy until after you have mastered grounding.

In the Microcosmic Orbit practice, we always meditate sitting in chairs with the soles of our feet solidly touching the ground. The legs and feet are the best ground wires to connect us to earth energy. We learn to sense the cool, blue, soft, Yin, gentle, kind sensation of Mother Earth's energy in a passive way as it percolates up through the feet and legs and enters the Microcosmic Orbit at the perineum. Even if you are in a room on the upper floor of a building, you will be able to ground through the building down into the earth, although direct contact with actual earth provides the strongest connection. Organic material like wood transmits a warmer quality of Chi than something like cement, which has a cold energy and can be draining. The earth's aura is so huge we take it for granted; you are swimming in it all the time. You can tune into it even if you are flying above the ground in an airplane.

We then allow this energy of Mother Earth to flow up the Governor Channel to the back of the head, pineal gland, and Bai Hui (crown) point and its corresponding point in the center of the brain, the thalamus gland. The crown is the most Yang part of our body, because it is closest to heaven (Yang). The ascending Yin energy of the earth helps cool, balance, relax, and refresh the hard-working Yang brain.

As the Microcosmic Orbit routes become more open and we are more easily able to receive and circulate the earth's Yin energy, we are then ready to open to other, more Yang energies with the confidence we are grounded enough to receive them safely.

In the Bible, the first human was called Adam. The name Adam means "earth creature." The Taoists were not the only ones to recognize our earthly connection! We are of the earth as part of our human birthright, regardless of our religion or philosophy. We therefore need never fear absorbing too much earth energy.

Mother Earth, the Great Recycler. The earth and its natural elements are unique in their ability to recycle and recharge energies. Dirty water can evaporate and become pure water. Trees take in carbon dioxide, which is poisonous to us, and convert it into the oxygen we need. Human and animal waste can be composted, transformed into fertilizer, and used to nurture new life.

When humans extract ores from the earth through mining, it drains the earth's reserves and energy. If mining is excessive, Mother Earth is often unable to fully recharge herself, and she becomes sick.

In Taoism, water and oil are regarded as elements of Mother Earth's blood. The minerals are like her organs, and the precious stones are like her glands. Trees might be considered the earth's veins and arteries. When we lose any of these, Mother Earth cannot properly recharge herself from the energies of the planets and stars. The sun, stars, and planets help provide what Mother Earth needs, as long as she has the strength to draw on their energies. When we drain the earth's energy, it is like taking apart a battery. As Mother Earth continues to lose her ability to recharge and recycle, we gradually lose our most powerful healing source.

Mother Earth, the Great Healer. Mother Earth that can transform our negative emotions and sick energies into nourishing energies for recharging herself. One way Mother Earth receives these sick energies is through our meditations, in which we send them down through the perineum and the soles of the feet, using mind/eye/heart power to direct them. If we dump them out in an emotional outburst, these energies simply infect the atmosphere until someone else walks by and picks them up, becoming sick or crazy.

Difference between feelings and emotions. Feelings and emotions are not the same, but they can be related. If a particular bad feeling is allowed to fester, it can eventually grow into a negative emotional state. The difference is that one can be more easily controlled than the other. Unchecked negative feelings can eventually lead to an uncontrollable emotional outburst. Although we may harbor feelings of anger, dislike, or distrust for others, we do not have to allow those feelings enough power to change our mental state. If we keep working to change negative feelings, we can prevent them from growing into negative emotions and possible outbursts. There is nothing wrong with good or bad feelings as long as we remain in control of them.

Most of us do not understand how this process works. People are all different; when we can iron out differences with other people, our angers and dislikes are controlled. There may be some bad feelings left, but no energy is allowed to empower them. If we instead pour out negative emotions in an outburst, there is no longer any way to change that energy, and its effect on the people around us usually creates more problems. Such an outburst is like pouring scalding water on other people. Once it is spilled, you cannot take it back.

Learning to feel negative energies. In Taoist practice, we start by feeling the different forms of Chi in the body, such as the energies of organs and glands and sexual energy. One of the most important steps in all exercises is to feel. This includes feeling good and bad sensations. We can nurture the good feelings to help nourish and maintain our bodies, and we can transform any bad feelings through the Inner Smile, Six Healing Sounds, and Microcosmic Orbit meditation. Taoists also use the inner eye to observe and direct negative energies down to Mother Earth, where they can be transformed into life-force. People who do not train themselves to feel and observe these energies cannot sense when a negative emotional outburst is likely to occur. They may not realize negative energies are accumulating to cause an emotional explosion. Once we release the energy behind an emotion in this way, it is of no use to us or to Mother Earth. It floats in space, waiting to attack those who are susceptible to it.

Humans help recharge Mother Earth. Humans are the only creatures who can absorb and utilize all Mother Earth's resources within their bodies. This makes us an important factor in healing the earth, as channels for healing forces. We draw in energies from the sun, moon, planets, and stars. These not only recharge us but also help recharge the earth. The magnetic power of our sexual energy actually attracts these energies, but we lose our Original Force and sexual energy through excessive ejaculations or menstruation, reducing our ability to draw in the heavenly forces. Additional stress weakens our channeling abilities even more. Internal blockages of the energy flow within our bodies can prevent Mother Earth from drawing in the external forces she needs to recharge.

Conserving, recycling, and transforming. Practicing the Microcosmic Orbit meditation is recycling. When you practice the Microcosmic Orbit and the Inner Smile, you compost any garbage energy and negative emotions within the body and recycle them into healthy life-force energy. If you instead release these energies from the body, dissipating the Original Force and sexual energy, there is no way for recycling to occur. We must to learn to conserve and recycle our own force so we can help others and Mother Earth.

Grounding and Iron Shirt Chi Kung

Although one is introduced to grounding and absorbing the earth's energy as an essential part of the Microcosmic Orbit meditation, mastery of the art of connecting to the earth comes through the more advanced practice of Iron Shirt Chi Kung I (Figure 7-4).

Iron Shirt Chi Kung was originally practiced to make the body capable of withstanding blows in combat without injury. It includes a variety of levels and techniques for achieving this. Today, it is mainly practiced for health and spiritual development.

Iron Shirt Chi Kung training emphasizes moving earth energy through the arm and leg routes of the Microcosmic Orbit pathway; this is known as the Greater Heavenly Cycle or Macrocosmic Orbit. For this reason, the Microcosmic Orbit Meditation is a prerequisite for the study of Iron Shirt Chi Kung.

In the practice of Iron Shirt Chi Kung, although you move the Chi through the same points as in the Microcosmic Orbit, the quality of the

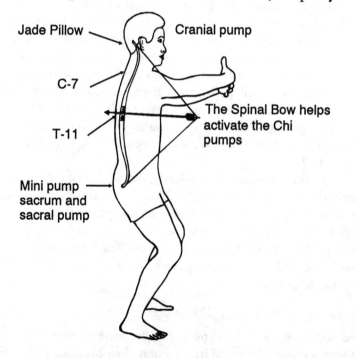

Jade Pillow

Cranial pump

C-7

The Spinal Bow helps activate the Chi pumps

T-11

Mini pump sacrum and sacral pump

Figure 7-4. Pushing the sacrum and slightly arching the spine will help activate the sacral pump.

Chi is thicker and cooler. This is because of the sensations of the elemental energy of the earth and water entering through the soles of the feet at Kidney-1 (Bubbling Spring or Yung Chuan point) and at Spleen-1 (on the medial side of the big toe), rising up through the perineum, and entering the spinal column.

Part of Iron Shirt training involves gently "packing" energy at the navel to increase the Earth Force in the body. This packing process is done carefully and without strain. One can then store the earth's Chi at the navel, which is the central area of the body and corresponds to the earth (the Five Elements of the Earth Force are correlated with the Five Directions: metal, west; water, north; wood, east; fire, south; and center, earth).

The originators of Iron Shirt Chi Kung reasoned that one's ability to withstand blows would improve if one could stand like a solid oak tree, as if rooted to the ground. Adversaries would have a hard time knocking down a well-rooted fighter, and the force of an opponent's blows would rebound, turning his force against himself.

To become proficient at Iron Shirt Chi Kung, one must seek the guidance of a competent teacher and then learn to perfectly align one's musculoskeletal structure with the magnetic force of the earth: gravity. One develops skill in Iron Shirt Chi Kung through daily practice in a variety of static standing postures. Each posture presents a slightly different energetic variation and teaches a new alignment skill. One thus learns to be grounded and rooted in a variety of positions, and to use the joints, bones, and meridian pathways to pulse the Earth Force into the physical body.

As you master Iron Shirt Chi Kung, you will become more and more sensitive to the subtleties and variations of earth energy, including weather, geology, power points, and so on, and you will learn to use them skillfully to your advantage, whether in business, daily life, or combat. Wearing your Iron Shirt will make you feel more confident, less easily intimidated; you will feel you can stand on your own two feet with the whole earth backing you up.

Grounding and Tai Chi Chi Kung

Once you have learned to connect to the earth's energy in the static standing postures of Iron Shirt, you may then progress to the moving practice of Tai Chi Chi Kung. Tai Chi Chi Kung teaches you how to

Figure 7-5. Tai Chi teaches us how to become rooted to Mother Earth through movement.

incorporate the sense of rootedness to the earth into the movements of everyday life (Figure 7-5).

Inner structure of Tai Chi and the Microcosmic Orbit. Training in Tai Chi Chi Kung emphasizes the "inner structure" of Tai Chi. Although all styles of Tai Chi and all true Tai Chi masters have this inner structure, few people achieve it today. This is largely because Tai Chi has become very popular, and in the hastiness to popularize and spread Tai Chi, the art has become watered down and divorced from its Taoist roots. Most students do not learn Tai Chi within the true holistic context of the Tao, which includes meditation, Chi Kung, and healing. Progress is painfully slow because, regrettably, most Tai Chi students learn only one isolated part of a whole Taoist system: relaxation. Learning the Microcosmic Orbit meditation and Iron Shirt Chi Kung first lays an excellent foundation for truly mastering the inner structure of Tai Chi.

Until I published my first book in English on opening the Microcosmic Orbit (*Awaken Healing Energy Through the Tao*, Aurora Books, 1983), many Chinese martial arts teachers made their students wait five or ten years before teaching them the Microcosmic Orbit as the "inner secret." I believe the process should be reversed: the master should teach the student the Microcosmic Orbit immediately, and then have Tai Chi training complement the inner work of meditation and amplify its power with integrated movement.

Activating the Chi pumps. The Tai Chi movements act as a slow-motion Chi pump that pulses a flow of Chi from the earth through the soles, legs, perineum pump, and sacrum pump, up the spine to the cranial pump, and back down the front of the body. The circular movements of the arms in Tai Chi enhance the opening of the channels and the flow of Chi through the arm routes of the Macrocosmic Orbit and the Belt Routes of the Fusion II formulas.

In addition, many of the specific points emphasized in Tai Chi Chi Kung are the same as in the Microcosmic Orbit meditation. For example, we constantly align our balance over the Bubbling Spring point on the sole of the foot and over the heel, and receive the Earth Force into the trunk through the Hui Yin (perineum) point. The angle of sacral tilt is crucial in allowing a clear doorway for the earth energy to move up into the spinal column. The alignment of the Chi Chung (T-11) point is vital in connecting the upper and lower body. The Ta Chui (C- 7) point must be open and aligned for the Chi to connect and flow from the torso to the arms. We also coordinate all the Tai Chi movements of our Three Bodies (physical, energy, and spirit) from the Lower Tan Tien (between the navel center, Door of Life, and sexual center).

The Tai Chi classics tell us to "sink the chest and pluck up the back." This becomes more meaningful when we know that "sink the chest" means to relax and lower the sternum by focusing on easing unnecessary tension at the heart point, and that to "pluck up the back" means to apply a backward counterforce at the Ta Chui (C-7) and Jade Pillow points.

The Tai Chi classics also tell us that "the head should be held as if suspended from above." This means that we want to align the Bai Hui (crown) point with the Hui Yin (perineum) point, so these points are effortlessly in line with the earth's gravity. When we practice, we feel the Universal Force coming in through the Bai Hui, and the gentle upward extension required in the Tai Chi classics is a natural result; it will automatically pull you up.

All these things seem very detailed and technical, but once you have grasped it, it becomes natural, a part of you. The purpose of Tai Chi is to teach you how to absorb the Chi through the major energy points, like the palms, soles, perineum, and mid- eyebrow, and to enhance your

Original Force. When you can do this, the detailed practices are not necessary.

When you finish a round of Tai Chi Chi Kung practice, your whole body may be tingling with sensations of warm or cool Chi. This is why we always stand still and quiet, circulate energy through the Microcosmic Orbit, and then collect energy at the navel after completing the movements of Tai Chi Chi Kung; allowing the Chi to flow through the Microcosmic Orbit helps us absorb and digest the Chi of Heaven, Earth, and the Higher Self that we draw in when we do Tai Chi correctly.

Through practicing the Microcosmic Orbit, you will develop a vivid kinesthetic familiarity with all the aforementioned points, points that are outside the scope of most people's normal body awareness. You will not only improve your mechanical sense of these points, but you will be aware of the degree of Chi flowing through them as well, an awareness that will help you accurately check and adjust your alignment as you practice your Tai Chi movements. This knowledge gives you one of the priceless tools you need to raise your skills in Tai Chi from run-of-the-mill mediocrity to the heights of martial arts mastery.

Tai Chi Chi Kung and self-defense. Tai Chi Chi Kung is practiced not only for health, strength, relaxation, and meditation; it is also a very effective art of self-defense. Once you can move earth energy through your bone and tendon structure, you become as immovable as a mountain in defense. When you attack, you have the strength of the earth behind each punch or throw.

Tai Chi masters are respected throughout the world for their powers and abilities. Much of this incredible skill comes from simply opening to the earth's energy, a power that is freely offered to everyone at all times. We need only learn how to tap it.

Tai Chi Chi Kung keeps the Chi pathways supple. In addition to teaching rooting and grounding, Tai Chi Chi Kung exercises the energy pathways of the body. Tai Chi Chi Kung practice helps keep the channels strong and supple and also aids in clearing blockages and tensions that would otherwise obstruct the smooth flow of Chi. Then Tai Chi Chi Kung is like doing "Microcosmic Orbit in motion."

With strong wiring and good grounding, you can progress more rapidly and with confidence to higher energy levels in Taoist meditation practice. The risk of negative side effects from the energy practices are minimized, and if they do occur, you have the tools to deal with them quickly and effectively.

PRACTICE
The Microcosmic Orbit:
Feeling Mother Earth's Energy

In this round of practicing the Microcosmic Orbit, you will learn the special techniques for connecting to the unlimited healing Chi of Mother Earth (*Di Chi* in Chinese). After beginning the Microcosmic Orbit meditation with Chi Kung Warm-Ups, the Inner Smile, and Warming the Stove, you absorb earth energy up through your legs to your "stove," or Tan Tien, and merge the earth energy with your own Original Energy. This will greatly strengthen and enhance your Original Chi. You can then circulate this combined, heightened energy through the Microcosmic Orbit.

You will also learn the practice of Fanning and Venting, an important method of purifying the body of sick energy by dispersing it down into the earth so the earth can absorb and transform it.

At first the practice may seem a little complex. Keep in mind that the details are for training purposes only. Once you have captured the sense of it, you will not need to go through all the steps; when you sit down to meditate, you will discover that the earth's energy comes to you effortlessly and automatically, as if it were happening by itself.

Figure 7-6. Picture the Original Force within you with a nose and a mouth and the ability to breathe in through them.

A. Preparations

1. Begin with Chi Kung Warm-Ups, Spinal Cord Breathing, and Spine Rocking.

2. Clear your emotions and warm up your internal organs with a round of the Six Healing Sounds. Do 2 or 3 repetitions of each sound.

3. Do the Inner Smile, with an emphasis on relaxing and developing awareness of your internal organs.

4. Follow the practice instructions for "Warming the Stove" in Chapter 4.

5. Make sure you feel your Original Force activated:

Condense your Chi in the Lower Tan Tien. As it becomes more concentrated, it will begin to expand, and you will feel pressure building at the spot of the Original Energy. Imagine the Original Energy has a mouth and nose and is breathing into your body through that spot (Figure 7-6). Now amplify the pulse you feel at the Original Energy spot. As you feel the pulse pumping, feel the suction drawing the sexual energy into the Tan Tien. Feel the sexual energy being drawn to you as if the Tan Tien were a powerful magnet.

6. Circulate your Chi in the basic Microcosmic Orbit to prepare yourself for receiving fresh energy from Mother Earth. You can use Small Sip Breathing, Internal Breathing, mind/eye power spiraling, or any of the techniques you have learned to enhance the sensation of Chi. Make sure you feel your Microcosmic Orbit is open before going on to the next step.

B. Feel the Force of Mother Earth Flow Through You

1. Massage the center of your palms (Figure 7-7), soles of your feet (Figure 7-8), perineum, and coccyx (Figure 7-9). Place the hands at the sides with the palms facing toward the earth, and place the soles of the feet flat against the floor. You can also put a marble or a small steel ball under each sole at the Bubbling Spring (Kidney-1) point to stimulate it.

Be aware of the Bubbling Spring point on the two soles. Picture two small pipes extended up to the Hui Yin point at the perineum, up to the kidneys and the Original Force (Figure 7-10).

Picture a pipe extending from the Lao Gong point on each palm to the heart center and down to the navel. The perineum, openings of the sexual center, anus, palms, and soles are gateways through which the nourishing energy of Mother Earth can flow into you.

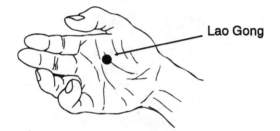

Figure 7-7. Massage the palm.

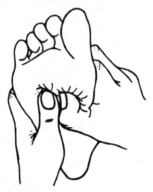

Figure 7-8. Massage the sole of the foot.

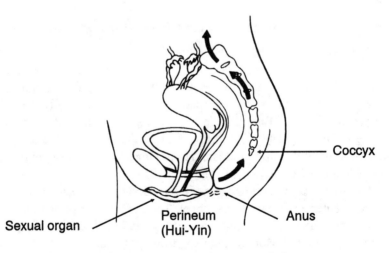

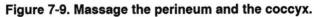

Figure 7-9. Massage the perineum and the coccyx.

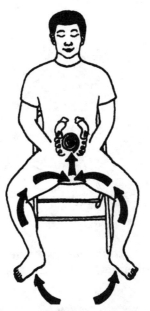

Figure 7-10. Rest. Be aware of the kidneys, and feel the Mother Earth force come up to fill the kidneys and the Original Force.

2. After a short time, you will begin to feel the palms and soles breathing by themselves. At the same time, you will feel the vagina and the perineum (Hui Yin) point start to naturally pull up and release in a pumping action, creating a suction in time with your breathing and/or the pulsing. You can also lightly contract and relax your eyes and pull up on the two gates of the sexual organs—the perineum and the anus—to help activate the pumping action (Figure 7-11). Do this 18 to 36 times, then exhale and rest.

3. Now focus your mind/eyes/heart about 95 percent on the Original Energy behind the navel, and about 5 percent on Earth Gates (perineum, sexual and anal openings, palms, and soles). Feel yourself grounded; feel connected to the earth. Relax. Feel your sitting bones connect to the earth. As you feel yourself sinking into the earth, you will also feel pulsing again. Water is the dominant energy of the planet, so you may sense Mother Earth's energy as a gentle blue force. The color blue is particularly healing to the bones and joints. Just relax and let it come in and up; feel the suction; feel the gentle blue earth energy pulsing into the navel, breathing in through the Five Earth Gates and pulsing and breathing into the Tan Tien ("stove") (Figure 7-12).

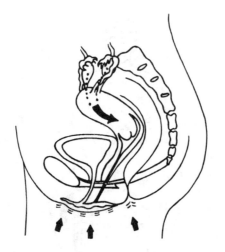

Figure 7-11. Lightly pull up the sexual organ, the perineum, and the anus.

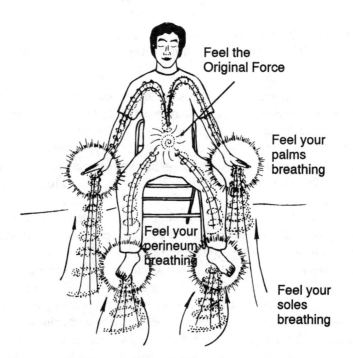

Feel the
Original Force

Feel your
palms
breathing

Feel your
perineum
breathing

Feel your
soles
breathing

Figure 7-12. Feel the five earth gates pulsing and breathing.

4. Mother Earth's energy strengthens the stove and enhances the Original Energy there. Feel the energy ball at the Tan Tien becoming more crystallized, more real. Your navel is connected to the earth now; your body feels connected to the body of Mother Earth.

5. Feel the Chi ball growing and expanding, filling the whole region between the navel, kidneys, and sexual center.

6. Finally, let the Original Energy radiate from the navel area and flow wherever it wants to go. As before, it may follow the path of the Microcosmic Orbit automatically, or it may flow in its own way. Just relax, and let it take its own course.

7. When you are ready to end your session, let the energy settle at the navel. Then finish and collect energy by spiraling at the navel.

C. Sedate the Heat of the Heart and Tonify the Kidneys' Yin

In this society, most people have overheating of the heart due to stress, pressure, impatience, and hatred. This drains out the kidneys' Yin, depleting the important reserve of basic life energy, the sexual energy. This exercise helps tone down the excess Yang so the cool earth Yin energy will rise automatically to the kidneys. Any time you feel the heart overheat, you can do this exercise to cool the heart (Figure 7-13) and strengthen the kidneys. This will make you feel calm yet energized.

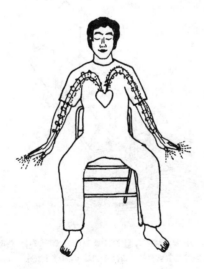

Figure 7-13. Sedate the heat of the heart.

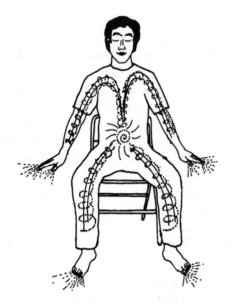

Figure 7-14. Exhale excess heat out to the tips of the fingers and toes.

Figure 7-15. Feel a nice, cool, gentle blue energy gathering like a pool of water around your feet.

1. Sit in the same position as above, palms facing down. Be aware of the heat in your heart.

2. Use the Heart's Sound, HAWWWWW. HAWWWWW down to the heart and let it spread inside both arms, down to the tips of the fingers. Do this 6 to 9 times. Feel the heart cool down.

3. HAWWWWW down to the heart and tips of the fingers; continue down to the tips of the toes (Figure 7-14). Use long, soft exhalations and feel comfortable.

Rest; be aware of the soles of your feet. Feel the Mother Earth Yin, gentle and kind. Blue energy will come by itself up the feet to the kidneys without any effort (Figure 7-15). Once the kidneys are filled with kidneys' Yin, the heart will calm and cool and balanced, the fire and water will be in harmony. The more you relax, the more Yin energy comes up through you with no effort. Do this 9 to 18 times.

NOTE: *The resting period is very important. Just rest and let the Mother Earth Yin energy come up to your kidneys. If you are very heated, sit in bathtub full of room-temperature water while you use this method.*

D. Transporting the Earth's Force Through the Microcosmic Orbit

While it is good to simply rest and allow the energy to flow in its own course through the body, you may want to use your mind to direct the Earth Force through the Microcosmic Orbit at this time. If so, please refer to the practice section in Chapter 6. The steps are the same, only this time you will feel your Original Chi reinforced and balanced by the earth's Chi.

You may notice the gentle blue Earth energy helps cool, smooth, and balance your Chi. Any time you feel any uncomfortable sensations of heat in the body during practice, just be aware of your connection to Mother Earth energy. Draw up more gentle blue energy from the earth and use your mind to direct it to that place of discomfort, pain, or sickness.

Yin Stage: Rest in the Original Chi

Rest. Just relax the mind and body. Find the neutral point in the center of the body; it could be at the navel, heart, or head, whatever feels the most neutral to you. Simply be there. Do nothing but absorb the fruits of having circulated the energy through the Microcosmic Orbit and having balanced your Chi flow. Allow the energy to do whatever it wants to do. It may reverse direction; it may flow to other areas of the body. The body may shake and vibrate, and you may hear high-pitched sounds. Spend five or ten minutes at this stage, giving yourself the chance to reap the benefits of your Microcosmic Orbit circulation: a sense of inner peace, calmness, and clarity. Let your physical body dissolve into your Original Chi, resting in the state of emptiness, making no effort whatsoever.

Gather and Collect Energy at the Navel

1. When you are ready to conclude your session, bring the energy to the navel and collect it, letting it return to the area behind the navel and in front of the kidneys to recharge your Original Force. Enjoy the comfortable, peaceful feeling you have created in your meditation. Feel the spaciousness inside your body and mind now that you have cleared out physical and mental tensions.

2. Conclude with Chi Self-Massage.

3. Get up slowly and carry this feeling with you into your activity. Whenever you start to feel sick or stressed, return your mind and your breath to the center. With regular practice, you can recapture this pleasant feeling at any time.

RETURNING SICK ENERGY TO THE EARTH

Fanning and Venting are ways of composting sick and emotional energies and returning them to Mother Earth. If you are able to transform them yourself, that is even better. But until you learn to regulate your own negative emotions with the Fusion of the Five Elements meditation, this will help you.

Fanning

Because tension causes a lot of sick, negative emotional energy to condense in the chest, the heart can easily become jammed. Long-term negative emotions such as hatred, impatience, and arrogance directly affect heart conditions and are a major cause of heart attacks. To protect yourself, you can activate the heart, draw the negative feelings and sick energy to the heart, and fan this energy out of the heart and body.

Purpose of Fanning

Taoists regard the soles of the feet, centers of the palms, fingertips, and tips of the toes as having a connection with the heart. Fanning

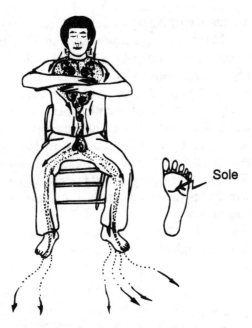

Figure 7-16. Fan sick energy and negative emotions from the heart to the soles of the feet.

negative and sick energy involves moving the energy from the heart down to the tips of the toes and fingers (Figure 7-16). The theory is that when the sick energy is fanned down to the toes and fingers, the soles and toes connect with Mother Earth, who can accept the sick and negative energy and then utilize and transform it into useful energy. If the negative energy is expressed as emotions and dumped from the heart onto someone else, it cannot be received by Mother Earth and put to good use. Instead, these emotions will be passed on to other people involved in the person's life, which can cause sickness for them as well.

Position and Practice

Fanning originates in the upper diaphragm and the mind. With the palms facing down, raise the left hand to the chest at the level of the heart center, about one and one-half inches from the top of the sternum. Place the right hand parallel to and above the left hand, aligning the Lao Gong points of both hands.

1. Practice the Heart's Sound (HAWWWWW) and feel the heat from the heart start to burn, drawing in any negative feelings.

2. Exhale this energy (using the Heart's Sound) as you slowly lower both hands. Feel the negative energies burn out. Continue to exhale the energy down to the perineum, palms, backs of both feet, and tips of the toes and fingers. Then perceive Mother Earth absorbing it. Rest the palms on the knees, fingertips pointed toward the toes. Look down to the toes and feel a cloudy, gray, and cold or chilly energy go out. Rest again. Be sure to take a long time to rest, because this resting time is very important.

3. Start over again by returning both hands to the heart level. Practice 18 to 36 times, for a total of five to ten minutes. As you clear yourself of the dirty, sick, negative energy, you will feel empty, but in a good mood. Feel the Heavenly Energy as a golden light coming down through the head and filling the body.

4. Rest for a while. You will also feel Mother Earth's Energy, a blue color, coming up through the soles of the feet.

Venting

Purpose of Venting

When negative emotions cause sickness in the organs, venting is another good practice to remove the undesirable energy. Venting gets rid of emotions and sick energy from all the other organs (Figure 7-17 and (Figure 7-18). Because fingers and toes are connected with all the organs and glands (Figure 7-19), sick energy tends to stagnate there, making them feel numb.

The kidneys connect to the soles, and the bladder to your little toes. Fear in the kidneys and bladder can be vented to change the color of their energy from a cloudy blue energy to a bright blue.

The liver connects to the big toes, and the **gall bladder** to the fourth toes. Anger can produce cloudiness in the liver and gall bladder's color, which can be changed from a cloudy green back to a bright, clear green.

The heart connects to the little finger, and the **small intestines** to the little finger. Hate can produce cloudiness in the heart's and small intestine's color, which can be changed from a cloudy red back to a bright, clear red.

The lungs connect to the thumb, and the **large intestine** to the index finger. Sadness and depression can produce cloudiness in the lung's and large intestine's color, which can be changed from a cloudy white back to a bright, clear white.

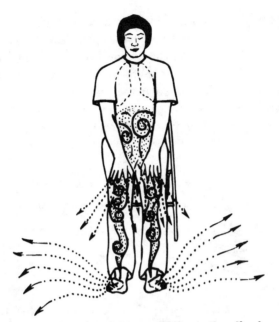

**Figure 7-17. Vent sick energy from the diaphragm
to the lower abdomen.**

**Figure 7-18. Vent sick energy from the organs
to the lower abdomen and the toes.**

The **spleen** connects to the big toes, and the **stomach** to the second toes. Worry can produce cloudiness in the spleen's and stomach's color, which can be changed from a cloudy yellow back to a bright, clear yellow.

The **pericardium** connects to the middle fingers. The purpose of the pericardium is to help cool down the heart.

The **Triple Warmer** connects to the fourth or ring fingers. It is closely connected to the glands and is the common repository for all the organs' excess energy.

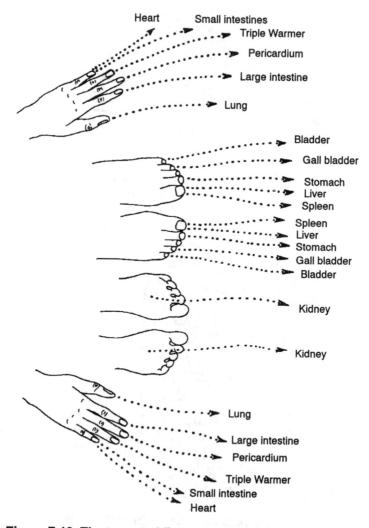

Figure 7-19. The toes and fingers correspond to the organs.

Position and Practice

After you finish Fanning as above, remain in the same sitting position to begin the Venting exercise.

1. Place the hands on the knees. Keep the fingers slightly spread and pointed toward the toes.

2. Place the feet parallel to each other and point the toes up. Be aware of the area two or three inches above and directly between the big toes. Be aware of the tips of the big toes, then of all the toes and tips of the fingers.

3. If you have sick energy affecting an organ, look at Figure 2- 19 to determine the toes or fingers that correspond to that organ. During Venting, you can emphasize the fingers or toes corresponding to the organ in which you have sick or emotional energy to send more of the energy out of the body. For example, if you have a heart problem, you can concentrate on the little fingers. Feel the cloudy gray energy exiting through those fingers.

4. Practice the Triple Warmer's Sound (HEEEEE) down to the navel, perineum, palms, toes, and fingers (Figures 7-22 and 7-23). Feel the vibration of the HEEEEE sound at and moving out of the tips of the fingers and toes.

5. Gradually feel you can see the steaming, dark, cloudy, cold or chilly, sick emotional energy emerging from the toes and fingers.

6. Picture it becoming brighter and brighter. Continue to look at the point between the big toes to see more sick energy and negative feelings emerge.

7. Be aware of the liver as you inhale fresh air, visualized as a green mist. See it become a bright green as it fills the liver, then the entire body, with green.

8. Be aware of the spleen and pancreas, and see them glow bright yellow as you inhale a yellow mist .

9. Be aware of the lungs, and see them glow with a white light as you inhale a cool white mist.

10. Be aware of the heart, and see it glow a bright red as you inhale a red mist.

11. Be aware of the kidneys; see them glow with a bright blue light as you inhale a cool blue mist.

Each organ is a "doorway" for a certain color and healing frequency. Practice filling the organ and then the entire body with different-colored mists or rays.

SUMMARY

Spend at least one to two weeks practicing with Mother Earth's energy before going on to the next stage. Cultivate a strong sense of the cooling and balancing of the earth energy; it will help you at all levels of Taoist meditation and Chi Kung practice. We speak of needing a good foundation to build something on, and there is no better foundation than the earth on which to build a strong, solid, and safe meditation practice.

Many people just do Chi Kung, generate heat, feel good, and never gather or condense the Chi. This is not good energy cultivation. Instead, skillful energy cultivation should be like farming. First the farmers plant their rice. Then they allow it to grow. But at this stage, they are not yet finished. They must let it come to ripeness, and then they must harvest it at just the right time, when there is no rain. Having harvested it, they must store it properly, so it will not get wet and sprout. If they store it improperly, within two weeks it will sprout and go to waste.

Some Chi Kung and martial arts practitioners do not create a place to store their energy properly. The energy becomes overly intense and flows in every direction, and they begin to burn themselves out or to become emotional and arrogant. They crave the coolness of Yin; it is common for such practitioners to overindulge in sex, alcohol, or drugs, or to associate primarily with people who are Yin so they can dominate them. They never learned that the purest, best, and most balanced source of Yin is right at their feet—Mother Earth's energy.

Once the farmers have gathered and stored their grain properly, they are still not finished. They have to grind it and take it to market; they have to create a channel to transfer the rice to its destination. If they do not take the rice to market, it is of no use.

In the same way, once your energy has matured through regular practice and has been gathered and stored, you need to direct it and open your energy channels so it can flow to wherever it is needed. Otherwise, it will tend to stagnate and cause problems. If you conscientiously follow the steps of practice in the right sequence, you can safely progress to the highest levels.

Chapter 8

THE COSMIC FORCE: Higher Self Energy and the Microcosmic Orbit

WHAT IS HIGHER SELF (COSMIC) ENERGY?

Heaven, Earth, and Humanity: The Grand Trinity

It is Taoist belief that humanity is as vital in the "grand scheme" of the universe as heaven and earth (the primordial energies of Yang and Yin). Taoists also observed that, unlike heaven and earth, which appear to last forever, the physical human life-span is limited. They reasoned that this was not always so, that humans have the ability to achieve immortality, and that our current mortality is the result of having lost our state of harmony with nature, the universe, and the Tao. We need only restore that harmony to be as immortal as heaven and earth and to fulfill our rightful destiny as part of the Grand Trinity.

The human soul is a living ray of the cosmic soul; it is as if the original cosmic beam of sound/light divided itself into 6 billion individual rays or souls on planet earth. That is why we speak of the energy of human beings as both human and cosmic energy. The universe is the macrocosm, and humans are a microcosm of the universe. The more accurately we reflect the natural patterns of the universe, the more we are in harmony with the Tao. The more we are in harmony with the Tao, the more easily we can open to, unite with, absorb, and enjoy the limitless energy of the universe. Harmony with the Tao is the key to immortality; Taoist sages therefore sought to understand these universal patterns and reflect them in their own being. Their goal was to become the process of the universe. Practically, this meant learning to tap the universal energies at all times, and, with this radiant force integrated into their being, to act for the purpose of helping all other creatures realize their own innate immortality.

Wu Chi

To understand ourselves as the microcosm, it is helpful to have a picture of how things unfold in the macrocosm. In the beginning, before heaven and earth even existed, there was a state of undifferentiated and un-manifest potential. The Taoists call this Wu Chi, or the Tao. In the Chinese picture character for this term, "Wu" means "nothing," and "Chi" means "absolute"; therefore Wu Chi means "absolute nothingness," a state before Yin and Yang even existed. Wu Chi is without boundary; it is pure openness, unobstructed, the possibility of infinite space, the vessel of the whole universe that is invisible and formless (Figure 8-1).

Yin and Yang

Then, somehow, something stirred in the Wu Chi. Wu Chi reached a certain critical mass, and it exploded and manifested. This Primordial Duality took two forms: Yang and Yin. In the first nanosecond of their birth from Wu Chi, these two forces were separate, and then they collided with immeasurable impact and fused. Their union resulted in a third force: Chi. The fusion of Yin and Yang and the Chi created by this fusion is called Tai Chi, or "Supreme Harmony" (Figure 8-1).

The Primordial Breath

The Original Chi of the Universe (said to have first manifested as inner sound and light) is also called Primordial Breath, Primordial Chi, Original Light, Clear Light, Source Chi, Light of Creation, or Neutral Force (Figure 8-1). In the Healing Tao, we access this energy from all three major forces in meditation. The Original Chi that emanates within our Cosmic or Higher Self energy is the easiest for us to access because it is closest in vibration to our "lower" or physical self and ego mind. It is from the essence of this Higher or Cosmic Self that we ourselves are made, just as individual particles of light crystallize from a long wave of energy. In the same way, the mind functions from these invisible cosmic waves of energy, even as it appears that the body is solid.

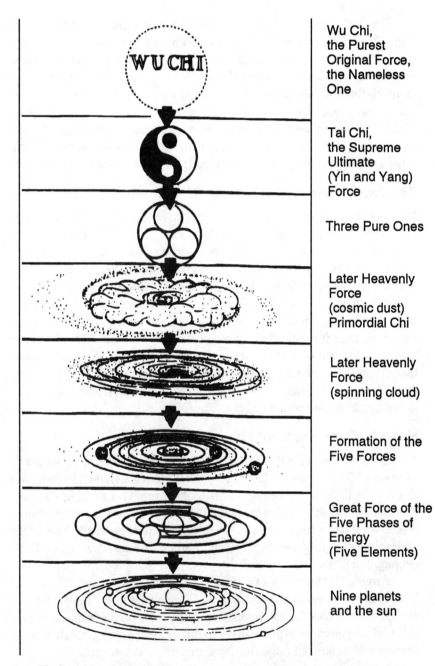

Wu Chi,
the Purest
Original Force,
the Nameless
One

Tai Chi,
the Supreme
Ultimate
(Yin and Yang)
Force

Three Pure Ones

Later Heavenly
Force
(cosmic dust)
Primordial Chi

Later Heavenly
Force
(spinning cloud)

Formation of the
Five Forces

Great Force of the
Five Phases of
Energy
(Five Elements)

Nine planets
and the sun

Figure 8-1. Wu Chi, Yin, Yang, and the Five Phases of Energy

The Original Chi of the Universe thus encompasses both Yin and Yang. It is the balance point, the child of Yin and Yang, the result of their union, the neutral force or matrix in which all creation occurs as a play of positive and negative forces. From the Original Chi of the Universe came all the multiple forms of matter and energy. According to the Big Bang theory, one of the first distillations of this energy was stars. Many of these early stars later became supernovas and exploded, sending their particles off into space. These particles joined with other particles from other galaxies, forming new molecules and new types of energies.

The Ten Thousand Things: The Birth of the Universe

Many of these particles clustered around stars and planets as they were drawn into the orbits of these heavenly bodies. Some of these compounds eventually drifted down to the planetary surface. In the case of our planet, some of the particles formed gases, which eventually became the earth's atmosphere. Others formed the beginnings of topsoil, making plant life possible. In this unique setting, conditions conducive to the formation of life were created, and eventually, along with plants and animals, humans emerged. Thus it is said that we are children of the stars. The essences and elements that compose our bodies are drawn from the cosmic dust that originated in the stars, and our minds are illumined by the living intelligence of the heavens, a stellar pattern imprinted on our individual genetic code at the moment of our conception.

Heaven, Earth and Man: The Three Pure Ones

"Man, Heaven, and Earth, all three, are mutually related, with the heart as master" (Huai-nan-tzu, Chapter 7, "On Seminal Essence, Breath and Spirit"). In the earliest Taoist writings of Huang Ti, Lao Tzu, Chuang Tzu, and the I Ching, dating from about 2500 B.C. onward, the first three forces to emerge from Wu Chi were called Heaven, Earth, and Man (Primordial Yang, Primordial Yin, and Primordial Light or Original Chi) (Figure 8- 2).

Around 700 years after the time of Lao Tzu (shortly after 100 A.D.), Buddhism was introduced into China. For the first time, Taoists had to compete with a new foreign religion for imperial favor and support. From the philosophical and meditative tradition of Taoism sprouted new branches of organized religious movements and Taoist sects.

Many of the energies previously recognized as impersonal forces of nature were remade into gods that could compete with the colorful deities imported from India. Thus, in the writings of Chang Tao-Ling (said to have been channeled information from Lao Tzu), the founder of religious Taoism and the first Taoist pope of the Heavenly Master sect, the energies of Heaven, Earth, and Man became known as the Three Pure Ones, the lords of Heaven, Earth, and Man. Chang Tao-Ling also said that by receiving these three spirits into the microcosm of the body, one becomes a child of the Tao.

In religious Taoism (Tao Na), the Three Pure Ones are deified as the three highest gods of the Taoist pantheon and are said to reside in the highest of the nine levels of the heavenly realms. The Three Pure Ones are also said to exist as giant stars in the center of the universe, constantly radiating their Chi, which pervades everything in time and space (Figure 8-3). Because of the popularity of religious Taoism, the names of the

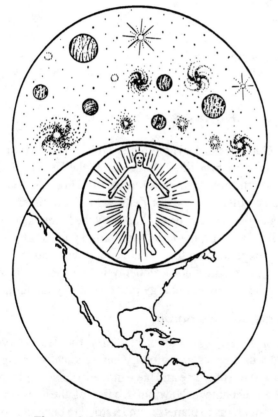

Figure 8-2. Heaven, Earth, and Man

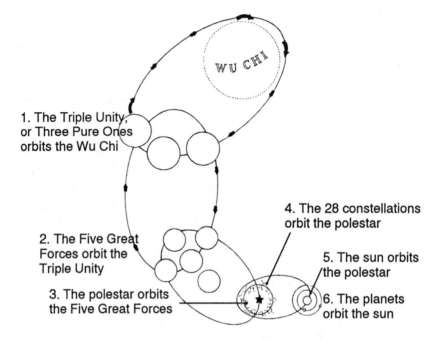

Figure 8-3. The universal orbit

Three Pure Ones became synonymous with Heaven, Earth, and Man throughout the many branches of Taoism. In the Healing Tao, however, although we often refer to these forces as the Three Pure Ones, it is not necessary to see them as gods or deities. You can understand them as primordial energies that can be explained by the language of physics and astronomy. In any event, the important thing is not what you believe; it is feeling and experiencing the cosmic energy that saturates your living being at every moment. Taoist alchemy is one method to regain your sensitivity to the patterns of energy movement in your subtle bodies.

The Universe as a Hologram

Within the last century (and particularly the last 25 years), new breakthroughs in physics and biology have radically changed the way scientists look at the universe and have moved Taoism and physics closer together. The mechanical, Newtonian view of the universe, in which everything from atoms to planets is understood to be made up of separate solid objects, has dissolved in light of relativity and field theory. What used to be called "things" are now viewed as both waves and particles;

our world is made up not of solid objects but of wavelike patterns of interconnections. The universe is now thought to be a dynamic web of interwoven energy patterns with an underlying yet unmanifest order as its foundation. The entire universe is seen as one inseparably interconnected whole.

Physicist-turned-metaphysician Barbara Ann Brennan says in her recent book, *Hands of Light*, "If the universe is indeed composed of such a web, there is (logically) no such thing as a part. Thus we are not separated parts of a whole. We are a Whole."

In 1971, Dennis Gabor received a Nobel Prize for constructing the first hologram, which is essentially a three-dimensional photograph made of light. Every part of the hologram is an exact reflection of the whole, and each part will rebuild the entire image. In his book *The Implicate Order*, physicist David Bohm maintains that the model of the hologram is the best way to understand the holistic view of the universe.

Contemporary biologists such as Karl Pribram theorize that our brain also works holographically—that it structures and transmits sensory impressions throughout the system so that each fragment can reconstruct the entire picture of the whole. Dr. Pribram goes on to apply the same holographic model of the brain's operation to describe the operation of the universe. If the universe is like a hologram, each part of the universe reflects the whole. Events that appear to be separated in time and space are actually simultaneous and occur everywhere in time and space. This coincides with the Taoist understanding that all the energies or "gods" that exist throughout the heavens also exist simultaneously within the microcosm of our human body. The Three Pure Ones, therefore, do not simply exist in some remote part of the universe; they are ever-present in us, too. They are an integral part of each human being.

The Microcosmic Orbit:
A Mirror of the Universe Within the Body

In Chinese, the Microcosmic Orbit is called *Xiao Jou Tien* (pronounced Shao Jo Tyen). This is translated as Smaller Heavenly Cycle. The Taoists saw the cosmos as having nine different levels or dimensions and also saw a perfect mirroring of the heavens contained in the human body. Little Heaven is the equivalent Chinese term for microcosm; it is the Taoist way of saying "As above, so below"—as it is in the universe, so it is in the human body. The practice of circulating light/energy in the Microcosmic Orbit is a way of reconnecting these different dimensions

313

of our selves, of rejoining our inner universe with the outer universe (Figure 8-4).

The Three Pure Ones are lords of the Three Tan Tiens. In traditional religious Taoism, the Three Pure Ones were also called the lords or Emperors of the Three Tan Tiens (literally, Cinnabar Fields or

Figure 8-4. God exists within us:
The Inner Universe and the Outer Universe

Elixir Fields), which were the three primary focal points in the human body for alchemical transformation of energy. The Three Pure Ones are said to reside and rule in these three places within each person: the Upper Tan Tien, or Palace of Ni Wan, in the brain; the Middle Tan Tien, or Crimson Palace, at the heart; and the Lower Tan Tien, or Yellow Court, at the navel area.

The Three Pure Ones become the Three Treasures in Man. On the human level, the Three Pure Ones become the Three Treasures: Ching (body essence and sexual energy), Chi (life-force energy), and Shen (spirit) (Figure 8-5). Shen is the most subtle and intangible of our Three Treasures and so corresponds to the Upper Tan Tien and the force of Heaven; it is predominantly Yang. Chi, the vital breath of life energy, is more subtle than Ching, yet more condensed than Shen. Chi corresponds to the Middle Tan Tien, the soul, and the Higher Self/Cosmic Energy. Ching, our life essence and sexual energy, corresponds to the lower Tan Tien. As it is the most condensed of our Three Treasures, it relates to the force of Earth, and is mostly Yin. All these have their Yin and Yang

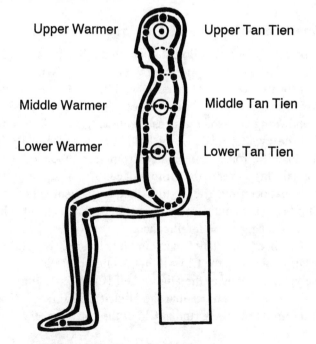

Upper Warmer   Upper Tan Tien

Middle Warmer   Middle Tan Tien

Lower Warmer   Lower Tan Tien

Figure 8-5. Three Tan Tiens

315

aspects, as even pure Yin contains a seed of Yang, which will grow as the Yin evolves. Mother Earth's physical planet is thus matched by a "Father" Spirit component of the Earth.

There is yet another set of correspondences between Heaven, Earth, and Man and the organs of the body. This is the Triple Warmer concept of Chinese medicine, which divides the human body into three zones of energetic activity. In this scheme, Shen corresponds to the parts of the body from the diaphragm up, to the heart, and to Heaven; Chi corresponds to the area between the diaphragm and navel, to the stomach/spleen, and to Man; and Ching corresponds to the parts of the body below the navel, to the kidneys, and to Earth. Chi Kung, herbs, Five Element nutrition, meditation, Chi Nei Tsang, and acupuncture help regulate the balance among these three centers of the physical body.

Although the Triple Warmers regulate the vital organs, it is in the alchemical cauldrons of the Three Tan Tiens or Elixir Fields that the vital substances of Ching, Chi, and Shen are brought to be refined, purified, and transformed in the Taoist inner alchemical path of spiritual development.

Human Genesis Reflects the Cosmic Unfolding

Our personal genesis follows a pattern similar to the beginning of the universe. Before conception, we were nothing (Wu Chi). A desire for human birth arose spontaneously within the Cosmic Soul. Then, our father (Yang energy) and our mother (Yin energy) made love, and their Yin and Yang orgasm essences combined, creating a brand-new cell, called the zygote, made up of both energies (Tai Chi). Our uniquely individual life-force Chi created from that union of egg and sperm (Original Chi) powered the trillions of cellular divisions (the ten thousand things) that occurred after fertilization, until eventually that one cell had multiplied to the countless number of cells that make up a human being, with form, energy, and intelligence.

The most important Chi in our body is our Original Chi (Yuan Chi). Our Original Chi is the Chi within the microcosm of our body that most closely corresponds to the Higher Self (Cosmic) Energy on the macrocosmic level. Remember that the Higher Self Energy (Cosmic Chi) is also referred to as the Original Chi of the Universe (Figure 8-6).

We Are Nourished Daily by the Cosmic Chi

Food and air are derived from Cosmic Chi. To sustain our life and to replenish our Original Chi, we need to take in other forms of Chi or energy on a daily basis. Much of the Chi we take in comes from the food we eat and the water we drink. All the food we eat originates with plant life, which in turn derives its energy from the topsoil, the atmosphere, and light. Thus, all the forms of nutrition we take in are related to Cosmic Chi.

Ions: Our subtle diet. We also take in Cosmic Chi in the air we breathe. This is primarily in the form of oxygen, but another subtle and less well understood form of Chi in the air is vital to the health of every bodily process: ions. Ions are electrically charged particles essential for the functioning of the nervous system and blood circulation. The electrical charges of the ions are conducted in the body by electrolytes or salts, such as calcium, potassium, and sodium.

Although these substances are primarily introduced into the body through food and drink, they interact with and are affected by the ions in the atmosphere. The earth's charge is positive. To balance this and maintain optimal human performance, we need negative ions. There are abundant negative ions in the air in the mountains and forests, by oceans, rivers, and waterfalls, after a rainstorm, and in grottoes. This is why sages of all traditions usually seek to live close to nature, for the Chi of nature

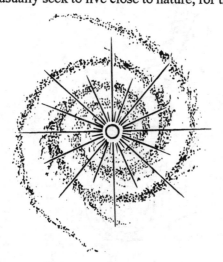

Figure 8-6. Cosmic Chi

is strong; it is conducive to clarity, health, and tranquility, all factors that nourish spiritual development and meditation.

In polluted cities and inside most houses, however, the negative ion count can decrease to near zero. When this happens, people often feel enervated and sapped of energy; negative moods are a common response as well. Many people use devices called ionizers, "ion fountains" that pump millions of negative ions back into the air and help restore the atmospheric ionic balance in their homes and offices.

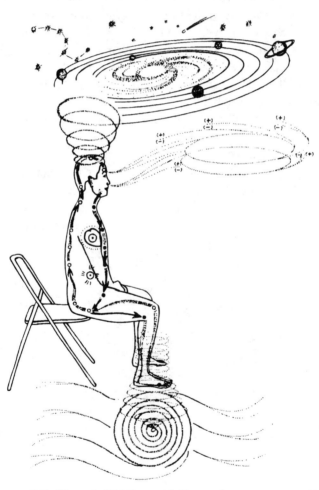

Figure 8-7. Absorb Chi through the major energy centers.

The Taoists discovered that breathing ions, cosmic particles, and Chi essence into the lungs alone makes it harder for the body to assimilate and use these energies. The most effective way to absorb them is through the major energy centers, the mouth, saliva, and skin (Figure 8-7). When we are young and healthy, we can absorb ions through our entire bodies, especially through the skin, palms, mid-eyebrow, and saliva (which attracts them). When our Original Force becomes weak and we lose too much sexual energy, it becomes harder for us to draw in ions from the air through the skin and these centers. By learning to open the energy centers and the pores of the skin through meditation and Chi Kung practices, we can absorb more Chi and thus maintain a higher level of health.

The food of meditation. Thus there are many forms of Chi, both visible and invisible, that we as humans require to stay healthy and balanced. Without your noticing it, regardless of your knowledge and beliefs, no matter what age, color, or sex you are, the Three Forces continuously supply you with life-force energy. It is given unconditionally, whether you are bad or good, young or old, rich or poor. The only question is how much use you are able to make of it.

All the great sages realized this. Jesus said, "Man does not live by bread alone." The Tibetan Buddhists speak of yogis no longer needing ordinary food but living instead on the "food of meditation." Similarly, at the higher levels of Kan and Li meditation, some Taoists are also able to abandon eating ordinary food and live on the Cosmic Chi alone. The real job of the true Tao master is to help you feel Chi and learn to absorb the subtle physical, energetic, and spiritual nutrients around you at every moment of your life.

Many of the ancient Taoists were great philosophers. They liked to explain and theorize about the origins of life and the universe and to explore intellectually the endless correspondences between the microcosm and macrocosm, between humans and the universe. This is important and helpful to a point, but if you are not able to put it into practice and learn how to use it, it will not add one minute to your life-span, nor will it help you at the hour of your death.

Using Higher Self/Cosmic Energy in Meditation

The Light of Creation

The light of creation, the Original Light, still saturates the universe and is simply waiting for us to capture it. On a subtle level, you can learn to access this Creation Light or Cosmic Chi during meditation through your mid-eyebrow, your palms, and the skin of the whole body, then absorb it into your system. Your respiratory and digestive systems take in energy from outside, process it, and send it to the heart, where it is distributed to every cell by the bloodstream. In the same way, we can absorb the Cosmic Chi and send it to the lower cauldron at the navel, where it will be "digested" and distributed to every part of the body through the energy channels.

This light shines from the Force to us. You may sense it with your inner eye as a benevolent golden cloud of light or luminous golden dust, very fine particles or waves of light floating in space in front of you at eye level and also radiating from your heart. Getting in touch with the Higher Self/Cosmic Energy in meditation can help strengthen and refresh your mind and spirit and can also help recharge and rebuild the Original Chi stored between your kidneys and navel.

Absorbing the Cosmic Chi will also heighten your practices of the Inner Smile and Microcosmic Orbit meditation. Using your mind to absorb light frequencies from external sources helps activate your internal light or soul. Just by connecting to the essences of the light frequencies, we start to awaken these different parts of ourselves; connecting with the Higher Self (Cosmic) energy causes a stepping-up of our corresponding energy on the human plane. It is usually not until you reach the higher meditation practices of Kan and Li that you reach your true soul level, where you actually merge with these energies. If Heaven Energy is related to your spirit body and Earth Energy is related to your physical body, then Man or Cosmic Chi is in turn related to your "soul body" or "energy body." At the level of Lesser Kan and Li, you are dealing with your own energies at a primordial soul level, at the level of Prenatal Chi.

At the beginning level of the Microcosmic Orbit, we are just starting to experience these energies, so we usually begin by connecting at a more simple mental level of visualization and inner focusing.

The Higher Self: Protector and Advisor

Once you establish the Original Force, you will automatically connect with the Higher Self. The Higher Self has been with us since birth, but we are not aware of it. We need to regrow our connection to it. If we have lost too much sexual energy, our life-force link to it becomes weaker and weaker. Once you feel the Original Force in the navel area and the golden light in mid-eyebrow, smile and be aware 6 to 12 feet above your head. You might feel a force or light above you. Simply let the force or light take form. It can be any form or color. Remember the form, so that next time you can recall it much faster. Let the form gradually touch you. Feel that you have a close connection with it. The place that it touches might open, and you can accept the Higher Self Energy into your body and merge it with the Original Force there. The place that the Higher Self touches will serve as a close connecting link between you and the Higher Self.

This Higher Self can give you advice, protection, and guidance in your life. If you can, constantly feel its presence.

PRACTICE: THE MICROCOSMIC ORBIT
Feeling Higher Self/Cosmic Energy

Now, in addition to receiving the Earth energy and merging it with your Original Chi, you will learn the practice of connecting with and absorbing the Higher Self (Cosmic) Chi through the doorway of your mid- eyebrow point. You will begin this process with the Cosmic Inner Smile, an enhanced practice of the basic Inner Smile. Then, after warming the stove and connecting to Mother Earth Energy, you will activate the mid-eyebrow point, draw in the golden light of the Higher Self/Cosmic Energy, and expand it to form a protective sphere or shield around your body. Having done this, you will combine the golden light with your own Original Chi and then circulate the golden light or Golden Elixir through the Microcosmic Orbit. The final new practice introduced in this chapter teaches you how to connect the Upper Tan Tien (or Upper Elixir Field) with the Middle Tan Tien (or Middle Elixir Field).

1. Preparations

A. Chi Kung Warm-Ups

1. Begin by loosening the spine with Chi Kung Warm-Ups: Spinal Cord Breathing, the Crane Neck, the Turtle Neck, Spinal Cord Shaking, and Spinal Cord Rocking.

2. Rest. Feel the spine become open and relaxed. As you inhale, imagine that you are breathing a white mist down to the navel and gathering it at the tip of the coccyx, then raising it into the spine to purify, cleanse, and brighten the spinal cord. When you exhale, feel that you are breathing out any impurities from the spine as a cloudy gray mist. This will help strengthen the bones.

3. Now be aware of a golden mist in front of you. Inhale; gather and condense the mist of golden light in the mouth a few times, and draw it down or swallow it to the navel. Gather it at the tip of the coccyx, as above, and rotate it as a golden ball of Chi 9 to 18 times. Then raise it into the spine to purify, cleanse, and brighten the spinal marrow. When you exhale, feel that you are breathing out any impurities from the spine as a cloudy gray mist. Repeat this 9 to 18 times.

B. The Six Healing Sounds

Practice 2 or 3 repetitions of each of the Six Healing Sounds to clear the emotions, warm up the organs, and prepare the body to receive fresh, pure energy.

C. The Cosmic Inner Smile

This simple version of the Inner Smile relaxes the Third Eye so that you can draw your Higher Self Force directly into the body. For a more detailed practice of the basic Inner Smile, please refer to Chapter 3.

In Taoist practices, it is very important to awaken the "mind's eye" so you can feel and see the internal organs, glands, bone structure, and the marrow inside the bones. This will greatly help improve the marrow's condition, and it will also help transform negative emotions into positive ones.

The organs, glands, and bone structure are not only the condensed essence of the Cosmic Force; they are also one medium by which to receive this force. Bones have piezoelectric properties, just like quartz crystals, which serve to amplify and receive the Cosmic Force of the

Higher Self. As you study the anatomical diagrams in this book, try to feel the organs, glands, and bones.

1. Sit properly, keeping the spine loose but straight. Tilt the head slightly forward and pull the chin in. Massage the mid-eyebrow point with the fingers. Then place the palms together (right hand on top) and hold them lightly in your lap. Close the eyes. Relax the Third Eye and the perineum as you slightly contract the sexual organs and the anus.

2. Be aware of the Higher Self (Cosmic) energy in front of you. Smile, and relax the mid-eyebrow. Inhale, and lightly contract the nostrils; simultaneously, gently contract and release the eye muscles in a pumping action. (The breathing should be slow and deep.) Feel these contractions amplify a pulsing sensation you will begin to feel at the mid-eyebrow. Feel a suction at the mid-eyebrow, and sense the golden light of the Cosmic Force run into the mid-eyebrow and be absorbed by it.

3. Begin smiling down the face, chin, and cheekbones as you lift the corners of the mouth. Feel the golden light flow to the places where you direct your smiling attention, and fill these places with loving energy.

4. Let the smiling energy spread down through the neck and down into the thymus gland, also known as the "little heart," which speaks directly to the Higher Self. Feel the thymus open like a flower. Continue to smile into the rib cage, starting from the top ribs down to the floating ribs. Smile deeper, into the marrow, and thank the marrow for producing white blood cells, a vital part of the immune system.

5. Smile into the heart and feel it open like a flower. Feel joy and happiness expand from its center, spreading out to all the other organs.

6. Spread this joy out to the lungs, liver, pancreas, spleen, and kidneys. Smile into these areas.

7. Smile down to the sexual organs. (Taoists acknowledge that the kidneys and sexual organs have a direct role in producing bone marrow.)

8. Return the attention to the Third Eye. Move the eyes around and feel them stimulate the brain. Smile, and feel the skull breathe. Draw the Cosmic Chi into the marrow.

9. Smile down the cervical vertebrae one by one. Feel yourself breathe into each, and feel them absorb the Cosmic Chi from outside into the spine and marrow.

10. Smile down to the thoracic vertebrae. Feel yourself breathe into each, and feel them absorb the Cosmic Chi into the marrow.

11. Smile down to the lumbar vertebrae. Feel them breathing and absorbing Cosmic Chi.

12. Smile down to the sacrum and the hips. Feel them breathing and drawing Cosmic Chi deep into the marrow.

13. Smile down to the femur bones, down to the tibiae, fibulae, and bones of the feet. Feel them breathing and absorbing Cosmic Chi into the marrow.

14. Finally, smile into the navel. You can use the hands to cover and help warm the navel, and also to strengthen the Original Force. When covering the navel with the palms, men place the left palm over the right; women place the right palm over the left. Mentally spiral the warm energy at the navel in any direction. (Focus one-and-a-half inches behind the navel.) Smile to your Original Chi.

2. Microcosmic Orbit Meditation

A. Warming the Stove:
Generating and Gathering the Force

Make sure you feel the Original Force activate before going on to the other stages of this meditation.

1. Practice Bellows Breathing at least 18 to 36 times.

2. Activate the kidneys. Feel the Door of Life between the kidneys and the navel become warm. Spiral with the hands and body into the kidneys and Door of Life.

3. Activate the sexual organs. Inhale into the sexual center. When you exhale, feel yourself breathing out the toxins, while at the same time retaining the energetic essence of the breath at the sexual center. Then pause for a while. Feel the energy expand and radiate outward. Breathe in and out in this way at least 18 times. Then lightly tap the sexual center with the fingertips to wake up the energy.

4. Now rest a moment. Feel the navel warm. Feel the kidneys and Door of Life warm. Feel the sexual center warm. As you inhale, feel the sexual organs, perineum, and anus very lightly pull up toward the Original Force.

5. Exhale, and push the diaphragm downward. Feel the pressure building at the Tan Tien. Picture the Original Energy with a mouth and nose, breathing into that spot (Figure 8-8). Now lightly contract the circular muscles of the irises and the muscles around the eyes. At the same time, lightly inhale and contract the muscles of the nostrils, as if

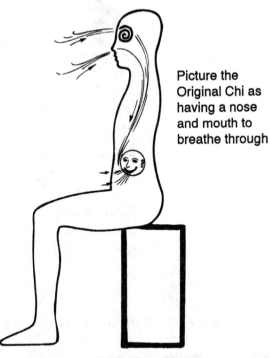

Picture the
Original Chi as
having a nose
and mouth to
breathe through

Figure 8-8. Warming the Chi Stove

you were smelling a lovely fragrance. Contract and relax the eye and nose muscles in this way, and feel those contractions amplify the pulse in the Tan Tien. As you feel the pulse pumping, feel the pulsing at the sexual organs. Feel this combined pulsing and pumping, condensing and expanding, creating a suction and drawing the sexual energy into the Original Energy at the Tan Tien. Feel the energy running into you. Spend at least 10 minutes warming the stove this way.

B. Basic Microcosmic Orbit Circulation

Direct the Chi from the Tan Tien out to the navel. Then use any method you like to circulate the Chi through the basic loop of the Microcosmic Orbit several times. This will provide a matrix in which to receive the energy of the Earth and Cosmic Forces.

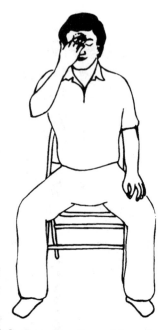

Figure 8-9. Opening the mid-eyebrow point

C. Feeling the Mother Earth Energy

1. Massage the palms and soles. Place the hands at the sides with the palms facing down toward the earth, and be sure the soles are flat against the ground. Also be aware of the Hui Yin (Functional Channel 1) point at the perineum.

2. After a short time, you will begin to feel the palms and soles breathing by themselves. Simultaneously, you will feel the vagina and Hui Yin (perineum) point starting to naturally pull up and release, pull up and release, in a pulsing and pumping action. You can time your breathing with the pulsing if you are having trouble feeling it. Do this 9 to 18 times. Then exhale and rest.

3. Now focus the mind about 95 percent on the Original Energy behind your navel, and about 5 percent on the Five Earth Gates (perineum, palms and soles, anus, and genital opening). Feel yourself grounded; feel connected to the earth. Just relax, and you will feel the pulsing again. Let it come in and up; feel the suction, and feel the gentle blue Earth Force pulse into the Tan Tien as you breathe in through the Five Earth Gates (Figure 8-9).

4. Feel the Chi ball growing and expanding in the Tan Tien, filling up the whole region between the navel, the kidneys, and the sexual center. Your Tan Tien is connected to the earth now; your body feels connected to the body of Mother Earth. Feel the Mother Earth energy strengthening the stove and enhancing the Original Energy at the Tan Tien. Once the Chi ball within the Original Force is full, it should automatically activate the mid-eyebrow. Alternately, you can lightly focus on the mid-eyebrow until you feel the pulsing.

D. Opening the Mid-eyebrow Point and Activating the Higher Self/Cosmic Energy

1. Raise the right hand to the forehead. Using the index finger of the right hand, touch the mid-eyebrow point and spiral clockwise with the finger and the power of the mind and eyes. You can also lace the fingers of the two hands together, extend the index fingers together, and touch the mid-eyebrow point. You will feel as though a drill is spiraling from your finger into the middle of your brain (Figure 8-10).

2. Lower the hands and breathe into the mid-eyebrow point. Feel it open as you exhale. Repeat this at least 3 to 9 times. Make sure you feel it open before you go on to the next step.

Using the power of the mind, eyes, and heart is very important. In the beginning, you can actually move the eyes to follow the fingers, spiraling the eyes in a clockwise direction.

3. Be aware of the Original Energy behind the navel. Feel the Original Energy activate, and feel the suction there.

4. As you activate the Original Energy, be aware of the Original Energy in the Tan Tien, and at the same time feel the mid-eyebrow point pulsing and activating on its own.

5. Raise both hands to the forehead, this time with the palms facing out. Feel the mid-eyebrow point, the eyes, and the palms actively pulsing on their own. Be aware of them as you picture a golden light gathering into a ball in front of your face. Feel the palms and mid-eyebrow breathe in this golden light (Figure 8-11).

6. Now project the awareness out to a favorite place in nature. Spiral counterclockwise with the power of the mind and eyes to connect with natural forces, such as a lake, an ocean, a forest, a waterfall, a mountain, a sunset, or a grotto. Picture them, and you will feel the Higher Self Force come from them to you like a benevolent and refreshing golden mist of light.

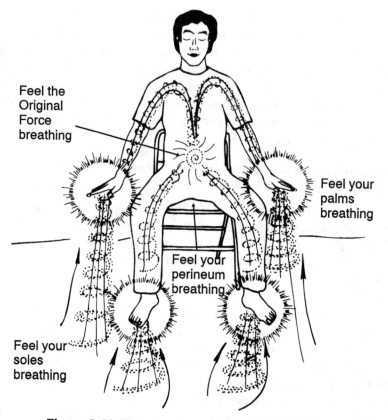

Feel the Original Force breathing

Feel your palms breathing

Feel your perineum breathing

Feel your soles breathing

Figure 8-10. Spiral and open the mid-eyebrow.

7. As you inhale, feel yourself bringing all the power of nature into your body. Exhale, and feel yourself breathing out all the toxins and poisons through the nose. Inhale again, and feel the nostrils lightly contract so that you stimulate the nerves that are connected to the hairs in the nostrils; as you inhale in this way, feel the power and beauty of nature fill your whole being. Feel that you are actually inhaling the essence of nature into the palms and mid-eyebrow, then exhale any impurities.

8. Breathe the energetic golden light down into the mouth, and with the light begin to form a golden ball of Chi energy there.

9. Breathe the golden light into the saliva; let it merge and fuse with the saliva. Notice how the saliva changes. It may become very rich, sweet tasting, and alive, charged with life-force. The golden light mixes with the saliva and is known as the Golden Elixir (Figure 8-12).

Figure 8-11. Breathe in the golden light.

**Figure 8-12. As you breathe in the golden light, mix it with the
saliva. Then swallow the saliva.**

10. Lightly knock the teeth together 9 to 18 times. Then lightly clench and release the teeth 9 to 18 times. Press and release the tongue against the palate 9 to 18 times. Press the upper and lower lips firmly together. Now swallow the elixir and follow the pathway of the golden light down with the mind. Picture a golden orbit that flows all the way down the front channel, through the perineum, to the coccyx; then feel it flow up the spine to the crown, and from the crown back down to the mid-eyebrow. Let it continue to flow through the Microcosmic Orbit pathway, circulating it through the Microcosmic Orbit 3 to 9 times.

11. Now picture a fine golden strand of light extending from either the Hui Yin point or the coccyx to the crown and mid-eyebrow, and feel it begin to expand (Figure 8-13). Gradually expand it into a golden pillar within the body. Continue to feel it grow longer and wider, expanding outside the body until it merges with your aura.

12. See yourself sitting within an oval-shaped form of this light, as if a golden ball were enveloping your whole body. Being enveloped by

Figure 8-13. Let the golden light flow in the Microcosmic Orbit.

a ball of golden light gives you a sense of comfort and safety within your own aura.

13. Hold this image as you breathe naturally. It will energize and protect you. Feel the golden ball acting as a buffer or neutral zone to prevent any psychic attack or disruption from the negative energy of others. Feel that the golden light can help you neutralize the negative energy or transform it into positive energy (Figure 8-14). Continue to hold this image for 5 to 10 minutes.

14. Picture the oval shape of the golden light around your body condensing into a thin shaft extending from the coccyx up the spine. Continue to condense this shaft into a small strand, then gather it into a golden Chi ball at the mid-eyebrow.

15. Finally, condense the Chi ball into a Chi dot. Let it flow down to the mouth, through the chest, to the navel. You can use the mind to guide the golden light through the Orbit 6 to 9 times.

Figure 8-14. The golden ball of light covers your whole body, acting like a buffer or neutral zone to protect and energize you.

E. Connecting the Upper Elixir Field and the Middle Elixir Field

1. Keep the fingers of the right hand on the mid-eyebrow center and move the left palm or fingers to touch the heart center. Inhale naturally and feel yourself breathing into the mid-eyebrow center. When you exhale, feel the energy of the breath drop down to the heart center (Figure 8-15).

Now focus on breathing in a golden mist. Exhale, and send the energy down to the area of the heart center. Follow your natural breathing patterns; do not force the breath or any movement of energy. With each breath, you are extracting and retaining the essence of the vital energy of life for your body's use. Do this from 9 to 18 times. Rest, and feel that the Upper and Middle Elixir Fields are open and connected.

2. This time when you inhale, feel the breath rising from the heart center up to the mid-eyebrow. Then, when you exhale, send it from the mid-eyebrow center down to the heart center. Use the breath to purify

Figure 8-15. Connecting the upper and middle Elixir Fields

the space between these areas. Follow your natural breathing patterns without using any force. Use the power of the mind, eyes, and heart to direct the current of life- force within the body. Do this from 9 to 18 times.

3. Now focus the mind about 95 percent on the Original Energy behind the navel and about 5 percent on the main Five Gates (perineum, palms, soles, and the mid-eyebrow and crown, not yet open). Use the mind/eye/heart power to condense and expand, and pulse the cosmic golden light and Mother Earth's gentle and kind blue energy into the Original Force. Be aware of the Higher Self above you. Feel your connection with it, and feel the Higher Self channel and absorb the force around you (Figure 8-16). Spend 10 minutes on this practice.

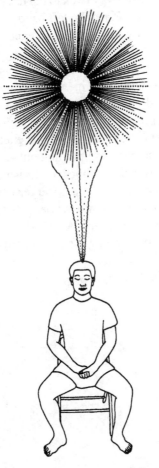

Figure 8-16. Make the connection to the Higher Self.

4. Rest, and feel the sensations of condensation and expansion, energy, lightness, peace, and balance. Now inhale, breathe the golden mist into the heart center, and exhale it into the Tan Tien. Gather it into the Tan Tien; picture it as the sun sinking into an ocean of stillness. Store this Chi, and keep it ready to call on for protection, or to energize you any time you need it.

3. Ending the Meditation: Collecting Energy at the Navel

1. When you feel ready to finish your round of meditation, use the mind to guide any excess energy back to the navel. You may also use the hands to guide the energy. Place the left hand on the navel and the right hand on the mid-eyebrow point. Feel the excess energy in the head or heart flowing between the two hands and beginning to flow strongly downward to the navel. It is important to take as much time as you feel you need to bring the energy down.

2. Focus the mind on the Original Energy behind the navel. Notice how quiet and peaceful you feel. Rest, and enjoy this feeling of being both relaxed and quiet in body and mind, yet energized at the same time.

3. Conclude the practice by spiraling outward 36 times at the navel and then spiraling inward 24 times to finish collecting the energy. Remember that the circles should be no larger than 6 inches in diameter, so the energy does not leak out into the heart or sexual organs. You may use your hands to help you spiral. At the abdomen, feel as though the intestines are physically spiraling, or use the mind alone as you become more familiar with the practice.

4. Finish with Chi Self-Massage.

Chapter 9

OPENING YOUR HEART: Shen and the Microcosmic Orbit

THE ROLE OF EMOTIONS IN THE HEALING TAO SYSTEM

The Taoist View of Spirit

Many religions are based on philosophy, faith, and belief. Each has its value, but each also has drawbacks. Focusing on intellectual understanding alone is limiting and stifling. And while faith and belief can sometimes provide a stimulus to motivate people who might otherwise feel that life is without hope, some religions have degenerated to the point where they rely on these means exclusively.

A real practice teaches one how to feel within and derive authentic knowledge based on personal experience. In the Healing Tao, we emphasize the practice of understanding nature, getting in touch with the natural forces, and getting in touch with oneself. Then the principles of philosophy will reveal themselves. Then one can have real hope based on what *is*, not on empty promises that can never be proven.

All religions speak about spiritual growth, but it is not always easy to understand exactly what they mean by spiritual growth, or even what they mean by spirit. By contrast, the Taoist view of spirit, or *Shen* in Chinese, is quite simple. To Taoists, one major aspect of the spirit is one's attitude, one's emotional energy. This idea is not foreign to the Western world. People often remark, "Well, you're in good spirits today," or "Let's have some team spirit!"

We also speak of a "spirited performance" or a "spirited horse."

If a spiritual teacher or leader seems gentle, fearless, joyful, kind, and just, then we naturally develop respect for his or her spiritual attainments. We find it pleasant, nourishing, and inspiring to be in the teacher's presence.

However, if a spiritual teacher seems angry, frustrated, arrogant, impatient, fearful, worried, or depressed, then we will be disappointed. We will not feel confident that this teacher can guide us to peace and happiness, because the teacher has not found peace within himself or herself and has not yet learned to get along well with others. From this example, it is clear that we do indeed equate spirit with emotions and mental attitudes.

The Virtues:
Energetic Essence of
Our Positive Emotions

In the Tao, we refer to the positive emotions as the *virtues*. However, the virtues are not merely positive emotions, which are limited to specific expressions in time and space. They are actually the true essence or seed Chi of our positive feelings, an aspect of our immortal soul essence, emanating from beyond time and space into our daily lives.

The virtues are our natural qualities; they are inherent in everyone. They do not have to be created in us; they need only to be uncovered, exercised, and nourished. This is the Taoist approach.

Our virtues have the nature of wisdom and love. They are wise because they reflect our interdependence with the Tao, with nature, with all life, and with the different parts of our own body; we cannot exhibit the virtues except in relation to another. The virtues are also wise in that they express love, the attitude that strengthens the positive bonds connecting everything in the universe. Thus the virtues promote life, health, and harmony. Cultivating the virtues is the basis of spiritual development in the Tao. We are born with these qualities in abundance.

The ancient Chinese correlated the virtues with the Five Elements, or Five Major Forces, as follows (Figure 9-1):

Metal: lungs; contracting force; courage; righteousness; appropriateness

Water: kidneys; gathering force; gentleness; generosity; alert stillness

Wood: liver; generating force; kindness; forgiveness

Fire: heart; prospering force; love; joy; happiness; gratitude; respect; honor

Earth: spleen; stabilizing force; in the center, openness; fairness; justice

A correspondence also exists between the virtues and the internal organs. In fact, the virtues reside in the organs and in the channels associated with them, which form an energy network throughout the body. The virtues are the product of the healthy Chi of each organ. They are each an essential component of our immortal spirit.

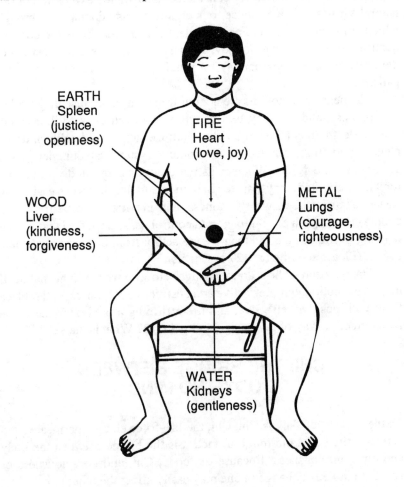

Figure 9-1. The Virtues with the Five Elements

337

Negative Emotions:
The Afflicted Expression of
Our Natural Virtues

The Five Elements are also correlated with negative emotions and specific organs. Our Chi can be adversely affected when we are subjected to prolonged stress, injury, unhealthy environmental factors, poor posture, or ill-treatment and abuse from other people. When the virtuous Chi associated with our internal organs is disrupted, it opens the door to the negative emotions, which are considered the afflicted expression of our natural virtues. So, in essence, our organs act as "doorways" through which emotions manifest. For example, the heart manifests the positive qualities of respect, love, and joy, but when its virtuous Chi is disrupted, the heart becomes the doorway for cruelty, hatred, arrogance, and impatience.

The negative emotions are not our true nature, because they lead to unhappiness, and—if they become chronic—eventually to illness and even to death. In contrast, the virtues nurture happiness, health, and life. Negative emotions can depress the immune system, sap our energy, and scatter our life force. When negative emotions repeatedly arise and remain unchecked, they start to become habitual. It becomes easier and easier for anger, fear, worry, sadness, and impatience to be triggered; people easily "push our buttons" and control us, and we find that we are reacting to life more often than we are acting from our wise and stable center. (Please see Figure 3-29 in Chapter 3.)

The question is: how do we change? How do we eliminate habits of negative emotion, our ineffective and destructive responses, and replace them with positive, effective, and life-affirming attitudes? What is the most effective way of reversing these patterns? What is the key?

CHI: THE BRIDGE BETWEEN BODY AND MIND

To the Taoists, the key is Chi. Chi, the life-force energy, permeates and activates the body and mind; in fact, it is the bridge between the body and our consciousness. Because the body, Chi, and consciousness or spirit are linked, a change in one may easily affect the other two.

Relaxing Your Attitude to Heal Your Body

Over the past two decades, there has been significant research indicating that emotional stress has a depressive effect on the immune system, and that it can aggravate chronic physical conditions such as hypertension and diabetes. Research also shows that the onset of cancer is often preceded by chronic anxiety, depression, anger, or other negative emotions. Stress management studies indicate that a change in attitude can cause an improvement in physiological indications of health. For example, Norman Cousins cured himself of a degenerative connective tissue disease by leaving the hospital, checking into a hotel, and treating himself with "laughter therapy" by watching old Marx Brothers movies. This is only one of many cases demonstrating that generating a happy and positive frame of mind can have a correspondingly positive effect on the body.

Relaxing Your Body to Heal Your Mind

Similarly, doctors and psychologists who specialize in stress management and relaxation training have discovered that many stress-related mental and emotional tensions can be relieved by relaxing their associated bodily tensions. Dr. Edmund Jacobson, inventor of the first biofeedback machine and the "father of progressive relaxation training," went as far as to say, "An anxious mind cannot exist in a relaxed body."

Directing Your Chi to Heal Both Body and Mind

In the Taoist classics, it is said, "The mind leads and the Chi follows; the Chi leads and the body follows." Because Chi is at the midpoint between the body and mind, directing the Chi enables us to make changes in both body and mind. Meditation, Chi Kung, Chinese medicine, Feng-Shui (geomancy), and the martial arts all emphasize controlling, refining, and directing the Chi for both physical well-being and spiritual development. For example, acupuncture, working exclusively with the Chi, can effectively alleviate physical pain and illness as well as mental and emotional disorders.

The Healing Tao System:
A Three-Pronged Approach

The Healing Tao system uses a three-pronged approach to emotional healing and transformation, comprising body, Chi, and mind. Depending on the personality of the individual student, one approach may work better than another. For example, some people are out of touch with their bodily tensions and sensations but are in touch with their thoughts and emotions. For this type of person, affecting and healing the body and Chi can be approached on a mind/emotion/spirit level, such as with the Inner Smile. Other people may be very much in touch with their physical side but out of touch with their feelings, thoughts, and energy. The doorway for such a person's opening to the totality of his or her being may initially be the Microcosmic Orbit, Tai Chi Chi Kung, Iron Shirt, or the Six Healing Sounds.

The Taoist approach follows the way of nature; we do not try to force the student to adapt to one method. Instead, we have many different methods to suit the nature, capacity, and needs of each student. Ultimately the goal is to know ourselves as we really are and to reclaim all aspects of ourselves on every level. And because part of who we are is our energy body, our Chi network, all these Taoist practices help us discover and sense Chi as part of our continuum of being: the Chi in our bodies, in other people, and the Chi of nature all around us.

Over centuries and millennia, Taoists have devised many exercises and ways of training to nourish all three interrelated aspects of our totality—body, Chi, and spirit. But it is not enough just to understand that working with emotional energy is important. You have to do it! If you practice, you will soon see results that transform your life.

FROM THEORY TO PRACTICE

Emotional Energy and the
Inner Smile

In the Healing Tao system, the practice of bringing the body, Chi, and emotions into balance starts with the Inner Smile.

We often get so out of touch with our bodies and emotions that we do not notice inner disharmony developing until it finally manifests as a serious illness. Practicing the Inner Smile daily provides a regularly scheduled time to look inside—to keep in touch with the state of our inner organs, our Chi, our breath, and our emotions. We can then spot problems at their inception, making it easier to "nip them in the bud."

Low self-esteem is becoming endemic. If we are not taught or encouraged to love ourselves, we cannot have a healthy, loving relationship with other people or with the earth; witness the state of society and the environment as proof of this imbalance.

The Inner Smile teaches us to recognize our inherent positive qualities, not just our negativity. With regular practice, we get to know ourselves as we really are; we can discover our virtues as well as our afflictions. This helps us form a more authentic and healthier self-image, one that stays in close touch with reality. The Inner Smile exercises our ability to love, starting with our own bodies. As we learn to love and accept ourselves, it becomes natural and easy for us to extend this love outward and begin to love and accept other people, creatures, places, and things.

As one of the best exercises for stress management and self-healing, the Inner Smile induces a state of deep relaxation. Deep relaxation dissolves physical and mental tensions that can cause energy blockages and unhealthy Chi. For this reason, the Inner Smile is always used as a preparation or warm-up in other meditation and Chi Kung exercises that circulate the Chi.

Working with Emotions in the Microcosmic Orbit Meditation

Chinese medicine recognizes that negative emotions can be caused by blockages in Chi flow. If an organ or its channel becomes blocked due to injury, poor posture, pollution, poor diet, prolonged stress, or illness, that organ may get too much or too little Chi. The virtuous qualities of that organ are distorted, and its negative emotions may increase.

Similarly, chronic outbursts or bouts of negative emotions can cause energy blockages in an organ or its associated channel. For example, it is well known in Western medicine that chronic worry can cause indigestion or stomach ulcers. It is equally well known in Chinese medicine that chronic anger and frustration is the primary cause of Liver Chi stagnation. It works both ways: negative emotions can cause energy blockages and imbalances, and blockages can cause a rise in negative emotions.

The Microcosmic Orbit meditation circulates Chi through the Governor Channel and the Functional Channel (Conception Vessel). These two pathways are the primary source, or reservoir, channels for all other Yang and Yin channels in the body. Circulating the Microcosmic Orbit helps keep the reservoirs full, ensuring a strong flow of Chi through the other channels and organs in the body. By eliminating the blockages, we can alleviate the negative emotions that were exacerbated by these blockages.

The Microcosmic Orbit is also an important component in the higher-level Taoist meditation formulas, which work with emotional transformation and healing, such as the Fusion of the Five Elements and the Kan and Li practices.

Opening the Heart

Taoists regard the heart as a cauldron, capable of taking in negativity and processing it into positive energy. It is also a place to blend all the energies of our virtues to create the higher-grade energy of compassion (Figure 9-2).

At the beginning of the Microcosmic Orbit, when we have just opened the heart, it tends to draw in negativity from other organs and the body for processing. We should be careful to handle these negative energies properly; otherwise they can combine in the heart (just like the virtues) and cause more negative feelings.

Because this initial opening of the heart is very small, when negative energies are jammed into it, they can be hard to get out. For this reason the practices of *venting* and *fanning* to help drain negative and sick energies into the earth is very important. (Please see detailed practice in Chapter 7.) Shining our virtues toward other people is also important. The more we give sincere love, kindness, gentleness, and respect to others, without any expectation of return, the more we can open the heart and transform negative energies into positive ones.

Massaging the sternum can also help release these negative emotions, stimulate the flow of lymph, and activate the thymus gland.

Emotional Energy and the
Six Healing Sounds

Together with the Microcosmic Orbit meditation and the Inner Smile, the Six Healing Sounds are an effective way of restoring and maintaining balance in your emotions and internal organs. When the thermoregulatory system of an organ becomes afflicted due to stress or other

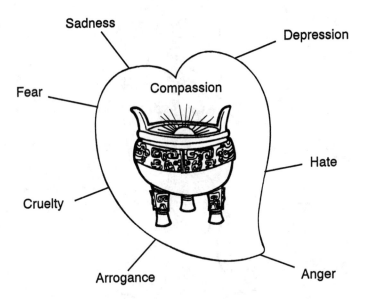

Figure 9-2. The heart is capable of transforming negative energy into positive energy.

factors, the organs may overheat. In this condition, negative emotions and other adverse health problems related to the organs may arise.

The Six Healing Sounds use a combination of movement, sound, and mental imagery to cool and restore balance to the organs. As with the Inner Smile, we observe what our inner state is and then let go of any negative emotions. At the same time, we nourish the virtue energy in each organ. Although both the Inner Smile and Six Healing Sounds use the power of the mind to bring change to our inner climate, the Six Healing Sounds also use the more physical approach of movement and sound, which may work better for some individuals or for certain types of ailments than mind power alone (Figure 9-3).

While the emphasis of the Inner Smile is on relaxation, the emphasis of the Six Healing Sounds is more on cooling, balancing, and detoxifying

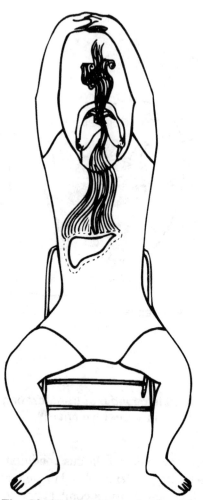

Figure 9-3. The Six Healing Sounds clear the negative energy out of the organs and grow positive energy.

the organs. These two excellent techniques for restoring physical and mental health and balance are a perfect complement to each other.

Fusion of the Five Elements

Once you have a firm foundation in the Microcosmic Orbit meditation, the Inner Smile, and the Six Healing Sounds, you are ready to progress to the more advanced formulas for transforming the emotions. When you begin the practices of the Fusion of the Five Elements, you will truly experience these "elements" as energy movements within your body. This will be your initiation into the beginning levels of Taoist Inner Alchemy.

Fusion of the Five Elements I:
Purifying the Negative Emotions

The Fusion of the Five Elements practice is divided into three levels. Only the first two levels focus on emotional transformation. In the first level, Fusion I, you will learn how the Five Elements, with their corresponding emotions, seasons, senses, organs, and colors, can actually be experienced, and then harmonized and fused. This meditation first neutralizes the Chi of negative emotions through applying the Controlling Cycle of the Five Elements. This clears an inner space so the virtue energy has room to grow. The Chi is then distilled, collected into a "pearl" or condensed ball of Chi, the essence of the body, and circulated through the Microcosmic Orbit to strengthen and heal all the centers in the body (Figure 9-4).

Fusion of the Five Elements II:
Nourishing the Chi of the Inner Virtues

In the second level of the Fusion of the Five Elements, this freshly transformed energy of the negative emotions is recycled and used to nourish the organs, strengthen them, and increase their associated virtuous emotions. This is accomplished by applying the Creation or Nourishing Cycle of the Five Elements to grow and increase the natural virtues at their energetic roots, the Chi in the organs. The energy of the positive emotions of all the organs is absorbed into the pearl and then circulated in four of the eight special channels: the Microcosmic Orbit (Governor and Functional Channels), the Thrusting Routes, and the Belt Routes. The Thrusting Routes run through the center of the body, linking the "chakra" centers. The Belt Routes spiral around the body, strengthening the aura and providing a form of psychic self-defense.

Fusion of the Five Elements III:
Regulating Chi Flow in the Energy Body

The third level of the Fusion of the Five Elements practice directs the pearl to open the remaining four of the eight special channels: the Yin and Yang Bridge Routes and the Yin and Yang Regulator Routes. Additional routes are opened as well, giving greater cohesiveness to the energy

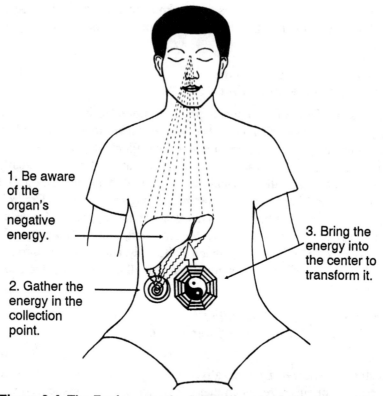

1. Be aware of the organ's negative energy.

2. Gather the energy in the collection point.

3. Bring the energy into the center to transform it.

Figure 9-4. The Fusion practice helps transform negative energy to positive energy in a more powerful way.

body and making the physical body more permeable to the Chi. Successful completion of this level gives one greatly heightened sensitivity to the energy body and the ability to move the Chi at will to any place in the body.

Advanced Fusion Formulas:
Projecting the Chi Beyond the Physical Body

Another important part of the Fusion of the Five Elements practice is learning how to temporarily separate the energy body and the physical body. In life, our three bodies—the physical body, energy body, and spirit body (consciousness)—all overlap and are generally inseparable. At death, the physical body is no longer a fit vehicle for holding the material Five Elements together, and Chi and consciousness are forced to leave. To avoid the traumatic disorientation and confusion that can occur at death when the energetic essence and consciousness are involuntarily thrust out of the physical body into unknown territory, we can familiarize ourselves with the "out-of-body realm" by temporarily separating the energy body from the physical body, as a "dress rehearsal" for death.

Consciousness always requires some sort of vehicle to manifest. Its gross vehicle is the physical body. Its more subtle vehicle is the energy body (sometimes referred to as the "subtle" body). We emphasized earlier that the virtues are the true energetic essence of our organs. Although we may identify ourselves more with our physical body than anything else in the world, it is our energetic essence, not our physical body, that survives after death and has the capacity to be immortal.

By regularly turning the awareness inward in the Fusion of the Five Elements practice, we gradually come to know our energetic essences as well as we know our face, our arms, and our legs. We learn to distill these essences into a pearl, as a sort of "space capsule" to carry our essential energy and consciousness out of the physical body. With regular practice, Taoists who follow the path of Inner Alchemy learn to move their energy body and consciousness in and out of their physical body as easily as one might walk from one room into another.

The Inner Elixir and the Outer Elixir

Just as it is important for the physical body to be strong so we can enjoy optimum health, it is also vital to strengthen the energy body so it becomes a sturdy vehicle for our consciousness. Strengthening Chi nourishes our health and spiritual qualities in this life and builds a strong energy body to carry us forth into the "afterlife" (which is, paradoxically, the here and now). We begin to strengthen the energy body through what is called in Taoist Inner Alchemy the Inner Elixir. It is called the Inner Elixir because we are working with the energies already within our own body and converting them into elixir—like healing essences. Through the meditation practices of the Microcosmic Orbit and the Fusion of the Five Elements, we detoxify, nourish, and integrate the physical body, the energy body, and the emotions.

After we have learned to develop and nourish ourselves through the Inner Elixir, we are ready to tap the Outer Elixir. The energies of the Five Elements also exist beyond the body—the energy of the earth, the planets, and the stars. This is the true or highest form of the Outer Elixir. Normally, we are incapable of absorbing and digesting the outer energies, but the points of the Microcosmic Orbit are connected to these energies.

By opening the Microcosmic Orbit and mastering the Fusion of the Five Elements, we develop the capacity to absorb and digest the energies from these external sources of Five Element Chi.

Once we have purified and transformed the negative energy of the organs back into usable life-force energy (Fusion I), distilled this energy along with the virtue Chi of the organs into the pearl (Fusion II), and opened all our reservoirs or special channels, giving us a larger energetic capacity, we can increase our virtue energies further by connecting with the external sources of Five Elements Chi and directing the external Chi toward its associated organs. Moving the pearl out of the physical body makes it easier for the pearl to absorb these energies. It becomes like an antenna that receives the external Chi and conducts it into the physical body. In this way, we again nourish our health in this life as well as strengthening the energy body and spirit in preparation for the next.

Your Microcosmic Orbit practice will change dramatically after you learn the Fusion of the Five Elements meditations. When you first practice the Microcosmic Orbit, the energy you move through your channels is raw energy. By contrast, when you reach the level of Fusion practice, the energy is more refined and condensed, and it is therefore much more powerful. The Fusion practice includes the Microcosmic Orbit, so it might be said that the Fusion meditation is simply a more advanced way of practicing the Microcosmic Orbit meditation.

The Way of Health and Immortality

Each stage of practice, from the Inner Smile to the Greatest Enlightenment of Kan and Li, is a vital step along the way to health and immortality. In fact, the Inner Smile, Microcosmic Orbit meditation, and Six Healing Sounds are used as an essential part of the Kan and Li meditations. So as a beginning or intermediate student in the Healing Tao, you need not be in a hurry to progress, nor do you need to be intimidated by the higher-level practices. The most important ingredient in success is daily practice. Soon you will discover that you have mastered the system. Your skills will develop naturally, and you will find it easy to add new steps. One step at a time, you will travel down the road to immortality.

PRACTICE
The Microcosmic Orbit:
Opening the Heart

This section emphasizes opening the heart and using the virtues of the heart to radiate cosmic Chi (or Higher Self energy) to the organs through the practice of the Cosmic Inner Smile. This is the same as the Inner Smile meditation, but it is more detailed, and more emphasis is placed on tapping into cosmic energy.

A. Preparations

Chi Kung Warm-Ups. Begin by loosening the spine with Chi Kung Warm-Ups: Spinal Cord Breathing, the Crane Neck, the Turtle Neck, Spinal Cord Shaking, and Spinal Cord Rocking.

Six Healing Sounds. Do 2 or 3 repetitions of each sound.

Prepare to focus inward. Sit in good meditation position on a chair. Once you are in a good sitting position, take a few minutes to focus and prepare yourself. Become aware of your surroundings. Feel the sensation of your feet touching the floor, of your clasped hands, of the chair beneath you. Be aware of the sounds inside the room, outside the room, and within your body. Be aware of your breath. Feel your body naturally expand as you inhale and contract as you exhale. Breathe in and out with awareness in this way 9, 18, or 36 times. Then rest.

Picture your spine as open and relaxed. As you inhale, imagine you are breathing a white mist from the earth into your spine to purify, cleanse, and brighten your spinal cord. Then breathe the golden mist of the Cosmic Force into the marrow in the same way. When you exhale, feel that you are breathing out any impurities from the spine as a cloudy gray mist. Repeat this 9 to 18 times.

B. Warming the Stove

1. Practice Bellows Breathing 18 or 36 times. Then activate the kidneys: feel the Door of Life, the kidneys, and the navel warm. Spiral with your hands and body into the kidneys and Door of Life. Activate and massage the sexual organs. Men, massage the testicles to transform sperm back into life-force. Women, massage the breasts to transform the blood (menstruation) into life-force. Inhale into the sexual center, and exhale, condensing the essence of the breath into the sexual center. Pause for a while. Feel the energy expand and radiate outward. Breathe in and out this way at least 18 times.

2. Rest a moment. Feel the navel warm. Feel the kidneys and Door of Life warm. Feel the sexual center warm. As you inhale, feel the sexual organs, perineum, and anus pull up toward the Original Force in the Tan Tien. Lightly push down as you exhale; feel the pressure building at the spot of the Original Force. Picture the Original Force with a mouth and nose, breathing into that spot.

3. Now amplify and feel the pulse in the area of the Original Energy. As you feel the pulse, feel the suction drawing the sexual energy up and combining it with the Original Energy. Feel the energy expanding within you. Spend at least 10 minutes warming the stove in this way. Adjust your breathing to be soft, long, slow, fine, and deep. Breathe in even cycles. The breath should gradually become so fine and light it would not move a down feather placed in front of your nostrils.

Make sure you feel the Original Force activate before going on to the other stages of this meditation.

C. Begin with the Basic Microcosmic Orbit

1. Move the awareness out from the Tan Tien to the navel. Then circulate your energy through the basic Microcosmic Orbit. You can try using the mind alone to guide the energy. If you prefer, you may use any of the previously mentioned ways to enhance the sensation of Chi in the Orbit: rotating, spiraling, touching the points with the hands, Small Sip Breathing, or Internal Breathing.

2. If the energy starts to flow on its own, stop trying to guide it and just allow it to move at its own pace. This is a good sign you have activated the Chi flow in the Microcosmic Orbit.

It is important always to establish the inner structure of the basic Microcosmic Orbit first, to provide a basis for the other energies you bring in through the more advanced methods of practice.

3. Use the mind/eye/heart power to guide the energy flow through the Microcosmic Orbit 9 to 18 times. When you are ready to conclude the session, bring the energy to the navel and collect energy, letting it return to the area behind the navel and in front of the kidneys to recharge the Original Force.

D. Cosmic Inner Smile

The purpose of the Cosmic Inner Smile is to expand your awareness out to nature, to Mother Earth and the universe, to connect to the unlimited Tao so you can realize your true infinite and abundant essence. But first you have to recognize the basic loving energy already inside you, the feeling of true unconditional love within the microcosm of your heart. Once you have love inside, you can easily connect to the universe.

Simply be aware, and feel the abundant Universal Love above and all around you. Use mind/eye power to draw in and condense this loving energy into the heart or any part of the body. Feel yourself overflowing with Universal Love. When you feel abundantly full, you can give freely to others. Conversely, if you have hatred inside, you will connect to more hatred outside; you will actually attract more negativity.

1. Be aware of the Cosmic Energy in front of you. Be aware of your tongue touching the palate. Smile to the energy in front of you; relax the mid- eyebrow. Feel the energy smile back to you. Breathe in; draw in and gather the smiling energy in your mid- eyebrow and mouth. Then breathe out and condense the smiling energy in your mouth until you feel a Chi ball forming and the tongue vibrating, as if electricity were flowing through it. Do this 9 to 18 times.

2. Contract the round muscles of the nostrils, eyes, and anus to amplify the sensation of pulsing and pumping at the mid-eyebrow. Feel the suction drawing in the golden light of the Cosmic Force. Absorb it into the mouth.

3. Let your smiling energy and the golden light combine and expand in the mouth.

4. Swallow the golden light down to the heart.

E. Opening the Heart

1. To help activate the heart's energy, raise the clasped palms and place both thumbs lightly against the heart's center (Figure 9-5). Draw more smiling energy from the source in front of you through your mid-eyebrow. Let it flow like a waterfall down to the thymus gland and into the heart. Smiling to the heart awakens the virtues of love, joy, and happiness (Figure 9-6). Spend as much time here as you need. Feel your heart relax and expand with loving energy, like a flower blossoming. Remember your best experience of love, whether emotionally or divinely inspired, and fill your heart with that feeling. Love your heart.

351

**Figure 9-5. Clasp the palms and place the thumbs
on the thymus gland.**

The heart is associated with the negative emotional energies of hastiness, arrogance, impatience, hatred, and cruelty. When you smile into the heart, these energies will dissolve, creating the space for the virtuous energies of love and joy to expand.

2. Do the Heart Sound: HAWWWWWW. When you exhale, feel a small flame or fire burning in the heart. After you have completed the Heart Sounds and activated the fire in the heart, the negative energies from all the other organs will come into the heart to be burned out and purified. Do 6 to 9 Heart Sounds (Figure 9-7).

(If you do not activate the fire in the heart, the energy you subsequently bring into it may jam up, and you may feel a tightness or pain in the chest and have difficulty breathing. Massaging the sternum will help keep the energy from jamming. Be certain to spend enough time generating a strong fire in the heart at this stage.)

3. Rest, and be aware of your loving heart. When you exhale, you may feel a cloudy, dull, dingy-red energy being released. Let any

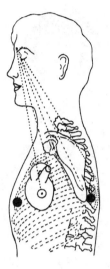

Figure 9-6. Be aware of the heart and the virtue energy.

negativity you find in your heart ride out on this breath. At the same time, retain the ruby-red essence lovingly in the heart.

4. Be aware of the Universal Love as a red mist above and around you, the force of the cosmos that corresponds to the positive energy of the heart. Breathe this lovely red healing, nourishing essence into the heart. Feel the heart grow a deeper and deeper red, like a ruby, as it is moistened and strengthened. Smile to the heart. Gradually feel it open like a red rose, giving forth a pure and fresh fragrance of love. At the

Figure 9-7. Open the mouth and round the tongue down to do the HAWWWWWW sound.

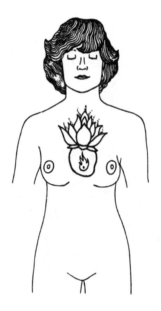

Figure 9-8. Feel the heart blossoming like a flower.

same time, open the palms and fingers outward like a flower blossoming and opening (Figure 9- 8).

5. Be aware of the small flame in your heart. Feel its heat and light, and let it gradually activate the loving Chi of the heart: joy, happiness, respect, and humility.

Inhale and draw more Universal Love from above you into the mouth and heart. Exhale, and condense this energy into the heart. Relax, and let the unconditional love expand and radiate. Do this 9 to 18 times, until you feel so much love within you that the love from your heart starts to overflow.

6. Let the love in your heart radiate to the lungs. Smile to the lungs until you feel them smile back to you. Be aware of the Universal Love around you and continue drawing it into the heart. Condense it into the heart and let it radiate and overflow out to the lungs. Completely fill the lungs with love and smiling energy. Feel the lungs glowing bright white, filling with courage.

7. Continue to radiate loving smiling energy down to the liver and gall bladder in the same way. Feel abundant kindness above and around you. Breathe in the kindness as a bright green mist into the liver and gall bladder. Condense this healing light energy into the liver and let it expand and radiate.

8. Continue down to the spleen and pancreas. Activate the feelings of openness and fairness of the spleen and pancreas. Fill the spleen and pancreas with loving, smiling, bright-yellow energy.

9. Continue down to the kidneys and bladder. Activate the feeling of gentleness within you. Fill the kidneys with gentleness, and with loving, smiling, bright-blue energy.

10. Be aware of the rainbow colors of love, kindness, and gentleness energy above and around you. Breathe in the rainbow light and draw the deepest state of love, peace, or bliss that you can imagine into the heart and all the organs. Breathe out and feel yourself absorb and condense this energy and these colors into each organ, filling every cell of your body with bliss and peace.

If you want to amplify the energy, hold the hands out with the palms facing the heart, left palm on the inside. Do this 9 to 18 times (Figure 9-9).

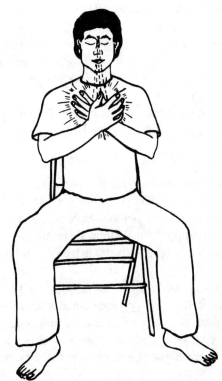

Figure 9-9. Face the palms toward the heart to help amplify the energy.

11. Strengthen the heart by repeating these affirmations to yourself:

"*Respect.* You lose nothing; eventually you will gain everything. *Disrespect.* You gain nothing; eventually you will lose everything."

"*Humility.* You lose nothing; eventually you will gain everything. *Arrogance.* You gain nothing; eventually you will lose everything."

F. Helping the Inner Peace Expand and Grow: Sending Love to Your Loved Ones

1. Hold the palms together near the heart's center. Picture a quiet, peaceful setting, like a beautiful sunset on a beach. Try to imagine the energy of that place, and gather it in front of you. Recall a pleasant experience from your past, or a feeling from a good dream or fantasy.

2. Once you feel your heart overflowing with love and peaceful feelings, recall your loved one. Let him or her take form in front of you. Smile to your loved one until he or she smiles back to you. Let your heart radiate unconditional love to your loved one.

Then continue to breathe peacefully. When you exhale, let the love radiate to your loved ones, your friends, your neighbors. Each time you inhale, expand the loving and peaceful feeling, and each time you exhale, send it out to the ones you love, the people you come in contact with daily.

3. Feel your loved one fill with your love. Gradually let your loved one rise higher and higher until he or she finally disappears.

G. Loving Your Enemy

When you have little love within you, it is hard to give love to both your loved one and your enemy. When you can connect to the Universal Love and link it to your heart, you will begin to have enough love to give others. You can gradually expand it further; let your loving heart energy radiate to those you hate, to the people who create trouble and obstacles in your life.

Generate the energy of forgiveness. Forgive each one, and hold him or her in your heart. In this way you are connecting to your higher heart, the Middle Tan Tien, the seat of unconditional love. Feel this love radiating through your own body and beyond. Feel the connection of those you dislike to the higher heart energy, the same place that yours comes from (Figure 9-10).

1. Let the one with whom you have conflict take form in front of you. Smile to him or her, and radiate love and peace to this person.

2. Ask him or her what you can give to make both of you more balanced. Breathe in the first color or thought form that comes into your mind, and let it radiate to this person. Let the color fill both of you so you are both vibrating in the same color. This color may be what has been lacking, the source of what is causing the two of you to be in conflict.

3. Breathe, condense, and draw more loving energy into the heart. Let your heart radiate unconditional love to this person. Every time you inhale, draw in more loving and peaceful feelings, and every time you exhale, send it out to him or her. Gradually you will feel the conflict between you start to dissolve, and you will feel you understand the person better.

4. Feel him or her fill with your love. Gradually let this person rise higher and higher, until he or she finally disappears in space.

5. Once you can dissolve these knots inside yourself, observe this person in real life. You will notice him or her beginning to change. Sometimes you will need a few more repetitions of this exercise to untie the knots inside you and between you. When you feel him or her change,

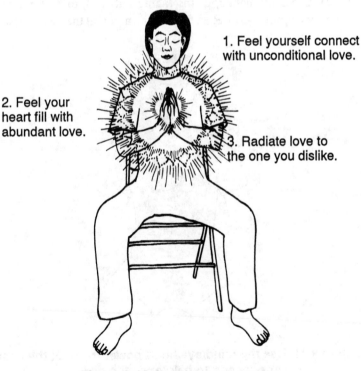

1. Feel yourself connect with unconditional love.

2. Feel your heart fill with abundant love.

3. Radiate love to the one you dislike.

Figure 9-10. Love your enemy.

357

it will be easier to find a time to sit down to talk and dissolve the differences.

H. Middle Line and Back

Next, let the smile and loving energy flow through the digestive tract. Then let the golden light of your Cosmic Inner Smile flow to the brain and down the spine. Finally, after letting your healing smile flow to anyplace in the body in need of loving and smiling energy, smile to the navel and Tan Tien.

I. Stabilizing the Middle Tan Tien:
The Cauldron at the Heart

1. Use smiling energy to activate the cosmic golden light energy. Breathe in through the mid-eyebrow and let the golden light radiate down to the heart. Use mind/eye/heart power to spiral the heart's energy of love, joy, and happiness 36 times clockwise out from the heart center and 36 times counterclockwise in toward the heart center (Figures 9-11 and 9-12). Cross the hands, palms facing outward, to help radiate the heart energy (Figure 9-13). Rest for a while and feel the heart expanding

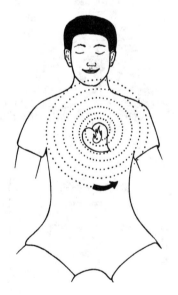

Figure 9-11. Use the mind/eye/heart power to spiral the heart energy and to help open the heart.

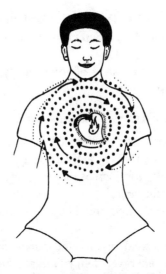

Figure 9-12. Continue to use the mind/eye/heart power to spiral the energy and to help open the heart more.

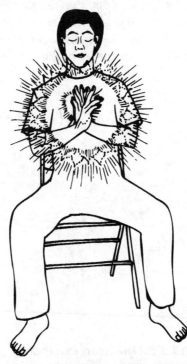

Figure 9-13. Cross your hands to help radiate heart energy.

and contracting (Figure 9-14). Be aware of both the cosmic golden light mixing in the mouth and the golden cord connecting the mouth to the heart.

2. Smell the sweet fragrance of love, purity, joy, and happiness radiating from the heart.

J. Love and Sexual Energy Combine as One

1. Be aware of the heart and sexual organs. Smile to the sexual organs, and feel your sexual energy activate. Recalling a good experience of love and sex can help you increase the orgasm feeling. At the same time, feel the love in your heart.

2. Inhale more love, joy, and happiness into the mid-eyebrow, mouth, and heart.

3. Exhale to the sexual organs and condense the loving energy together with the sexual energy. When you relax, the energy will expand, feeling as if it is exploding there. Feel the loving fire combine with the dense and watery sexual desire. The fire will not dry up the water, nor will it let the water sink or leak out. Feel the sexual energy become light with life, joy, and a peaceful orgasmic feeling (Figure 9-15).

4. Repeat 9 to 18 times, feeling the tremendous amount of orgasm and bliss inside, as the loving energy of the heart and the watery sexual

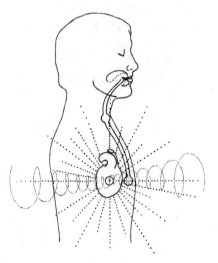

Figure 9-14. Feel the heart expanding, contracting, and radiating love.

energy combine within you. Let this energy expand like steam through the whole body and up to the crown.

5. Extend out and connect to the cosmic energy of your Higher Self. Become aware of your cosmic orgasm (the combination of love, sexual energy, and cosmic energy) or bliss above and around you. Breathe the blissfulness into the heart, the sexual organ, and the whole body. Let every cell fill with the energy of the cosmic orgasm. Love and sex are the most basic energies of life.

6. Now breathe the blissful energy into the mouth and body. Exhale and condense it down into the Original Force behind the navel in the Lower Tan Tien. Relax and let the energy expand inside you. It will radiate to wherever your body needs it.

7. Repeat 9 to 18 times, until you feel the Original Force combining with the cosmic orgasm and expanding inside you.

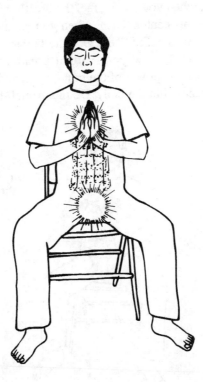

Figure 9-15. Combine the loving energy and the energy of sexual desire.

K. Connecting the Middle Elixir Field and the Lower Elixir Field

1. Keep the left palm on the heart's center and move the right hand to the lower abdomen with the palm up, just below the navel. Inhale naturally, and feel yourself breathing into the heart's center. When you exhale, feel the energy of the breath drop to the Tan Tien.

2. Now focus on breathing in a golden mist through the mid-eyebrow down to the heart. Exhale, and condense the energy down to the Tan Tien. Follow your natural breathing patterns; do not force the breath or any movement of energy. With each breath, you are extracting and retaining the essence of the vital energy of life for the use of your body. Do this from 9 to 18 times.

3. Rest, and feel the Middle and Lower Elixir Fields open and connected (Figure 9-16).

4. This time, when you inhale, feel the breath rising from the lower abdomen to the heart center. Then, when you exhale, send it from the heart center down to the Tan Tien. Use the breath to purify the space between these areas. Follow your natural breathing patterns without using any force. Use the power of the mind, eyes, and heart to direct the current of life-force within the body. Do this from 9 to 18 times.

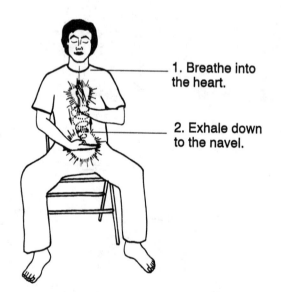

1. Breathe into the heart.

2. Exhale down to the navel.

Figure 9-16. Connect the Middle and Lower Tan Tiens.

5. Rest in the Original Force at the Lower Tan Tien. Feel the sensations of expansion, energy, lightness, peace, and balance.

L. Connecting to the Energy of Mother Earth

1. Place the hands at the sides with the palms facing down toward the earth, and be sure that the soles are flat against the ground. Be aware of the Hui Yin point at the perineum. After a short time, you will begin to feel the palms and soles breathing by themselves. At the same time, you will feel the vagina or scrotum and Hui Yin point starting to naturally pull up and release in a pumping or pulsing action in time with your breathing. Do this 3 to 9 times. Then exhale and rest.

2. Now focus the mind about 95 percent on the Original Energy behind the navel, and about 5 percent on the Five Gates (perineum, palms and soles). Feel yourself grounded; feel connected to the earth. Just relax, and you will feel pulsing again. Let it come in and up. Feel the suction; feel the gentle blue Earth Energy drawn in through the Five Gates pulse in the navel.

3. Feel the Chi ball growing and expanding, filling the whole region between the navel, the kidneys, and the sexual center. Your navel is connected to the earth now; your body feels connected to the body of Mother Earth. Feel the Mother Earth energy strengthening the stove at the Tan Tien and enhancing the Original Energy there.

M. Activating the Cosmic (Higher Self) Chi

1. Breathe into the mid-eyebrow point. Feel it open as you exhale. Repeat this 3, 6, or 9 times. Make sure you feel it open before you go on to the next step.

2. Be aware of the Original Energy behind the navel. Feel the Original Energy activate, and feel the suction there. Simultaneously be aware of the mid-eyebrow point pulsing and activating on its own. Feel the golden light coming in. Now project the awareness out to a favorite place in nature: a lake, an ocean, a forest, a waterfall, a mountain, or a grotto. As you picture them, you will feel the Higher Self Force come to you from them, like a benevolent and refreshing golden mist of light.

3. Now breathe the energetic golden light down into the mouth. Condense and form a golden ball of Chi energy there. Do this a few times until you feel the tongue has an electrical charge. Breathe and merge the golden light with the saliva. Notice how the saliva changes. It may become very rich, sweet tasting, alive, and charged with life-force (Figure 9-17).

4. Swallow the saliva, and, with the mind, follow the pathway of the golden light downward. Picture the golden light flowing through the throat center to the heart and navel and around the perineum to the coccyx. Then feel it flow up the spine to the crown, and from the crown back down to the mid- eyebrow. Let it continue to flow through the Microcosmic Orbit pathway. Feel the ball of light gradually expand until it covers your whole body. Feel it energize and protect you.

The Taoist way is not to worry about the whole world, but simply to concern yourself with the people and things around you. Make sure the people who are part of your life can feel your loving energy, rather than spreading your love so thin that nobody can feel anything.

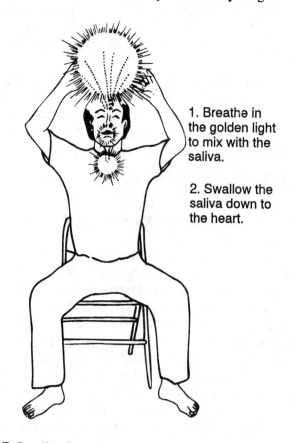

1. Breathe in the golden light to mix with the saliva.

2. Swallow the saliva down to the heart.

Figure 9-17. Swallowing the golden light and the saliva.

N. Ending the Meditation: Collecting Energy at the Navel

1. Place both hands over the navel. Continue to focus the mind on the Original Energy behind the navel. Rest, and enjoy this feeling of being relaxed in body and mind, yet energized at the same time.

2. Conclude the practice by spiraling outward 36 times at the navel and then inward 24 times to finish collecting the energy.

3. Finish with Chi Self-Massage.

A LOVING STATE

Remember the feeling of this practice. If at any time in your daily life you should feel down or depressed, impatient or hasty, anxious or afraid, frustrated or angry, you can recall the feeling and experience from your practice of Opening the Heart. Be aware of your heart, and feel the flame burning out any impatience or hastiness and generating joy and happiness. In just a few minutes, you will feel that you have more energy and Chi. The success of this method of recalling depends on your daily practice. The more you practice, repeat, enhance, and remember it, the more easily you can enter a loving state. This is the easiest way to cultivate Chi.

Practice at this stage for at least 1 to 2 weeks before going on to the next stage.

Chapter 10

SEXUAL ENERGY AND THE MICROCOSMIC ORBIT

Since the early Han dynasty (206 B.C. to 220 A.D.), Taoists have known that sexual energy, Ching Chi (or simply "jing"), has tremendous creative and rejuvenative powers. Not only did they acknowledge that sexual energy is the foundation of human life, but they also observed that sexual energy is the wellspring of creative genius, drive, and self-healing power. They believed, with good reason, that mastery of the Tao of the bedroom arts could lead to happiness for both sexes, as well as improved health, longevity, and even immortality.

There were many references in the Han literature and thereafter to men who had mastered this art and lived in robust health to the ripe old age of 150 or more. In China, longevity has always been much sought after, for in Chinese society, as people grow older, more respect is paid to them. If one stayed healthy and fit, becoming elderly could be a great joy, the best time of one's life. The Chinese were particularly inspired by the example of the legendary Yellow Emperor, Huang Ti. Huang Ti is regarded as the sage-father of Taoism and of Chinese medicine because of his early and profound observations on medicine and physiology. He wrote them down in the famous *Huang Ti Nei Ching* (*The Yellow Emperor's Classic of Internal Medicine*), which after several millennia is still revered as the basic textbook for Chinese medical studies. In addition to his medical pursuits, Huang Ti was also intensely interested in the Tao of Love. According to the famous Han dynasty Chinese historian Ssu-ma Chien, Huang Ti held the throne for one hundred years. During this time, he intensively practiced the Tao of Love without emission, and as a result "ascended into Heaven in broad daylight as an Immortal." In an early Taoist sexual manual, Peng Tzu is quoted as saying, "The Yellow Emperor made love with control...and ascended as an Immortal, while normal people make love without control and only shorten their lives as a result. If a man loves the beauty of women and ejaculates frequently, he will damage his body and encounter all kinds of diseases. By doing this, he is actually seeking death."

Following Huang Ti's example, Taoists desiring to attain longevity and immortality have practiced making love without emission. They have studied the ancient sexual manuals of the Plain Girl, the Select Girl, and the Dark Girl, which describe Huang Ti's conversations with three women sexual initiators into the Tao of Love. These and other early Taoist erotic handbooks were generally kept secret; they were reserved for rulers and initiates who would use the heightened power gained through mastery of their sexual energy to increase their wisdom, compassion, and justice.

Sexual attitudes have changed since those times. Beginning in the 1960s, many people in the "baby-boomer" generation broke free from sexual repression and traditional values and explored the length and breadth of sexual freedom and liberation. After a time, what seemed to be lacking for many was not simply more new sexual partners but a strong spiritual basis for life, love, and relationships. AIDS, herpes, and other hard-to-cure venereal diseases have encouraged a fresh look at the advantages of monogamy. During this period, many people have also become aware of what the East has to teach about reconciling their sexual desire with their yearning for spiritual development.

The West has benefited the East, too. My master, I Yun, encouraged me to study Western anatomy and physiology to bring the ancient Taoist teachings up to date with modern discoveries. Natural science and the Tao do not conflict; the ancient Taoists were scientists who closely observed nature. They made great discoveries in the fields of astronomy (one of the world's first accurate calendars), chemistry (gunpowder), and biology (the circulation of blood) centuries before similar discoveries were made in the West. Now the world is more open; the time for secrecy is past. East and West can share their knowledge for the benefit of all the people on earth.

The Abundance of Sexual Energy

The human body goes to great efforts to keep us in a state of reproductive readiness, with the amazing power to create new life on a regular basis if we so desire. In the average male, each ejaculation of semen contains

200 to 500 million sperm cells, and every one of them has the potential to become a human being. Add to this the fact that most men ejaculate thousands of times in their lives, and the potential becomes astronomical. With one ejaculation, if every sperm cell met a willing egg, one man could repopulate the entire United States. With twenty ejaculations, that same man could become the father of the entire world's population!

Women are born with a store of 450,000 to 700,000 eggs. During their fertile years of menstruation, between 360 and 450 eggs make their way out of the ovaries in their journey down the Fallopian tubes to the uterus. On its trip to the womb, the egg may encounter a sperm cell and be fertilized. If no fertilization occurs, the uterine lining is sloughed off, and the egg and lining passes out with the menstrual blood once a month.

The Importance of Conservation

Despite the body's extravagant reserves of trillions of sperm cells and hundreds of thousands of eggs, it is rare for a man and woman to produce as many as a dozen offspring. If nothing is done with the rest of the reproductive Chi, it is simply lost. Some may argue that this is the way of nature, but to the Taoist, whose goals are longevity and immortality through the transformation of the abundant supplies of energy within the body, the indiscriminate loss of one's rich reserves of Ching Chi is a tremendous waste.

Thus, for the past several thousand years, Taoists have developed and practiced ways of conserving Ching Chi. But Ching Chi is not simply hoarded; it is masterfully recycled, returned as a powerful nutrient to enrich both body and spirit. The major pathway for this recycling process is the Microcosmic Orbit.

HEALING LOVE THROUGH THE TAO

In the Healing Tao system, the main applications of Ching Chi are improving physical and mental health, harmonizing and enhancing sexual relationships, and nourishing spiritual growth. This body of practices is called Healing Love Through the Tao, or Seminal and Ovarian Kung Fu. "*Kung Fu*" literally means skill or ability gained through hard work and discipline. Healing Love Through the Tao offers rewards that can transform your life beyond your wildest dreams, but you have to study, strive to understand what you have learned, and then practice hard if you want to reap those amazing benefits (Figure 10-1).

Before starting Healing Love, it is absolutely necessary that one first learn how to circulate the basic life-force Chi through the Microcosmic Orbit. Once the Orbit is opened, practicing Healing Love methods further opens the Microcosmic Orbit by circulating Ching Chi through the same pathways. The Microcosmic Orbit practice is also accompanied by the meditations of the Inner Smile and the Six Healing Sounds. All three meditations are emphasized throughout the Taoist system, and their mastery is essential to the successful practice of Healing Love. People who rush to practice sexual cultivation techniques motivated by sexual lust alone may endanger their physical and emotional health if they do not first accomplish these preparatory practices that clear the energetic pathways of the body and mind.

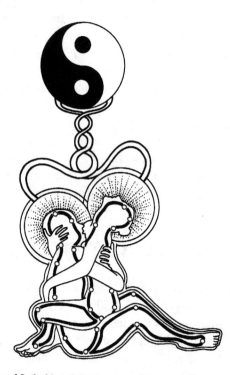

Figure 10-1. Healing Love with couple

The two pillars of Healing Love are conservation and transformation. Although the principle of conservation applies to both men and women, the actual practices of conserving sexual energy differ. The main way that men lose sexual energy is through ejaculation. Women, by contrast, lose little sexual energy through orgasm, but instead lose Ching Chi primarily through menstruation and childbearing.

In both men and women, the major loss of Ching Chi occurs when the sperm cells or egg actually leave the body. Therefore, to conserve sexual energy, the Healing Love practices emphasize retaining the sperm and egg except when procreation is desired, and learning to reabsorb, transform, and recycle the Ching Chi of the egg and sperm. Several practices help accomplish this process.

Western folk wisdom has long agreed with the Taoists regarding the importance of conserving sexual energy. For example, most athletic coaches caution their athletes to refrain from sexual activities before an important competition or game. Similarly, in his famous book *Think and Grow Rich,* Napoleon Hill devotes an entire chapter to the necessity of conserving sexual energy to achieve great success in life.

Nonetheless, until recently Western biologists have clung to the belief that male sperm are produced relatively easily and "cheaply" by the body, with no significant drain produced through frequent ejaculation. This dogma was solidly challenged by recent scientific research reported in the December 3, 1992, *New York Times* by Natalie Angier. A scientist studying worms found that the simple act of making sperm substantially shortened the male worm's life-span. Wayne A. Van Voorhies, a graduate student researcher at the University of Arizona in Tucson, discovered that male nematodes live much shorter lives than their mates and traced that discrepancy directly to sperm production.

When he experimentally altered the male worms so that "they lost their capacity to make sperm while retaining their taste for intercourse, the altered nematodes lived at least 50 percent longer than the normal, fertile males. The results suggest that creating sperm is far more difficult than scientists had imagined, demanding a diversion of resources that might otherwise go into ensuring a male's long-term health." Commenting on this study, other scientists maintained, according to the report, that it is possible "at least a fraction of the difference in life span between men and women just may be linked to sperm production," noting that women, on average, live about six years longer than men.

The study found that normal male worms prevented from mating lived about 11.1 days. Males allowed to mate at will, a state requiring steady sperm production, lived only 8.1 days. But the altered males, freed from the demands of sperm production and allowed to mate as they pleased, survived almost 14 days. Hermaphrodite worms, which normally produced both eggs and sperm, lived an average of 11.8 days regardless of how much sex they engaged in. However, the altered hermaphrodites, still producing eggs but not sperm, lasted 19 days.

Although scientists aren't certain how much of the worm research applies to humans, over the past four thousand years Taoist masters have devised time-tested methods of making love without emission. The research suggests Taoist methods of conservation are far different than suppression of sex promoted by celibate priests, monks, and nuns of many religions. While Taoists are renowned for their longevity, celibate monks and nuns are not generally long-lived. One recent study found celibate Catholic priests experienced a 300 percent higher rate of prostate cancer than the normal population, indicating, from the perspective of Taoist medical knowledge, the adverse effects of "stagnant Chi."

Testicle and Ovarian Breathing

Healing Love practices of Testicle and Ovarian Breathing teach one how to recapture and recycle Chi that has gone into the reproductive system, returning it to nourish the rest of the body before it is lost through menstruation or ejaculation. This energy can heal the organs and glands, strengthen the brain, bones, and nervous system, energize the body, and further open the Microcosmic Orbit. Women often report great relief from symptoms of premenstrual syndrome (PMS), as well as lighter, shorter, and less painful periods. Since Testicle and Ovarian Breathing recycle the Chi of the sperm cells and eggs, it is important to suspend the practice if procreation is desired. A high level of mastery offers a noninvasive form of birth control. Men should read *Taoist Secrets of Love* (Aurora Press, 1984) and women can read *Healing Love Through the Tao* (Healing Tao Books, 1986) to get the full details on these and other sexual techniques listed in this chapter.

Scrotal and Ovarian/Vaginal Compression

The practice of Scrotal and Ovarian/Vaginal Compression uses special breathing and muscle contractions to pack fresh Chi into the reproductive organs, which strengthens, energizes, and flushes the entire area. Regular practice can reduce mental problems. In men, it strengthens the prostate and testes; in women, it strengthens the ovaries and cervix and increases the power of the vaginal muscles.

Egg Exercise for Women

Many women today have never experienced an orgasm. According to recent sexual research, vaginal muscle tone, particularly that of the pubococcygeal muscle (PC muscle), is directly related to orgasmic potential. In one experiment, doctors measured the clenching power of the PC muscle and compared it with orgasmic ability. Totally nonorgasmic women registered a pressure of an average of 7.43 mmHg (millimeters of mercury) on a Kegel perineometer, whereas clitorally but not coitally (vaginally/G-spot) orgasmic women measured 12.31 mmHg. Women who were both clitorally and coitally orgasmic measured 17 mmHg.

In the Healing Tao, women can strengthen their vaginal muscles with the Egg Exercise. The Egg Exercise involves inserting a small jade egg into the vagina and learning to tighten the vaginal muscles to move the egg around. Developing the vaginal muscles not only increases a woman's orgasmic capacity, it also increases her male partner's pleasure. In the harems of the ancient emperors of China, the queens and concubines who learned the Egg Exercise from their Taoist physicians kept it a closely guarded secret, for it improved their ability to please the emperor. Becoming a favorite consort raised a woman's rank and standing among the many concubines in the harem. All other factors being equal, those who had mastered the Egg Exercise (Figure 10-2) had a definite edge on the competition.

In addition to its benefits in the boudoir, the Egg Exercise is a marvelous exercise for health. When one strengthens the ability to pull energy up, one can then draw more healing Mother Earth energy and sexual energy upward to balance and strengthen all the systems of the body. The Egg Exercise is also used as an aid in Ovarian Breathing, the Orgasmic Upward Draw, and Bone Marrow Nei Kung to increase the marrow.

Orgasmic Upward Draw

In *Everything You Always Wanted to Know About Sex (But Were Afraid to Ask)*, David Reuben, M.D., describes orgasm as it is typically understood by Western sexologists: "For orgasm to occur," he writes, "the full

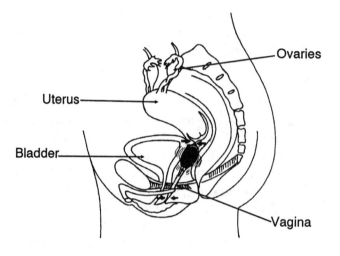

Figure 10-2. Egg Exercise

force of the body's entire nervous system must be concentrated on the sexual organs. Successful orgasm requires that every microvolt of electrical energy be mobilized and directed toward the penis and clitoris-vagina."

Although this description confirms that the very nature of sexual arousal gathers and focuses the Chi (electrical energy) of the body, Reuben goes no further than a discussion of what Taoists refer to as "genital orgasm." Taoists say that orgasm energy is the best distillation of the body's essences, drawn from all our organs, glands, and cells by the amazing electrochemistry of the arousal process. The body thinks we are going to create new life, a child, so it releases its premium energies to start that new life. But for most people these days, the sexual act is usually aimed at recreation, not procreation. In ordinary sex, this energy is directed toward the genitals and then simply lost in what we call an "outward pour" orgasm. Men lose far more energy than women in the sexual act, but both men and women ordinarily release energy at orgasm.

Taoists recognize the tremendous opportunity for inner alchemical cultivation during sexual arousal. The Taoist orgasm takes this intense focus of energy that has been drawn to the sexual organs and spreads it throughout the body. With this sexual "electricity," many other centers in the body are activated and revitalized. This is called an "inward pull" orgasm, achieved by the Orgasmic Upward Draw.

In the practice of the Orgasmic Upward Draw, all the Chi and hormones activated and released during sexual arousal are recaptured and circulated throughout the body. This shifts the orgasmic experience from a localized genital "outward pour" orgasm to a total-body "inward pull" orgasm. The inward-pull orgasm is more intense, blissful, and longer lasting. It enlivens and nourishes every system of the body, especially the brain, sensory organs, nervous system, and internal organs and glands (Figure 10- 3).

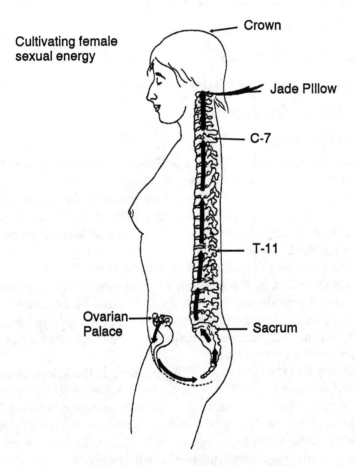

Figure 10-3. Orgasmic Upward Draw

Controlling aroused sexual energy is like trying to control a team of seven wild horses. Therefore, one usually practices the Orgasmic Upward Draw as a solo practice first. Once one has learned how to control one's powerful aroused sexual energy, one can use the same techniques when making love with a partner.

Dual Cultivation

Harmonizing Sexual Relationships

Male belongs to Yang.

Yang's uniqueness is that he gets aroused quickly,

But he also quickly retreats.

Female belongs to Yin.

Yin's uniqueness is that she is slower to be aroused,

But she also is slow to retreat.

—Wu Hsien, Han Dynasty Taoist

Balancing Kan and Li (Water and Fire, male and female) on the sexual level. Taoists say men are naturally Yang and are like fire: quick to get hot and quick to burn out. Women are naturally Yin and are like water: slow to bring to a boil, but once hot, they hold their heat for a long time. The art of Healing Love balances Yin and Yang so that both partners are totally satisfied.

In Dual Cultivation (practice with a partner), the first goal is to control male ejaculation. A man's ability to make love more frequently and for longer periods of time not only increases his pleasure but enhances his ability to satisfy the woman. The second goal is for the woman to become fully aroused and orgasmic. The couple must support each other to achieve these goals.

Intimacy and the exchange of Yin and Yang in the Microcosmic Orbit. Because men are more Yang and women are more Yin, they can help bring each other into better balance through exchange of their Chi during lovemaking. To do this, both partners need to have opened their Microcosmic Orbit as the first step toward balancing the Yang channel in the spine and the Yin channel running down the front of the body. Then, during their lovemaking, a man and a woman can circulate their aroused Chi through their own and their partner's Microcosmic Orbit.

If both partners have opened their Microcosmic Orbits, the natural polarity between man and woman is greatly amplified and the energetic flow much more powerful, because these two master channels feed all the vital organs and their associated meridians. This balancing and nourishing exchange of Yin and Yang energies is the heart of the Healing Love practice and is part of what eventually leads the dedicated student beyond sexual pleasure to longevity and immortality (Figure 10-4).

When you can open and receive the loving energy of your partner, and in turn have your partner open to receive your energy, you will experience a blending and intimacy unlike anything you have known before. You will grow to love each other more each day, and your mutual

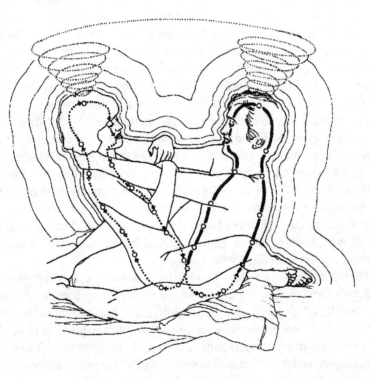

Figure 10-4. Yin and Yang sexual energy exchange

love will enrich those around you. In this way, sexual love blossoms and matures into a deeper, spiritual love.

Dual Cultivation and Spiritual Development

Spiritual development is directly related to emotions and attitudes. As we have already mentioned, the emotions are housed in the bodily organs. Through the Inner Smile, the Six Healing Sounds, and later in the meditation of the Fusion of the Five Elements, we can learn to get in touch with our emotions at their source, our internal organs. We can then process, release, and transform our negative emotions and nourish our positive, constructive, and wise emotions.

The term *Dual Cultivation* is also used in ancient Taoist texts to describe a single person cultivating his or her dual Yin and Yang sexual energies. This kind of higher internal practice, known as the Alchemical Marriage, or self-intercourse, is covered in the chapter on Kan and Li.

The multiplying power of sexual energy. Healthy sexual union is often called "making love," and from the Taoist point of view, that is exactly what we are doing. Sexual energy is creative energy; it has the ability to multiply other energies exponentially. At conception, Ching Chi activates the initial two human cells—one egg and one sperm—to multiply into the trillions of cells that make up a mature human.

Just as it stimulates multiplication on a cellular level, our Ching Chi or sexual energy expands and intensifies our emotions and attitudes. This is why sexual pleasure is popularly considered the highest bliss known, and why the feeling of "being in love" is so intense and all-encompassing. On the negative side, it is also why lovers' quarrels are the most intense, and why so much fear, frustration, anger, worry, and depression often surround sexual performance. Many murders are related to the sexual issues of rape, jealousy, infidelity, and marital frustration and resentment stemming from sexual dissatisfaction.

Therefore, in Taoist Dual Cultivation practices, it is important to first dissolve and cleanse the organs of any negative emotions. Using the skills developed through the Inner Smile, Six Healing Sounds, and Fusion practices, one connects with the positive virtue qualities of one's spirit expressed through the organs. The sexual energy is then drawn up into that organ, and the effect is like throwing gasoline on a fire: the sexual energy takes the positive virtue quality being expressed by the organ and expands it manyfold. This multiplying ability can transform individual love into love for all creation. With practice, we can raise our virtues from an ordinary level to the transcendent level of those of a saint or an immortal. This is the highest purpose to which we can direct our sexual energy—the goal of enlightenment.

Dual Cultivation and Sexual Healing

Throughout the ages, Taoist physicians have prescribed certain lovemaking postures and techniques for healing various ailments and for tonifying specific systems in the body. Some positions are more beneficial for the man, others for the woman, and still others are equally beneficial for both. In general, one partner is active while the other partner is passive. The active partner passes healing energy to the passive one.

These positions are described in detail in the *Su Nu Ching* (*The Book of the Plain Girl*). Several of the important postures are included in *Healing Love Through the Tao: Cultivating Female Sexual Energy.*

The *Su Nu Ching* does not go into detail about the circulation of energy in these positions. Once you learn how to control and direct your sexual energy through Testicle and Ovarian Breathing and the Orgasmic Upward Draw and have learned how to circulate and exchange it with your partner, the positions are not crucial. Energy can be directed at will, using mind power alone, to whatever place needs healing in your partner or yourself, regardless of position.

Sexual Energy, Tai Chi Chi Kung, and Iron Shirt Chi Kung

It is difficult to have a fully satisfactory sex life if you are not physically fit. Iron Shirt Chi Kung I and Tai Chi Chi Kung help strengthen not only the muscular system but also the skeletal, endocrine, digestive, cardiovascular, excretory, urinary, integumentary (skin), and nervous systems. By frequently exercising the perineum and anus, Iron Shirt Chi Kung builds and tones the love muscles in the pelvic floor, making it easier to accomplish the Orgasmic Upward Draw.

With regular practice of Tai Chi Chi Kung and Iron Shirt Chi Kung, greater amounts of Chi are generated, absorbed, and circulated. One feels fit, powerful, full of Chi energy, and unencumbered by physical weakness. With greater stamina, sensitivity, and flexibility, one is physically able to experiment with more postural variations in lovemaking, increasing the opportunities for new and undiscovered pleasures. Each practice brings a unique variety of energy—Earth, sexual, and vital-organ Chi—into the Microcosmic Orbit.

Even a physical disability need not be an obstacle to exercise; one can still exercise to the fullest extent possible. A well-known Tai Chi master once commented, "Anyone who is still breathing and is conscious can benefit from Chi Kung practice!"

Sexual Energy and Bone Marrow Nei Kung

Bone Marrow Nei Kung focuses on the relationship between the sexual energy and the skeletal system, which has long been acknowledged in traditional Chinese medicine. Bone Marrow Nei Kung strengthens the reproductive organs and releases Ching Chi and sexual hormones throughout the body. This energy is captured and stored in the bones.

Sexual Energy Massage

Massage is beneficial for every part of the body, including the reproductive organs. Regular Sexual Energy Massage stimulates the nerve receptors in the reproductive organs, enhances blood circulation, and increases the production of sexual hormones. Sexual Energy Massage differs for men and women, for the obvious reason that their sexual organs are different: male sexual organs are primarily external, while female sexual organs are mainly internal. Men learn a variety of techniques for massaging the kidneys, testes, penis, perineum, and scrotal sac. Women learn special techniques to massage the breasts, kidneys, ovaries, and uterus while using the mind and senses to activate the viscera and endocrine glands, in the same way as in the Orgasmic Upward Draw (see *Bone Marrow Nei Kung*, pp. 112- 116).

Bone Breathing

Sexual Energy Massage stimulates the production and release of sexual hormones. The sexual hormones are part of what is called Ching Chi in Chinese physiology. In addition to being related to the skeletal system, these hormones are related to many bodily processes, including aging. Taoists seek to keep the Ching Chi strong to retard the aging process and promote rejuvenation and longevity.

Abundant Ching Chi is essential in the Taoist process of regrowing the bone marrow. The red and white blood cells of the body are produced in the bone marrow. One effect of the aging process is that the marrow begins to dry up, to be replaced by fat. This puts more stress on the remaining marrow to continue to produce an adequate supply of new blood cells. By regrowing the marrow, a rich supply of blood cells is assured. This helps maintain a strong flow of oxygen to all the body cells and builds a strong immune system.

Most bodily systems become stronger, more sensitive, and more responsive with regular exercise, and the reproductive system is no exception. We were never taught to exercise our sexual organs in school. The idea of doing so may sound strange at first, but the rewards of these practices are stronger and healthier organs, improved hormonal balance, and enhanced sexual performance and response.

Power of Sexual Energy

Sexual energy is one of our most powerful energies. Most people do not know how to use it, aside from procreation, so this rich source of energy is lost to them. For millennia, Taoists have developed skillful methods of conserving, balancing, and transforming sexual energy for improved physical and mental health, happier and more satisfying relationships, and rapid spiritual growth.

The conservation and transformation techniques and principles learned in the Microcosmic Orbit and Healing Love Through the Tao classes serve as a foundation for success in many other advanced practices of the Healing Tao.

PRACTICE
The Microcosmic Orbit:
Connecting Loving Energy with
Sexual Desire

In this round of practice, you focus on further opening the Functional Channel (Conception Vessel), with special emphasis on connecting the heart and sexual centers and on cultivating the connection between the Middle and Lower Tan Tiens. Almost every system of spiritual development recognizes the necessity of activating both the sexual energy and the heart. However, few systems explain how these two forces—compassion and sexual desire—can be harnessed together for spiritual development.

When you combine opening the heart and activating your sexual energy with the Original Force, you will feel your Original Force change. You will notice the change both in quality and quantity and will have a sense of peacefulness, delight, security, and comfort.

The compassion energy of the heart is cultivated to a deeper level with the second level of meditation in the Fusion of the Five Elements. Also, to fully awaken and control your sexual energy, you must master the practices taught in Healing Love Through the Tao. This book presents more advanced levels of the Microcosmic Orbit. Readers who have already mastered Fusion and Healing Love should accomplish this stage of combining energies with ease. Nonetheless, if you are still a beginner and practice well at the level of this book, you will reap many of the benefits.

The following sequence can be used when cultivating sexual energy and circulating it to the Orbit.

1. Chi Kung Warm-Ups. Begin by loosening the spine with Chi Kung Warm-ups: Spinal Cord Breathing, Iron Bridge, Crane Neck, Turtle Neck, Spinal Cord Shaking, and Spinal Cord Rocking. Then rest. Feel the spine open and relaxed. As you inhale, imagine breathing a white mist from the earth into the spine to purify, cleanse, and brighten the spinal cord. When you exhale, feel you are breathing out any impurities from the spine as a cloudy gray mist. Repeat this 9 to 18 times.

2. Six Healing Sounds. Practice the Six Healing Sounds.

3. Focus inward. Prepare yourself by sitting in good meditation position on a chair.

Become aware of your surroundings. Feel the sensation of your feet touching the floor, your hands clasped, the chair beneath you. Be aware of the sounds inside the room, outside the room, and within your body.

Be aware of your breath. Feel the body naturally expand as you inhale and contract as you exhale. Breathe in and out with awareness in this way 9, 18, or 36 times.

4. Warm the Stove.

5. Open the basic Microcosmic Orbit.

6. Practice the Cosmic Inner Smile to align with your Higher Self.

7. Open the heart.

Activate the Sexual Center

Women: Transform blood into Chi.

1. Rub the hands together until they are warm. Cover and press the breasts with the palms and start to massage outward (Figure 10-5). Be aware of the vagina and the pineal and pituitary glands. Circle inwardly up and outwardly down 18 times as one set. Rest with the fingers lightly

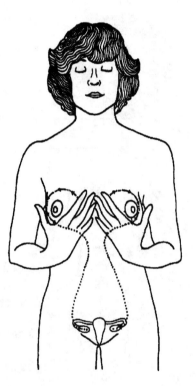

Figure 10-5. Massage the breasts outward.

touching the nipples and gather the energy from the breasts, sexual organs, and pineal and pituitary glands into the heart center. Repeat 2 to 4 times (Figure 10-6).

2. Reverse the direction and gather the force back into the nipples. Make a connection to the back, on both sides of the spine between the T-5 and T-6 spinous processes, and connect down to the kidney. Do 2 to 4 sets. (Refer to Chapter 5, Figures 5-34 and 5-35.)

3. Move the hands to massage and lightly shake the kidneys 9 to 18 times. Rest and feel the kidneys warm. The massaging, shaking, and resting is one set. Do 2 or 3 sets.

4. Move the palms to the lower abdomen and massage the groin up to the ovaries. Then massage the area around the liver, gall bladder, and

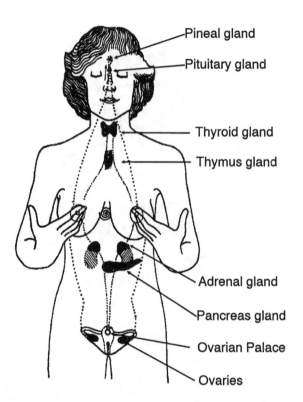

Pineal gland

Pituitary gland

Thyroid gland

Thymus gland

Adrenal gland

Pancreas gland

Ovarian Palace

Ovaries

Figure 10-6. Touch the nipples with the fingers and gather the breasts' and sexual glands' energy into the heart center.

spleen, and return to the groin again. Start in an outward direction from the lower part, circling in and up to the top, and back out and down 36 times. Then reverse the direction and massage 36 times (Figure 10-7).

5. Move the palms down and cover the sexual center (Ovarian Palace) (Figure 10-8). Using mind/eye power, lightly contract the circular iris muscle and the muscles around the eyes. Feel them stimulate the vaginal muscles (the first sexual energy gate), the opening of the cervix (the second sexual energy gate), and the anal muscles to lightly contract as well. This helps gather the sexual energy you have activated.

6. Pause for a while. Feel the energy expand at the sexual center.

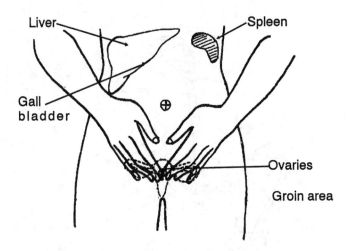

Liver

Spleen

Gall bladder

Ovaries

Groin area

Figure 10-7. Massage the groin and the waist areas.

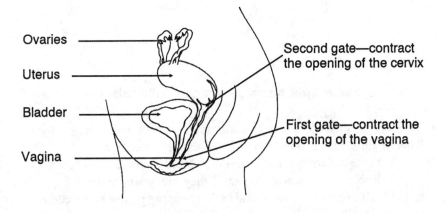

Ovaries

Second gate—contract the opening of the cervix

Uterus

Bladder

First gate—contract the opening of the vagina

Vagina

Figure 10-8. Close the two sexual gates.

Men: Transform Ching (sperm) into Chi.

1. Rub the palms together until they are warm. Massage and lightly shake the kidneys 9 to 18 times. Rest and feel the kidneys warm. Use mind/eye power to gather energy from the kidneys. Inhale deeply into

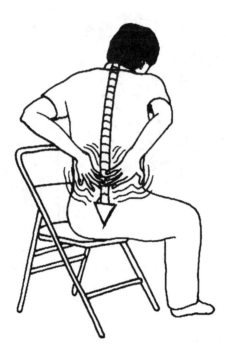

Figure 10-9. Massage and shake the kidneys.

the kidneys, then exhale and condense the breath and energy into the Door of Life. This is one set. Do 2 to 4 sets (Figure 10-9).

2. Make the connection from the kidneys to the sexual organs.

3. Rub the hands together until they are warm and massage the testicles 18 to 36 times. Rest, and feel the energy gather in the center of the testicles. Do 2 to 4 sets (Figure 10-10).

4. With the left palm, hold the testicles; with the right palm, massage in a clockwise circle around the navel 36 to 81 times. Change hands: now the right palm holds the testicles, and the left palm massages in a counterclockwise direction 36 to 81 times (Figure 10-11).

5. Move the palms down and cover the sexual center. Using mind/eye power, lightly contract the circular iris muscle and the muscles around the eyes. Feel this stimulate the perineum, the tip of the penis, the urogenital diaphragm, and the anal sphincter muscle to lightly contract

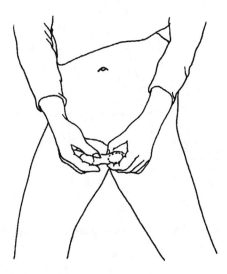

Figure 10-10. Finger massage of the testicles

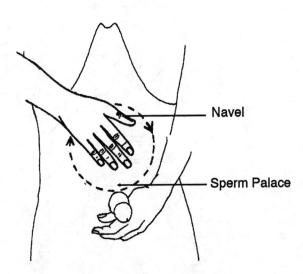

Navel

Sperm Palace

Figure 10-11. The left hand holds the testicles. The right hand massages the lower abdomen.

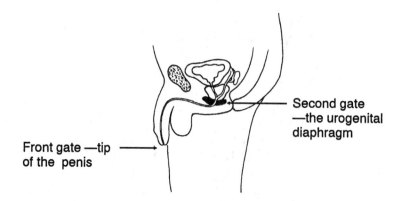

Second gate
—the urogenital
diaphragm

Front gate —tip
of the penis

Figure 10-12. Close the two sexual gates with mind/eye power.

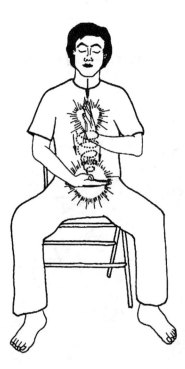

Figure 10-13. Connect the heart and sexual center.

as well. This helps gather the sexual energy you have activated (Figure 10-12).

6. Pause for a while. Feel the energy expand at the sexual center.

Men and women: Continue together, practicing in the same way.

7. Feel the joy, love, and happiness in your heart. At the same time, focus on your sexual energy at the sexual center. Be aware of the multiplying quality of your sexual energy, of its ability to expand and increase other energies many times.

8. Move the left hand up to touch the heart, and the right hand down to touch the sexual center, palm facing up (Figure 10-13).

9. Become aware of the Universal Love above you. Inhale, and draw this love into your heart, filling it with love. Feel the heart overflowing with love. Exhale down to the sexual organs. Feel the loving energy from the heart and the sexual energy combine into a blissful orgasmic feeling. Repeat 6 to 9 times, or until you feel the orgasm and blissfulness pervade your body.

10. Feel a connection like a pipeline between the sexual center and the heart. Draw the sexual energy up into the heart, and feel the joy, love, and happiness expand until it feels as though it is filling all heaven and earth (Figure 10-14).

11. Feel the love and sexual energy combine into an orgasm and gradually travel up the spine to the crown. Then feel it expand to connect with the Cosmic Orgasm.

12. Inhale; gather the Cosmic Orgasm into the mouth and the Original Force (navel area). Exhale and condense it in the navel area. Feel the heart and sexual energy drawn in also. Rest, and let it expand to the whole body. Feel every cell fill with this blissful energy, the most important energy in our cells. Spend 5 to 10 minutes absorbing and condensing the Cosmic Orgasm (blissful feeling).

Connect to Mother Earth Energy. Draw up Mother Earth Energy and circulate it through the Orbit.

Protecting the aura. Form a golden egg around the body for protection. Circulate the golden healing light of your Higher Self through the Microcosmic Orbit.

Widen the Functional Channel (Conception Vessel)

1. Return the awareness to the mid-eyebrow point. Draw in more golden light from the Higher Self Force. Use the mind to spiral at the

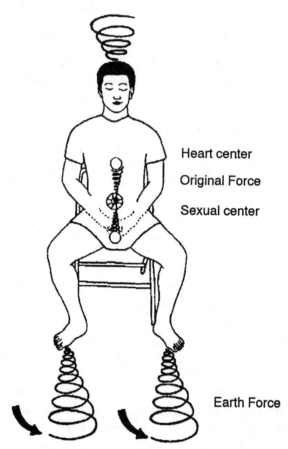

Unconditional Love

Heart center

Original Force

Sexual center

Earth Force

Figure 10-14. Draw the heaven/earth, heart, and sexual energy into the Original Force.

mid-eyebrow point. Feel the mid-eyebrow point expanding and filling with energy.

2. Rub the tip of your the back and forth to massage the palate. Rest and be aware of the tongue and the palate.

3. Inhale, press the tongue to the palate, and draw Chi into the mid-eyebrow and the mouth. Exhale, condense the Chi in the mouth, then relax and let the Chi expand in the mouth. Feel the tongue's strong connection to the palate. Do this 9 to 18 times.

4. Rest, then touch the tip of the tongue to the roof of the mouth just behind the teeth and slowly begin to move the tongue toward the back of the mouth. Continue until you feel a tingling, metallic, or electric sensation where the tongue and palate touch. This means you have made a good connection and successfully linked the Governor and Functional Channels at the upper "Magpie Bridge."

5. Knock the teeth together 18 to 36 times, then lightly clench and release them. This vibrates the bones and activates the bone marrow to transport Chi through the denser matter of the bones. Let the energy radiate to the palate. Spiral there with the mind and eyes 36 times each way. Inhale and exhale into the palate 3 to 9 times, using the word "Chi" to increase the energy there.

6. Generate some saliva in the mouth, swallow down, gently breathe the energy down, and spiral at the throat point. Feel the energy flowing down and expanding at the throat point. Repeat 3 to 9 times.

7. Gently breathe the energy down and rotate a Chi ball at the heart point. Feel the energy flowing down and expanding at the heart point. Feel the connection between the mid-eyebrow and heart, like a pipeline. Repeat 3 to 9 times.

8. Gently breathe the energy down and rotate at the solar plexus point. Feel the energy flowing down and expanding there. Repeat 3 to 9 times.

9. Gently breathe the energy down and rotate at the navel point. Feel the energy flowing down and expanding at the navel point. Repeat 3 to 9 times.

10. Gently breathe the energy down and rotate at the sexual center point. Feel the energy flowing down and expanding there. Feel your sexual energy activating and becoming even more energized as you bring additional energy in. Repeat 3 to 9 times.

11. Gently breathe the energy down and rotate at the perineum point. Feel the energy flowing down and expanding at the perineum point (Figure 10-15). Repeat 3 to 9 times.

12. Continue to focus on the Hui Yin (perineum point). Inhale deeply; then, as you exhale, release the energy through the perineum and down through the legs, soles of the feet, and down into the earth (Figure 10-16). Repeat 2 to 3 times. Feel as if you are releasing down into the center of the earth. Now be aware of the gentle blue Earth Energy rising through the soles and legs like a soothing, healing, and refreshing blue mist. Let it rise to merge with the Original Energy behind the navel. Use

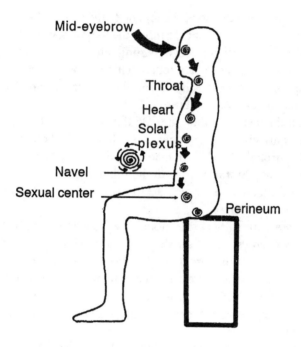

Figure 10-15. Widening the Functional Channel

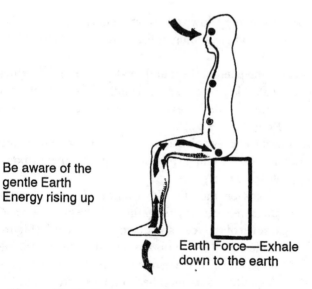

Be aware of the
gentle Earth
Energy rising up

Earth Force—Exhale
down to the earth

Figure 10-16. Connecting the heart channel to the Earth Force

the mind to warm the navel, kidneys, and sexual organs. This activates the Original Energy and helps you digest and assimilate the Earth Energy. Rest for a few minutes and enjoy the feeling of being peaceful and energized.

End the Meditation: Collect Energy at the Navel

1. Place both hands over the navel. Continue to focus the mind on the Original Energy behind the navel. Rest, and enjoy this feeling of being relaxed and quiet in body and mind, yet energized at the same time.

2. Conclude your practice by rotating outward 36 times at the navel, and then rotating inward 24 times to finish collecting the energy.

3. Finish with Chi Self-Massage.

Summary

Continue with this level of practice for at least several weeks before moving on to the practices in the next chapter.

In this practice we have concentrated on making the connection between the sexual energy and the heart energy. The higher levels of this practice occur after you have completed the Fusion of the Five Elements meditations and Healing Love through the Tao.

In this chapter we have also focused on opening and strengthening the Functional Channel (Conception Vessel) from the mid-eyebrow to the perineum. Having the Functional Channel open provides a vitally important vent for the energy you will bring up the spine and draw down from heaven in the following chapter. Be sure to practice until you really feel the energy descending from the mid-eyebrow all the way down to the navel and perineum.

As outlined in previous chapters, spend at least a week mastering bringing the energy down from the mid-eyebrow point to the heart point. Then spend a week mastering bringing the energy from the heart point to the navel point and sexual center. Finally, spend a few more days establishing a firm connection from the sexual center to the perineum.

Many systems teach the student to bring energy to the crown but do not say anything about providing a vent for it in case of excess Chi in the head, nor do they emphasize bringing the energy back down. In the Healing Tao, it is our experience that this can lead to many negative side effects, including the phenomena of Kundalini psychosis and "cooking your brain"—having so much Yang Chi in the head with nowhere else to go that the brain literally overheats and the tissue begins to cook.

Therefore, we cannot overemphasize the importance of having the Functional Channel completely open in preparation for bringing energy into the crown point. Be certain to spend as much time as you need to open the Functional Channel before proceeding.

Chapter 11

HEAVENLY CHI AND THE MICROCOSMIC ORBIT

CONNECTING WITH THE UNIVERSAL FORCE

What Is the Universal Force (Heavenly Chi)?

Since the dawn of time, people all over the world, including the Chinese, have been fascinated with the heavens—with the movements and mysteries of the sun, moon, stars, planets, comets, and meteors. They have instinctively felt that what happens in the skies above is somehow intimately related with life on earth, and that by better understanding the heavens, they could better understand themselves. From this conviction, generations of study eventually gave birth to the sciences of astrology and astronomy, alchemy, and physics.

Many world religions and philosophies, including Taoism, believed that humanity actually came from the stars, that human life originated not on earth but at some other place in the universe. Although there are myths and legends in many cultures supporting this belief, modern science has no way yet to either prove or disprove it. But interestingly, today's astronomers and physicists do theorize that life on this planet was seeded from other stars, that the forces vitalizing the inorganic elements into life forms originated elsewhere in the universe.

The Heavenly Force Is
Related to Our Spirit

Whatever the case may be, it is an ancient belief of humankind that the higher, more spiritual forces of the universe are in the heavens. Christians, Buddhists, and Taoists believe, as did the ancient Egyptians, that if one practices the virtues during this life, it is possible to be reborn in "Heaven," a purer and holier place, perhaps far away in space or merely in a different dimension that is impervious to profane vibrations. In the sacred and spiritual atmosphere of heaven, virtue and spiritual cultivation are much easier to practice than on earth.

Heaven Is Linked with
Immortality

Taoist literature speaks of immortality as its ultimate goal and describes such people as the Yellow Emperor "ascending to Heaven in broad daylight as an immortal." Chinese art often depicts a sage riding off into the clouds on the back of a crane or dragon. Immortality thus seems to be linked with one's ability to access the pure heavenly realms and actually to go there in one form or another. Some describe attaining heaven as a one- way street and maintain that the Immortals go there never to return. But more often, Taoists see a more compassionate pattern to the universe, in which the sages who have attained immortality, as well as the primordial gods, continue to interact with humanity, going back and forth between heaven and earth. Thus, it is said that an Immortal can take thousands of different forms at once, manifesting as whatever is needed by humanity at any given time (Figure 11-1).

To attain this type of immortality, a refinement of one's entire being is necessary. The impure aspects of one's body, Chi, and consciousness must be brought under control and transformed into purer forms. Spiritual mastery means that one's true nature, or original spirit, must be awakened to its heavenly connection. Recognizing our connection and place in the universe, our awakened original spirit becomes the rightful master of our personality, thoughts, feelings, and will. Then we are in accord with the Tao, and as a result we can be effortlessly and naturally in harmony with ourselves, our families, society, nature—with every-thing.

**Figure 11-1. Taoist Immortal riding off into a cloud
on the back of a crane**

Cultivating the Immortal Tao

The fading away of the Tao is when openness "Wu Chi" turns into spirit, spirit turns into Chi, and Chi turns into form. When form is born, everything is thereby stultified. The functioning of the Tao is when form turns into energy, energy turns into spirit, and spirit turns into openness [Wu Chi]. When openness is clear, everything thereby flows freely.

Therefore ancient sages investigated the beginnings of free flow and stultification, found the source of evolution, forgot form to cultivate energy, forgot energy to cultivate spirit, and forgot spirit to cultivate Wu Chi.—Tan Jing-sheng, "Transformational Writings," 10th Century (trans. by Thomas Cleary, *Immortal Sisters*)

The Three Pure Ones of Heaven, Earth, and Humanity correspond to our Three Treasures in the human body: Shen (spirit), Ching (sexual energy), and Chi (life-force energy), respectively.

Heavenly Chi Is the Ordering Force of the Macrocosm

Heaven, or the Universal Force, is the most ethereal of the Three Pure Ones. It corresponds and is linked to our spirit, or Shen, which encompasses our consciousness, thoughts, and emotions.

In ancient Taoist writings, the term *Heaven* is often used to mean the ordering principle of the universe, or universal law, the law the ten thousand things have to follow. Sometimes Heaven is even used as a synonym for Tao. Heaven is the Yang principle of the universe; it is represented in the first hexagram of the I Ching as the Creative principle, being the first of the Three Pure Ones to emerge from Wu Chi. Heaven is thus the initiating force of all creation. (Please see Figure 8-1.)

Spirit Is the Ordering Principle of Our Inner Universe

Just as the Universal Force (Heavenly Chi) is the ordering principle of the Three Pure Ones in the macrocosm, our spirit or consciousness is the ordering principle of our being in the microcosm of the body. As we said in a previous chapter, our individual consciousness is one ray of the light of universal consciousness. The bodily form and Chi may dissolve at death, but with cultivation, the spirit can be immortal; it can transcend the realms of Yin and Yang to reunite with Wu Chi. Thus it follows that the spirit or consciousness should be the ruler of the body and the Chi.

This relationship of the Three Treasures is reflected throughout Taoist practice; for example, in the Tai Chi classics it is said, "The mind leads and the Chi follows; the Chi leads and the body follows."

This is not to say that these three (spirit, Chi, and body/Ching) do not interact and mutually influence each other. A wise ruler must listen to and respond appropriately to the limitations and requests of his ministers and subjects; one who does this is a skillful ruler indeed. Sensual pleasure is not evil in itself. The Taoists have always emphasized moderation as the key. If we can enjoy pleasures without being ruled by or addicted to them, they add to our joy and enrich our lives. Nonetheless, it is important that the servant not become the master, which happens in those of low spiritual cultivation. Sensual pleasure and the passions (such as greed, hatred, and heedlessness) become the dictating motivations of their lives, to the extent that they lose their spiritual integrity and their harmony with themselves, with those around them, and with the Tao.

Different Aspects of Shen (Spirit)

The ancient Taoists realized, just as did Freud, Jung, and other modern psychologists, that we have many parts to our consciousness. The word *Shen* can have several different meanings, depending on the context. Two different meanings in particular are most important for the understanding of Inner Alchemy.

The first meaning is that Shen is our mind and resides in the heart, rather than the brain. It refers to our whole range of mental activities, emotions, and spiritual aspects—not only those associated with the heart, but with all the other organs, glands, and systems as well.

The second view is that Shen is our Original and unconditioned Spirit, connected to Wu Chi as light rays are connected to the sun.

Shen Is Our Mind and Resides in the Heart

It is said in Chinese medical texts, as well as Taoist scriptures, that the Shen resides in the heart. In this context, Shen is more related to the ordinary mind, to the normal range of mental activities and consciousness. In fact, *Hsin* or *Xin*, the Chinese word for the heart, is often used as a synonym for mind. The heart thus affects mental activity, emotions, memory, alertness, thinking, consciousness, and sleep. Strong and balanced Heart Chi will promote a strong mind and a happy personality.

The heart governs the blood, and the blood flows to every cell in the body. In Chinese medicine, the mind itself is related to the blood, in that the blood pervades the body, communicating with every cell, maintaining life and supporting metabolism throughout the organism.

If the heart becomes weak and unbalanced, one's mind will be scattered and lacking in concentration, and one's emotional state will be unstable. It may be hard to "open one's heart" to other people, and health as well as interpersonal relationships can suffer. Recent medical research by Dean Ornish, M.D., indicates that keeping the heart closed to others can actually increase one's risk of heart attack.

The broader context of Shen refers to the entire complex of our mental, emotional, and spiritual consciousness. Shen thus relates not only to the heart, but also to the internal organs, glands, brain, memory, nervous system, senses, emotions, subtle bodies, and all the various aspects of our personality, both conscious and subconscious.

We have already mentioned that the internal organs each house a part of our consciousness. In addition to the positive and negative emotions of each organ, the five viscera also relate to other specific aspects of our spirit (Figure 11-2):

The liver controls the Hun, our higher-level or ethereal soul.

The lungs control the Po, our lower-level or corporeal soul.

The spleen controls the I, our thinking and intelligence.

The kidneys control Zhi, our will power.

The heart controls the Shen, our spirit/consciousness.

The Liver and the Hun Soul. The liver houses the Hun, sometimes translated as our higher-level soul, or Ethereal Soul. The Hun is divided into three parts (Hun sub-souls) and is said to give us our positive Yang human nature. The Hun is thus considered to be the essence of the five virtues. The Hun is the subtle yet substantial expression of our higher-level consciousness and is the seed of our immortal spirit body. It is like the Chi aspect of our spirit. Through inner alchemical refinement, the Hun becomes a strong, stable vehicle for our spirit; it is the basis of our subtle immortal spirit body, in which we can travel to the heavens.

The Lungs and the Po Soul. Our lower-level, corporeal or Po soul is divided into seven parts and resides in the lungs. It is that part of our consciousness that is the most earthbound, the most Yin, physical, material aspect of the soul. It is the part that fixates on things as being solid, separate, physical, and distinct. Not seeing how all things are connected and related in the grand scheme of things, this part tends to be the most selfish, and is related to the passions or negative emotions. The Po is connected to the physical body; it cannot leave this plane at death but stays with the bones in the tomb, and it is therefore sometimes called the White Essence Soul. The Po is related to the nervous system, limbic system, senses, sensations and feelings, and Ching. It is very much affected by sadness. When a person is being treated for sadness and depression in traditional Chinese medicine, the points corresponding to the lungs and the Po would be treated. Much of the energy of the Po can be sublimated and transformed into the Hun.

The Spleen and the I. The spleen houses the I (pronounced Yee), our thought or intentions. It is thus particularly related to our intellectual and scholastic thinking, formulation of ideas and intentions, memory, studying, and concentrating. When Spleen Chi is strong, the mind will think clearly and memorization will be quick and easy. Too much study, mulling things over, pensiveness, or worry drains and weakens the spleen. Similarly, weak Spleen Chi dulls the mind, concentration, and memory.

Some recent Tai Chi authors have mistranslated the "I" of the Spleen as "mind" or "will" instead of intention. *Mind* is too broad a term, as all

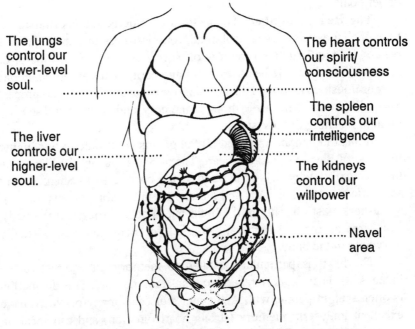

The lungs control our lower-level soul.

The heart controls our spirit/ consciousness

The spleen controls our intelligence

The liver controls our higher-level soul.

The kidneys control our willpower

Navel area

Figure 11-2. The internal organs each house a part of our consciousness.

the organs participate as a part of the mind; the Spleen houses only one part of the mind, that associated with intention. "Will" is also very distinct from intention; the difference between intention and will is clearly illustrated by the old saying, "The road to hell is paved with good intentions." It is easy to have good intentions, such as losing weight, quitting smoking, or meditating at dawn every day, but intentions alone do not accomplish the deed; it takes willpower to carry out intentions. In both Taoist Internal Alchemy and traditional Chinese medicine, the willpower is associated with the kidneys, not the spleen.

The Kidneys and the Zhi (Willpower). The kidneys house the Zhi, or willpower. The kidneys nourish the brain and are related both to brain function and short-term memory. They are also the seat of our Ching Chi, as well as the strength of purpose that often accompanies sexual drive. Both good short-term memory that keeps us focused and mindful of our goals, and the drive and ambition to achieve them (an aspect of Ching) are thus related to the kidneys. If the kidneys are strong, the willpower will also be strong; if the kidneys are weak, short-term memory may be poor, and a person may lack willpower and be easily distracted from his or her goals.

The Heart and Shen. The heart is considered the coordinator or ruler of all the various aspects of mind, consciousness, and spirit. For this reason, in traditional Chinese it is often referred to as the Emperor or Master Controller. The heart regulates and coordinates all the functions of consciousness mediated through the five organs; it directs and processes our intention, willpower, thought, memory, and nervous and sensory input in reaching life decisions.

It must be emphasized that all the organs contribute to this higher meaning of Shen, not just the heart. The nervous system, the blood—in fact, virtually every cell of the body—are connected to Shen. Recent scientific research has indicated that the chemical components for consciousness exist not only in the brain but in cells throughout the body. This creates the biochemical potential for consciousness virtually anywhere in the body.

The heart is particularly related to memory. In contrast to the kidneys, the heart is more related to long-term memory. This distinction is often seen in people with Alzheimer's disease, many of whom have excellent long-term memory (strong heart function) and can recall in great detail events from their childhood, but poor short-term memory (weak Kidney Ching/brain marrow).

Our Original Shen Is Our True Nature

A second level of meaning for Shen is our Original Shen (Yuan Shen), Original Mind, or Original Spirit. It differs from the meaning of Shen as our ordinary mind, which can be conditioned by relative experiences and circumstances. In Western religious terms, it might be compared to the difference between our individual soul and that part of us that is the Universal Spirit. Our Original Shen is unconditioned and limitless. It is often compared to a mirror or crystal ball, which is clear and empty and can thus reflect entire worlds. The Taoists sometimes referred to this mind as the Uncarved Block, because it has not been affected by the world and is full of potential. This is our true, highest spirit, the ray of the light of Wu Chi, unborn and undying. Therefore it is also called our immortal spirit (Figure 11-3).

We have opened the gates of immortality when we connect with or wake our Original Spirit. At first, we may only glimpse it in a flash; later, with practice, we may be able to maintain lucidity in our Original Spirit

Figure 11-3. Our Original Spirit

during meditation, first for short periods, then for longer and longer periods. Often at the beginning, as soon as we get up from our meditation seat, we resume our normal habitual patterns of thinking and quickly lose touch with our Original Spirit.

With more practice, we can maintain the light of our Original Spirit throughout the day. In this way the higher mind, coming from the light of Wu Chi, rules in the hierarchy of our being. All aspects of body and mind become servants of this highest Universal Mind; we can connect with the Tao whatever we do and wherever we go. When we can exist in this consciousness without lapse in the midst of every moment of daily life, we have reached the highest level of immortality; we have returned to the source, to our true origin, to Wu Chi.

Traveling to the Celestial Realms

On the path to Wu Chi, we must practice regularly to transform our ordinary state into an immortal state. One very important factor is the place where we practice. Although it is good to reach a stage in your practice where you can practice anywhere, in any circumstances, some places are more conducive to practice than others, and it is good to take advantage of them when you can. These places are usually quiet, protected from the elements and from danger, with good air and beautiful and inspiring scenery. It is also good if sages or yogis have meditated there before, or if the site is blessed or holy. (If you are planning an extended meditation retreat, it is helpful if there is a town or community not too far away and people who can bring you any necessities and provisions.) Once you have become familiar with such a place, however, it is not necessary to be there physically; you can make the connection through the mind.

Just as certain sites on earth are more conducive to practice, the Taoists seek to travel to the heavenly realms where the Immortals live (Figure 11-4). There, sages can guide their practice, and in this celestial and rarefied atmosphere, attainment of the highest fruits of spiritual realization is not far off. For this reason, Taoists seek to strengthen and refine their Three Treasures. By so doing, they may be able to attain the highest levels of immortality and visit the heavenly realms during this very life, traveling in their soul and spirit bodies and then returning to the physical body. If they do not attain immortality during this life, they

Figure 11-4. Travelling to the Celestial Realms

will already have prepared a purified vehicle for their consciousness to use at death to carry them to the heavenly realms.

Because the physical body is mortal, Taoists seek to transform the Ching, or physical essence of our energy, into Chi, and to refine Chi into Shen, ultimately to merge with Wu Chi. In doing so, Taoists also learn to absorb, digest, and transform energies from nature to use for these purposes. We have already spoken of the Earthly and Cosmic Chi, so now let us take a closer look at Heavenly Chi, examining both what it is and how it may be used by the Taoist adept.

Varieties of Heavenly Chi

A simple way of thinking of Universal Force or Heavenly Chi is to perceive it as the Chi of the sun, moon, planets, and stars. There are many types of Heavenly or Universal Chi. Each type has its own correspondence with our microcosm and is used in different ways.

Chi of the Sun and Moon

The sun has very strong Chi that has an obvious and undeniable effect on life on earth. It is the essence of Greater Yang and is related to the heart and the fire element. The earth revolves around the sun and in one year completes a 360-degree circle. This solar cycle, called the Yellow Route, is divided by the Taoists into 24 solar periods, beginning with the Spring Equinox. Each period lasts 15 days and is considered a single season. Each period also has a special name that describes the climate in that phase of the year. (Please see Figure 1-11.)

These periods also correspond, within the microcosm of our bodies, to the 24 separate vertebrae of the spine: the 5 lumbar, 12 thoracic, and 7 cervical vertebrae (the sacral and coccyx vertebrae are not included, as they are fused together); they also correspond to 24 primordial energies in the body (the circulation of the Chi through the 12 ordinary Chi channels on both sides of the body). Taoists have 24 sets of Chi Kung practices that correspond to these 24 periods and are practiced at those times to connect with the unique Chi of each season. (More details are provided in the Tao Body/Mind/Spirit Chart in the catalogue chapter.)

Despite this solar breakdown, the Chinese calendar is based on the moon, beginning 4681 years ago on the first new moon during the reign of the Yellow Emperor, Huang Ti. The moon is the essence of Yin and is related to the kidneys and water. Absorbing lunar energy helps one cultivate a strong Yin essence.

There are specific days of the solar cycle during which the sun and moon energies are particularly potent and accessible. The ancient Taoists observed that on the solstices and equinoxes, which mark the seasonal changes, the sun seems to stop in its movement. They called these stops Doors, and, according to ancient lore, the Taoist alchemical practitioner must pass through these doors to be received by the lord who grants the fruits of immortality unique to each celestial region.

The Spring Equinox is called the Golden Door and is the most important door of access to the sun. The Summer Solstice is called the Palace of Universal Yang; it marks the peak energy of the sun (the longest day of the year). The Autumn Equinox is called the Eastern Well and is the most important door of access to the moon. The Winter Solstice is called Great Cold or the Palace of Eternal Frost and marks the peak of the lunar energy (the longest night of the year).

The Solar essence is gathered during the lunar month of the Spring Equinox on the 3rd, 9th, 17th, 21st, and 25th day of the month in which the sun enters the Golden Door. Gathering the Lunar essence is done during the lunar month of the Autumn Equinox on the 3rd, 15th, and 25th day of the month in which the moon enters the Eastern Well. There are optimal days for meditation and Chi Kung practices that draw the energy or "breath" of the sun and moon. The key days for gathering the Solar essences are at the solstices and the equinoxes, and the best days for gathering the Lunar essences are the new and full moon days. However, one can still draw the solar and lunar energies on other days; it will simply not be as powerful as on the key days.

These are advanced practices begun at the level of Greatest Kan and Li and should not be undertaken until you have mastered the basic and advanced practices of the Microcosmic Orbit, as well as Fusion of the Five Elements, Lesser and Greater Kan and Li, Healing Love, and Iron Shirt. (For a simple level of these practices, see "Most advanced mind/eye training"in Chapter 4.)

Once you have reached this level, the Chi you are circulating in the Microcosmic Orbit has become highly refined, and the eight Extraordinary or "psychic" channels, including the central or Thrusting Channel, have been opened as well. At this level you can thus more consciously direct the process. You are using more of yourself; there is more room for venting and storing the energies; and there is less likelihood of energy stagnation, heat, or malabsorption.

Chi of the Planets

In the Fusion of the Five Elements advanced formulas, we connect to the Chi of the nearby planets, which in turn directly enrich the Chi of our associated internal organs. The planet Jupiter is associated with wood and the liver; Mars with fire and the heart; Saturn with earth and the spleen; Venus with metal and the lungs; and Mercury with water and the kidneys. These five planets in turn draw their energy from the Grand Force of the Five Elements, the Five Primordial Emperors or Stars that originated from the Three Pure Ones (see "Heavenly Chi," below). Because the bodily organs are related to the planetary energies, we can build the essential energies of the organs when we connect to the planets in the Kan and Li Meditations. Drawing on the planetary energies helps empower, strengthen, and protect not only the physical body but the energy body as well. (Please see Figure 5-3.)

We prepare ourselves for Fusion of the Five Elements and the Kan and Li practices with the Inner Smile and the Six Healing Sounds. These foundations teach us to feel our organs, to get to know their colors and qualities, to begin to connect to the energy of each particular element. In addition, the Microcosmic Orbit practice opens the way for circulating the planetary energies through the body so they can be better absorbed and digested. Neglecting these basics can lead to disappointment and trouble. A strong mastery of the Microcosmic Orbit, Inner Smile, and Six Healing Sounds paves the way to safe accomplishment of the higher-level practices.

Heavenly Chi of the Stars and Constellations

The Three Pure Ones, the first forces to emerge from Wu Chi, gave birth to five huge "stars"—the Wu Tai, or Five Grand Forces of the Five Elements. These five huge elemental forces gave birth to the entire universe, including trillions of stars. According to Taoist cosmology, they created the North Star, which created smaller stars, among which were the stars making up the 28 major constellations. The constellations are grouped according to the four directions and the center, and these five groups are known as the Five Houses.

Stars and constellations have their own unique energy that corresponds to the body and our Chi. For example, just as the polestar or North Star is considered the stillpoint or central axis around which the heavens revolve and which is the doorway to heaven, our lower Tan Tien is our central axis and is the doorway to the core of the body. In addition, the various bones of the skull are connected to the energy from the seven stars of the Big Dipper and the North Star and can easily draw these energies. The 28 Constellations in the Four Quadrants of Heaven are related to the Five Elements, the Five Seasons, the Five Directions, and the five organs of the body.

The Microcosmic Orbit Meditation and Stellar Heavenly Chi. The first step in opening to the stellar energies is in the Microcosmic Orbit, where we open the door to the Heavenly Chi by focusing on the North Star and the Big Dipper energies, concentrating on their light, their color, and the associated feeling of their energy. Our main doorway to

Heavenly Chi at this level is our crown or Bai Hui point. Internally, the hypothalamus is the point of correspondence to the Bai Hui. The back of the Crown point is also known as Kun Lun Mountain, the highest peak of humans and in heaven. The pineal is the point most sensitive to the light of heaven.

Once we are able to open to and tap the outer energy sources of the North Star and Big Dipper, we can use them to bring ourselves into balance by absorbing and blending them in much the same way we would adjust the temperature of the water in the bathtub by adding hot and cold as necessary to bring it to a perfect temperature. If we find we are too Yin, we can draw more Heavenly Chi; if too Yang, we can draw in more Earth Chi. In this way, we can harmonize our Yin and Yang energies with the Microcosmic Orbit practice.

Kan and Li Meditations and Stellar Heavenly Chi. At higher levels of practice, the Kan and Li practices and beyond, we explore the many other stellar connections between the heavenly macrocosm and the microcosm of the body. For example, in esoteric Judaism, it is said that when God created Adam, Adam was as big as the entire universe. Then God placed his hand on Adam's head, and Adam became small. Similarly, in higher-level Taoist meditations, you imagine that you are the legendary first man, Pan Gu, and that you have a giant body, billions of light-years from head to toe.

When this is done properly, you become the Cosmic Being, whose Crystal Palace is the North Star, who has constellations and planets for vital organs, whose heart is the sun, whose kidneys are the moon, and whose Tan Tien is the planet earth. This Cosmic Being—the mind of Tao—beams its exquisite rays to one cell of its being, the human sitting on a chair on planet earth, meditating on the stars. This practice cultivates our True Knowledge and awakens our Real Senses; it develops cosmic consciousness and opens our three Tan Tiens to receive energy from their heavenly counterparts. Thus, Kan and Li teaches us how to tune to different frequencies from the stars as well as the earth, and to the different levels of consciousness associated with them. Eventually, we become who we really are by returning to the source.

Returning to the Source

"Heaven, Earth and I are living together, and all things and I form an inseparable unity."—Chuang Tzu

In the science section of a recent issue of *The New York Times*, an astronomer was quoted as saying that life on this planet was seeded from other stars. We are thus connected to the stars through our bodies; the human form itself is a product of stellar energy and matter. Realizing that our essence is of the stars, the Taoists devised methods to tap the macrocosmic energies of the Three Pure Ones, the Five Elements, the North Star, the Big Dipper, the 28 Constellations, and the planets. The purpose is to enhance the processes corresponding to these energies within the microcosm of our bodies—to promote our health, refine our spirits, and eventually reunite us with our source, the Wu Chi.

Deep within our subconscious minds we still carry memories of the unity and bliss that preceded our entry into the dense vibrations of the earth plane. Here it becomes easier to see our individuality, but more difficult to perceive our interconnectedness with the universe, than when we are in our energy or spirit body. Yet because of the subtlety of these latter bodies, many people are unaware of Chi and even forget that life has a spiritual side.

> When openness "Wu Chi" turns into spirit, spirit turns into Chi, Chi turns into form, and form turns into sexual energy [Ching], then sexual energy turns into attention. Attention turns into social gesturing, social gesturing turns into elevation and humbling. Elevation and humbling turns into high and low positioning, high and low positioning turns into discrimination.

> Discrimination turns into official status, status turns into carriages. Carriages turn into mansions, mansions into palaces. Palaces turn into banquet halls, banquet halls turn into extravagance, extravagance turns into acquisitiveness, acquisitiveness turns into fraud. Fraud turns into punishment, punishment turns into rebellion. Rebellion turns into armament, armament turns into strife and plunder, and strife and plunder turns into defeat and destruction.--Tan Jing-sheng, *Transformational Writings*, 10th Century

The ultimate purpose of Taoist practice is to return to our original state—the source, the Wu Chi. One way of returning to the Wu Chi is through the practice of Internal Alchemy. Taoist Inner Alchemy begins with opening, cleansing, and purifying the energy pathways of the body through the Microcosmic Orbit meditation, Iron Shirt Chi Kung, and Healing Love techniques. The second stage of Internal Alchemy works directly with the Five Elemental Forces within our bodies and also within the earth through the practices of Fusion I, II, and III, Tai Chi, Five Element Nutrition, and Chi Nei Tsang (massage). These techniques begin to clear the way for advanced work with the energy body and the spirit body, the subtler aspects of our being.

Later stages of Internal Alchemy continue expanding our consciousness or awareness beyond the physical body into the vastness of inner and outer space. In the advanced disciplines of the Healing Tao, students begin to work more consciously with the Five Elemental Forces emanating from the cosmos. Advanced practices involve collecting and absorbing energy from different sources in the universe while traveling in the energy and spirit bodies. Yet it is important to understand that as we do the advanced practices, such as Greatest Kan and Li, we are using Water and Fire to dissolve the ego/mind's arbitrary boundaries between our inner world and outer space; we travel to the farthest reaches of the universe in order to return to the center of our own Tan Tien.

Wu Chi is beyond the boundaries of time and space, so for us as Taoist practitioners to "return to Wu Chi," we must broaden our minds and empty ourselves; we must let go of the fixed, limiting concepts of Newtonian physics and realize that we are the universe. A leap like this is not so easy! Generations of Taoist masters have refined and mapped the simplest and safest approaches. Because it is impossible to realize the Wu Chi in one step, the journey is divided into several stages.

Five Stages of Cultivating
Heavenly Energy in the
Healing Tao

First Stage: The North Star

The first stage utilizes the material aspects of the physical body to refine, strengthen, and transform energy into the immaterial forms of the spirit bodies. If successful, the first stage brings the practitioner to the North Star (or Polaris), which is the first station and the center of the visible constellations from the earthly perspective. Polaris is also known as the polestar because all constellations that are visible from the North Pole seem to rotate around it. The position of the earth's axis (marked by the North and South Poles) relative to the plane of the earth's orbit determines which star appears to be at the center of the constellations. Over thousands of years, as the axis gradually shifts its position, it points to different stars. (In 3000 B.C., the polestar was Thuban; thousands of years from now, it will be Vega.)

Taoists reach the North Star by expanding their energy and spirit bodies beyond the earth's sphere. This requires practitioners to learn to draw efficiently on the stars and the universe as sources of energy to fortify these bodies. The North Star and the seven stars of the Big Dipper are of primary importance for this purpose. Their energies can be identified with practice, because the stars of the Big Dipper radiate a red light, whereas the North Star emanates a violet light. The force of this violet light penetrates all matter, including the planets and other stars. It is important to note, however, that the violet light emanating from the North Star indicates the doorway of heaven; it is not the highest heavenly force. The light of the highest Heaven Force is clear.

Three steps are required to complete the first stage.

Taoist practice begins in the body. The first step of stage one is to upgrade and maintain your physical health while stabilizing your financial and social conditions. Your body is a vehicle for processing energy; the healthier you are, the more energy it can process, and at a faster rate. Your health and processing capabilities will be greatly enhanced through the Microcosmic Orbit, Six Healing Sounds, Inner Smile, Healing Love, and Iron Shirt Chi Kung practices. Your finances and social interactions should be stable so you can create space in your life for these disciplines. (It is difficult to concentrate if you do not know where your next meal is coming from.)

Travel beyond the body and beyond earth. Next, you will learn how to use accumulated energies for traveling beyond the earth plane to the moon, sun, and planets. This is similar to the way a space shuttle uses a booster rocket to push it beyond the earth's gravitational field. In Taoism, the Microcosmic Orbit and Fusion practices begin the process of creating the energy body, to help boost the immortal body (spirit body) beyond this world while you still remain present in it. The healthier you are internally, the more power you will be able to generate to expand your consciousness beyond the confines of the physical body and the field of planet earth. When you can expand beyond this reality and return, you will gain the raw materials necessary to build a more powerful energy body and spirit body for longer journeys. (Please see Figure 1-14.)

Travel to the stars. The higher practices involve traveling to and from the stars and constellations—particularly the North Star and Big Dipper—using the energy and spirit bodies. During these journeys the physical body does not actually leave the earth. Rather, our consciousness merges with the earth, in its capacity as a heavenly body, which allows us to use it as an expanded ground connection so we may safely absorb the higher radiations and vibrations from the stars.

Second Stage: The Great Forces of the Five Elements

Beyond the polestar lies the second station of the ascending Taoist, comprising the *Great Forces of the Five Elements* (origin of the Five Elemental Forces). These are represented as a group of five stars beyond our visual perception. Practitioners who attain the level of the Five Elements become one with the forces animating the universe. When the Five Elements are transcended, the Taoist enters the realm of the *Triple Unity*. This stage is achieved through the three levels of Kan and Li enlightenment practice.

Third Stage: The Three Pure Ones

In Taoist cosmology, the Three Pure Ones are symbolized as three massive stars beyond the Great Forces of the Five Elements. In actual practice, this level establishes union with the three forces of Chi, or vital energy; Ching, or vital essence (sexual energy); and Shen, or vital spirit. The universe unfolded from the unity of the Wu Chi into the multiplicity of stars, planets, and life. Taoists trace back this process of unfolding primal energy through the practice of *Sealing the Five Senses*.

Fourth Stage: Primordial Yin and Yang

The next level beyond the Three Pure Ones reestablishes a union with the forces of Yin and Yang (male and female). All multiplicity is returned to the original polarity, preparing the way for complete reabsorption into the Wu Chi. This stage is achieved through the practice known as the *Congress of Heaven and Earth*. (Please see Figure 1-4.)

Fifth Stage: Wu Chi

The attainment of Wu Chi is sometimes symbolized in Taoist cosmology as a physical journey, yet Wu Chi is always present within each individual, beyond the diversity of energy configurations. These energies, when passed through the filter of time and space, were polarized to appear separate from the Wu Chi. Primordial Yin and Yang energies dissolve back into their source, thereby ending the illusion of separation. The process of realization involves becoming fully conscious of the intrinsic identity of all universal energy. This stage is achieved through *Reunion of Heaven and Man.*

PRACTICE
Microcosmic Orbit Meditation:
Opening the Governor Channel and Connecting with the Heavenly Chi

1. Preparations

Chi Kung warm-ups. Begin by loosening your spine with Chi Kung Warm-Ups: Spinal Cord Breathing, Iron Bridge, Crane Neck, Turtle Neck, Spinal Cord Shaking, and Spinal Cord Rocking. Then rest. Picture your spine as open and relaxed. As you inhale, imagine you are breathing a white mist from the earth into your spine to purify, cleanse, and brighten your spinal cord. When you exhale, feel that you are breathing out any impurities from your spine in the form of a cloudy gray mist. Repeat this 9 to 18 times.

Practice the Six Healing Sounds.

Preparations for meditation. Begin by sitting in good meditation position on a chair. Once you are in a good sitting position, take a few minutes to focus and prepare yourself.

1. Become aware of your surroundings. Feel the sensation of the feet touching the floor, of the hands clasped, of the chair beneath you.

2. Be aware of the sounds inside the room, outside the room, and within your body.

3. Be aware of the breath and of the tongue touching the palate. Feel the body naturally expand as you inhale and contract as you exhale. Breathe in and out with awareness this way at least 9 to 36 times.

2. Microcosmic Orbit Meditation: Opening the Crown

A. Activating and Connecting the Energies

1. Begin with the Cosmic Inner Smile.

2. Cosmic Inner Smile to your heart. Open your heart and continue the Cosmic Inner Smile. When you get to the sexual organs, spend more time connecting the loving energy of your heart with the sexual energy of desire. Combine their energy with your Original Force at the center.

3. Activate your Original Energy (Warming the Stove).

4. Circulate energy in the Basic Microcosmic Orbit.

5. Activate and connect with Mother Earth Energy.

6. Activate and connect with the Higher Self (Cosmic) Energy.

7. Expand the golden light to cover your body.

8. Activate your Functional Channel by spiraling through each point. Return your awareness to the mid-eyebrow and connect all the points to open the Functional Channel: drawing and spiraling energy to your mid-eyebrow point, palate, throat, heart, solar plexus, navel, sexual center, perineum, down to the soles and back up to the perineum.

B. Widening the Governor Channel to the Crown

In this phase, you move the energy up the spine point by point. You use Small Sip breathing and spiraling with the mind and eyes to assist the energy. Use whatever other methods you like to assist the energy: sound, color, touching. It is not important what method you use, but rather that you focus your awareness on all aspects of your being and energy and have the sense of Chi moving up your spine.

> **CAUTION:**
> **IF YOU HAVE HIGH BLOOD PRESSURE, GLAUCOMA, OR ANY OTHER HEALTH PROBLEM THAT WOULD BE ADVERSELY AFFECTED BY HOLDING YOUR BREATH, DO NOT USE THE SMALL SIP BREATHING METHOD. USE SOFT INTERNAL BREATHING INSTEAD, OR SIMPLY USE YOUR MIND TO GUIDE YOUR CHI.**

1. Opening the sacrum. Massage and shake the coccyx and sacrum, especially the eight holes of the sacrum, in a circular fashion until you feel warmth there. Massage 9 times in one direction and 9 times in the other (Figure 11- 5).

Inhale a small sip into the mid-eyebrow, and feel the suction as you lightly pull in the eyeballs and pull up on the perineum. Take a small sip, and delicately pull up on the anus; inhale another small sip and pull up on the back part of the anus. Slightly tilt the tip of the sacrum inward as you inhale 5 more small sips into the sacrum. As you exhale, condense the energy in the coccyx and feel the pulsing at the sacrum.

Exhale, and condense the energy at the coccyx. Keep the mind focused on the tip of the coccyx. You may also rotate a Chi ball inside the sacrum 9 to 18 times in each direction. For some people, this may suffice to stimulate the movement of Chi up the spine to the crown.

Although we will not mention it further in the instructions, you can pull up on the perineum, anus, and back part of the anus each time you do Small Sip breathing, to draw energy up from one point to the next, all the way up the Governor Channel to the crown. Also, remember to do each point 9 to 18 times.

2. Opening the Ming Men (Door of Life) center. Inhale a small sip, and draw the energy from the perineum through the sacrum and up to the Ming Men point between the kidneys. Spiral the energy into the Ming Men using mind/eye power. Take 3 to 9 more small sips and breathe more energy up from the sacrum to the Door of Life 9 to 18 times. (Please see Figure 5-32.)

Now exhale, condense the energy at the Ming Men. Let the energy expand as you rest, breathing naturally. Just relax and feel the line of energy radiating up the perineum, coccyx, sacrum, and Door of Life.

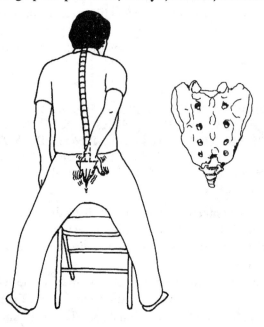

Figure 11-5. Massage the coccyx and sacrum.

3. Opening the Chi Chung (T-11) center. Focus the mind on or touch the T-11 point. Inhale a small sip, and draw the energy from the perineum up to the Door of Life and T-11. Spiral the energy into T-11. Take 3 to 9 more small sips to draw the energy up to T-11, spiraling more energy into T-11 with each sip. (Please see Figure 5-33.)

Exhale and rest. Feel the line connecting the perineum to the Door of Life and T-11, and feel the energy flow up to the T-11 point. Spiral at T-11 with your mind and eyes.

4. Opening the Wing Point (Shen Dao or T-5) center. Focus on the Wing Point opposite the heart (below T-5). Inhale a small sip, and draw energy from the perineum up to T-11 and to your Wing Point. Then take 3 to 9 more small sips to draw more energy up to your Wing Point, spiraling the energy into the Wing Point with each sip, using mind/eye power. (Please see Figure 5-35.)

Then exhale, condense the energy, and allow it to expand as you rest. Now feel the energy flowing by itself up into the Wing Point. Feel the point expand and grow energized.

5. Opening the Da Zhui (C-7) point. Focus on the C-7 point. Inhale a small sip, and draw the energy up from the perineum to the Wing Point and then to C-7. Take 3 to 9 small sips into the C-7 point, using mind/eye power to spiral more energy into the C-7 point with each sip. (Please see Figure 5- 36.)

Exhale and rest. Feel more energy continue to flow up into C-7 on its own.

6. Opening the Jade Pillow (Yu Chen) point. Focus on the Jade Pillow point. Touch and massage the hollow at the back of your head. Inhale a small sip, and draw the energy up from C-7 to the Jade Pillow point. Take 3 to 9 more small sips to draw the energy up from the perineum to C-7 and the Jade Pillow, spiraling more energy into the Jade Pillow point with each sip. If you wish, you may rotate a Chi ball there in both directions using mind/eye power. (Please see Figure 5-38.)

Exhale and rest. Feel more energy flowing up by itself into the Jade Pillow point.

7. Opening the crown point (Bai Hui). Focus on the crown (Bai Hui) point. Inhale a small sip of breath and draw the energy from the perineum up to the Jade Pillow point through the back of the crown and up to the top crown point. Take 3 to 9 more small sips to draw more energy up to Bai Huni spiraling more energy into the Bai Hui point with each sip. Exhale and rest. Feel the energy flowing, radiating by itself into the crown point. Using mind/eye power, rotate a luminous ball of Chi in both directions 9 to 18 times.

C. Connecting with the Heavenly Force

Not only do we draw Heavenly Chi in through the crown point, we also practice opening this point as a doorway for the soul and spirit to leave at the time of death. Some people have never closed their crown from infancy. The rest of us must practice so this doorway is clear.

If you exit through the crown, you need not return to earth after you die; you can continue to the heavenly realms. But do so, you need to practice opening the crown well before death.

D. Kun Lun Mountain (Back Part of the Crown)

The back part of the crown connects to the pineal gland in the brain and is the doorway by which the soul and spirit depart for the North Star at the time of death. The North Star is the easiest gateway to enter heaven, as it is aligned with the axis of the earth and the North and South Poles. Likewise, when we become aligned with the axis in our body, we become aligned with the violet light of the North Star, the violet light of unconditional love. (Please see Figure 5-42.)

E. The Crown

The middle of the crown connects with the hypothalamus and is the pathway to the Big Dipper. The light of the Big Dipper is a vibrant red, which reflects the vitality of the life-force manifesting.

The mid-eyebrow point connects to the pituitary gland and is the doorway to the Higher Self (Cosmic) Energy. It draws in the golden light, as mentioned earlier. Taoists refer to the area of the brain where the pineal gland, hypothalamus, and pituitary gland are housed as the Crystal Room. (Please see Figure 5-46.)

1. Activate the back of the crown by tilting the chin in slightly. This tilting aligns the pineal gland with the back of the crown, which is now the highest point of the body. At the same time, touch and press the back of the crown with the fingers. Again, tilt the chin and press very lightly and easily.

2. Touch the middle of the crown and look up as if at the middle of the crown. Gently press and look up, and you will feel it open (Figure 11-6).

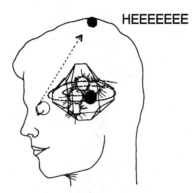

HEEEEEEE

Figure 11-6. Activate the back part of the crown.

3. Breathe in deeply, then exhale, softly whispering the Triple Warmer Sound: HEEEEEEEE; the sound should be vibrated toward the back part of the crown subvocally. At the same time, raise the arms above the head with the palms pointing up. Release the energy through the crown and extend upward with your Chi, as though extending a pipeline toward the North Star. Feel it go up through the sky, through the earth's atmosphere, out into space; keep going until it reaches the North Star. You will know you have made the connection when you are aware of the violet light of the North Star, or feel some other sensation or pressure on the crown. Do this 9 to 18 times. Rest and feel the sensation or pressure as energy is absorbed into the crown (Figure 11-7).

Be aware of the center of the crown and the Big Dipper. Use the Triple Warmer sound as above to help activate the energy of the Big Dipper's seven stars and draw in the red essence of the Dipper. Do this 9 to 18 times (Figure 11-8).

4. Look up and begin to move the trunk of your body in a circular pattern. Feel that you are creating a vortex of energy above your head as you circle. At the same time, turn the palms downward and angle them so they point toward the back of the crown. As you circle the body, feel relaxed and open. Picture the North Star, and let its light come to you, the violet light of unconditional love. Allow it to flow into the back of the crown and deeper inside, to the pineal gland. Feel it energizing, cleansing, and refreshing your brain.

5. Be aware of the red light of the Big Dipper. It is the higher astral fire of the earth. Picture the Big Dipper, and let the red light come to you. Let it flow in through the middle of the crown and into your brain, and

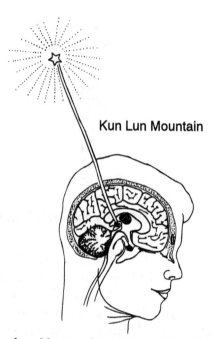

Kun Lun Mountain

Figure 11-7. The pineal has a close connection to the North Pole and North Star.

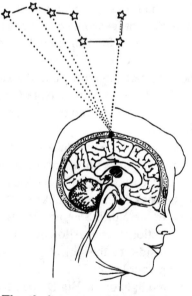

Figure 11-8. The thalamus and hypothalamus connect to the Big Dipper.

then down into your whole body. Feel your blood energized by it. The natural polarity to this astral fire is the blue water energy of the earth. Breathe in the blue light and let it neutralize the red light and gather this original energy at the Tan Tien.

6. Be aware of the universal violet light of the North Star flowing through the crown and down into the body. It may help to visualize a violet pearl at the crown, which you rotate in both directions. Now spiral the violet light down into your brain, first 9 times clockwise, then 9 times counterclockwise. The natural polarity to this universal violet light is the white light of your individual (Po) soul. Allow them to mix at the solar plexus. Rest for a few moments. Enjoy the peaceful, joyful feeling. Let the light flow anywhere in your body that needs healing (Figure 11-9).

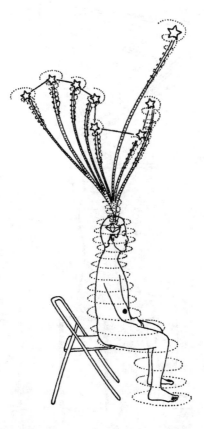

**Figure 11-9. Spiral violet and red light energy
through the whole body.**

F. Connecting the Crown to the Mid-Eyebrow

1. Be aware of the crown and the mid-eyebrow point.

2. Inhale as though you were breathing in through the crown point; draw the violet light of the North Star in with the breath to the Crystal Room. Then exhale through the mid-eyebrow point.

3. Be aware of the golden light in front of you, the energy of mountains, oceans, lakes, waterfalls, and forests. Breathe that energy in through the mid-eyebrow point to the Crystal Room. Exhale through the crown. Repeat these last two steps 3 to 9 times (Figure 11-10).

Then rest. Feel the line of connection between the crown point and the mid- eyebrow point.

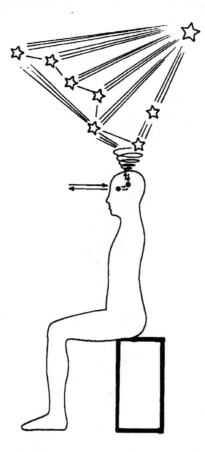

**Figure 11-10. Make connections from the crown
to the mid-eyebrow.**

G. Bring the Energy Down the Functional Channel to the Navel

Heavenly Energy is very Yang. The brain is also naturally Yang, because it is the part of the body that is closest to heaven. When we bring more Heavenly Chi into the brain to nourish the body, it is especially important to circulate this energy, to bring it down to the navel and to ground and balance it with the more Yin energies in the body. Then this energy can be very beneficial.

If you leave this Yang energy in your head, your brain may become too Yang. You may feel headachy, dizzy, spacy, lightheaded, or notice a sense of heat or pressure in your head. In the following steps, you will learn how to take extra care to bring the energy down.

1. Touch the tip of the tongue to the roof of the mouth. Inhale lightly (Figure 11-11), and press the tongue against the palate. Exhale and relax

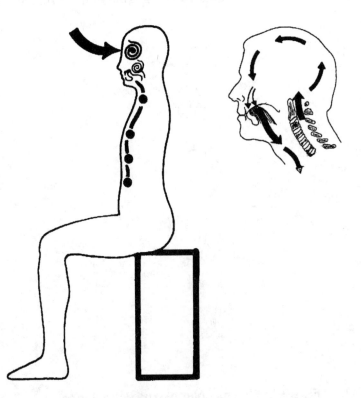

Figure 11-11. Touch the tip of the tongue to the roof of the mouth.

the tongue as you condense the energy. Repeat 18 to 36 times. Lightly touch the tongue to the palate. Move the tip of the tongue from the front of the palate slowly toward the back until you feel the sensation of Chi contact: vibration, metallic taste, electric shock, tingling, or even slight pain. The tongue has an opening and will draw the Chi down.

2. Swirl the tongue around the gums and generate a pool of fluid; we call this the Jade Nectar, the high-potency Yin fluid of the body. Gather the Heavenly Chi into this fluid, stirring the Yang energy in with the Yin fluid. Swallow, and let the energy flow back down the Functional Channel through the throat point, heart point, and solar plexus. Use the mind and eyes to spiral at each point until you feel the points open and connect to each other.

3. Rotate a white Chi ball at the solar plexus and be aware of the bright sunshine radiating from it (Figure 11-12). Feel it connect to the larger sun above you. Let the bright light shine out from the solar plexus.

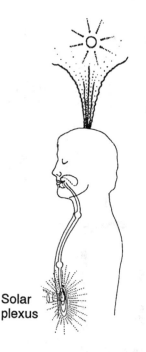

Solar plexus

Figure 11-12. The solar plexus connects to the white light and radiates out.

You can focus it like a spotlight to strengthen any weak areas in your aura.

4. Place the right hand in front of the solar plexus, palm in, and feel the radiance of the light. Inhale; draw the white light of your earth (Po) soul into the mid-eyebrow and solar plexus. Exhale and condense the energy there. Rest, and let the energy expand and radiate from the solar plexus to the palm. Eventually, you can move your palm farther away and still feel the light. Do this 9 to 18 times.

A strong solar plexus will strengthen your spiritual willpower and will help protect you from the negative energy of others. You also can send your sunshine to other people when you connect with the unlimited source of light. This will help change the negative energy they direct toward you. The radiant white light of the solar plexus will make you more visible to higher forces, and the higher masters will be able to identify you and protect you more easily.

5. Go slowly, spending enough time at each point to feel it open (Figure 11-13), and to feel that you have strongly drawn the energy down

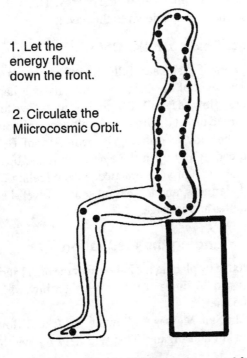

1. Let the
energy flow
down the front.

2. Circulate the
Miicrocosmic Orbit.

Figure 11-13. Chi flows in an orbit.

from the previous point. Feel the Chi flowing down like warm honey, filling each point with radiant, glowing energy. Notice a pleasant and expansive sensation in each point. If you wish, you can also use the power of the Inner Smile to relax, open, and further energize each point.

6. Finally, bring the energy back to the navel.

7. Now just be aware of the Original Force, and rest. Feel the pulsing at the place of your Original Force. Keeping 95 percent of the awareness on the Original Force, put 5 percent of the awareness on the soles of the feet, the crown points, and the mid-eyebrow point. Feel the pulsing. Feel that the Original Force has a suction force to pull energy into it, to absorb that energy and merge with it. (Please see Figure 2-9.)

8. If you complete the steps above and still feel you have a great deal of energy in your head, repeat the steps again as many times as necessary, and use the hands to help guide the energy back down. Remember that the left hand will draw energy toward it, and the right hand will move energy away. Therefore, you should place the right hand on the place where the energy is stuck, and place the left hand on the center toward which you want to guide the energy. This will enable you to bring the excess energy back down to the navel.

H. The Yin Stage: Resting in Wu Chi

Then rest. Allow yourself to sit peacefully in total blackness and be open to receiving the clear light of the Original Chi. Whatever happens, let it happen; let the energy flow as it will. The energy may move to other parts of the body. Don't try to direct it; allow the intelligence of your life-force to nourish and heal the body according to its own wisdom. Be careful not to fall asleep; you can lightly open the eyes. Just relax, be neutral and open, and absorb the fruits of your practice: a deep feeling of peacefulness, an expanded alertness, and a pleasant sense of well-being. Spend at least 5 to 10 minutes at this stage.

Ending the Meditation

Conclude your practice by placing the hands over the navel and collecting energy. Spiral outward 36 times at the navel, then inward 24 times to finish collecting the energy.

Finish with Chi Self-Massage, allowing the Chi to flow from the fingertips into the skin and organs. This will help relieve the stiffness caused by sitting.

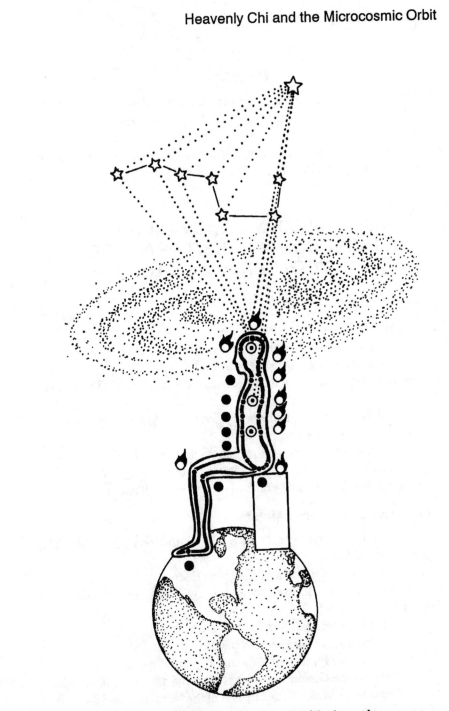

Figure 11-14. Feel yourself in touch with the universe, cosmic, and earth force.

Regularity

Practice at least 20 minutes a day consistently. Being consistent is the most important part of your practice. A little every day is better than a long session one day and nothing the next. Avoid extremes. If you go to one extreme, you will tend to swing to the other. Do at least a little practice every day, and you will continue to deepen your practice of the Healing Tao.

OVERVIEW OF ADVANCED MICROCOSMIC ORBIT PRACTICE WITH HEALING LIGHT

Preparations

1. Start with Chi Kung Warm-Ups.

2. Practice the Six Healing Sounds; see the color of each organ.

3. Focus inward with the Inner Smile.

4. Breathe in the white mist to cleanse the marrow of the spine and brain.

5. Activate your Original Energy: Warm the Stove

(a) Begin with Bellows Breathing.

(b) Activate and massage the kidneys and open the Door of Life.

(c) Activate and massage the sexual centers.

(d) Gather the Original Force in the lower Tan Tien.

The Microcosmic Orbit Meditation

1. Circulate your energy through all the points of the Basic Microcosmic Orbit.

2. Draw in the blue light of the Earth Energy.

3. Activate the mid-eyebrow and draw in the golden light of the Higher Self.

4. Open the heart with the Cosmic Inner Smile.

5. Combine sexual desire with pink loving energy.

6. Activate the Functional Channel from mid-eyebrow to sacrum.

7. Activate the Governor Channel from the sacrum to the crown.

8. Draw in the violet Heavenly Chi of the North Star and the red Chi of the Big Dipper.

9. Bring the energy down to the mid-eyebrow and solar plexus, and fuse it with the Original Chi at the navel.

The Yin Stage

Rest in the blackness and be aware of the clear light of the Original Chi.

Collect the Energy at the Navel

Chapter 12

SUMMARY

In Chapters 6 through 11, we have outlined the practice of the Microcosmic Orbit step by step, from basic to advanced. In this chapter we present a summary of the entire practice.

GUIDELINES FOR PRACTICING THE MICROCOSMIC ORBIT

The Seven Phases of the Microcosmic Orbit

In the first few weeks after having been introduced to the entire Microcosmic Orbit meditation, it is very important that you try to practice diligently. You can divide your practice into several sections. Your training should be progressive—that is, once you have mastered one section, you can progress to the next. Be sure to spend at least one or two weeks on each section, allowing enough time to master each part thoroughly before adding the next section. Remember that you should *always* do the Chi Kung Warm-Ups before beginning meditation; it is very important to loosen the spine before meditation.

We have divided the entire Microcosmic Orbit practice into seven phases.

1. Warming the Stove: Activating the Original Energy in the Lower Tan Tien. The first phase is the practice of activating your Original Force. You should practice this phase for one to three weeks or more if you need to, until you can actually feel the Original Energy. Once you do feel the energy, practice circulating it in the basic Microcosmic Orbit.

Many people who open the basic Orbit circulate at the outer level of the skin or aura. Regardless of whether you are just beginning or have been practicing for years, it is possible to circulate the Orbit so that it

431

penetrates more deeply into the organs, bone marrow, and brain. As you penetrate more deeply, your aura will extend outward and you will become more radiant. Simultaneously, your capacity to absorb the various energies, such as Heaven and Earth Chi, into the Orbit will increase.

Your practice will become simpler with time. Once you have gained some experience with circulating through the Orbit, you can go through the entire basic Microcosmic Orbit in two breaths: inhaling up the spine and exhaling down the front. Many beginners open the Orbit after practicing the Inner Smile and the Six Healing Sounds, using this two-step breath method to "kick-start" the Microcosmic Orbit and activate the two channels. This practice can be enhanced by rocking back and forth: rocking back as you inhale up the spine, and rocking forward as you exhale down the front. This rocking can be done sitting or standing.

The Two Step Breathing method can be expanded to include tapping into the universal wells of energy in nature. We have outlined more advanced Nine Breath and Five Breath methods at the end of this chapter.

2. Connecting to the Mother Earth Force. The second phase begins with the Chi Kung Warm-Ups, Warming the Stove, the Inner Smile, and activating your Original Energy, and then focuses on connecting to Mother Earth Energy. The grounding techniques you learn at this stage are absolutely essential to the subsequent stages of the Microcosmic Orbit. Earth Energy is the first of the Three Forces that you will connect with, so it is vital to spend one to three weeks at this stage until you can begin to strongly feel and assimilate the Mother Earth Energy. Real rooting of the entire body is a discipline learned in Iron Shirt and Tai Chi Chi Kung and takes years to master fully.

Once you have successfully activated your own center of Original Chi and have established your grounding by connecting to Mother Earth Energy, spend at least one week circulating whatever Chi you have been able to gather through the basic Microcosmic Orbit. It may still feel very faint at this point; you may only feel it in a few places, such as the navel, Third Eye, or sexual center. Don't be discouraged. Often some of the energy will be circulating, but you will not be able to feel it at all the points. The goal is to change the flow from a small stream of Chi into a strong river. This happens gradually over time with regular practice; the practice will naturally deepen.

3. Activating the Higher Self (Cosmic) Energy and the golden light ball. In the third phase you begin widening and charging the Microcosmic Orbit by drawing in the Higher Self frequency through the Third Eye point. It is essential that you absorb and digest this higher-level frequency by grounding it with Earth Energy at the navel and feet and fusing it with Original Chi at the Tan Tien, then circulating this mixture in the Orbit.

4. Opening the heart with the Cosmic Inner Smile. The fourth phase teaches you to use the power of the Cosmic (Higher Self) Energy to help open the heart. You also use this energy to enhance the Inner Smile. This further amplifies and deepens the purification and transformation of the emotional energy; it changes the quality of energy flow in the Orbit.

5. Clearing the Functional Channel and connecting the three Tan Tiens. In the fifth phase, you concentrate on deepening the flow of Chi in the Functional Channel (Conception Vessel) and on opening and connecting the heart with your sexual energy. The Functional Channel is the channel for the flow of Water or Yin energy, which softens and dissolves blockages in your basic Orbit.

6. Clearing the Governor Channel and connecting to the Heavenly Chi. In the sixth phase, you strengthen the opening of the Governor Channel, bring the energy up to the crown, and connect with the Universal Force. The powerful light burns out impurities in your basic energies.

7. Connecting the crown and mid-eyebrow and joining the two channels. The seventh phase connects the Governor and Functional Channels and brings the energy back down the front to the navel, balancing Water and Fire, Yin and Yang.

Once you have completed these seven phases, you practice them all together.

Deepening the Microcosmic Orbit: A 100-Day Training Program

To master the seven phases of the Microcosmic Orbit, we recommend a 100-Day Training Program. By spending about two weeks at each phase, you can complete all seven stages in about 100 days. This program will benefit anyone seeking to improve his or her life and health and to circulate the Orbit at a deeper level. Everyone is at a different level of practice. Some who have had a great deal of meditation experience open up the Orbit with a few hours or days of practice. Although it may not take a full 100 days to experience results at the various stages, it is still helpful to follow the program to deepen and reinforce your understanding and abilities in the practice.

Diet. During the 100 days of the program, you should eat a diet high in fiber, whole grains, fresh vegetables, and fruit. Limit intake of meat, poultry, fats, caffeine, and dairy products. This helps clean out your system, gives you more energy, and aids in the purification of your energy.

Sex. For best results, you should conserve your sexual energy during the 100 days. If you dissipate your sexual reserves, you will not have enough sexual energy to transform into Chi. Healing Love practice is very important.

Rest. Try to work less, rest more, and practice the Inner Smile throughout the day to reduce your level of stress. This helps conserve energy to enhance your practice.

As Your Practice Matures, Your Energy Will Move More Quickly and Easily

At the beginning, it is important to go through the steps of the Microcosmic Orbit meditation slowly and carefully in detail as you have been instructed in this book or in the workshop. As you mature and grow in your practice, however, you will find that your experience changes. One of the first changes you will notice is that you can do the practice more quickly. Your neural pathways become trained. As they become familiar with the meditation the more you practice, they will begin to activate very quickly and easily.

Another change you will notice is that your energy will begin to flow more readily. You will find you can move your energy more and more using mind power alone. When this happens, you can dispense with whatever methods seem unnecessary; you need no longer use your hands, Small Sip Breathing, or spiraling at the different points. It is fine to use these methods if you wish, but once you have reached the stage where you can move the Chi with your mind alone, the other methods are no longer an essential part of the practice.

Your Energy Will Flow Smoothly
Without Stopping at the Points

You may also find that your Chi will flow smoothly through the Microcosmic Orbit by itself, with no conscious effort on your part and without stopping at any individual points or centers. This is a good sign. The most important sign of increasing skill is that your energy flows smoothly and with little effort through the pathways. After you have mastered the steps, you need not concentrate on each point as you move through the Microcosmic Orbit; you can simply let it flow. However, it is fine to spend more time at places you want to energize or heal.

SUMMARY
Open the Basic Microcosmic Orbit:
Mind/Eye Rotating, Touching,
Breath, and Color

We suggest you try using all the modalities to discover which ones work best for you.

1. *Spiral or rotate a Chi ball at the points with the mind and eyes.*

2. *Touch the points with the fingers to draw Chi to the physical body.*

3. *Hold the hands a few inches away from the body to increase the flow in the aura energy field and draw in the outer energies.*

4. *Focus on the breath as you move it around the Orbit.*

5. *Visualize different colors to stimulate your energy body and to help open the Microcosmic Orbit.*

It is not necessary to use every single method; in the beginning, choose the technique that appeals to you most. These techniques are only for training your body/mind and can be dropped once you have established a sense of the Chi flow. If you fix on any one method, such as breathing, you will limit your growth later on and may prevent the quality of your Chi flow from deepening. Eventually the feeling you are seeking to generate from these methods will be there effortlessly and spontaneously.

Chi Kung Warm-ups

Do Spinal Cord Breathing at least 9 to 18 times. Do the Crane Neck exercise, then Spine Shaking and Spine Rocking to the left and right.

Rest. Picture the spine open and relaxed. Breathe a white mist into the bones to brighten, strengthen, and wash the spinal cord and bones. Breathe in a golden mist to strengthen and wash the marrow. When you exhale, feel that you are breathing out a cloudy gray mist, letting go of all impurities and diseases and any kind of negativity.

Sit in good meditation position on a chair. Then take a few minutes to focus and prepare yourself.

Become aware of your surroundings. Feel the sensation of your feet touching the floor, of your clasped hands, of the chair beneath you. Be aware of the sounds inside the room, outside the room, and within your body.

Be aware of the breath. Feel the body naturally expand as you inhale and contract as you exhale. This increases the flow of blood and Chi. Breathe in and out with awareness, feeling the veins and arteries expand and contract. Do this Veins and Arteries Exercise 18 to 36 times.

Activating Your Original Energy: Warming the Stove

Activate the Navel Chi

Begin with Bellows Breathing, at least 18 to 36 times. This activates the energy. Rest, and use mind/eye power to gather the energy into a Chi ball. Store the energy by condensing it into a Chi dot or pearl at the navel.

Open the Door of Life Between the Kidneys

Inhale, and pull the stomach in toward the right kidney. Spiral with the whole body into the kidney. Feel the energy activate in the right kidney and the Door of Life. Then do the same with the left kidney. Do this at least 18 to 36 times on each side. Cover the kidneys with both palms to gather the Chi in the kidneys and condense it into the Door of Life. Feel the Door of Life open and warm.

Place the right hand over the navel and the left hand over the Door of Life. Feel the Door of Life, kidneys, and navel become warm. Inhale, and gather the energy into two Chi balls with mind/eye power. Exhale, and condense it into two Chi pearls in the kidneys.

436

Activate the Sexual Center (Ovarian or Sperm Palace)

Women: Transform Blood into Chi

(1) Rub the hands together until they are warm. Cover and press the breasts with the palms, and start to massage outward. Circle inwardly up and outwardly down 18 times. Rest and gather the sexual, glands, and breast energy at the heart center. Do two to three sets.

(2) Reverse the direction for 18 repetitions and gather the force back into the heart center. Make a connection to the back, on both sides of the spine between the T-5 and T-6 spinous processes, and bring it down the spine to the kidneys and the Door of Life. Do two to three sets.

(3 Massage and lightly shake the kidneys 9 to 18 times. Rest; cover the kidneys and feel them warm. The massaging, shaking, and resting is one set. Do three sets.

(4) Move the palms down to the lower abdominal area and massage the ovaries and the waist (liver and spleen area). Start in an outward direction. From the lower part, circle in and up to the top, and back out and down 36 times. Then reverse the direction and massage 36 times.

(5) Move the palms to cover the sexual center. Using mind/eye power, lightly contract the circular iris muscle and the muscles around the eyes. Feel them stimulate the vagina and anus to lightly contract as well. This helps gather the sexual energy you have activated in the Ovarian Palace.

(6) Pause for a while. Feel the energy expand at the sexual center.

Men: Transform Ching (Sperm) into Chi

(1) Rub the palms together until they are warm. Massage and lightly shake the kidneys 9 to 18 times. Rest and feel the kidneys warm. This is one set. Do three sets.

(2) Make the connection from the kidneys to the sexual organs.

(3) Rub the hands together until they are warm, and massage the testicles 18 to 36 times. Rest; gather and condense the energy in the center of the scrotum. Do two to three sets.

(4) *With the left palm, hold the testicles; with the right palm, massage the lower abdomen up to the navel and circle downward in a clockwise direction 36 to 81 times. Rest and feel the energy. Reverse the hand positions and the direction of the circular massage. Now the right palm holds the testicles and the left palm massages in a counterclockwise direction 36 to 81 times.*

(5) *Move the palms to cover the sexual center. Using mind/eye power, lightly contract the circular iris muscle and the muscles around the eyes. Feel them stimulate the perineum, sexual organ, and anus to lightly contract also. This helps gather the sexual energy you have activated.*

(6) *Pause for a while. Feel the energy expand at the sexual center, the Sperm Palace.*

Gather the Force in the Lower Tan Tien

Cover the navel with the right hand and place the left hand over the sexual center. Feel the navel, sexual center, and Door of Life warm. Breathe a small sip into the navel, breathe into the Door of Life, and then breathe into the sexual center. Breathe into each spot and exhale, but retain the essence of the breath at each place. Gather a Chi ball in the navel, the Door of Life, and the sexual center. Condense them into three Chi dots or pearls and draw into the Lower Tan Tien, merging them to form one Chi ball. Feel them condensing together.

Stop the leakage of energy and conserve the Chi. Fix 95 percent of the awareness and senses on the Chi ball in the Tan Tien, 5 percent on the navel, Door of Life, and sexual center. Using mind/eye power, lightly contract the circular iris muscle and the muscles around the eyes. Lightly close the sexual organ gate and the anus. Exhale down and feel a pressure created at the Tan Tien. Exhale, and feel that you can condense and retain the essence of the breath at the center.

When you can hold your mind and eyes and feel the lower gates all seal toward the Original Force, you will feel you have "stopped the leakage and conserved the Chi." You can practice this at any time in your daily life. Whenever you feel tired, turn the mind and eyes inward to the Lower Tan Tien and lightly close the sexual organs and the anus. You will immediately feel an increase in your Chi energy.

Spend at least 10 to 15 minutes at this stage to allow the Original Energy to build up in the Tan Tien. Feel it pulsing and breathing inside. If you want to finish, gather the energy in the navel.

Connecting to Mother Earth Energy

1. *First increase the Original Force by fixing the mind and eye power there. Look for the sensation of vibration and pulsing and the feeling that the Original Energy has a mouth and nose and is breathing along with you. Feel the vibration and the breathing; the vibration may start to extend up to the mid-eyebrow point, crown, palms, and soles.*

2. *Turn the palms facing the ground. Inhale, pull up, and very lightly contract the eye muscles, sexual organs, perineum, and anus. Exhale, and completely relax the sexual organs, perineum, and anus. Repeat 9 to 18 times. Feel the suction in the palms and soles of the feet.*

3. *On the last exhalation, breathe out into the fingers and toes. If you have any sick energy or negative emotions, you can purge them out and let them drain into the tips of the fingers and toes. Let the sick energy drain down into Mother Earth.*

4. *Feel the qualities of Earth Energy: a nice, soft, gentle, kind, blue energy rising up through the legs like a mist from the earth to your Original Energy in the Tan Tien.*

5. *To sedate the heat of the heart and tonify the kidneys' Yin, do the Heart Sound, HAWWWWW. From the heart let the sick or excess heat spread to the inside of both arms and leap down to the tips of the fingers and toes. Do this 6 to 9 times. Feel the heart cool down. Rest, and be aware of the soles of the feet. Feel the qualities of Mother Earth Yin—nice, soft, gentle, kind, blue energy rising by itself like a mist through the legs to the kidneys and the Original Energy in the Tan Tien. Spend at least 5 to 10 minutes at this stage to allow the Original Energy to build up. Feel it pulsing and breathing inside, and draw the Mother Earth Force in and up to the Original Force.*

Activating the Mid-eyebrow and
Drawing in the Higher Self (Cosmic) Energy

1. *Feel your Original Energy expand from the Tan Tien until it begins to activate the mid-eyebrow. Lightly raise the hands to face out, or if you wish, you can touch the mid-eyebrow with the tips of fingers and spiral there. Spiral with the mind and eyes as well.*

2. *Expand outward and connect with the forces in nature: the ocean, sunset, full moon, forests, waterfalls, mountains, lakes, clouds, thunder. Feel yourself connecting with this ion-rich energy and draw it into your mind's eye as a glowing golden light. Breathe that golden light into the mid-eyebrow, eyes, and mouth. Feel the energy build up; feel it condense into the saliva.*

3. *Swallow the energized saliva. Feel it go down as a form of golden liquid Chi and merge with your Original Energy, strengthening and adding to your supply of Chi.*

4. *Imagine gathering the golden light in the coccyx. The golden light then rises up through the spine, up to the crown. Feel the golden light expand and cover the whole body; feel the whole body covered and protected by a golden ball of light energy. Put the hands over the heart. Feel that you are sitting safely in the golden light. Any negative feelings directed toward you, or any psychic attack, will be deflected by the golden light.*

Opening the Heart: Cosmic Inner Smile

1. *Now do the Heart Sound to clear out any negative emotions. Inhale, and exhale making the Heart Sound, HAWWWWW. The sound helps activate the flame to burn out any negativity in the heart. Rest, and feel the heart open. Repeat the Heart Sound at least 6 times.*

2. *Place the palms in the prayer position, facing each other at the level of the heart. Feel love, joy, gentleness, and kindness radiate out to the lungs. If you have a favorite affirmation for loving yourself and others, you may use it here.*

3. *Do the Pleasant Fragrance meditation. Open the hands like a flower blossoming, and smell the fragrance of the loving energy in your heart. Smell the joy and happiness energy; breathe in the fragrance of the gentleness and kindness Chi. Let it radiate to the lungs. Smile and draw in more cosmic golden light down to the lungs, and feel the courage in the lungs activate.*

4. *Radiate more loving energy from the heart to the liver, spleen and pancreas, kidneys, and sexual organs, in sequence. Feel the organs relax and open, and notice the positive qualities of the energy as each one smiles back to you. Allow the heart to receive and absorb the energy of each organ. Feel the heart glow even more strongly.*

5. *Middle line: Smile the cosmic golden light down into the digestive system. Gather the saliva in the mouth and radiate the cosmic smiling energy into the saliva, transforming it into a soothing, healing nectar. Swallow the saliva, smiling into it as it flows down to the stomach; feel it soothe and refresh the esophagus. Finally, smile down to the intestines and anus. Express your gratitude for their important role in maintaining your good health.*

6. *Back line: Draw in more cosmic golden light and smile into the brain. Move the eyes as if looking back inside the brain and spiral the Chi in the brain with mind/eye power. Smile down the spine from the cervical vertebrae to the coccyx. Feel the spinal cord open, loose, and filled with light.*

Combining Loving Energy with Sexual Desire

(1) *Smile once again to the heart, and feel the heart radiate more loving energy down to the sexual organs.*

(2) *Inhale into the heart center. Feel the heart open and more love, joy, and happiness radiate from it. Hold for a while and swallow the saliva down to the heart. Exhale down to the sexual center. Feel the fire of your loving heart energy coming down to activate and blend with the cooler water of your sexual energy, transforming it into blissful orgasm energy. It may also feel like an expansive light, a heightened*

*or tingling feeling of energy, or a rising warm mist. Do this 6
to 9 times.*

(3) *Be aware of the sexual organs. Women: inhale and lightly
contract the vagina. Men: inhale and lightly pull up the
testicles. Feel more loving energy floating down from the
heart to combine with your sexual energy. Gather the force
into the sexual center.*

(4) *When you feel you have gathered enough energy at the
sexual center, use the mind's eye to create a luminous pink
pipeline from the sexual center up to the heart. Inhale again
into the heart, and inhale love down the pink tube into the
sexual center. Hold for a while, then exhale up the tube to the
heart center. Do this 6 to 9 times. Rest and breathe naturally.
Feel the pipeline from the sexual organs to the heart. Feel the
sexual passion expanding the heart's loving energy.*

(5) *Feel the heart and sexual energies pulsing together into a
gentle orgasmic energy. Feel them radiating a pink light, and
bring the energy into the Original Force.*

(6) *To develop this phase more deeply, refer to the practices of
Testicle/Ovarian Breathing and the Power Lock exercises in
the Healing Tao books on male and female sexual practices.*

Opening the Functional Channel:
Connecting the Three Tan Tiens

In this part of the practice, we want to clear the space between the Third
Eye, heart, and navel and connect from the mid-eyebrow to the perineum
along the path of the Functional Channel. For best results, spend a week
connecting the mid-eyebrow to the heart, and then up to a week connecting the mid-eyebrow to the navel, sexual center, and perineum. As soon
as you feel the connection at one point, allow the momentum of the
energy flow to continue to the next one. Those with high blood pressure
or insomnia should focus only on the navel and soles of the feet.

1. *Feel the pulsing and breathing between the navel and
kidneys. Draw more energy in from the mid-eyebrow.*

2. *Inhale into the mid-eyebrow and rotate. Gather a mouthful of
saliva and merge the golden light into the saliva. Swallow the*

saliva as you exhale down to the heart. Rest, and feel the mid-eyebrow connect to the heart center. Do this 6 to 9 times.

3. *Inhale into the mid-eyebrow hold and rotate for a while. Inhale a small sip down to the heart and hold for a while. Exhale up to the mid-eyebrow. Rest, and feel the space in between has been cleaned out. Do this 6 to 9 times.*

4. *Inhale to the mid-eyebrow and down to the heart, and exhale to the navel center. Do this 6 to 9 times. Reverse the process, inhaling from the mid-eyebrow down the front channel to the navel and exhaling to the mid-eyebrow. Rest, and feel the space in between has been washed out and opened. Use mind/eye power to gather the energy into the three Tan Tiens, and feel them pulsing and breathing together.*

5. *Repeat the above procedure with the sexual center. Inhale to the mid-eyebrow, heart, and navel and exhaling to the sexual center. Reverse by inhaling to the mid-eyebrow, heart, navel, and sexual center and exhaling to the mid-eyebrow. Do this 6 to 9 times.*

6. *Repeat the same procedure with the perineum.*

7. *Repeat the same procedure with the toes. Inhale all the way to the perineum and exhale down to the toes. When the perineum center is activated, it works like a powerful suction pump. When you contract and pull up the perineum, it automatically draws down the Cosmic Energy from the mid-eyebrow, which you can then release down to the earth.*

Opening the Microcosmic Orbit and Connecting All the Points

Activate the Original Energy at the Lower Tan Tien

Return to your awareness of your Original Energy at the Tan Tien. Feel it pulsing and breathing. Focus there until again feel your Chi pulsing or vibrating from the Tan Tien up to the mid-eyebrow.

Open the Governor Channel

In this phase we connect from the perineum up to the crown and the mid-eyebrow. Spend a few days moving the energy to each point, until you feel some connection and opening: from the perineum up to sacrum, Door of Life, T-11, and C-7. Some people may need to spend more time. Spend up to a week moving the energy from the perineum up to the Jade Pillow and back part of the crown, and a few more days to move it from the crown down to the mid-eyebrow. Students who have previous experience with meditation will find they progress much more quickly.

1. *Inhale, and lightly pull up the perineum, and feel it draw the energy down from the mid-eyebrow. Inhale again, and draw the Earth Force from the ground up until it meets mid-eyebrow energy at the perineum. Hold for a while. Inhale a small sip, and contract the anus and sexual organ up to the coccyx and the sacrum. Hold for a while. Rotate a Chi ball at sacrum, then exhale down to the toes.*

    Rest, and feel all the points on the channel from the mid-eyebrow down to the toes are connected.

2. *You can stimulate the movement of energy up the Governor Channel by using small sips of breath between the points. Inhale up to your Door of Life and hold for a while. Then exhale down to the fingers and toes and feel the navel, sexual center, perineum, soles of the feet, sacrum, and Door of Life pulsing and connecting.*

3. *Do the same with the T-11 center 6 to 9 times.*

4. *Do the same with the C-7 center and up to the Jade Pillow point, touching and rotating at each point.*

5. *Rest a moment, and then inhale up to the back part of the crown point. Raise the hands above the head with palms facing up. Keep the spine and neck straight as you turn the eyes up and use the OM sound or the HEEEEE sound. Feel a vibration go up the spine, and feel yourself connecting the energy of the North Star to the back part of the crown and the Big Dipper to the center of the crown. The violet and red light descending to you is the love of Father Heaven. Feel you are like a child, returning to and resting in the Fatherly love again.*

6. *Turn the palms to face down toward the crown. Feel the palms projecting energy down into the crown. Rotate the energy into the crown with your head, eyes, and palms. Feel the crown open. Be aware of a pipeline connecting the back part of the crown to the North Star and the crown to the Big Dipper.*

7. *Turn the palms down toward the mid-eyebrow. Feel the palms projecting more Chi into the mid-eyebrow to help open the mid-eyebrow and connect to the crown.*

Allow the Chi to Flow Down the Functional Channel

1. *Now direct the Lao Gong points in the center of both the palms toward the face, and feel the energy descend to the palate point. Use the mind, eyes, and hands to rotate at the palate point. Knock the teeth and press the tongue to the palate 9 to 36 times each.*

2. *Lower the hands. Line up the Lao Gong points of both hands and direct the palms toward the throat center. Inhale through the nose, then exhale into the throat center. Feel the palms project energy into the throat center, opening the center, and use the mind, eyes, and hands to spiral at the throat center.*

3. *Continue down the Functional Channel in this way, using the palms' energy in combination with the mind and eyes to open the heart point. Inhale into the throat center, and exhale down to the heart. To activate the flow of Chi to the heart, either cross the hands at the wrists with the fingers touching the heart, or hold them a few inches away. Be aware of the red color at the heart point.*

4. *Move the hands down to the solar plexus point. Touch the point with all 10 fingers, then slowly pull them away from the body, rotating with the mind only. Inhale into the heart, and exhale into the solar plexus point. Feel a bright sun inside, and gradually radiate it to protect you and your aura.*

5. *Activate the five major pulses. Line up the palms and focus them toward the navel. Feel the palms activate more Chi in the navel. Inhale into the solar plexus point, and exhale to the navel. Put the mind 95 percent on your Original Energy (Lower Tan Tien) and turn your eyes, mind, and heart toward*

445

the Lower Tan Tien. Lightly contract the sexual organs, perineum, and anus. Feel the Chi ball expanding from the navel and starting to vibrate the crown, mid-eyebrow, perineum, soles, and palms. If you have time, spend 10 to 15 minutes at this phase alone. The more you can feel your Original Energy activate, the more you will be able to heal yourself and maintain vibrant health.

6. *Lightly use the mind to guide the flow in the Microcosmic Orbit down to the perineum, up to the sacrum, and up to the crown. Gently draw down more Heavenly Energy to the palate. Press and relax the tongue against the palate and feel the energy come down to the throat center, the heart center, the solar plexus center, and back to the navel. Do the circulation for 18 to 36 orbits.*

7. *Continue circulating energy around the Microcosmic Orbit in this way a few times. Do the circulation for 18 to 36 orbits. When you are ready to conclude your session, gently guide the energy back to the navel.*

Yin Stage: Rest in the Original Chi

Rest. Just relax the mind and body. Find the neutral point in the center of the body; it could be at the navel, the heart, or the head, whatever feels the most neutral. Simply be there. Do nothing but absorb the fruits of having circulated the energy through the Microcosmic Orbit and having balanced your Chi flow. Allow the energy to do whatever it wants to do. It may reverse direction; it may flow to other areas of the body; the body may shake and vibrate; you may hear high-pitched sounds. Spend 5 or 10 minutes at this stage, giving yourself the chance to reap the fruit of your Microcosmic Orbit circulation: a sense of inner peace, calmness, and clarity. Let the physical body dissolve into your Original Chi, resting in the state of openness and emptiness, making no effort whatsoever.

Conclusion

Collect the energy at the navel by lightly spiraling at the lower abdomen 36 times outward from a small to a bigger spiral (clockwise for men, counterclockwise for women), and then spiral 24 times inward in the reverse direction. Rest.

Rub the hands together until they are warm. Then rub your face with your hands. This is the best cosmetic there is. The hands are warm with the Chi from your meditation, so when you rub your face, it brings fresh energy to invigorate the flow of Chi and blood to the skin.

Finish with a thorough round of Chi Self-Massage.

Intermediate and Advanced Levels of the Microcosmic Orbit Meditation

Once you have opened all the centers and connected them, your mental powers will increase tremendously. As you practice more, you will find the Chi flows quickly and easily through the Microcosmic Orbit. At this stage, you can begin to streamline your practice. Instead of focusing on opening the centers, you will shift the attention to letting the Chi flow smoothly through the channels. The summaries that follow are simple guides to the practice of the Microcosmic Orbit once you have solidly opened the basic Orbit.

Nine Sip Breathing: Activating Internal Breathing

Start with Chi King Warm-Ups and Warming the Stove. Then you can go right to the Cosmic Inner smile and opening the heart. Gather the energy into the Tan Tien.

1. *Inhale, and draw the energy into the Tan Tien. Hold the breath gently for a few seconds without straining, and feel your Original Energy expand into the navel, kidneys, and sexual organs.*

2. *Exhale, and release the energy down through the navel, sexual center, perineum, legs, and toes into Mother Earth. Feel the soles of the feet pulsing as you hold the exhalation for a few seconds.*

3. *Inhale the cool blue Earth Energy up through the soles, legs, perineum, sacrum, and spine, all the way to the crown.*

4. *Exhale out through the crown and up to the North Star and Big Dipper. Feel the crown pulsing.*

5. *Inhale the violet and red light through the crown and spiral or rotate it around the top of the head and the brain.*

6. *Exhale out through the mid-eyebrow, connecting with the Higher Self Energy.*

7. *Inhale the golden light in through the mid-eyebrow.*

8. *Exhale the golden light down the Functional Channel to the navel.*

9. *Inhale into the navel, and feel the energy merge and combine with your Original energy. Repeat the entire cycle. As you advance, the physical breath becomes less and less, and the internal breath and mind become more and more. The way to achieve this is to relax and spend more time in the neutral state or pauses between the inhalations and exhalations. You can continue to circulate in this way for 9, 18, or more rounds. If you like, you can simplify the practice even further, as follows:*

Five Sip Breathing: Connecting Heaven and Earth

1. *Inhale, and expand the Original Energy at the navel with the pulsing of the perineum, sexual organs, and kidneys.*

2. *Exhale from the navel, out through the perineum, and down through the legs to the earth.*

3. *Inhale Earth Energy in through the soles, and perineum, and up the Governor Channel to the crown.*

4. *Exhale through the crown and connect to Heavenly Energy.*

5. *Inhale and breathe Heavenly Energy in through the crown and down through the Third Eye, palate, throat, and solar plexus to the navel. Feel it combine with your Original Energy.*

6. *Repeat the cycle by exhaling from the navel down through the feet into the earth. You can continue in this way for as long as you like, balancing your own energy with the Yin and Yang energies of Earth and Heaven. Gradually the outer breath becomes quieter, less important. As the breath quiets down, so does the mind; you become more aware of circulating these energies from the effortless stillness of the mind. Enter the Yin stage, and rest in Wu Chi. End the meditation by gathering the energy at the navel. Conclude with Chi Self-Massage.*

Circulating the Light in the Orbit

Now you will use only the mind and inner eye to guide the Chi through the Microcosmic Orbit. Do not follow any breathing patterns; allow the body to breathe with its own natural rhythm.

1. *Repeat all the preparations, Chi Kung Warm-Ups, and the Inner Smile. Then breathe the white mist into the bones to brighten and strengthen the spinal cord, bones, and marrow. When you exhale, feel you are breathing out a cloudy gray mist, letting go of all impurities, diseases, and negativity.*

2. *Activate the pulsing of your Original Energy at the Tan Tien. At this stage, simply focusing the awareness on your Original Energy at the Tan Tien should activate the pulsing of your Original Chi. Spend as much time as you can Warming the Stove. See if it begins to glow or radiate with a white or golden light.*

3. *Use the mind to create a pink tube between the heart and sexual center. Feel the compassion energy of the heart pulsing together with your sexual energy in the pink tube. Use the mind to guide this energy down to the perineum, through the backs of the legs, and out through the soles to connect to Mother Earth.*

4. *Draw the gentle blue light of the earth up through the soles, legs, perineum, sacrum, Door of Life, T-11, T-5, C-7, Jade Pillow, and crown.*

5. *Expand out through the crown to connect with the light of the North Star and the Big Dipper. Absorb the red light rays of the Big Dipper into the crown and circulate this red light into the Orbit. After you feel the red light circulating in the Orbit, expand it to fill the entire body and aura. Allow it to meet the cool, watery blue light of Mother Earth, and feel both dissolve into the Original Energy at the navel.*

6. *Draw the violet of the North Star down into the crown. Spiral it around in the brain, absorbing it into the Crystal Room. Circulate the violet light in the Orbit and expand it to fill the whole body. Feel its vibration fuse with the white light of your earthbound soul and dissolve into the Original Energy in all three Tan Tiens.*

7. *Then move the awareness down to the mid-eyebrow point. Extend out through the mid-eyebrow to connect with the golden light.*

8. *Draw the golden light into the mid-eyebrow. Then use the mind to direct the golden light rays down the front channel to the palate point, throat center, heart center, and solar plexus center, and back to the navel. Circulate the light up the back channel and around the Orbit several times. Return to the navel, absorb the golden light into the Lower Tan Tien, and feel it activate and further expand your Original Energy.*

9. *Continue to circulate your Chi in the Microcosmic Orbit 3, 6, 9, or more times. The more you relax, the more easily you can feel the qualities of the different forces.*

Rest in the Wu Chi in total blackness, but notice that this dark void is full of energy. Relax and do nothing. End the meditation by gathering the energy at the navel. Conclude with Chi Self-Massage.

SUMMARY

You can practice this final level of the Microcosmic any time and any place. As you practice more, you will find it easy to do whether you are standing, sitting, lying down, riding in a car, or walking. Eventually you will be surprised to discover you are automatically circulating the Microcosmic Orbit almost all the time without even thinking about it!

You also can practice the Cosmic Inner Smile any time you need to recharge by feeling smiling and loving energy inside, above, and around you, drawing this energy in to fill the whole body.

Daily awareness of your connection with the Higher Self will give you the strength, power, and wisdom to run your life.

Chapter 13

THE MACROCOSMIC
ORBIT AND
THE FIVE PULSES

OPENING THE MACROCOSMIC ORBIT

Once you have successfully completed the Microcosmic Orbit, the next phase of practice is to extend the energy circulation through the arms and legs. This practice is traditionally called *Da Jou Tien* or the *Macrocosmic Orbit.*

You will feel a pleasant sense of wholeness when you integrate the arm and leg routes, because your awareness and Chi will fill the entire body, not just the torso and head.

1. Begin with Chi Kung Warm-Ups and preparations for meditation.

2. Activate your Original Chi: Warm the Stove.

3. Use mind and eye power to begin circulating energy through the Microcosmic Orbit. You do not need to connect to the Three Forces (Universal, Higher Self, and Earth) yet. Circulate energy through the entire Microcosmic Orbit 3 to 9 times.

4. On the last round, bring the energy down the front channel and pause for a moment at the perineum.

5. Inhale deeply, and exhale down the backs of the thighs, dividing the energy into two pathways. Spiral at the backs of the knees (Weizhong, Bladder 40).

6. Use the mind to continue guiding your Chi down the calves and around the outer ankles. Let the Chi revolve around the ankles several times. Then guide the Chi down to the soles of the feet and spiral at the Bubbling Spring (Yung Chuan) point. This is the first point of the kidney channel. Concentrating here strengthens the kidneys, lowers the blood pressure, calms the mind, and relieves fatigue. Concentrate on the Bubbling Spring points until you feel a strong sense of energy there.

7. Draw earth energy up to the tops of the big toes. Use the mind to activate the two points at the base corners of the big toes. Both the Liver and Spleen meridians originate at the big toe (Da Dun, Liver 1; Yin Bai, Spleen 1). Concentrating here strengthens and energizes those organs. When you feel a numbness or a sensation like an ant bite at these points, move on to the next points.

8. Connect to earth energy and direct the Chi up along the shin bone (tibia) to the fronts of the knees. Spiral and revolve the Chi to encircle the kneecaps; this activates the Eye of the Knee points and strengthens the knees. It also invigorates the stomach and spleen and their meridians. In addition, it helps open the knees to prepare them for further passage of energy in the higher-level Taoist formulas. Hold your focus at the knees until you feel a sense of warmth or tingling.

9. Draw the energy up the insides of the thighs and back to the perineum, up to the coccyx and sacrum, and on to the Door of Life, T-11, and the Wing Point below T-5.

10. From the Wing Point, divide the Chi into two routes and direct it across the scapulae, under the armpits, and down the insides of the arms to the inner elbow crease. The lung, heart, and pericardium channels pass through here; focusing on the inner elbow creases invigorates the meridian circulation and strengthens these organs.

11. Direct the Chi down the insides of the forearms to the Lao Gong point (Labor Palace, Pericardium 8) in the middle of the palms. Concentrate here for a while; feel the energy flow out to the tips of the middle fingers.

12. From the tips of the middle fingers, direct the Chi over the backs of the palms and up the backs of the forearms to the outsides of the elbows. Feel the Chi flow continue up the backs of the upper arms and over the shoulders, and reconnect to the Governor Channel at either T-5 or C-7. In either case, move the Chi from T-5 up to C-7 and on through the Governor Channel up the back of the neck to the crown. Then allow it to descend to the tongue and follow the Functional Channel to the navel.

This completes the Macrocosmic Orbit. Repeat at least 3 to 9 times.

FIVE PULSES PRACTICE
Activating and Connecting the Five Heart Pulses

The Five Pulses practice develops greater ability to feel, gather, and absorb the natural forces. By first becoming like a child, innocent and open, you learn to activate the palms, soles of the feet, perineum, crown, and mid-eyebrow. Eventually you will learn skin breathing, in which the skin opens wide to receive Chi from all around you.

Activate the Organs' Chi

Imagine you are like a child, able to receive unconditionally the Father Heaven and Mother Earth Forces. With daily practice of conserving, moving, and directing the life-force through the Microcosmic and Macrocosmic Orbits, your mind power will increase, and you will easily expand your awareness to the extremities and external forces.

The fingers are connected to many acupuncture meridians. The finger joints are also related to the internal organs and the corresponding senses and emotions. In fact, the entire body is mirrored in the hands and fingers. (Please see Figure 7-17 in Chapter 7.)

Because the tips of the fingers and toes have little resistance to Chi flow, stimulating them also stimulates the organs. The tips of the fingers and toes have many tiny veins and arteries. When we are weak or sick, Chi and blood do not flow well, and circulation to the extremities becomes stagnant. Often the first place we feel cold is in the hands and feet. To warm the whole body quickly, we can warm the hands and feet. By stimulating the flow of Chi and blood in the hands, we can benefit many other parts of the body.

How to Bring Chi to the Hands and Palms

1. Be aware of the palms. Inhale, and lightly contract the sexual organs, perineum, anus, and buttocks. (Note: Hold the breath comfortably; exhale any time you feel uncomfortable.) Emphasize pulling up on the left and right sides of the anus; this helps guide the Chi directly to the left and right hands. Hold the breath and hold the contractions. Lightly clench the teeth and press the tongue to the roof of the mouth as you rub the hands together.

2. Continue to rub the hands while holding the breath and contracting the lower parts. Feel the face and palms getting hot. Guide more Chi to the palms to activate them. Exhale and breathe naturally a few times.

3. Inhale again, hold the breath, and contract the lower parts as above. Press the palms together, then rotate the palms back and forth against each other. Do this 18 to 36 times (Figure 13-1).

4. Massage the Lao Gong points in the centers of the palms. Use the thumbs to press the middle of the palms in a circular motion. Massage each palm at least 18 to 36 times.

5. Using the right fingers to hold the left thumb, pull from the base of the thumb toward the tip. Repeat 6 to 9 times. Do this with the index, middle, ring, and little fingers. Do the same with the right hand.

Massage the Feet

Like the hands, the energy meridians of the feet and soles are connected to the entire body. Massaging the feet stimulates the organs and glands and increases the circulation to the extremities. If you find any painful points, massage them until the pain goes away. This clears blockages of Chi flow.

1. Take off your shoes and stockings.

2. Rub the hands together until they are warm. Rest the left foot on the right knee. Massage the left foot up and down, left and right, until it feels warm.

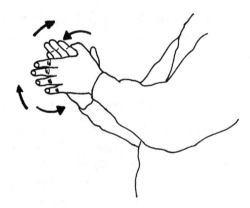

Figure 13-1. Rub the hands together

3. Massage the kidney point (K-1; also called Bubbling Spring or Bubbling Well). Taoists regard Bubbling Spring as the "heart of the foot" because it has the closest connection to the healing Mother Earth.

4. Use both thumbs to massage the sole of the foot. Flex the foot to reach the deeper parts. Dig in deep; press and spiral around the sole with the fingers.

5. Using the fingers of the right hand, hold the left big toe and pull from the base to the tip. Repeat 6 to 9 times. Do the other toes the same way.

6. Repeat the same steps with the right foot.

Activate the Chi

1. Lace the fingers together.

2. Press the palms together, tighten, and relax. Feel the heat produced (Figure 13-2).

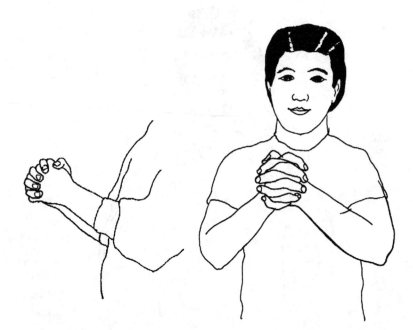

Figure 13-2. Lace the fingers and squeeze the palms together.

3. Press the fingers and the palms against each other. Rest, and be aware of the Chi in the palms and fingers. This activates the organs' Chi as well as the Chi in the hands.

4. Use the awareness to scan the heart, then the lungs, liver, pancreas, spleen, and kidneys. Feel the warmth inside each organ and its connection to the fingers.

Activate the Chi at the Palms and Fingertips

1. Hold the hands in front of the chest at heart level, palm to palm, until you feel heat build up.

2. Gradually separate the hands until the palms are about 1 inch (3 centimeters) apart. The fingers should be slightly curled, their tips facing each other, as if you were holding a big egg (Figure 13-3).

Figure 13-3. The fingers are slightly curled as though you are holding a big egg.

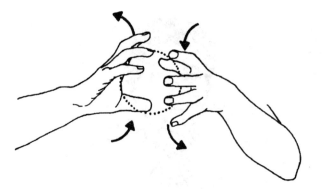

Figure 13-4. Slowly circle the tips of the fingers around each other.

3. Look at the point between the two palms. The mind and eyes will help gather the force into the palms and fingers. Gradually feel a ball of energy growing between the hands.

4. Slowly move the hands in and out without touching them together. Slowly circle the fingertips around each other. Feel the radiating Chi, heat, or aura of one hand repelling that of the other. Some people may feel a gentle electric shock, an expansion, or a coolness in the fingertips. As you practice more, these sensations will intensify (Figure 13-4). The abundance of energy at the fingertips activates Chi in the organs and glands.

5. Holding the palms and fingers 1 to 2 inches apart, be aware again of the Chi ball forming between the palms. Start to move the right palm up and down, left and right, but not so far that you lose the energetic connection between the palms (Figure 13-5).

6. Once you can clearly feel the Chi in the palms, move both palms together, up and down, left and right.

7. Move the palms about 3 inches apart. The fingers will curve as if you were holding a ball 3 inches in diameter. Hold this position until you feel a Chi ball build up (Figure 13-6).

8. Twist the palms in opposite directions. You will feel Chi pressure or sense a ball of energy.

9. Go back to the original holding-the-ball position. Gradually pull the palms apart until you feel the Chi diminish, then move them together until you can feel the Chi again. As you pull out and press in, feel the Chi

Figure 13-5. Move the palms up and down to feel the Chi.

Figure 13-6. Holding a big Chi ball

ball expand and contract. People whose hands are usually warm may have a less dramatic sensation of heat or Chi. With continued practice, everyone will feel more Chi.

10. Rest with the hands in the lap, palms up. Be aware of the palms and soles. Feel the palms and soles breathing together with the external breath (Figure 13-7).

Activate the Original Force

Use the palms to massage around the navel clockwise, gradually expanding the circle to the cover the whole abdomen. Rest and feel the warmth at the navel.

Activate the Door of Life and Gate of Heaven

1. Lightly contract the sexual organs, perineum, anus, and buttocks 3 to 6 times.

2. Gather the sexual essence at the sexual center, behind the pelvic bone.

3. Use your physical breath to breathe into the perineum and the Door of Life. Notice whatever quality is there: coolness, soreness, numbness, or sexual arousal. Expand the sexual energy and gather its essence into a ball of light at the perineum. Concentrate the light ball into a dot of light about the size of a small marble.

4. Visualize a small silver pipe extending up through the spinal cord from the perineum to the crown. Feel the Chi rise through the pipe to the crown, the Gate of Heaven.

5. Feel the crown warm and expand, or see a light at the crown point. Condense the light or the feeling into a dot.

6. Split your attention between the dot at the crown and the dot at the perineum. Picture the spinal cord as a shining silver pipe connecting these two shining dots.

7. Gradually draw one dot down and the other up so they meet at the Tan Tien. Feel the energy condense further as these dots come together. The dots may give out more light (Figure 13-8).

Once the base and crown have been connected by the pipe, you stop losing life-force and sexual essence and activate your true knowledge and wisdom. The feeling of Chi or arousal will gradually feel stronger and move up more clearly to the brain. Joy and peace will gradually fill the brain and the whole body.

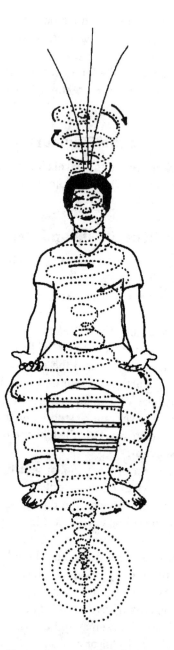

Figure 13-7. Place the palms on the lap facing upward. Feel the palms of the hands and the soles of the feet breathing.

Connect Heaven and Earth

1. Be aware of the two dots, silver pipe, and navel center. Then bring the awareness down to the perineum. Feel the perineum and soles breathing. Picture the silver pipe dividing at the perineum and extending down into both soles. Condense the feeling or light into a dot at each sole.

2. Exhale through the soles and extend the silver pipe into the ground. Picture the pipe connecting to a cool blue lake. Feel an energy full of gentleness and kindness rise through the pipe to the soles and on up to the perineum.

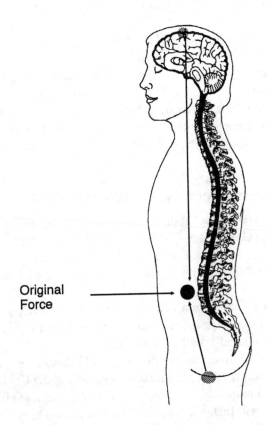

Original Force

Figure 13-8. Gather the perineum and crown energy into the Original Force.

3. Feel the energy rise up the spine through the silver pipe to the crown. Extend the pipe out the crown and connect it to the North Star and Big Dipper, or focus on a dot infinitely high above the head.

4. Feel the energy descend to the crown and navel center. As you inhale, draw down the golden light of your Higher Self or the violet or red light of the Heavenly (Universal) Force, and draw up the Earth Force as a blue light. Draw both forces to the navel. It may help to visualize the energies as colored dots.

5. Exhale through the palms and the soles down through the center of the earth to a light dot infinitely far away. Inhale from that dot, drawing energy into the palms, soles, and navel. Do this 6 to 9 times. As your mind power increases, repeat with a light dot infinitely far away above the crown.

6. Feel the palms, soles, crown, and perineum connected at the Tan Tien (the Original Force center) by the breath.

7. Circulate the energy you have gathered at the navel through the Microcosmic Orbit: down to the perineum, through the legs and out the soles to connect with the Earth Force, back up through the soles and legs to the perineum, up the spine to the crown, out the crown to connect with the Universal Force, down through the crown, and down the Functional Channel to the navel.

Activate the Mid-Eyebrow, the Wisdom Center

1. Focus on a light ball or dot at the navel center. Inhale, and let the dot rise to the mid-eyebrow, the Wisdom Center. Exhale from the mid-eyebrow to a golden light dot at infinity.

2. Inhale the light dot, drawing it into the mid-eyebrow and down to the navel. Repeat 9 to 18 times.

3. Rest at the navel center for a while. Be aware of all five pulses: at the heart, crown, mid-eyebrow, perineum, soles, and palms (Figure 13-9). Feel them inhaling and exhaling together.

4. Remember the positive feelings of being a child: soft, relaxed, and open. Feel the skin and pores open and breathing, absorbing Chi into the organs, glands, and marrow. The more you relax and the less effort you use, the more you will feel your whole body pulsing and breathing. This pulsing activates Chi flow and circulation of blood and lymph.

5. When you want to stop, gather the Chi back to the navel, and spiral and condense the Chi there.

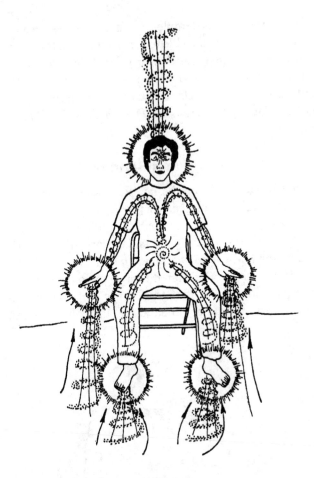

Figure 13-9. Activate the five pulses.

Using the Palms to Absorb Chi

The hands and fingers are among our most wonderful possessions. With our hands we can build, create, and repair things, as well as heal ourselves and others. When the palms are trained to feel Chi inside and outside the body, you can use them to absorb Chi from nature and the universe. When you practice using mind/eye/heart power to gather, condense, transform, and move the life-force through the Orbit, this ability becomes stronger. You can use the palms to absorb Chi from places of concentrated higher

463

energies, such as churches, temples, mountains, forests, caves, grottoes, and waterfalls. When you are able to absorb and transform these energies for your use, you no longer need energy from other people.

You can use the palms to test a place or a ceremony to determine whether it has power or Chi. Use the right palm to gradually spiral toward the person conducting the ceremony. Draw in the Chi and feel its strength and qualities.

Drawing and Sending Chi

1. Place the left palm on the lap. Raise and extend the right hand with the elbow slightly bent, palm facing down.

2. Be aware of the palm and fingertips. Inhale very slowly, drawing the Chi in front of you into the palm and fingers. Allow the Chi to travel up the arm to the mid-eyebrow and down to the navel (Figure 13-10).

3. Exhale. Push the Chi from the navel up to the chest, out the arm, hand, palm, and fingers. Do this 9 to 18 times. Repeat 9 to 18 times using both hands. Then rest and continue to feel the palms breathing (Figure 13-11).

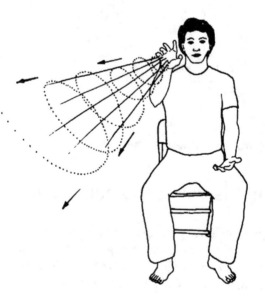

Figure 13-10. Draw Chi into the palm and fingers.

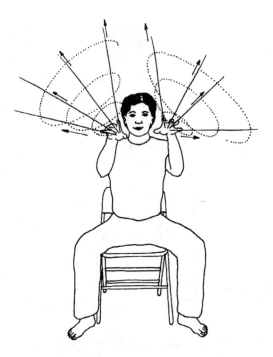

Figure 13-11. Draw Chi into both palms and fingers.

Testing the Chi

This method can help you find a good house, hotel, or place to stay by telling you whether its energy promotes or conflicts with your own energy. The same method can be used with objects you are considering acquiring.

1. Raise the right hand in front of you at chest level. If you are in a group of people, you can hold the hand near your navel area.

2. Spiral the hand clockwise in a circle 6 to 10 inches in diameter to draw energy from the place or object into the palm and direct it to the navel center. Evaluate the quality of the energy. Eventually you will have no need to use your hand to draw the Chi; you will be able to do it with mind/eye power alone (Figure 13-12).

465

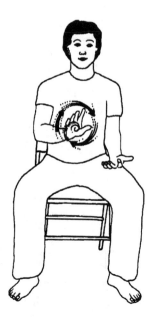

Figure 13-12. Test the Chi by spiraling your hand clockwise.

Gathering Spiritual Energy

Highly developed masters are connected to a higher force or source of spiritual energy. The energy is transferred to those who respect the master and are open enough to receive it. In the beginning of your practice, you can receive this higher force from your teacher. As your practice becomes stronger, you can gather it yourself.

1. Put both hands in front of you near the chest or navel, fingers lightly spread. Direct the palm toward the person conducting the meditation. Sense the spiritual energy. It feels different from other types of Chi, like a floating form of condensed energy. It is not spread out evenly like energy from the sun, the moon, mountains, or a holy site.

2. Spiral the energy clockwise into both hands. You can practice with just one hand until you feel the Chi strongly, then add the other hand (Figure 13-13).

3. When you feel the spirit or Chi come to you, absorb it into the palms, mid-eyebrow, and crown, and store it in the Crystal Palace or heart center.

Figure 13-13. Gather the spiritual energy with both hands.

Blocking Unwanted Chi

In our everyday lives, we encounter negative emotional energy in the form of anger, hate, and aggression. To reject this type of energy, people automatically raise their hands in front of their chests. To enhance the effectiveness of this response, in the Healing Tao we teach people to use smiling energy and mind/eye/heart power to repel any unwanted Chi.

When you sense Chi you do not want, cross the hands in front of the chest or navel with palms facing out. Quickly uncross the palms and bring the hands out to the sides to cut and block the unwanted Chi. Use mind/eye power to send the Chi to a distant place. Do not send it in the direction of a nearby person, or the person will pick up on it and feel uneasy. If there is a forest or a stand of trees in the vicinity, send it there. Trees transform negative energy into healing energy (Figure 13-14).

Sensing Other People's Energy

If you are thinking about interacting with someone and want to make sure his or her energy is positive and congenial with yours, look the

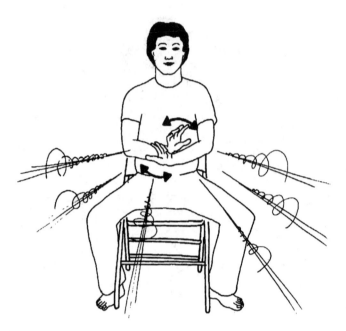

Figure 13-14. Block out the undesirable Chi by waving the hands.

person directly in the eye. The eyes are windows of feeling and expression. Draw the person's Chi into your Third Eye, in the middle of the forehead, and into your mid-eyebrow point. Does the energy feel good to you or not?

During this contact, use your whole body like sonar to feel the energy coming from the other person. With practice, you can even feel the location of sickness or pain in the other person's body. You may feel the sickness in the corresponding part of your own body.

You may feel disturbing energy as a cold or chilly sensation coming from a person's abdomen or back. Try to direct it away from you, so it does not affect your own energy. With daily practice, you can repel sick energy easily.

Chapter 14

ONENESS WITH THE TAO
A Daily Practice Guide

Inner Smile

Begin Your Day with the Inner Smile

Practicing the Inner Smile as soon as you wake up will improve your whole day. If you love your own body, you will be more loving toward others and more effective in your work. After you have learned the Inner Smile well, it only takes from 5 to 10 minutes to smile down to your entire body.

Try to maintain the sensation of the Inner Smile throughout the day. Keep reminding yourself to practice the Inner Smile. It is one of the best stress reducers in the world.

Protect Yourself with the Smiling Aura Field

Although they are unseen by the majority of people, there are subtle energies or "psychic forces" around us that have a strong influence on our health and well-being. Negative psychic energies from others can create stress and even cause illness. When a person has strong emotions toward you, the psychic energy associated with them disturbs the balance of your energies, jeopardizing your health. The Smiling Aura, a beautiful emanation of our highest energetic frequencies, protects us from the negative vibrations of others. Practice of the Inner Smile enhances this Smiling Aura.

By remaining conscious of the smiling energy in the mid-eyebrow, face, and navel, and especially the solar plexus, you can create a strong sunlight radiance and intensify the Smiling Aura field around your body to act as a shield to keep out negative vibrations. The Smiling Aura field can also help you transform your own negative energies into positive life-force. For instance, if you feel anger, smiling energy gives you the ability to smile into that emotion until it is transformed into kindness. With practice, you can use this force to transform hatred into love, sadness into courage, and fear into gentleness. After a while, the process becomes automatic.

Six Healing Sounds

Best Times to Practice the Six Healing Sounds

Practice the Six Healing Sounds before going to bed at night to slow down the body, promote sound sleep, and cool any organs that are overheated. You may also use these sounds to enhance any of the other Taoist exercises, such as the Microcosmic Orbit and the Inner Smile, whenever you wish. For health maintenance, do three repetitions of each sound per day. Be sure to rest for at least 1 to 3 breaths between each repetition. Once learned, the Six Healing Sounds take only 10 to 15 minutes to complete.

Transform Negative Emotions

Before you go to sleep, use the Six Healing Sounds to clear out any negative emotions and let the positive emotions grow. Feel a sense of openness as you relax your own mental activity and connect with Universal Consciousness. This will also reduce bad dreams during your sleep, allowing the body to recharge through its connection with the Heavenly Force. If you have any problems, stress, or illness, this is the best time to allow the Universal Consciousness to help you find the solution. When you wake up, smile inward and look for the answers that arise spontaneously.

Do More Sounds When Appropriate

If you have health problems related to a specific organ, do more repetitions of that sound. In each season, the organ associated with that season is more vulnerable, so it is advisable to do more repetitions for an organ during its particular season. In the fall, do more Lung Sounds; in winter, more Kidney Sounds; in spring, more Liver Sounds; in summer, more Heart Sounds; and during Indian summer, more Spleen sounds. Increase in multiples of 3: for example, from 3 repetitions to 6, 9, or even 18.

Follow the Natural Order and Do All the Sounds

The order of the Six Healing Sounds follows the natural progression of the seasons. Always begin with the Lung Sound and follow it with the Kidney, Liver, Heart, Spleen, and Triple Warmer Sounds, in that order.

Practice to Relieve Fatigue

If you are tired or depressed, whether at work or at home, practice the Six Healing Sounds to clear out the fatigue or low mood. If you do not have time to do three repetitions each, or it is late at night and you are very tired, do them once each. You can also do the Six Healing Sounds without the hand positions. It is always better to do a little practice each day than none at all.

Microcosmic Orbit Meditation

Open Your Heart in the Morning

Taoist tradition says to open your heart before you open your eyes. To open your heart, smile down to the heart area until you feel it open like a flower blossoming. Feel love, joy, and happiness radiate from the heart and spread to all the organs. When you wake up, do not immediately open your eyes and jump out of bed. In the Taoist system, we believe each organ has its own soul. When we are asleep, the souls of our organs are at rest too, and they take awhile to awaken. Also, sometimes they leave the body while you are asleep to travel to other realms and need time to return when you wake up. If you are too hasty, you can injure the souls of the organs.

Overcome Your Biorhythms and Astrological Chart

In Taoism, we believe that when you control your Chi (life- force), you control your life and future. Until you attain this level of mastery, forces such as the positions of the stars (astrology) and the peaks and valleys of your own energy system (biorhythms) heavily influence your life. To be aware of these forces and eventually overcome them, check your energy levels each morning. While you are still lying in bed, concentrate on your navel until you feel it become warm. Direct the energy to flow down to the perineum and up the spinal cord in the Microcosmic Orbit, then direct it back to the navel. If you can move through the Microcosmic Orbit quickly and smoothly, your physical, emotional, and mental energy levels are good.

On days when the Microcosmic Orbit moves slowly or not at all, the physical, emotional, and/or intellectual energies are in a low cycle, and your body's defense system is low. This may be associated with your biorhythm cycle or your astrological chart. In either case, you may discover you are out of balance and more prone to accidents and illnesses. By consistently practicing the Healing Light meditation, you can eventually overcome your biorhythms and astrological influences.

Before Eating is the Best Time to Practice

Practicing the Microcosmic Orbit meditation is beneficial any time of day. When you have just learned the meditation, it is best to establish the habit of practicing 15 to 20 minutes in the morning before eating, and again in the evening before eating. It is easier to relax and enter a meditative state when the stomach is empty (but not when you are very hungry).

If it is physically difficult for you to sit for 20 minutes at the beginning, you can practice lying down, as long as you are rested enough not to fall asleep. If this time feels too long for you at the beginning, practice for shorter periods, increasing the time as you become used to sitting and your concentration improves.

Check Yourself for Blockages Daily

if you move Chi through the Microcosmic Orbit and feel an obstruction or blockage along the path, take a little more time to focus on the obstruction until it clears up. Chronic disease begins with a blockage of energy flow to the organs or glands along a major energy pathway (acupuncture channel). When the Chi flow to a major organ or gland is blocked, that organ either receives less energy, blood, and nutrition, or Chi and blood become stagnant, resulting in pain.

If the blockage continues over a long period, the organ or gland gradually works less effectively, until its function is critically impeded. By the time a doctor learns that the organ is not functioning well, it may be working at as little as 10 percent of its capacity. The malfunction can even lead to surgery or removal of that organ. To prevent such a catastrophe, as well as great expenditures of time and money, simply check yourself every day. Keep the channels open and maintain and strengthen your Chi by practicing the Healing Light meditations.

Diet, Sleep, Medicine, and Food Supplements:
Listen to Your Body

When you recycle and conserve your Chi by circulating it in the Microcosmic Orbit daily, you will have more life-force. As a result, you may find you require less food, fewer vitamins and food supplements, lower doses of medication, and even less sleep. If you continue to consume the same amounts and sleep as much as before, too much energy may collect. This can produce excessive heat in the head, which can cause insomnia. You may also find that as your body begins to heal itself, you inadvertently overdose on your medication, and that can cause serious problems. Take time to listen to your body. It will let you know just how much food, vitamins, or medication you need.

If you can maintain peace and quiet and a thankful heart at mealtimes, your stomach will be well prepared for the meal; digestion and assimilation will improve as a result. (In the Healing Tao Five Element Nutrition practice, you will learn the correlation between food and the seasons, as well as other valuable information regarding digestion and the Tao of nutrition.)

Transform Negative Emotions into Healing Energy
and Wisdom

When you practice the Inner Smile, you release negative energies trapped in the organs. As you concentrate on the navel and bring the accumulated Chi there, energy from the negative emotions also collects there. With the Inner Smile and Microcosmic Orbit meditations, you can refine, enhance, and circulate this energy through the main centers of the body, transforming the negative energy into vital healing energy.

For example, if you are angry, you may feel hot, explosive dull green or dingy red energy in the liver area. Use mind power to collect that energy and spiral it into the solar plexus center. Direct the negative energy down to the navel, smile to it, then move it through the Microcosmic Orbit. As it moves through the sacral center, Door of Life, T-11, and Jade Pillow, watch the color change into a clear, bright, luminous green; feel it transform into usable life-force energy.

If you are fearful, you may feel a cold and contractive blue-black energy from the kidneys in the lower back. Use mind power to gather and spiral this energy into the Door of Life. Smile to it, then move it through the Microcosmic Orbit. Observe with your inner eye how the color changes from dull blue to bright, clear blue; feel it transform into usable life-force energy.

If you are sad or depressed, you may feel a cool and heavy grayish-white energy afflicting the lungs and being reflected in the upper back. Use your mind power to gather and spiral this energy at T-5 (center opposite the heart). Smile to it, then move it through the Microcosmic Orbit. Observe with your inner eye how the color changes from dull white to bright, clear white; feel it transform into usable life-force energy.

Each organ can produce negative Chi that can be transformed into vital, positive energy and wisdom. At this level of meditation, you may perceive this transformation in terms of change in color and sensation. In later practice, during the second level of the meditation called Fusion of the Five Elements, you will learn very precise and advanced methods for transforming negative emotions into positive life-force energy.

Breathe Naturally

Awareness of natural breathing is part of the Six Healing Sounds practice. With the Inner Smile and Microcosmic Orbit, the breath takes care of itself.

Many meditation systems rely on the breath to guide the energy. But the energy often flows a lot faster than the breath. If you let the body breathe by itself, the energy can flow as fast as it wants.

In fact, you will develop your own breathing patterns during the practice—the breathing suitable to your body. This may change; from time to time your breathing may become rapid or jumpy or may slow down, all of which are normal during meditation.

If your breathing changes while you are meditating and you don't like the change, tell yourself to go back to normal breathing, and you will. If there is a change in breathing and you are curious about it, you can simply observe it and see what happens.

Tips for Daily Practice

Practicing daily to maintain and increase Chi is one of the most important components in staying healthy and growing spiritually. After we have begun to practice and have accumulated more Chi, we need to know how to use it wisely. We should avoid things that drain or destroy the life-force, such as tobacco, alcohol, coffee, drugs, and junk food. Daily cultivation and conservation of Chi includes practice of good life-style habits, such as eating right, exercising regularly, and getting enough rest.

1. Daily practice is the most important part of the cultivation and conservation of life-force. With daily practice of the Inner Smile, you will feel joyful, loving, kind, open, gentle, and courageous the first thing in the morning. Extend all these good feelings and energies to your family, friends, neighbors, and the people around you. This will increase your life- force.

2. Learn to conserve sexual energy, one of the major components of your life-force. Learn to recycle it to revitalize the brain and the organs. This is taught in the Healing Love practices.

3. Learn to conserve Chi by talking less. Although we often think of Chi as energy, it is also intimately related to the breath. Too much talking dissipates your Chi. Speak less, and when you must talk, speak only constructively to help others.

4. Constantly be aware of the navel center and the Original Force. Use the mind to keep the navel warm. This increases your life-force.

5. You may know by now that peace is not found in the outer world; peace is found within. Guard the senses. Looking outward all the time and chasing after things drains Chi and weakens the mind. Learn when to let go of fame, excitement, and money, so you retain more mental strength and spiritual life-force.

6. Learn how to forgive by using the Six Healing Sounds to transform anger into kindness. This conserves Liver Chi. Holding onto anger burns up a tremendous amount of the Chi the liver needs for other functions. You may think forgiveness is being nice to others, but it is actually being nice to yourself, because it helps you maintain your life-force.

7. Eat more fresh steamed vegetables, fiber, and foods with high water content; eat less spicy food. This conserves the Blood Chi.

8. Consciously swallow your saliva 50 to 100 times each day. This increases digestive Chi, lubricates and moistens the organs, helps prevent tooth decay, eliminates gas, and maintains the intestines in good condition.

9. Don't eat to your full capacity. Eat no more than two-thirds of your stomach's volume; when you begin to feel full, stop eating. This gives the stomach room for digestion and conserves Chi in the stomach and intestines.

10. Worry less. Worry can sometimes help solve problems, but usually it makes them worse. Do more inner Chi cultivation so you have

less time to worry and more Chi to face your problems. This conserves Heart and Spleen Chi.

11. Keep your life-style moderate. Don't overdo things; be moderate in work, sex, exercise, social activity, reading, and watching television. Excess activity drains your reserves of Chi. Living moderately conserves Chi and gives you energy for the important things.

Chapter 15

TROUBLESHOOTING GUIDE
Helpful Hints and Home Remedies

This chapter provides answers to common questions and solutions to problems that may occur in relation to your practice of the Microcosmic Orbit meditation. If you are feeling an energetic disharmony and the information in this chapter does not solve the problem, contact the certified Healing Tao instructor nearest you. If there are no Healing Tao instructors nearby, contact your local acupuncturist; acupuncturists are familiar with the treatment of energetic problems.

If you are unable to contact any of these resources to satisfactorily solve your problem or answer your questions, then get in touch with the national Healing Tao Center in New York.

Overcoming Difficulties with the Healing Light Meditation

How will I know when my Orbit is open?

Many people report feeling some Chi sensations up the spine yet nothing down the front channel. Because the five channels up the back are close to the spine, even if the energy is a little diffused, many students do feel sensation somewhere along the spine. However, there are seven channels coming down the front of the body, spread widely across the chest. Sometimes the energy diffuses, and the descent of the Chi is not felt until it reaches the navel.

Others report feeling energy at the sacrum and crown, but nothing on the spine in between. This is because there are fewer nerve endings on the skin surface of the back, and we are not used to paying attention to subtle sensations there. With practice, you will gradually gain more sensitivity and begin to feel energy along the spine.

Some people feel intense sensations of Chi when they first open the Microcosmic Orbit, and then little or nothing thereafter. When a dry river bed is filled by a sudden flash flood, the contrast between the bed's dry state and its wet state is very dramatic; yet once it is filled, if the river rises or falls a few inches, it is hardly noticeable. It is the same with your Microcosmic Orbit. A lack of sensation does not mean no Chi is flowing; it may just mean you need more practice to increase your awareness of the often subtle Chi sensations.

Most people have some sensations during their meditation. These may be warmth, heat, or tingling at the sacrum, Ming Men, Third Eye, or tip of the tongue, or cold or numb areas. Some people feel an effervescence like champagne bubbles. You may experience mild electric-like shocks anywhere in the body; the body may shake rhythmically or suddenly jolt. The hands, feet, or whole body may become unusually hot; in fact, you may feel strong sensations of heat anywhere in the body. Those who are visually oriented may see a light inside their heads, or points along the orbit may light up. If you have any of these sensations, you can conclude that energy is circulating.

I don't feel anything during the meditation. What's wrong?

It may take some people longer than others to open the channels of the Microcosmic Orbit. Exactly how long it takes depends on the individual's energy level and the number of blockages in each channel. If after two weeks you have not completed this meditation successfully, reverse the energy flow one center at a time, starting at the last point reached. Spend one week concentrating on each center in reverse order. Your Microcosmic Orbit should then be clear and open.

Although most people have some sensation that tells them their energy is circulating, several of my students have been practicing for years without any specific sensations. Why do they continue to meditate? Because they feel so much better afterward! Their health has improved.

I have had students tell me they felt nothing, but I could see a substantial difference in their energy before and after meditation. When they came to class they looked tired and preoccupied. After the medita-

478

tion, their eyes sparkled, their skin glowed, and there were a happy expressions on their faces.

The Microcosmic Orbit seems to be running the wrong way; it is coming up the front and going down the back.

This sometimes happens at the beginning, when the Yang energy in the back is not strong enough to overcome the rising Yin energy in the front.

It is nothing to worry about. There is no wrong way. Some people, especially women, have very strong Water energy and run it backward, using Water energy to clear the channel. Just keep meditating. After a while, the energy pattern will probably change, and you will feel the energy running up the back and down the front.

When I sit for 20 minutes, my mind wanders, and I get antsy.

Many people are troubled by what is sometimes called "monkey mind"; their thoughts jump all over the place, and they find it hard to concentrate. The Microcosmic Orbit meditation is actually well suited to people with this tendency.

When you practice the Microcosmic Orbit, you are constantly changing your state of consciousness. These changes can be observed with an electroencephalograph. The waves generated in the brain as you read and try to understand this book are called "beta." Beta waves indicate a state of mental alertness and active thinking. The first stage you enter in meditation is called "alpha." The next deeper state is called "theta." Theta is the state of purring cats as well as deep meditation.

In doing the Microcosmic Orbit meditation, you are first in beta as you tell yourself what you are going to do: "I am going to do the Inner Smile." When you actually begin the practice, you probably enter the alpha state. After a period of smiling to the thymus and heart, for instance, you tell yourself, "Now I'll smile to the lungs." At that point, you have gone back to beta. When you direct your attention to the lungs and return to the meditation, you will go down at least to alpha. So in the course of a meditation you can transfer easily from beta to alpha to theta, perhaps back to beta, and then more quickly into alpha and theta again.

My students with "monkey mind" had great difficulty when they tried other methods that involved watching the breath or emptying the mind. But because of the shifts in consciousness as well as the shift in focus to all the varied points along the Microcosmic Orbit, the "monkey mind" is satisfied.

If you put your attention at the navel and then after a few minutes your mind wanders or you get restless, tell your mind to focus on the Sperm or Ovarian Palace, Ming Men, or any point you like. After a while you will find you are able to maintain your concentration at a point for longer periods. Counting from 1 to 9 and 9 to 1 can also help. The spiraling technique galvanizes your attention and your energy at a specific point.

If your body feels restless or if you become aware of stiffness in your back, you can calmly adjust your posture by gently bending or stretching without disturbing your meditation.

Sometimes during meditation my breathing seems to stop. Is this something I should be concerned about?

The Six Healing Sounds use awareness of the breath as part of the method. In practicing the Inner Smile and Microcosmic Orbit, the breath takes care of itself.

Many meditation systems rely on the breath to guide the energy. But the energy often flows a lot faster than the breath. If you let the body breathe by itself, the energy can flow as fast as it wants.

In fact, you will develop your own breathing patterns during the practice—the breathing suitable to your body. This may change; from time to time your breathing may become rapid or jumpy or may slow down, all of which are normal during meditation.

If your breathing changes while you are meditating and you don't like the change, tell yourself to go back to normal breathing, and you will. If there is a change in breathing and you are curious about it, you can simply observe it and see what happens.

I have been seeing a psychotherapist and am on medication. Is it safe for me to practice the Microcosmic Orbit?

Whenever you are under the regular care of a physician, psychotherapist, or other healthcare practitioner for *any* chronic mental or emotional problem, you may wish to consult your practitioner first to determine whether meditation might adversely affect your condition. If your practitioner gives you the go-ahead, you should still advise your meditation instructor of your condition before beginning training.

When meditation may be inappropriate. If you are in an extremely unstable period emotionally or mentally, or are suffering from severe schizophrenia or any serious mental or emotional problems, you should not practice the Microcosmic Orbit. It may bring more Chi to the problem areas and aggravate them instead of helping. Limit yourself to the Inner Smile and Six Healing Sounds. Even with the Six Healing Sounds, if they release more emotional energy than you can digest, *stop right away.* Later, when you feel more stable and able to deal with the traumas locked in your body, you can resume your practice.

When meditation may be beneficial for psychological problems. The Microcosmic Orbit meditation can be helpful in treating many psychological conditions and problems. The practice helps you slow down and become calmer, more relaxed and centered. Because of its calming effects, it is particularly helpful for stress and the negative emotions brought on by prolonged stress, nervous tension, and irritability.

The Microcosmic Orbit is the treatment of choice for Kundalini psychosis, in which too much energy rushes up to the head and becomes stuck there. We have had several cases in the Healing Tao where people previously confined to psychiatric hospitals due to lack of understanding and misdiagnosis of this phenomenon were completely restored to health through practice of the Microcosmic Orbit alone. In other cases, people learning the Microcosmic Orbit were able to give up powerful psychiatric medications with no further problems. We will say more about Kundalini syndrome later in this chapter.

The Microcosmic Orbit, Six Healing Sounds, and Inner Smile are also particularly helpful in dealing with low self-esteem, low energy or chronic fatigue syndrome, shyness, and emotional problems caused by blocked energy in the organs.

I sometimes become sexually aroused when I practice. Is this good, bad, or neither?

Sexual arousal is a healthy sign that you have an ample amount of sexual energy. It is also a sign your Microcosmic Orbit is open (at least to the sexual center) and that the Chi is flowing strongly.

However, if you have not yet learned the Taoist methods to redirect your sexual energy, arousal during meditation can be very distracting. By learning Testicle/Ovarian Breathing and the Power Lock exercise (taught in the Healing Love Through the Tao workshop), you will easily be able to draw the sexual energy up from the sexual organs to the sacrum and on up the spine through the Governor Channel to the brain. This conserves and recycles sexual energy usually lost through ejaculation or menstruation. By circulating the Ching Chi, or sexual energy, through the Microcosmic Orbit pathway, you can transform it into life-force energy to nourish the whole body.

If you have not yet learned these techniques, you can take several Small Sip breaths and pull up on the perineum, anus, and back of the anus, and draw the sexual energy from the genitals around to the sacrum. Then use the mind, eyes, spiraling, and Small Sip breathing to draw the energy around the Microcosmic Orbit and back to the navel.

Once the sexual energy is drawn away from the genitals, the arousal itself will subside and should no longer be a distraction. If it recurs, repeat the process of drawing the sexual energy up the spine.

Should I become celibate to obtain the highest results from the Microcosmic Orbit meditation?

Many religions recognize that sexual energy is important to spiritual work and accordingly require celibacy of serious practitioners. In Taoism, celibacy is not essential, but conservation of sexual energy is vital. For this reason, we often teach Taoist methods of conserving sexual energy, known as Healing Love Through the Tao, in the same seminar with the Microcosmic Orbit.

Even so, it takes time to master the techniques of conserving sexual energy. Try to abstain from orgasm for at least the first 100 days of practice while you are learning the Microcosmic Orbit. This will build up a reservoir of Chi to aid in opening the Orbit. This is somewhat more important for men than women, because men lose more energy through orgasm (with ejaculation) than women. The 100 days of celibacy are a recommendation, however, not a requirement. Taoism teaches moderation. It is important to maintain harmony and balance in one's life. Changes in life-style should feel natural; if it is too stressful for you or your partner to abstain, respect your needs and those of your partner. Simply recognize that while it may take longer to accumulate energy if you are having sex to orgasm, you are preserving balance in other areas of your life.

Is it safe for me to practice the Microcosmic Orbit during my menses?

Women's cycles are very personal; each woman's constitution is unique, so it is difficult to make any overall pronouncement. Generally, if you are not having any problems with your menses, it is fine to practice the Microcosmic Orbit during your period. In fact, many women have reported their practice of the Microcosmic Orbit has reduced or eliminated menstrual problems such as PMS, cramping, skipped periods, scant menstrual flow, and pain.

If there is substantial bleeding during your period, however, bringing more Chi to the area of the uterus could increase the flow. If you experience excessive flow, observe the effect of your meditation practice. If the problem seems aggravated by meditation, discontinue the Microcosmic Orbit during your menses and instead emphasize the Inner Smile and the Six Healing Sounds.

Warming the Stove creates heat in the lower abdomen. If the heavy period is caused by excess heat in the blood, Warming the Stove could aggravate the excessive bleeding. However, many problems of painful menses and cramping are diagnosed in Chinese medicine as being caused by "internal coldness." In these cases, Warming the Stove would be helpful.

Female Healing Tao students who also practice Iron Shirt Chi Kung should not practice the packing process during their menses, but they can still benefit from other parts of the practice: standing, holding the postures, circulating energy without packing, and bone breathing.

Many female practitioners of the Healing Tao also report experiencing profound improvements in their overall health and menstrual cycles from Ovarian Breathing, a more advanced practice that circulates unaroused sexual energy through the Microcosmic Orbit pathway. Ovarian Breathing is described in *Healing Love Through the Tao: Cultivating Female Sexual Energy*.

Sometimes my body starts shaking and vibrating when I meditate. Other times it involuntarily jerks suddenly and strongly. What is happening?

There are several reasons for shaking, jerking, and vibrating involuntarily during meditation and Chi Kung practice. There is a Chinese saying, "The Chi moves and the body follows." When Chi flows strongly and suddenly into areas previously blocked, it sometimes moves the body spontaneously and causes the practitioner to jerk.

Sometimes the meditation posture may be slightly off, blocking an energy channel. In this case, the body sometimes spontaneously and involuntarily moves to open the channel and allow the Chi to flow in. The body displays its own wisdom in these matters, bypassing the control of the conscious mind.

In other cases, the body starts moving rhythmically to help "pump" the Chi through the body. When practicing the Microcosmic Orbit, many people rock back and forth spontaneously in time to the flow up the Governor Channel and down the Functional Channel. This is also common among Jewish worshipers, who call it "davening." It is frequent among one Christian religious sect that drew its name from the experience: the Shakers.

Yet another reason is that we have begun to absorb Chi from Heaven, Earth, and the Higher Self, and our channels are widening to absorb additional bursts of Chi. This is similar to what happens when you suddenly increase the water pressure in a hose: the hose jerks and moves around.

The shaking process is beneficial. In fact, special forms of Chi Kung encourage the shaking process; one is even called *Spontaneous Movement Chi Kung*. Shaking releases nervous tension and helps Chi penetrate deeply into the body.

If the shaking becomes too violent or powerful, however, you can stop it by simply mentally ordering it to cease.

When Chi fills the organs, there may be specific shakings that occur:

The heart rules the blood vessels. When the heart fills with Chi, the body jumps up and down like a monkey at play.

The liver rules the tendons. When the liver fills with Chi, the legs and big toes may cramp as the Chi swims joyfully like a fish in an ocean of divine ecstasy.

The spleen rules the muscles and flesh. When the spleen fills with Chi, the muscles twitch like a bird hopping from branch to branch, and the place where the Chi rests feels like fire.

The lungs rule the skin. When the lungs fill with Chi, you will feel sensations of prickling, itching, and heat all over the body, as if ants were crawling all over you, especially on your face. This indicates the lung Chi is moving around.

The kidneys rule the bones. When the kidneys fill with Chi, you will hear the sound of moving bones. As the Chi moves up the spine, you will sometimes also feel sexual arousal.

Will I get better results in my practice if I become a vegetarian, or is it helpful to eat meat?

In the beginning of your practice of the Microcosmic Orbit meditation, it is best to purify yourself. It is helpful to reduce the amount of meat, fish, and poultry you eat and to increase the amount of fiber in your diet to clear the digestive tract. If you are not totally vegetarian, we recommend that during your first 100 days of practice your diet consist of about 80 percent steamed vegetables and grains, 10 to 15 percent fish, and only 5 percent meat and chicken.

If you are doing a lot of practice, your metabolism and blood circulation will improve, as well as your Chi circulation. Heat is a common byproduct of this increase. If this happens, it is important to eat less warming food, such as meat and grains, and more cooling and cleansing food, such as high- water-content vegetables and fruit, and a moderate amount of fruit juice (but not too much; fruit juice can be overly cooling) to keep from overheating.

If you are not experiencing excess heat and are doing a lot of Tai Chi or physical Chi Kung practice along with intensive meditation, it can be beneficial to eat more building foods, such as meat and poultry. The Chinese have traditionally been partial to meat as a building food. There are also plentiful building foods, however, in a well-designed nonmeat diet; over the millennia, many Taoists have successfully practiced as vegetarians. Many Olympic athletes in recent years have also been exclusively vegetarian while training.

Modern research has implicated excessive meat consumption as a major factor in increasing the risk of heart disease and cancer. Meat eaters have a risk of heart attack over 300 percent greater than that of vegetarians. Taoists concerned with the balance of nature recognize that meat production is a major factor in the destruction of the world's rainforests. The Taoist path is the way of moderation. Be conscious of the implications of your life- style, and use your own good judgment as to what your needs are.

In any case, it is inadvisable to jump suddenly into a strict vegetarian diet without first educating yourself about it, because the changeover can create imbalances that may add to your problems. See Maneewan Chia's forthcoming book, *Five Elements Nutrition*, or consult a Healing Tao instructor.

I have heard meditations that work with energy are dangerous. Is the Microcosmic Orbit meditation safe?

The major adverse side effect of energy meditations is having too much energy get stuck in the wrong places. The most common places for energy to get stuck are the head and heart.

In the Healing Tao, we teach the Microcosmic Orbit in a safe and systematic way. Because we emphasize both and upward and downward flow of energy, there are fewer problems than with other systems. We also teach appropriate safeguards to prevent difficulties. If you follow the stages as we have outlined, respect the precautions, and use common sense, you should have only positive experiences with the Microcosmic Orbit.

In this troubleshooting guide, we outline common problems. If you show any adverse signs you feel may be related to your practice, use good judgment and immediately apply the appropriate remedy.

Meditation practice is like medicine. It can be tremendously healing if used according to directions, but if you are careless and do not treat it with respect, you can incur negative side effects. Energy practices are powerful, like fire. Fire can warm your home, provide light, cook food, and run machinery; it can benefit you in many ways. But you must treat fire with respect. If you handle carelessly, it can destroy your home, burn you, even kill you.

Don't be foolhardy in your practice of meditation. Respect the system, respect your teacher, and follow the appropriate safeguards given throughout this book.

Sometimes I feel very tired after meditation. Why is that?

Sometimes when energy has been blocked for a while and the channel is suddenly opened, energy rushes into the previously blocked area. While the energy is flowing where it needs to go, it may feel as if steam has been let out from where it was before, or as if there has been a release of pressure.

If you feel tired, rest. Allow your body to heal itself. You have already aided the process by opening the door for the energy to flow. Healing and restoring balance in the body requires a lot of energy; it is natural to feel tired as a result. The fatigue usually disappears in a few weeks.

After practicing the meditation regularly for several months now, I find myself experiencing powerful emotions like anger, sadness, and fear. I thought meditation was supposed to make me more peaceful!

Emotional traumas often create energetic blockages or areas of chronic tension in the body. These tensions are created as "psychological armoring," to protect us from threatening situations we are unable to process at the time. We often maintain these tensions for years, holding patterns we may be completely unaware of.

When we practice the Microcosmic Orbit, we are beginning the work of opening up all the energy blockages in the body. Moving energy through these areas of tension is a conscious attempt to relax these areas and bring them back to life. As we do this, we often reexperience the emotions of the original trauma. A certain part of us may feel frightened, vulnerable, almost naked, as if the meditation is stripping us of our protective armor.

If you are to be truly free and no longer a slave to the old reactions of your unconscious, you need to process your emotions daily and let go of old anger, fears, and grief. Nonetheless, it is important to respect your emotional strengths and abilities in dealing with these old, repressed traumas. Many victims of physical and sexual abuse have completely shut out the memories of these incidents from their conscious minds, recollecting them only years later after something triggers the memories. This kind of severe trauma can be painful and difficult to deal with, so progress at your own pace.

As their meditation practice unlocks old emotional problems, brings them to the surface, and starts the process of healing and releasing, many people find it helpful to seek some form of counseling or therapy to aid recovery. Others find they are able to handle the release with meditation alone. A good counselor can be of great help in speeding the emotional healing process. You should respect your own needs.

How long should I practice the Microcosmic Orbit meditation before moving on to the higher levels of practice?

This is a highly personal matter, less a question of time than of accomplishment. Some people are ready to move on almost immediately, whereas others may practice for months or years before they are ready to move to the next stage. Generally speaking, once you have thoroughly mastered the Microcosmic Orbit instructions and have spent some time practicing, you can continue with such practices as Testicle or Ovarian Breathing, the Power Lock Exercise, and Fusion of the Five Elements meditations. These practices are advanced variations of the Microcosmic Orbit; the main difference is that they are moving a different form of Chi through the Orbit.

In fact, sometimes students who don't feel Chi moving in the Microcosmic Orbit or who don't have the sense of having opened the pathways *should* move on anyway. The sensation of sexual energy (Ching Chi) moving in the pathway is much more vivid and pronounced for many people, as is the sensation of the pearl formed in the Fusion practice. The more advanced practices may therefore actually help them open the Microcosmic Orbit.

Turning Awareness Inward Highlights Health Problems

Taoist meditations bring your attention back into yourself. The mind/body connection becomes stronger, and you can learn to foresee dangers to your health. Some people mistakenly blame newly discovered problems on the meditations. It would be wise to recognize that in most cases internal disorders have their roots in past experience, not in the practices that make us aware of them. The truth is that the meditations only expose these problems.

Nonetheless, when we begin to circulate energy, we sometimes encounter congestion. The situation is something like a roadblock: it isn't a problem until you try to drive your car past it! The following section describes common symptoms associated with congestion in particular organs. If you experience any of these symptoms, try the simple remedies suggested. These remedies are intended to alleviate the underlying problem, not just the symptoms.

Simple Remedies for Organ Congestion

Liver congestion. Symptoms of liver congestion include headaches due to perverse heat in the liver, being easily angered, constipation due to the heat of the liver, and painful eyes. The liver is congested and the Wood meridians are blocked, creating pain.

One reported remedy is the Chinese herb pill called Niu Huang Chieh Du Pien, packaged eight to a bottle. The average dose is two to four the first night and two the following nights. After you finish one bottle, wait for the effects. Heat and anger may be reduced or may cool other emotions. You may have diarrhea, so avoid taking this pill before a long trip. (The pill is also available in a coated form, 20 in a bottle, enough for three treatments.)

Avoid the following: oily, greasy, or fried foods; butter and cheese with a lot of cream; alcohol; and hot and spicy foods. Do not overeat.

Beneficial foods include green leafy vegetables and lightly cooked black seaweed.

Do 9 Liver Sounds. Repeat as many times as necessary.

Spleen/stomach/pancreas congestion. Symptoms of spleen/stomach/pancreas congestion include indigestion due to heat in the stomach and intestines, feeling over-full or bloated after eating, pieces of food in the stool, abdominal discomfort, and dislike of having the abdomen touched.

A reported remedy is the Chinese herb pill called Huang Lien Shan Chin Pien, supplied eight pills in a bottle. Normal dose is two to four the first night and two the following nights, then wait for the results. Heat and emotions may be reduced. You may have diarrhea, so do not take this formula before a long trip.

Avoid the following: fried foods and foods rich in butter or cream; raw or cold foods; sugar, meat, and eggs.

Beneficial foods include mild soups; soft cooked cereal, such as rice cream; and kudzu drink or arrowroot.

Do the Spleen Sound 9 times. Repeat until you feel better.

Lung congestion. Symptoms of lung congestion include dry or sore throat, oral and nasal boils, toothache, yellowish or reddish urine, constipation due to heat, and depression. These stem from internal conditions due to perverse heat in the lungs and are not to be confused with similar symptoms caused by the flu.

A reported remedy is the Chinese herb pill called Ching Fei Yi Hua Pien, supplied eight to a bottle. Normal dose is two to four the first night and two the following nights, then wait for the effects. The heat and emotions may be reduced. Avoid taking these before a long trip.

Beneficial foods include relaxing teas and boiled pears.

Lightly tap the chest area all over with your palm.

Practice the Lung Sound 9 times. Repeat as many times as necessary.

Disharmony of the entire system. Symptoms include feeling faint due to sudden disharmony in the energy system at that moment, or from exhaustion.

Remedies: Immediately lower the head between the knees, or lie down with the feet slightly elevated. Press these points: Large Intestine 4 (at the base of the V-shaped web between the thumb and the first finger), Stomach 36 (on the lower calf).

If you are applying the points on another person and he or she faints completely, press Governor Channel 26, Renzhong, between the nose and the upper lip. Cover the person with a blanket and give some hot tea.

Signs of Detoxification

As the healing benefits of the Inner Smile, Six Healing Sounds, and Microcosmic Orbit begin to manifest, you may also find the process includes detoxification. For instance, with the Six Healing Sounds you may find yourself belching, yawning, and passing gas as you practice. That is an immediate form of detoxification and a good sign the practice is working.

You may find from time to time that you experience other signs of detoxification. The most common are listed below.

Diarrhea. You can distinguish the diarrhea of detoxification from the diarrhea of illness. For one thing, you will probably have the episode of diarrhea at the same time you would normally have a bowel movement. It will not be accompanied by the common signs of sick diarrhea: intestinal pain, fever, weakness, cold sweat, and so on. In fact, when the diarrhea is over, you may even feel more energetic. Some of my students say they have diarrhea at the time of a normal bowel movement perhaps three days in a row, and then no more. Or it may return from time to time as they reach new levels in their practice.

Sleeping a great deal. You may find yourself sleeping for long stretches after you start the practice. This is another way the body handles detoxification. Also, at the beginning, your energy may be doing a lot of repair on your body, and you may feel tired after meditating. As long as this marathon sleeping (10 to 15 hours) doesn't last more than a few days, it is nothing to worry about.

Recurrence of old illnesses. One of the more disturbing signs of detoxification is the resurfacing of an old illness. This can happen with any type of disease, but it seems to be more common with skin and lung conditions, particularly those treated with drugs to suppress the symptoms. It is like trying to keep a bunch of Ping-Pong balls underwater. When you take away the suppression, they bounce to the surface.

For many of my students, these recurrences are a way for the old diseases to fight their way out of the body entirely, but feeling sick or being disturbed by skin rashes is not pleasant or easy to tolerate. My only encouragement is that this is often the end of their old affliction. If the condition is not too troublesome, try some of the recommended herbs and dietary treatments mentioned in the previous section. Of course, if the problem appears serious or goes on too long, you should consult a health practitioner.

If it is physically possible, do not stop meditating when you are ill. Accelerated healing will continue to take place as long as you meditate for even 20 minutes a day.

Those who have had broken bones or surgery may experience some pain as energy flows through these areas. For the first time since the injury or surgery, energy links are being reestablished. The pain is often short-lived, intense but brief; then it vanishes and does not recur.

Circulation of Energy Prevents Blockages and Maintains Safety

Follow the Natural Patterns of Yin and Yang

Chinese medicine has roots in Taoism; it emphasizes developing and maintaining internal harmony and strength to help the body heal itself. All meditations, internal exercises, and martial arts of the Healing Tao system are based on these same concepts. They are gentle and safe because they circulate Chi, which enhances the body while recycling stagnant or negative energies. Taoists believe in the law of Yin and Yang: energy in nature moves in an appropriate and balanced way. The sun rises, and so it must set. The moon waxes and then wanes. If the sun remained still for several days or more, everything on one side of the planet would burn, and everything on the other side would freeze. If the moon remained still, its gravitational effect would upset the balance of the oceans. This is why the balancing of Yin and Yang energies is so important.

In the microcosm of the body, when you bring energy up to the head and the heart, you must also bring it down again to avoid overheating these vital organs. Circulating energy regularly through the Microcosmic Orbit regulates the body's energies and maintains internal balance as an essential part of practice. The Healing Light meditation is useful in restoring health, but it also acts as a safety valve for other practices. Circulating Chi with this exercise protects the practitioner from dangerous side effects of drawing in too much energy.

Don't Cook Your Brain; Don't Cook Your Heart

There is an old Taoist saying:"Don't cook the brain, and don't cook the heart." This means do not leave energy too long in the head or the heart. Under certain conditions, the body's Yin and Yang energies may separate, and the hot Yang energy will rise to the higher centers of the heart and brain. If it is not consciously circulated, it can overheat these organs and possibly damage them. When this hot energy is drawn down to the navel, the head and heart centers remain cool, and a surplus of Chi becomes available to the body.

Overheating the Brain: Kundalini Syndrome

Causes of Kundalini syndrome. Other systems advocate building up a great deal of energy through such practices as celibacy. This energy may spontaneously rise up the spine to the brain, resulting in Kundalini syndrome. When this powerful Yang energy surges up all at once, the body doesn't know how to handle it; all kinds of syndromes, psychoses, and damage to the organs and senses can result.

Kundalini syndrome can also occur if one focuses the attention for too long on the mid-eyebrow or Third Eye without having opened the Functional Channel to provide a Yin pathway for grounding, venting, and recycling the energy.

Symptoms of Kundalini syndrome. Complications that arise because of energy congestion in the head include sudden baldness, headaches, ringing in the ears, seeing flashing lights, and psychosis. These problems can occur if energy flows up the spine without being released through the skull or circulated down the front channel to the navel. Incidents of this syndrome have caused acute suffering, especially to those who sought treatment from Western physicians, because Western medicine does not address the flow of energy in the body. (For more information, read *The Kundalini Syndrome* by Lee Sannella, M.D.)

Avoiding and treating Kundalini syndrome. To avoid such problems, you need to open both channels of the Microcosmic Orbit and store all accumulated energies at the navel. The Microcosmic Orbit meditation balances Chi flow by circulating energy up through the warm vital centers and down through the cooler centers before it is stored in the navel. This naturally harmonizes the Yin and Yang (cold and hot) energies, in contrast to the emphasis in Kundalini practice on the Yang upward movement of energy without grounding it in cooling Yin energy.

It is also far better to bring the energy up gradually and in a controlled manner. The situation can be likened to trying to get water to the top story of a tall building. One possibility is to install a big pump on top of the building. It will work, but with a lot of difficulty. A better way is to install a pump at ground level and add more small pumps all the way up the building, so each pump sends water to the next pump.

Likewise, in Taoist practice we learn to activate several different pumps: at the perineum, anus, sacrum, adrenal glands, seventh cervical vertebra, and base of the skull (part of the cranial pump together with the crown) to help pump energy up the 24 vertebrae. Sending energy up the spine to the higher center daily and bringing it down the front enhances the organs and glands, reduces side effects, and more fully utilizes the vital life-force. In the Taoist way, Awakening Healing Light is an ongoing process. It does not happen suddenly, leaving you with no room to handle the excess.

Overheating the Heart

The main cause of the heart overheating is an excess of negative emotions blocked in the heart. Sometimes if people concentrate on the abdomen too long, either because of gastrointestinal problems or because they don't feel any Chi there, the energy rises up the front and overheats the heart as well. In women, Chi in the Functional Channel tends to rise up the front of the body to the head. When heart energy is not clear and open, the Chi can't pass through; it jams up in the pericardium, overheating the heart's cooling system. The heart then overheats, causing irritability, chest pain, and an accelerated heart rate.

1. To solve this problem, first move the concentration to the Door of Life. Feel the heat drain from the heart back to T-5 or T-6 and down to the Door of Life. Feel the heart cool down.

2. If this doesn't help or the heart still beats fast and causes profuse sweating, shift the concentration to the mid-eyebrow and move down to the navel and Door of Life. Moving the concentration back and forth should release the congestion of the heart.

3. Practice more of the Six Healing Sounds for the lungs, heart, and liver. Do each 6 to 12 times and feel the organs cool down.

4. Feel love, joy, and happiness to open and cool the heart. Impatience, hastiness, and hate overheat the heart and can lead to heart failure or heart attack.

5. Massage the sternum and between the ribs to help release the jamming-up of heat and energy in the heart.

6. Practice Fanning and Venting the excess heat out to the tips of the toes and fingers.

Chapter 16

THE TAO OF HEALING AND HEALTH MAINTENANCE

ONENESS WITH THE TAO

In the forest, a microcosm in the vast universe, all parts work together to form a harmonious whole. The forest produces vapor and attracts rain. The rain helps the trees, plants, and vegetables grow. The plants produce oxygen and fruit for humans, animals, and birds. Humans and animals produce carbon dioxide to be used by the plants to make food; our droppings fertilize the trees, plants, and vegetables. When we destroy our forests, the cycle and its balance are disturbed, and everyone suffers.

In Taoism, the human body is also considered a microcosm of the universe. Just as with the forest, the health of the body depends on a balance among its constituent parts. From the perspective of Taoist Five Element theory, the elemental forces within the body nourish and support one another as they simultaneously keep each other in check.

In terms of Western physiology, the body's systems and organs are also seen to support and promote each other; all bodily processes are controlled through a series of feedback loops. Despite the similarity in understanding between East and West, this holistic perspective is not integral to the Western medical approach. Medications and surgery are prescribed for specific parts of the body without full consideration of the ramifications for the entire being. The result is often that while the original presenting symptoms are "cured," annoying side effects crop up as evidence that the treatment has disrupted the harmonious interdependence of the body's systems. Dissatisfaction with this approach is precisely why today more and more people are seeking alternative systems of medicine and healing.

THE MICROCOSMIC ORBIT HELPS INTEGRATE THE WHOLE BODY

Some of the safest and most effective ways of healing were discovered by the ancient Taoists. Many students ask me about their problems and illnesses, and I always answer, "Just do the Microcosmic Orbit; this will connect the parts of your body as a whole. Seek balance first, and many problems will be solved."

One of my students was referred to me by a physician. The student showed me two sheets describing his illnesses: high blood pressure, diabetes, back pain, headache, and so on—problems that would be considered unrelated in Western medicine. I gave him one solution for all those varied manifestations of disharmony: the Microcosmic Orbit meditation. He asked me why. I said, "The first thing you have to do is complete the Orbit. Once the energy is flowing freely, you can take in more energy to heal your body. When you do the practice, don't focus on your sickness, or on wanting to heal the illness. Just keep your mind on the opening the Orbit, on absorbing more energy into it to help balance the energy in the body, and on taking care of the body as a whole. When all the parts are stronger and healthier, they will help each other."

Later in this chapter we present some special formulas for specific problems, but the most basic healing power comes from activating the Original Force and practicing the Microcosmic Orbit, Inner Smile, and Six Healing Sounds. Once you can feel Chi, you can use the energy prescriptions to deal with specific problems.

PREVENTION AND MAINTENANCE IS THE BEST WAY TO HEALTH

The *Nei Jing*, a second-century B.C. Taoist medical classic attributed to the Emperor Huang Ti, states, "Maintaining order rather than correcting disorder is the ultimate principle of wisdom. To cure disease after it has appeared is like digging a well when one is already thirsty, or forging weapons after the war has already begun."

In the Healing Tao, we emphasize daily practice to get in touch with the organs, the glands, and all the other systems of the body. The Inner Smile creates a positive feeling inside that is important for health maintenance and self-healing. When you have a clear awareness of your body, if anything goes wrong you can detect it at an early stage. As soon as you are aware of a potential problem, take a moment to practice and overcome the negative feeling or sickness. In this way, you can very easily take care of any problem that arises.

WORKING WITH COMMON PROBLEMS

Once you fall ill, it takes more time to heal. The Healing Tao approach roots out the problem slowly, without covering or suppressing it. You may not see results right away, but with regular training, you can stop pain and overcome colds and other acute illnesses quickly. Using mind power to concentrate on the painful and sick areas, you will gradually feel improvement. Don't give up on long-term or chronic illnesses; continue to practice, and you will slowly get better.

The Microcosmic Orbit and the Common Cold

The Microcosmic Orbit helps activate the lymphatic flow, spleen, and thymus glands, all important parts of the immune system. Many students, once they are regularly practicing the Microcosmic Orbit meditation, find they seldom get colds or the flu.

The moment you feel you are going to catch cold or become sick, take a few moments to concentrate on the navel and make it warm. Then guide the energy flow in the Orbit, absorbing more energy from the earth, stars, and Cosmic Force. Directing Chi flow down through the nose expels coldness and dampness in the body. When your body is warm and the energy is flowing through the nose, you have already overcome the cold or flu. This is one of the best means of prevention and self-maintenance.

When you feel cold throughout the body, or even if only your hands and feet are cold, concentrate on the navel. Picture the sun in front of you and absorb its warmth into the navel. Feel the rays of the sun radiating into your body, hands, and feet.

A second method is to picture a small fireball at the navel. Start with it very dim; as it gradually becomes brighter and hotter, it warms the hands, feet, and whole body.

With a third method, you imagine you are standing on two fireballs. The heat from the fireballs gradually rises from the feet to the navel and radiates throughout the body.

Fever

If you have a fever, imagine you are covered with ice or are in a crystal ice palace. Gradually feel the body cooling down. This can help reduce the fever.

Chi Can Help Overcome Pain

From the perspective of Taoism and Chinese medicine, pain is created when Chi or blood stagnates anywhere in the body. The cure is straightforward: because Chi also moves stagnant blood, to alleviate pain, get the Chi moving. Acupuncture and acupressure are so famous for their effectiveness in treating pain because these healing modalities are specifically centered around restoring the balance and flow of Chi.

Chi Treatment for Lower Body Pain

When you have pain in the lower back and legs, inhale, drawing energy from the earth through the soles of the feet. Guide this energy into the areas of discomfort. Raise the palm over the painful area. Breathe and pack more Chi into the pain, then exhale all the pain into the earth very slowly through the toes (Figure 16-1).

Chi Treatment for Upper Body Pain

You can use the same method of breathing and packing into painful areas in the upper body, holding in the pain's energy until you feel hot, then exhaling it out to the arms and through the tips of the fingers (Figure 16-2).

Constipation

With the stresses of modern life—heavy consumption of meat and refined foods, drugs, drinking, sedentary living—many people suffer from constipation. Due to life-style excesses and not enough time for rest and renewal, the liver can become swollen and strained. The intestines

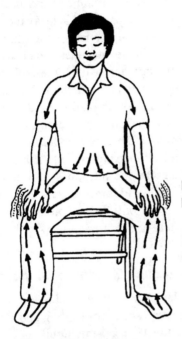

Draw Chi to the painful area

Exhale the pain down to the toes

Figure 16-1. Lower back pain

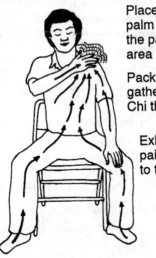

Place the palm over the painful area

Pack and gather the Chi there

Exhale the sick, painful energy down to the tip of the toes

Figure 16-2. Upper body pain

then become deformed, swollen in some places and constricted in others, making it difficult for food to pass. Toxins stay too long in the intestines and are reabsorbed into the body, causing a multitude of health problems. Stress also causes cramps in the intestines and obstructs the flow of food.

Several different approaches help reestablish healthy peristaltic movement in the intestines, which causes food to move through smoothly. First, you can use the power of the mind to bring more Chi and movement to the area. Second, you can use embryonic breathing (described below) to move the whole abdomen. You can also train the muscles of the large intestine to create a wavelike movement, or you can use the fingers to massage the intestines in a clockwise spiral. Daily practice of the Inner Smile and forgiveness is very important. When you practice forgiveness, it not only helps you let go of negative emotions such as grief, anger, hurt, and depression; it also helps you get rid of the waste in your body.

Using Chi to Reestablish Movement in the Intestines

Meditating on the solar plexus, navel, and Sea of Chi, below the navel, directs more Chi to the intestines for healing and restoring balance.

1. Prepare as for the Microcosmic Orbit.

2. Activate the Original Chi in the Tan Tien. Picture the small and large intestines filling with Chi. When you concentrate on the center, lightly rock the spinal cord in the lumbar area.

3. The solar plexus is connected to the area of the Chi Chung point (T-11). Focus your mind on T-11, and rock in that area until you feel the intestines moving with you.

4. Concentrate on the navel, which connects with Lumbar 2 and 3. Rock in this area until you have the sensation of warmth, vibration, and the intestines moving.

5. Move lower, to the center called the Sea of Chi, which connects to Lumbar 4 and 5. Rock and spiral until you feel the Chi open and flowing.

Practice Embryonic Breathing (Womb Breathing)

1. Sit or stand with the back slightly curved. Inhale and tighten the sexual organs, perineum, anus, and buttocks. Lightly draw in the chin and straighten the neck.

2. Exhale completely in three consecutive outbreaths. Feel the stomach flatten to the back and feel the sexual organs being pulled up.

3. Move the upper abdomen in and out 9 to 18 times: hold the exhalation, but expand and contract the upper abdomen as if you were breathing. Relax and breathe naturally. Close the eyes, being aware of the warmth and fresh Chi flow in the abdomen and the intestines.

4. Repeat the same procedure, but instead move the navel area 9 to 18 times.

5. Repeat the same procedure, but move down to the lower abdominal area. It is important when you rest to be aware of the abdominal area, using the mind to picture the intestines having strong, vital Chi flow and feeling pleasant and warm.

Spiral and Massage the Large Intestine

1. Start by touching the fingers to the right hip corner, where the cecum and ileocecal valve meet. Focus the mind on training the muscles around that area to spiral clockwise and upward.

2. When you feel you can control the muscles, move up along the ascending colon and gradually up to the right corner (hepatic flexure) under the right rib cage. Spend more time spiraling in this area, because it is a curve through which food has more difficulty passing.

3. Move along the transverse colon to the corner below the left rib cage, where the transverse colon meets the descending colon (splenic flexure). Spend more time spiraling clockwise, emphasizing the downward direction. (Please see Figure 5-7.)

4. Continue down the descending colon to the sigmoid colon and rectum.

5. Once you master this technique, you can use the mind to move a wave from the cecum on the right hip up to the right corner under the ribs, across to the left corner under the ribs, and down to the left hip. Continue to do this until you feel Chi in the large intestine. You may feel as though energy is moving in it, or you may feel as if you want to move the bowels.

Exercise the Corners of the Large Intestine

1. In a standing position, keep the hips stationary and twist the waist to the left. Feel the cecum and ileocecal valve at the corner of the right hip tighten or twist. Twist to the opposite side, and feel the ascending and descending colons twist.

2. Return to the starting position.

3. Twist to the right and feel the tightening of the sigmoid colon and anus. On the opposite side, feel the ascending and transverse colon twist.

4. Do this 9 to 18 times. Rest, and feel the open, warm, good feeling at the four corners. This exercise strengthens the corners of the large intestine.

Abdominal Massage

Abdominal massage helps relieve constipation as well as cramps, knots, and tangles in the abdomen.

Lie face up. Start at the left side of the navel. Using the middle and index fingers of both hands, massage in a clockwise circle. Circle at least 9 to 36 times, or more if necessary, then reverse the direction. Move around the navel, gradually spiraling out to cover the whole abdomen. Feel for knots and lumps. Sometimes you need to shake the lumps to break them up.

For more details, please see *Chi Self Massage: The Taoist Way of Rejuvenation* and Chapter 5 of *Chi Nei Tsang: Internal Organs Chi Massage.*

Regular Intestinal Cleansing

Twice a year, the intestine should be cleaned out by a brief fast or eating only vegetables for a few days. Consult a colon specialist. Having a colonic a few times a year can be helpful, but it may be too cold for people with a weak or Yin constitution.

Daily Intake of Fiber

Daily intake of more fiber, such as vegetables and fruit, helps clear out the colon.

Beware of Salt

Be aware of salt intake since eating too much salty food can cause constipation.

Smoking and Drinking

Many students come to me because they want to quit smoking, drinking, or taking drugs. My prescription is the same as for anyone else: Learn the Six Healing Sounds, Inner Smile, and Microcosmic Orbit. After you practice for a while, the bad habits will simply start to evaporate.

A smoker who does the Lung Sound conscientiously will, like any other student, begin to really appreciate the lungs. He or she will begin to consider the lungs even before lighting up. When you really love your lungs, you do not want to hurt them any more with irritating smoke.

When you feel better and more balanced through the practice of circulating the energy and receiving higher, more refined force, you will not need stimulants. Many students give up smoking and drinking after learning the practice of circulating Chi. Once the body experiences better energy, it does not like to go back to the lower kind of energy.

While working, if you need more energy, close the eyes, concentrate on the mid-eyebrow, spiral until you feel energy there, and bring it down to the navel and kidneys. Spiral until they feel warm, and then move the energy in the Orbit. You can stop at T-11, the adrenal glands center, and make it warm. With this technique, you can have more energy right away.

Simply close the eyes and do the Inner Smile into the organs and glands until the whole body fills with Chi.

Occasionally taking a moment during work to lightly rock and twist the spinal cord will recharge your energy. How fast you recharge depends on your daily practice; if you practice regularly, it is much easier to obtain more energy in a short time.

Shaking the kidneys (described below) and massaging the adrenal glands invigorates kidney and adrenal function so you have more energy throughout the day.

1. Place the thumbs near the spine between T-11 and T-12.

2. Inhale, expand the back, and push the spine toward the back. Press the thumbs in.

3. Exhale and curve the spine inward. Continue to press the thumbs into the glands (Figure 16-3). Do this 6 to 9 times.

Shaking the Kidneys to Relieve Fatigue

This practice is highly beneficial. It is especially invigorating when you feel tired.

Form the hands into loose fists. Use the back of the fists to very lightly hit the back in the kidney area, under the rib cage. Never hit the kidneys forcefully, as this can injure them. Do this from 9 to 49 times (Figure 16- 4).

Cover the kidney area with the palms. Gently shake the kidneys up and down to increase Chi flow and blood circulation. Do this from 9 to 49 times.

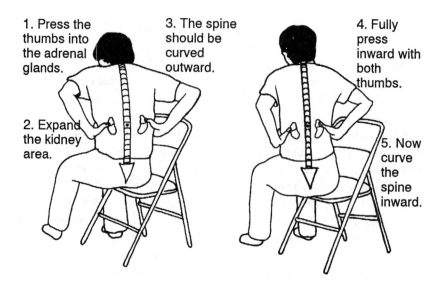

1. Press the thumbs into the adrenal glands.

2. Expand the kidney area.

3. The spine should be curved outward.

4. Fully press inward with both thumbs.

5. Now curve the spine inward.

Figure 16-3. Activate the adrenal glands.

Physical Weakness, Old Age

The mid-eyebrow point, the center between the eyebrows, is connected to the pituitary gland. The pituitary gland is known as the "master gland" because it controls many other glands and activities in the body. This gland is situated in the Crystal Palace in the brain, near several of the other major glands, such as the pineal gland, thalamus, and hypothalamus. (Please see Figure 3-45.) Stimulating the pituitary also helps activate other glands. With aging or weakness, the pituitary gland becomes less active. Concentrating on the mid-eyebrow point brings more Chi or life-force to reactivate this center.

Although it is important to activate this center, remember that you are seeking balance, not excess. More is definitely not better in the case of the mid-eyebrow point. Because this is in a naturally Yang area of the body (the head), once you have activated this point, be sure to guide the Chi back down to the navel, where it can be safely stored for future use.

1. You can use the fingers to touch the mid-eyebrow point. (Please see Figure 5-48.) Smile and lightly rub the point. Use the power of the mind and eyes to spiral there until you feel a sensation of expansion or warmth. When the area feels energized, use the mind to guide the energy down the front channel to the navel.

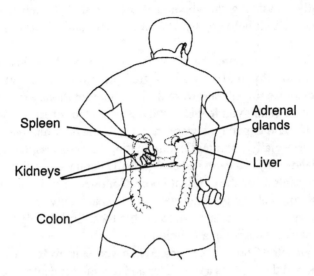

Spleen

Adrenal glands

Kidneys

Liver

Colon

**Figure 16-4. Lightly hit your back over both
kidneys with loose fists.**

2. Practice looking at the sunrise and sunset (see Chapter 4, "Most advanced mind/eye training," for instructions and important safeguards). Gather the sun essence into the saliva and swallow it upward to the pituitary gland. Close the eyes and picture a sun glowing bright in the Crystal Palace. (Please see Figure 5-46.)

3. Practice gathering the moon essence (see Chapter 4, "Most advanced mind/eye training"). Gather the moon essence into the saliva and swallow it upward to the pituitary gland.

Nervous Tension and Headache

Nervous tension can be caused by long-term stress. Stress works like a pressure cooker: if it is prolonged, it can cause the organs to overheat. Clenching in the abdominal area turns into physical knots and tangles. Stress can also cause insomnia and headaches (Figure 16-5).

Daily practice of the Inner Smile and Six Healing Sounds helps relieve overheating and pressure. During work, if you can constantly remind yourself to smile down, this will release tension before it builds to an extreme level. Rocking and twisting the spinal cord is important as well.

Lightly massaging the abdominal area around the navel to help release tension will help greatly. Practice the abdominal massage techniques.

1. Start with Warming the Stove. Emphasize the abdominal area by spiraling and physically moving the intestines clockwise and counterclockwise to generate warmth. Feel the vibrations expanding in the navel area. When you feel Chi, move to the Door of Life. Warm the Door of Life, and expand the warmth to the kidneys. Strengthening the kidneys is especially important in eliminating nervousness, because the adrenal glands are physically and energetically connected to the kidneys.

2. Concentrate on the Original Force. Continue to smile down to the navel until you feel Chi pressure starting to expand outward.

3. Move the awareness down to the big toes. Curl the big toes, as if you were clawing the floor, a few times.

4. Concentrate on the big toes. When you start to lose your concentration, curl the big toes a few times and resume concentrating on the

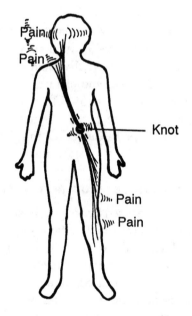

Figure 16-5. A knot in the abdomen can cause pain in distant areas of the body by pulling and creating tension.

Original Force. Gradually you will feel the nervous tension and headache go away.

5. Be aware of the big toes throughout the day. Pick up small objects, such as a pencil, with the toes. Rest, and shift the awareness between the toes and navel. This takes only a few minutes (Figure 16-6).

6. Using the knuckles, massage around the temporal bone at the side of the eyes. (Please see Figure 5-48.)

7. With the thumbs, massage the back of the head on both sides at the Wind Pond points (Gall Bladder 20) (Figure 16-7). When you massage upward, inhale; when you massage downward, exhale. Massaging the Wind Pond points helps relieve headaches, colds, flu, and eye pain. End by lightly tapping the whole head with the fingertips. This reduces the tendency to rely on medicine.

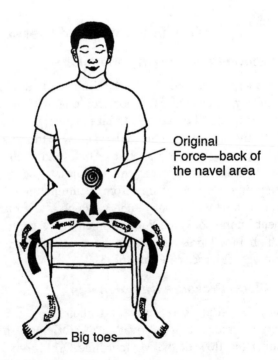

Original Force—back of the navel area

Big toes

Figure 16-6. Original Force and big toes

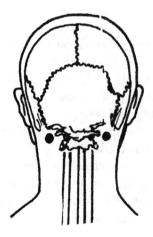

Figure 16-7. Wind Pond points

High and Low Blood Pressure

High Blood Pressure (Hypertension)

Anyone with high blood pressure should avoid holding the attention at the pituitary/pineal/Third Eye point for long. After holding the awareness there during the Microcosmic Orbit practice, be sure to take extra care to return the energy from the mid-eyebrow to the navel. If you have high blood pressure, keep the attention "below the belt." The navel, Ming Men, and soles of the feet are all appropriate places for your attention. These points keep the energy from accumulating in the head. They are also associated with kidney energy, which is associated with the Water element. In the body, the Water element helps control the Fire element, and high blood pressure would be considered excess Fire in Taoist physiology. (Please see Figure 5-33.)

Low Blood Pressure (Hypotension)

For low blood pressure, the points higher on the body are preferable centers for focus. After activating the Original Chi at the navel and initiating the flow of the Microcosmic Orbit, move your focus to the pituitary/pineal/Third Eye point during meditation. Spending more time focusing Chi at the mid-eyebrow can raise your energy and elevate your blood pressure. (Please see Figure 5-48.)

You can also spend some time focusing at the Chi Chung (T-11) point, especially if the low blood pressure is from adrenal exhaustion or undersecretion of the adrenal glands. Keep the concentration on this point and focus the awareness on the adrenal glands. Feel them filling with fresh Chi, becoming invigorated with new life-force. You may feel a surge of adrenaline as they activate. Smile to the adrenal glands and kidneys many times during the day to wake them up. (Please see Figure 5-33.)

Insomnia

Some of the causes of insomnia include worry, nervousness, overwork, not getting enough exercise, becoming overtired, eating too much late at night, and experiencing too many negative emotions at work and in one's family life. These make the energy too active at night, causing not only insomnia but nightmares. For a good night's sleep, the energy needs to be settled and calm.

During work that requires a lot of thinking and planning, much of the energy and blood gathers in the head, leaving less energy and blood in the hands, legs, and abdominal area. This can result in poor circulation. At night the brain remains overstimulated, and the person cannot sleep.

Our Shen, or spirit, goes deep within us at night; it is said to rest in the blood. If we are still agitated or hot when we go to bed, the spirit does not have a comfortable "bed" in which to rest, and we will sleep uneasily.

The Six Healing Sounds

To solve the problem, you need to address the negative emotions that cause overheating of the organs. The Six Healing Sounds are particularly helpful for this. You should always do the Six Healing Sounds before going to sleep to clear out any unresolved tensions and process any negative emotions that have come up during the day. Practice until you feel the organs cool, the emotions quieting down, and the positive virtuous energies of the organs emerging. Then you will be quiet, relaxed, and peaceful and can go to sleep. The Triple Warmer Sound is especially effective for insomnia.

Practice Forgiveness

Forgiving people is the best way to release negative emotions. Each night, be aware of any anger, resentment, disappointment, or hurt feelings you are still harboring. Envision the person who engendered your feelings during the day. Picture a pink light descending from heaven and surrounding this person. Feel yourself letting go of your hurt feelings and forgiving him or her. When we continue to harbor a grudge, it hurts us as much as or more than it hurts the other person.

Avoid Excitement at Night

Avoid watching exciting movies or reading exciting books before going to bed. Also avoid vigorous types of Chi Kung, martial arts, or other exercise shortly before bedtime. Very relaxing exercises such as stretching, Hatha Yoga, or Tai Chi are all right for most people, but some will find even these too stimulating.

Check Your Sleeping Position

The position in which you sleep is very important. Here are several good alternatives:

1. If you are used to sleeping on your back, place a small pillow under the knees and cross the feet. Cover the navel with the palms.

2. Using abdominal breathing, count your breaths. This gathers and condenses the force in the Tan Tien, so the Chi does not run up to the head. It also helps excess Chi already in the head to descend.

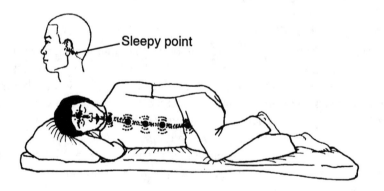

Figure 16-8. Sleeping position

3. If you usually lie on your side, start on the right side. Place the right thumb behind the right ear, where there are several acupuncture points to help insomnia. Place the other hand on the hip, and use abdominal breathing (Figure 16-8).

Shake Out the Body to Relieve Tension

In a standing position, shake from the knees, and feel a vibration up through the body. Shake all the excess Yang from the top down to the bottom and into the ground.

Stand and relax the knees. Be aware of the knees. Let the body begin to rock. Gradually shake from the knees up through the whole body. Rock and shake until the body relaxes and feels warm. Feel the fingers and toes fill with Chi; feel them swelling and pulsing. This circulates the Chi and blood flow throughout the body. Direct the excess heat to the feet (Figure 16-9).

If you can stand longer, concentrate on the navel area. Using abdominal breathing, breathe 36, 72, or 108 times. Feel yourself calming down and relaxing. Rest and collect the energy.

Figure 16-9. Rock and shake the whole body.

Autonomic Nervous System Out of Balance

Use standing meditation. You will need to stand for 10 or 20 minutes.

Stand with the legs slightly wider than shoulders' width apart, the toes slightly turned in. Raise the arms in front parallel with the feet, palms facing down. Spread the thumbs and fingers evenly. Feel Large Intestine 4 point open. The knees should be slightly bent, but don't strain to go too low in the beginning.

Start with very gentle deep breathing. Grasp the floor with the toes during the whole period of practice. Let the body rock back and forth slightly. Use skin breathing and bone breathing, concentrating the energy into the Original Force. Finish by gathering the Chi back to the navel.

Respiratory Disease, Asthma

The most important part of the healing practice is using either sitting or standing meditation to gather and condense Chi into the Original Force.

Spend 20 to 30 minutes focusing the mind on the Original Force until you feel Chi pressure starting to spread through the body.

Move the awareness to the C-7 point (Ta Chui.) (Please see Figure 5-36.) Spend 5 to 10 minutes concentrating on the C-7 point. Massage around the point. On both sides, about one-half inch out, there is a point called Stop Wheezing (Ding Chuan) to stop asthma. Massage this point every time you think of it.

It is important not to let the neck get cold or be exposed to wind. Wear a scarf, turtleneck sweater, or high-collared coat whenever the weather is cold or windy.

Recovery from Stroke or Partial Paralysis (Evil Wind Attack)

Paralysis is a common result of stroke. People who find it hard to sit up or walk often lose the courage to deal with their lives. To facilitate recovery, call the Healing Tao Center to obtain the name of a Chi Nei Tsang practitioner near you. Failing that, here is a program that may be suitable for certain persons. This practice is especially useful if you are forced to take long periods of bed rest.

1. If you are able to stand, you will obtain the fastest results, but you will also do very well sitting up. If you are unable to sit or stand, you will also benefit from this practice if you perform it lying down. If it is comfortable, put your legs over the side of the bed so your feet rest on the floor; this will enable you to gather strength and healing from earth energy. Find a comfortable position whether standing, sitting, or lying down. In the beginning, if you are sitting, you can rest against the back of the chair for support or put a pillow behind your back. You may also place a pillow on the floor to help raise the feet higher if that is more comfortable.

2. Start by Warming the Stove and activating the Original Force. Fix the mind there until the Chi pressure becomes so great that it starts to move. Let the Chi move or shake the whole body (Figure 16-10).

3. Move the awareness down to the soles of the feet. Hold it there, practicing condensing breathing 18 to 36 times. Inhale into the point, and on the exhalation hold the essence of the energy at that point even as you release the breath. Rest, and bring the awareness back up to the Original Force in the Lower Tan Tien. Practice condensing breathing 18 to 36 times there as well. Then bring the awareness back down to the soles again. Spend 10 to 20 minutes practicing in this way.

4. Raise the palms to chest height, facing each other. Feel Chi moving across from palm to palm, As the pulsing between the two palms increases, feel it moving in waves up the arms until the whole body begins

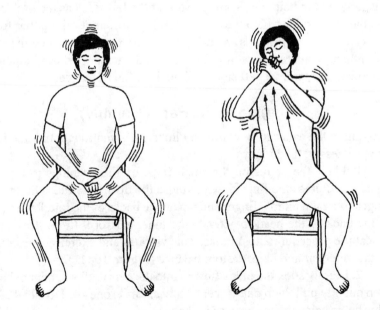

Figure 16-10. Let the Chi move and shake the whole body.

to rock back and forth. Feel that the palms have a repelling force pushing them away from each other and a drawing force attracting them back together. Feel the pulsing of the palms and the attracting and repelling force each time you breathe. Let the arms move in and out in this way 18 to 36 times. This helps open the six major channels in the fingers, hands, and arms. (Please see Figure 7-21.)

5. If you have shoulder, knee, or hip problems, you can gather the force in both palms and cover the problem place with the hands. Use the waist to move the hands in circles 2 to 3 inches above the place. Feel the place starting to pulse and vibrate.

6. If you feel the sick place has sick, cold energy, gradually grab the sick energy. If it is in the lower body, drag it down to the toes; if in the upper body, drag it down to the fingers. Repeat 3 to 6 times, or until you feel that place warming, pulsing, and vibrating.

7. Vent the sick energy. Bring the hands to the sides, fingers pointed down. Use the HEEEEE sound to vent the sick energy down to the ground. Finish by massaging the area. Then take off your socks and massage the soles of the feet. (Please see Figure 7-22.)

8. If you are unable to raise the foot on one side, you can massage the good foot to help the paralyzed side. If the left side has the problem, use the right side to help it to get better. If you cannot raise either foot, you can massage the hands and palms to benefit the foot on the same side as the hand you are massaging. In this way the upper part can help heal the lower part, and the left side can help heal the right side.

Ringing in the Ears (Tinnitus)

Ringing in the ears can be caused by imbalance, malfunction, infection, or weakness of the kidneys.

1. Place the palms on the small flaps by the openings to the ear canals, and press the flaps down to close the openings. Place the index fingers over the middle finger and tap on the backs of the middle fingers to the back of the head to activate the inner ear for 9 times. Rest, and repeat the procedure 2 to 4 times. This vibrates and exercises the bones of the inner ear and helps restore balance (Figure 16- 11).

2. Lightly stick the index fingers into the ears until you cannot hear, then quickly pull them out. Repeat 9 times; this is one set. Do 2 to 4 sets. This helps balance the pressure in the ears.

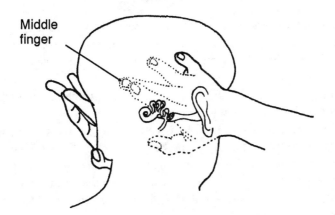

Middle
finger

Figure 16-11. Activate the inner ear.

3. Massage the muscles in the area around the kidneys with the palms, then gently tap the area with loosely clenched fists. This strengthens the kidneys.

4. Rest for a moment. Then breathe a blue mist from the atmosphere into the kidneys.

5. Ringing in the ears can be accompanied by lower-back pain. Once the back problem is attended to, the ringing in the ears may correct itself.

Dizziness, Motion Sickness, Disequilibrium

This problem can keep people from traveling by car, ship, and airplane.

1. Use the same practices for treating ringing in the ears to strengthen the kidneys and inner ears.

2. Practicing while standing is best. Place both hands at the sides, with the middle fingers touching the index fingers. Be aware of the Original Force until the Chi activates.

3. Move the awareness down to the space between the little toes and the fourth toes. Use the fingers to massage this area to focus the awareness and strengthen the concentration. Occasionally return the awareness to the Original Force and then move it back down to the feet again.

4. Exhale down to the navel area a few times, and gather energy there.

5. Massage the Wind Pond point (Gall Bladder 20) at the back of the ears, and repeat the ear exercises.

515

Eye Problems

To heal nearsightedness, eyes that are sensitive to the wind, blurry vision, or gradual decline of vision, you first need to increase the Chi level in the body. When the Chi in the body grows weak, the eyesight also declines.

Start by activating the Original Force and strengthening the whole body. Use the sitting or the standing practice.

1. Hold the hands out as if you were holding a basketball, with armpits open and palms facing each other. (Please see Figure 13-6.)

2. When you feel the Chi in between the palms like a magnetic power pulling the hands toward each other, slowly move the palms in and out. Feel the strong pulsing between the hands, and use the mind to form a Chi ball there.

3. Once you feel the electromagnetic field strongly, slowly raise the palms up near the eyes, 2 to 3 inches away. Close the eyes.

4. Project the Chi into the eyeballs for 10 seconds. Then count to 9 as you slowly pull the hands away, as if you were pulling strands of silk thread from a cocoon. Don't let the strand of Chi be broken. Do this 9 to 18 times.

5. Spiral the palms clockwise 9 times and counterclockwise 9 times. Feel the Chi move in the eyes.

6. Move the left palm to the back of the head, and with the right palm in front, project the Chi through the center of the eyes. Feel the left palm receiving the Chi. This strengthens the optic nerves. Do this 9 times.

7. Move both palms 2 to 3 inches in front of the eyes and hold them there. Project Chi into the eyes for 5 minutes.

8. Cover the eyes with both palms until you feel heat, expansion, or pain in the eyes.

9. Massage the bridge of the nose. Use the fingers to guide the Chi from the eyes down to the nose, neck, and navel.

10. Still standing, relax the entire body and mind, especially the eyes. Smile to the eyes until you feel the tension melt away. Slowly and gradually open the eyes; don't open them suddenly.

Baldness and Hair Loss

Abnormal hair loss is often caused by excessive mental activity, resulting in too much energy becoming trapped in the head. It can also be caused by wearing synthetic clothing that does not "breathe." In either case, the body has no way to release excess heat, and the heat rises and kills the hair roots.

1. Start by developing the Chi in the palms. Sit or stand with the palms facing each other.

2. Slowly raise the hands up to the head, palms still facing each other.

3. Lower the left hand to shoulder level, and turn the palm face up. Slightly bend the right hand at the wrist so the right palm faces the head. Lightly touch the head and raise the hands up six to ten inches above the head. Turn the head to look at the left palm.

4. Gradually shift the weight to the left leg or left side of the body and raise the left palm above the head. Bring the right palm down to shoulder level with the palm facing up. Look at the left palm. Breathe into the left palm and feel it draw in the Chi around you.

5. Project Chi out from the right palm onto the scalp and reverse. Do this 9 to 18 times.

NOTE: *The body is not turning; only the head turns. This increases Chi flow in the head so the Chi does not become jammed there. You will gradually see the hair start to grow back.*

6. When you are finished, do a few repetitions of the venting exercise to bring the excess heat from the head down to the feet.

7. Drawing sexual energy up to the crown is also important to promote strong hair growth. Please refer to Chapter 10 for details on sexual energy practices.

Neck Problems

Neck problems are often caused by sitting for long periods at a computer terminal or working too long with an improper neck position. This causes stiffness and pain in the neck or shoulder muscles and many related problems as well, such as insomnia, nervousness, and headaches.

Do the rocking and shaking exercise, concentrating on the knees. Starting at the knees, shake the whole body, especially the neck.

Do the Crane Neck exercise 9 times. When the neck pulls in, press the tongue up firmly to the palate and inhale. When extending the neck, exhale and relax the tongue. Then reverse the direction of the circle (this is then called the Turtle Neck exercise) and repeat 9 times. (Please see Appendix, Figures A-20 and A-21.)

Massage the C-7 point. This is a very effective way to strengthen the neck.

Premenstrual Syndrome (PMS)

PMS is often caused by blood and Chi stagnating and thus not flowing well. This stagnation is often rooted in an imbalance or weakness of the liver and spleen.

Start by shaking the whole body loose. This activates Chi and blood flow.

Rest. Use the right palm to cover the area below the navel and place the left palm over the right. Concentrate on the Original Force, and move the Chi down to the pelvic area. Feel the ovaries and cervix become warm. (Please see Figures 10-7 and 10-8.)

Gradually bend down, letting the body shake up and down, and very slowly reach to touch the big toes, allowing the knees to bend as much as necessary. Massage the big toes, especially the lower corners of the nails where the Liver and Spleen channels begin. Do this 6 to 9 times. This also strengthens the back and relieves menstrual cramps. (Please see Figures 5-70.)

The Egg Exercise and Vaginal Breathing are also very important in treating and preventing PMS.

Infertility in Women

There are many possible causes of female infertility; it is best to check with a Western physician and/or a traditional Chinese medical physician to diagnose the actual cause. It can be caused by a stagnation of cold in the ovaries and cervix. If so, the following exercise may be helpful.

Meditate on the Original Force and move the Chi down to the Ovarian Palace. Picture a red-hot Chi ball, fiery and expanding, and let the heat spread through the lower abdominal area below the navel. This warms the ovaries and cervix so the sperm can survive more easily. We have had many reports of success in conceiving a child from couples who were unable to do so prior to learning this practice.

Overeating, Diabetes, Digestive Problems

Be aware of the navel area. Bend down and rotate the upper body from the waist in a circle to the right, back, left and front. Don't rotate from the neck; this can make you feel dizzy. Repeat 36 times (Figure 16-12).

Figure 16-12. Rotate in a circle around the abdominal area.

Note: *Use the waist as an axle. Exhale when bending down, and inhale when rotating up. When rotating back, there is no need to bend back.*

This exercise helps correct digestive problems and may make the body more balanced so you will not feel the need to overeat. It can also strengthen the sexual organs and correct adult-onset diabetes.

Male Sexual Problems (Nocturnal Emissions, Impotence, Prostate Trouble)

1. Wearing loose trousers and loose-fitting underwear (or no underwear), sit on the edge of a chair, so your sexual organs can hang freely.

2. Inhale, and lightly draw Chi from the sexual center (above the pubic bone) up to the Door of Life. Touching the tongue to the palate, lightly pull up the energy from the perineum and anus to the Door of Life.

3. Hold the breath for a moment, then exhale and relax. Release the Chi down toward the perineum and anus, relax the tongue, and release

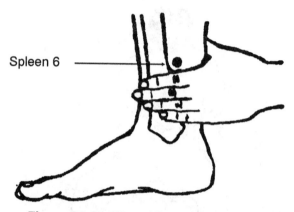

Spleen 6

Figure 16-13. Three Yin Crossing Point

tensions from the whole body. Feel the Chi spread to the sexual organs. (Please see Figure 2-9.) Do this 9 to 18 times.

4. When you are ready to conclude, gather the Chi at the navel, with the left palm covering the navel and the right hand on top. Rotate the palms around the lower abdomen 36 times clockwise and 24 times counterclockwise.

5. Massage the navel and Door of Life 18 to 36 times. Use the palms, not the fingers.

6. Massage the Three Yin Crossing point (Spleen 6), located three finger- widths up from the inside ankle. This is the junction of the Liver, Spleen, and Kidney channels, the three Yin channels of the legs. Massage with both thumbs here in a circular motion 36 times; this increases the kidneys' Yin energy and the Original Force, the major storage of sexual energy for men. Reverse directions and repeat 36 times (Figure 16-13).

Illness and Medication

Recovering from Illness or Injury

Most of this book is addressed to normal, healthy adults. If you are sick or have a chronic disease, you need to intensify your meditation schedule. Healing requires a great deal of energy, and meditation increases your energy.

I recommend meditating twice a day for an hour each time. Although we have all read testimonials about miracle cures, a disease that has taken a long time to develop usually takes awhile to go away. Often, people with serious chronic diseases begin to notice improvement in the second month of practice.

If you are very weak and debilitated, you may find it difficult to meditate for long periods at first. If so, don't tax your strength. Practice for shorter periods, rest, and resume when you are able. Instead of limiting your meditation to two hour-long sessions, you can practice for many short periods during the day. You will quickly and easily build up to meditating for longer periods.

If you are too weak or injured to meditate sitting up, you can do the practices lying down and still reap great benefits. Nonetheless, it is best if you can practice sitting up if you are able to do so comfortably and painlessly. You are less likely to fall asleep, and the sitting position strengthens the spinal column, muscles, bones, and nervous system. It also aligns the body directly with the Universal, Earth, and Higher Self energies, but with practice one can tap into these forces even while lying down. In fact, because many people are lying down in bed at the time of death, it is important, whether sick or well, to do at least some meditation practice lying down, in preparation for death. When death comes, we will be ready to meet it peacefully and gracefully, in a meditative frame of consciousness.

Medication

If you take regular medication for your illness or to control pain, do not stop after learning the Microcosmic Orbit meditation. As you start to meditate, you may find you need less medication. Consult your physician on the best way to reduce the dosage. Western medicine is often very powerful, and if the body is used to it, you may need to reduce the amount gradually rather than stopping suddenly. Occasionally, people find health problems are cured or controlled by meditation, and they are able to stop taking medicine eventually. Always use common sense and caution, and consult your health care provider when adjusting medication.

Healing the Emotions

Fear

Fear is produced in the kidneys. The area around the Door of Life, the kidney point, may feel cold when you are afraid. You should always try to keep this area warm. If you feel fear and are cold, collect the energy

521

at the Door of Life and circulate it in the Microcosmic Orbit. (Please see Figure 5-33.)

Collecting the energy means making a spiral the way you do at the navel at the end of your meditation. This technique enables you to respond to your emotions more quickly and gives you a way to defuse them. If you don't deal with an emotion when it arises, it may trigger other emotions or eventually manifest as a disease or physical disorder.

Anger

Anger is produced in the liver and is often triggered by fear. For example, if you are driving down the street and a car pulls out in front of you, you will probably feel frightened as you brake and steer to avoid hitting the car. But will you stay frightened? Chances are, you will roll down your window and yell something nasty at the other driver. If you can stay with your fear, spiraling and then circulating it, you can avoid involving the kidneys and liver. (Please see Figure 5-59.)

Anger energy radiates from the solar plexus. When you are angry, your solar plexus is often tense. Spiral the anger energy at the solar plexus, collecting it and circulating it in the Microcosmic Orbit until the anger is gone.

Sadness and Depression

Sadness and depression are created in the lungs, but they accumulate at the heart center. You may feel the heart center sinking, and you won't be able to raise it. Collect the sadness and depression at the heart center or at the Wing Point (Shen Dao, below T-5 on the spine directly behind the heart center), and move it through the Microcosmic Orbit. (Please see Figure 5-35.)

Sadness and depression are not as volatile as fear and anger. You can be sad and depressed without even realizing it, and you may resist doing anything about it. Also, the process of clearing out sadness can be slow. You may feel better on the inhalation and then sad on the exhalation. Don't be discouraged. Keep collecting and circulating, and you will start to feel yourself lighten up. It may take 30 minutes to an hour before you feel better, but you will learn a new technique that is faster than any other therapy, and safer than medication.

Collect the energy by using the mind to move it in circles, or use the hands if it helps ground you. Eventually you will be able to direct the collection process with the mind.

Worry

Worry is generated in the spleen and weakens the spleen. Worry is often brought on by thinking or studying too much, or by becoming mentally inflexible. It can also be aggravated by working while eating or eating on the run, and by a hectic life-style generally.

Collect the worry energy by spiraling at the navel and drawing the worry energy out of the spleen. Then circulate it in the Microcosmic Orbit until you no longer feel worried.

You can always use the Six Healing Sounds to focus on the appropriate organ and draw out the negative energy. The colors of the emotions and the organs (described in Chapter 14) also provide a convenient and helpful "handle" for grasping and moving the energy. If you are sensitive to the inner color frequencies, you can use these as well.

SELF-HEALING

In the practice of the Tao, self-healing involves training the mind/eye/heart power to take in more Chi and transform it to heal ourselves. This does not mean using the mind or imagination alone. We train the body and mind to use our own Chi, nature's Chi, the universe's Chi, and the earth's forces to provide healing energy. Although these energies can be drawn in and circulated through the Microcosmic Orbit, they can also be drawn in through the bone marrow.

Marrow Washing is a good way to get rid of sick energy daily. It is one of the best ways to strengthen immunity, as it increases the white blood cell count. The white blood cells are responsible for seeking out and destroying cancer cells and foreign substances in the body such as bacteria and viruses. If you have pain or sickness, you can do this 2 or 3 times a day.

Heavenly Marrow Washing

1. Turn the eyes inward and look up to the crown. Be aware of the crown and feel a sensation of numbness there.

2. Be aware of the mouth. Move the tongue around to generate saliva. Once you have gathered a copious amount, swallow the saliva, pulling upward by lightly tightening the throat. Feel the energy push up to the crown. Do this 3 to 6 times.

3. Rest, and feel the crown pulsing and breathing. Feel a sensation of numbness there.

4. Be aware of the North Star and the Big Dipper. Feel the violet and red light descend to the crown and penetrate slowly into the skull and marrow, and through the neck, cervical vertebrae, clavicle and sternum, ribs, thoracic vertebrae, lumbar vertebrae, bones of the pelvis, sacrum, coccyx, and bones of the legs and feet. Feel that this heavenly light is purifying and washing away any disease or illness, flushing all bacteria or viruses out of the body. Let it wash away any stresses, negative attitudes and emotions, or nervous tensions you are holding onto. Feel it drive out any destructive or negative entities or spirits that may be feeding on you.

5. Rest, feeling completely purified. Now that the light has cleared away all negativity, let it fill you with its healing power.

Earth Marrow Washing

1. Be aware of the sexual organs and anus. Contract them, and gradually be aware of a feeling of arousal, numbness, soreness, or an urge to urinate.

2. Gather the energy into a dot around the sexual center.

3. Be aware of a connection, like a pipe, between the perineum and the soles of the feet. Extend it down into the earth.

4. Gradually feel a cool blue or whitish energy rising from the ground like a pure cleansing steam or mist. Feel it ascending through the soles of the feet and marrow of the leg bones.

5. Feel this cool energy travel up through the hips, coccyx, sacrum, lumbars, thoracics, rib cage, sternum, cervicals, and skull. With your inner eye, watch the bone and marrow light up and glow.

6. Feel this purifying the whole body, releasing and cleansing any tensions, pain, negativity, or illness (Please see Appendix Chapter, Figure A-16).

Cosmic Marrow Washing

Be aware of the mid-eyebrow point. Spiral, expand, and contract at this center until you feel numbness or see a flash of golden light. Spread the sensation and light through the skull, down the neck and the chest to the spine and legs. With your mind's eye, see the bone structure and marrow glow with golden light.

Holding the Breath, Spiraling, Swallowing Saliva

This practice can be used to bring more Chi to any part of the body. The example here focuses on liver problems or strengthening the liver.

1. Be aware of the liver and the mouth. Move the tongue around to activate the saliva. Suck the mouth in and out to mix the saliva with the golden light force that you breathe in from the Higher Self (Cosmic) energy in front of you.

2. Inhale to the lower right ribs. Feel them expand around the liver.

3. Hold the breath there. Hold the breath only as long as you feel comfortable.

4. Using mind/eye power, spiral in the liver area. Start expanding counterclockwise and then spiral in clockwise.

5. When you feel out of breath, swallow the saliva toward the liver and breathe out slowly.

6. Close the eyes and be aware of the liver glowing with bright green light. Feel kindness come forth.

7. You can do this 3 to 6 times. Do the same with any other organ or part of the body you wish to strengthen or heal.

Grabbing the Sick Energy

1. Smile and relax the body, focusing especially on any area of sickness, pain, or injury.

2. Put the center of either or both palms 2 to 3 inches above the sick area.

3. Be aware of the sick area; use the mind and palms to spiral clockwise 49 to 108 times around it.

4. Rest, and slowly move the palms up and down, left and right, around the sick or painful area, until you feel you can grab something. Once you feel you have a good hold, drag it with the hands down to the feet and out the toes, if it is in the lower part of the body. If it is in the upper part, drag it down to the hands and out the fingers. Do the grabbing 3 to 7 times.

Mind/Eye/Hands Guide Chi
to the Places That Need Healing

After you finish the Microcosmic Orbit meditation and your hands feel warm and full of Chi, you can use this Chi to heal any place you want. You can do this sitting, standing, or lying down.

Preparations

1. Hold the palms facing each other near the navel.

2. Use mind/eye power to direct Chi to the palms. Feel the warm, expanding, numb sensation and feel the heat from each palm radiating to the other palm. Use mind power to draw more Chi from the atmosphere into the palms.

3. Gradually raise the palms 2 to 4 inches in front of the eyes; with practice you can find your own "Chi feeling" distance. Move the palms closer and farther away. Don't move so far that you don't feel the Chi. Do this 10 to 20 times. If you have little time, you can reduce the repetitions to 5 to 10 times.

Palms Project Chi to the Eyes

1. Move both palms together toward the right. Follow with the eyes, but don't move the head. When you have moved the eyes to their limit, stop for a while and then move the palms and eyes back to the front. Repeat 10 to 20 times. Move slowly so you can feel the Chi.

2. Do the same on the left side, 10 to 20 times.

3. Repeat the exercise, moving both hands up and down 10 to 20 times. Project the Chi feeling to the eyes, and have the eyes follow the hand movements.

4. Start circling the eyes to the right, following the movement of the palms. Do this 10 to 20 times. Then reverse direction, circling the eyes to the left following the palms, 10 to 20 times.

Eye Power Training

Choose a distant object. Look at the object and close the eyes, until you can see the object as though it were a projected picture. Open the eyes wide and look at the object for a while and close the eyes. When you close the eyes, draw the eyes' power back to the eyes. Do this 10 to 20 times.

Use the hands to massage the eyes and around the eyes.

Project Chi to the Face and Senses

Move the palms above the head. Be aware of the crown and palms. Feel the Chi from the palms activate the Chi in the crown and spread it throughout the body.

Move the palms down to the face. Move the right palm slowly down the right side of the face and the left palm down the left side. Then move both palms back up. Feel the face expand with Chi and blood flow.

Project Chi to the Throat

Move the palms down to the throat. Project Chi to the throat center and thyroid and parathyroid glands, and feel the throat expand. Feel the throat breathing, or be aware of the sound of breathing in the throat.

Project Chi into the glands. Feel it activate the glands; enjoy the warm, expanding feeling in the throat.

Project Chi to the Chest

Be aware of the lungs. Visualize the lungs. Move the palms down the chest, radiating Chi into the lungs. Project the Chi from the palms into the lungs, feeling them expand and contract. Move the chest left and right to massage the lungs.

Project Chi to the Heart

Focus both palms on the heart area. Hold them there and project Chi to the heart. Feel the heart moving and expanding together with the rib cage. If you feel too much Chi in the heart, do the Heart Sound 3 times to eliminate the excess.

Project Chi to the Liver, Pancreas, Stomach, Spleen

1. Move both palms to the right side near the edge of the rib cage and project Chi to the liver. Picture the liver, and feel the liver moving. You can move the muscles around the liver to lightly massage it. Feel the warm and pleasant sensations there, and feel the Chi flow around and through it.

2. Move the palms to the solar plexus center below the sternum. Project Chi and feel the stomach and pancreas moving or expanding.

3. Move the palms to the left side on the edge of the left rib cage. Project the Chi until you feel Chi and movement in the spleen.

Project to the Kidneys and Adrenal Glands

Move the palms to just slightly above the navel on either side. Project Chi into the kidneys, making the muscles move left and right like a wave to massage the kidneys and adrenal glands. Twist and spiral the lumbar region left and right.

CAUTION: IN THIS CHAPTER AND IN OTHER PARTS OF THIS BOOK WE PRESENT MANY TRADITIONAL TAOIST METHODS OF SELF-HEALING. THIS BOOK IS NOT IN ANY WAY IN-TENDED TO TAKE THE PLACE OF REGULAR CARE AND CHECKUPS BY A QUALIFIED PHYSICIAN, NOR DO WE MAKE ANY WARRANTY OF THE EFFECTIVENESS OF THESE METHODS.

HEALING IS ALWAYS AN INDIVIDUAL MATTER AND SHOULD TAKE PLACE UNDER THE GUIDANCE AND ADVICE OF A QUALIFIED HEALTH- CARE PROVIDER.

Appendix

SPINAL CORD BREATHING
Opening the Channels of the
Spinal Cord

The spinal cord is a major pathway for energies from the earth and sexual center to move up to the higher centers of the body. Taoists regard each junction between the vertebrae as storage places for Chi. They also see the spinal cord contains the largest concentration of marrow in the body (Figure A-1). The bones are regarded as Yang; the nerves are regarded as Yin.

When we exercise and shake the spinal cord loose, mentally stimulating the nerves, we generate an electrical current (Figure A-2) that flows more intensely during practice. When Chi travels up the spinal cord, the health of the spine and brain improves greatly as the absorbed energies are refined into life-force. Keeping the spine relaxed and properly aligned with the shoulders and hips is important to prevent or release energetic obstructions. The more relaxed the spinal cord is, the more easily energy will flow.

The Spinal Cord's Connection to
Vital Parts of the Body

The nerves of the coccyx and sacrum are connected to the lower limbs, kidneys, bladder, sexual organs, external genitalia, rectum, and large intestine (partially).

The lumbars (L-1 to L-5) in the lower back are also connected to these areas.

The nerves of the thoracic vertebrae in the middle back (T-5 to T-12) are connected to the stomach, liver, gall bladder, pancreas, spleen, adrenals, small intestine, and abdominal blood vessels.

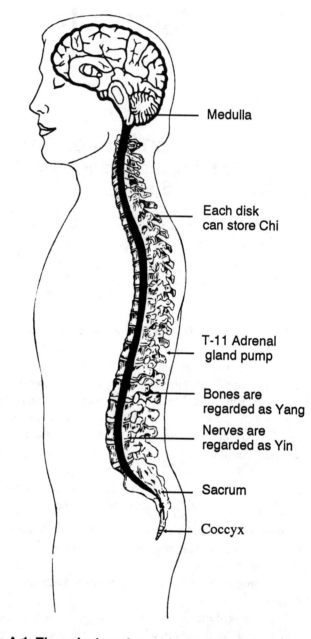

Figure A-1. The spinal cord contains the largest concentration of marrow in the body.

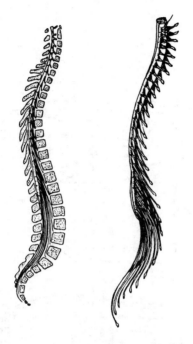

Figure A-2. The nervous system runs through the spinal cord.

The nerves of the upper thoracic vertebrae (T-1 to T-4) are connected to the heart, larynx, trachea, bronchi, and lungs.

The nerves of the cervical vertebrae (C-1 to C-7) are connected to the organs, glands, and upper limbs.

Meditative practice

Look carefully at a good anatomy book, then close your eyes and try to see these connections as well as feel them (Figure A-3). Smile down along the spine, covering these connections with smiling energy.

Practice: Spinal Cord Breathing Exercise

The Spinal Cord Breathing exercise helps relax the spine while activating the sacral and cranial pumps and adrenal and thymus glands.

Spinal Cord Breathing also helps relax the muscles of the back so you can remain comfortable while sitting for long periods of time. It can be practiced sitting or standing (Figure A-4). Find a suitable chair and relax, keeping the spine comfortably straight without allowing it to touch the back of the chair.

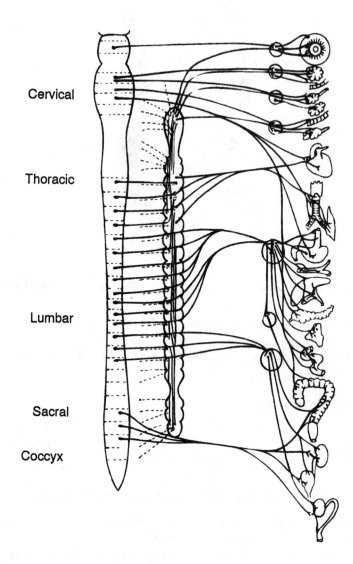

Cervical

Thoracic

Lumbar

Sacral

Coccyx

Figure A-3. The spinal cord is connected to vital parts of the body.

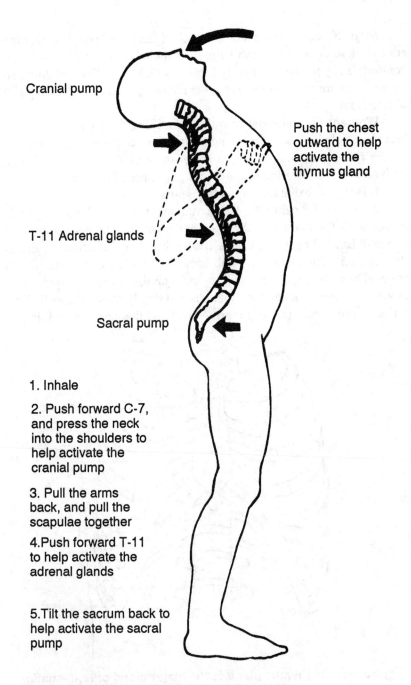

Cranial pump

Push the chest
outward to help
activate the
thymus gland

T-11 Adrenal glands

Sacral pump

1. Inhale

2. Push forward C-7,
and press the neck
into the shoulders to
help activate the
cranial pump

3. Pull the arms
back, and pull the
scapulae together

4. Push forward T-11
to help activate the
adrenal glands

5. Tilt the sacrum back to
help activate the sacral
pump

Figure A-4. Spinal Cord Breathing

Men: If you sit, use a straight-backed chair, and sit on or near the edge of it so the testicles can hang over the edge freely. (If this is not comfortable, you can sit slightly farther back.) Wear loose clothing so the testicles are unrestricted and the male energy can flow without any obstructions.

Women: Sit comfortably without touching the back of the chair. Wear loose clothing so there are no obstructions of the perineum and the energy flowing through it. If you prefer to sit on the floor, use a thick cushion so the circulation of the legs is not impeded too much.

1. Begin by exhaling and feeling yourself relax.

2. Inhale, and gently tilt the sacrum and the head all the way back as you arch the middle of the back and push the abdomen and chest outward. Expanding the rib cage activates the adrenal and thymus glands (Figure A-5). Simultaneously pull back the shoulders and fists (which are held near the shoulders), pulling the scapulae together (Figure A-6) as you press the neck into the shoulders and lightly clench the teeth. This activates the cranial pump (Figure A-7). Hold this position and tighten

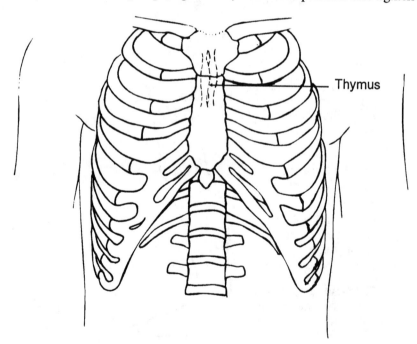

— Thymus

Figure A-5. The thymus gland is the major gland of rejuvenation and of the immune system.

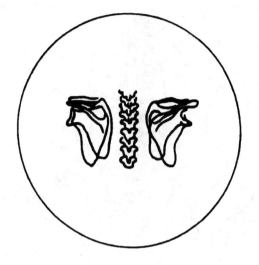

Figure A-6. By expanding and contracting the rib cage and the scapulae, we can help activate the thymus gland.

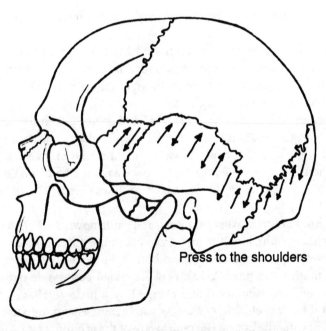

Press to the shoulders

Figure A-7. The cranial pump becomes activated when you press the neck to the shoulders and lightly clench the teeth.

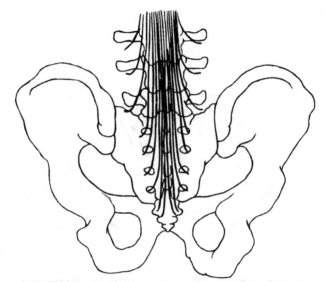

Figure A-8. Tilting the sacrum in and out will help activate the sacral pump and exercise the nerves.

the muscles. Tilting the sacrum activates the sacral pump and exercises the nerves (Figure A-8).

3. Exhale, and push the sacrum and head forward, rounding the back. As you do this, bring the elbows forward, close the forearms and fists into the chest, and bring the chin down to the sternum (Figure A-9). Don't tighten any muscles. Just relax.

4. Repeat. Inhale, tilt back the head and sacrum, arch the back as you push out the abdomen, and retract the shoulders and fists. Then exhale as you round the spine forward, tuck the chin in, and bring the arms to the front. Continue arching the back as you inhale and bending forward as you exhale. Do this 9, 18, or 36 times (Figures A-10, A-11, and A-12).

5. Spinal marrow washing. Rest, and smile down the length of the whole spine. Breathe in white mist from the mid-eyebrow, golden light from heaven through the crown, and blue light from the soles to help wash the marrow (Figures A-13). Feel the spinal cord tingle out to the nerves as they are stimulated and charged by a higher voltage of Chi (Figure A-14). Feel electricity flow as you breathe energy into the area. Feel the Chi enter the bones. Become aware of the sacrum, cranial pump, and adrenal and thymus glands. Feel them become loose and warm as they begin to vibrate.

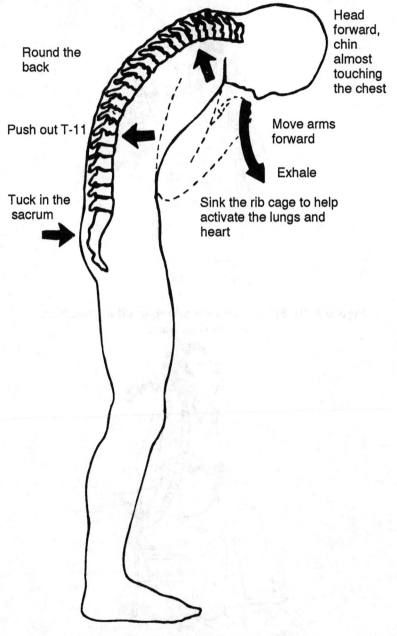

Round the back

Push out T-11

Tuck in the sacrum

Head forward, chin almost touching the chest

Move arms forward

Exhale

Sink the rib cage to help activate the lungs and heart

Figure A-9. Spinal Cord Breathing

Figure A-10. Spinal Cord Breathing in sitting position, bending forward

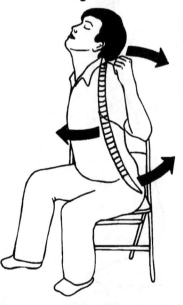

Figure A-11. Spinal Cord Breathing in sitting position, bending backward

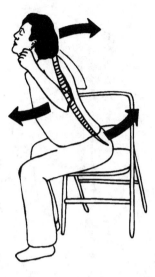

Figure A-12. Spinal Cord Breathing from a sitting position

Golden light descends from the heavens through the crown to help wash the marrow

Breathe in a golden mist to strengthen the bone marrow

Breathe in a white mist to strengthen the bones

Smile down the entire length of the spine

Blue light ascends from the earth to wash the marrow and strengthen the joints

Figure A-13. Bone Marrow Washing

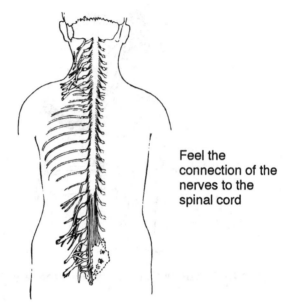

Feel the connection of the nerves to the spinal cord

**Figure A-14. Nerves are conductors of Chi. Visualizing
their connection to the vertebrae will increase the flow of the Chi.**

SPINAL CORD ROCKING

Rocking movements are very free and flexible. Each person is different, so once you learn the pattern of each exercise, just let the body express it naturally and enjoy the freedom of movement. The explanations may sound complicated, but the motions are really very easy. The more you let go of tensions, the more you benefit.

NOTE: *Pay attention during each resting period. Feel the Earth Force enter the soles of the feet and travel up through the legs, bones, hips, sacrum, spine, rib cage, and brain. Feel this force washing the marrow as you absorb it into the bones. Round bones produce red blood cells, which carry oxygen and nutrients to the cells. Flat bones, such as the ribs, skull, and scapulae, produce white blood cells, which serve as the body's main defense system against disease.*

During each resting period, practice Heavenly Force Marrow Washing (or Fire Force Marrow Washing) by drawing Chi into the marrow of the bones (Figures A-15 and A-16): Become aware of the crown and feel numbness or heaviness spreading down into the brain, skull, neck, collar bone, sternum, and rib cage. Feel the nerves penetrate the bones as you generate more Chi.

Silkworm Rocking

Rock the spine like a silkworm climbing a tree. Use soft, gentle, slow movements of the body. The spinal cord should move like a little wave.

1. Start by smiling to the spinal cord. Try to feel the spine. Then close the eyes and visualize the spine (Figure A-17).

2. Rock from the base of the spine gradually up to the head. Rock from the coccyx up to the sacrum, fifth lumbar vertebra, twelfth thoracic vertebra, cervical vertebrae, and up to the skull. Move as if you were creating a wave with the spine, like a silkworm (Figure A-18).

3. Rock back down gradually from the head to the coccyx (Figure A-19).

Men should practice 3, 6, or 9 times; women should practice 2, 4, or 6 times. Rest, and smile to the spine. Feel the spine absorb Chi into its marrow and radiate it up to the brain. Feel the spine become warm and relaxed.

Crane-Neck Rocking

This movement emulates a larger wave in the spine than Silkworm Rocking (Figures A-20 and A-21). (It is an extended version of the Silkworm exercise.) Create a wavelike motion, loosely bending the middle and lower spine. While rocking, pay attention to the Door of Life and the L-2 and L-3 lumbars. Feel the wave move from the lumbars up to the neck (Figures A-22 and A-23).

1. Start by arching lumbars L-2 and L-3 to the front as you stretch the neck to the back.

2. Stretch the neck like a crane. Stretch the chin out, curve it in, and touch it to the throat. At the same time, push back the lumbar area, creating a wavelike movement.

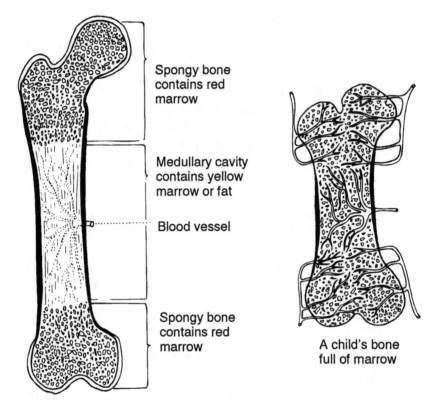

Spongy bone
contains red
marrow

Medullary cavity
contains yellow
marrow or fat

Blood vessel

Spongy bone
contains red
marrow

An adult's bone

A child's bone
full of marrow

Figure A-15. The bones of a child are made exclusively of red marrow with abundant blood vessels, while adult bones have red marrow at the extremities and a central area containing fat (yellow marrow).

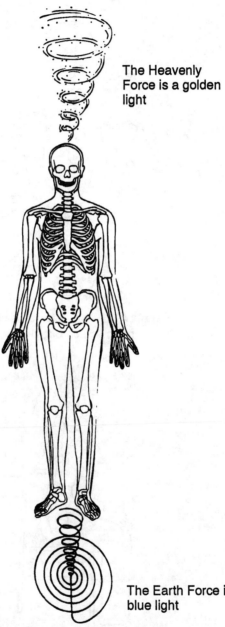

The Heavenly Force is a golden light

The Earth Force is a blue light

Figure A-16. Draw the Heaven and Earth Forces through the bone structure to help wash the bones.

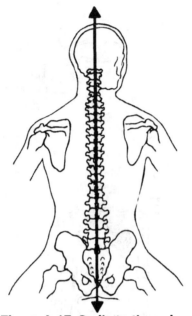

**Figure A-17. Smile to the spine
from top to bottom.**

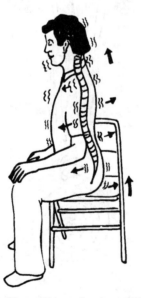

**Figure A-18. Move the spinal cord like a wave
from the base up to the head.**

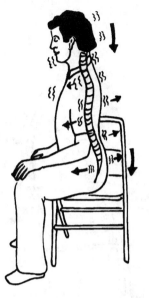

Figure A-19. Reverse from the head down to the sacrum.

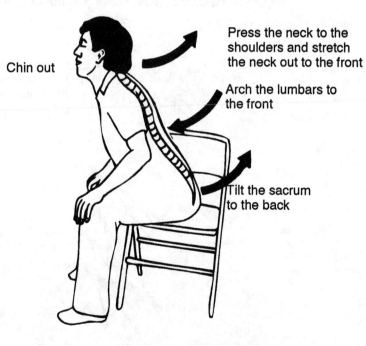

Chin out

Press the neck to the shoulders and stretch the neck out to the front

Arch the lumbars to the front

Tilt the sacrum to the back

Figure A-20. Crane Neck, curving spine out

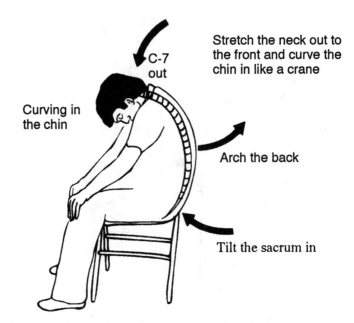

Stretch the neck out to the front and curve the chin in like a crane

C-7 out

Curving in the chin

Arch the back

Tilt the sacrum in

Figure A-21. Crane Neck, curving spine in

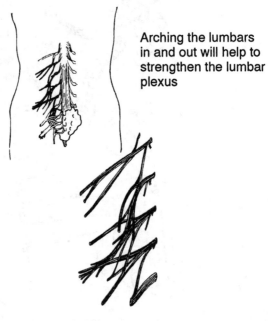

Arching the lumbars in and out will help to strengthen the lumbar plexus

Figure A-22. Lumbar plexus

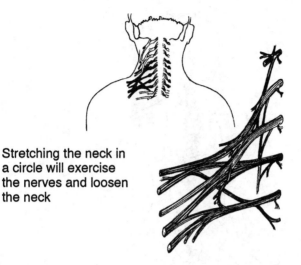

Stretching the neck in
a circle will exercise
the nerves and loosen
the neck

Figure A-23. Brachial plexus

3. Rest, and smile down the length of the spine. Feel the spine and the brain breathing in Chi from the earth and the universe. Feel the spine become warm and relaxed.

4. Do this exercise from 18 to 36 times.

Rocking Left and Right

1. Start rocking the body from left to right, gradually expanding the motion from the base of the spine (coccyx) up through the sacrum, lumbars, thoracic vertebrae, cervical vertebrae, and up to the head. Start by rocking from each section individually, then move up to the next section (Figures A-24 and A-25).

2. From the top of the head, rock left and right down through each section, one by one, until you reach the coccyx. Rest, and smile down the length of the spine. Feel it become warm and loose. Feel the spine absorb Chi into the marrow and brain to increase the life-force in the bones.

3. Do this exercise from 18 to 36 times.

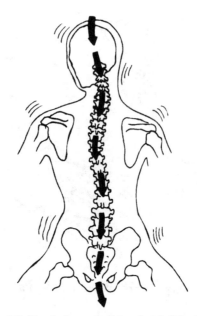

**Figure A-24. Rock from left to right. Start rocking
each vertebra up to the head.**

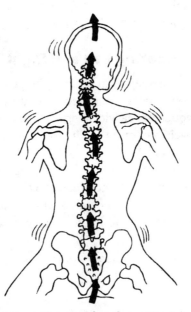

**Figure A-25. Reverse the rocking from the head back down
to the base.**

Circular Rocking (Twist-Rocking)

Follow the above procedures.

Starting from the coccyx, use soft, slow, circular movements to rock the body from left to right. To get a feeling for this exercise, start by moving one shoulder forward and the other backward, alternating these movements as you move the upper body. Begin Circular Rocking by gradually circling upward through each section, one by one, until you reach the head. Then rock back down to the coccyx. Do this exercise 18 to 36 times (Figures A-26 through A- 29).

Combined Movement Rocking

Combine all the rocking forms into a continuous movement. You may emphasize or interchange particular motions. Each movement should also contain all the other movements to some degree. Rock left and right, front and back, and practice Crane Neck and Circular Rocking at the same time. Let the body decide which motions it wants to emphasize. Each person will have a distinct and original pattern.

Rocking the Organs and Glands

The spinal cord has nerves branching out to all the organs, glands, and bones (Figure A-30). When you smile down to the organs, try to feel this connection.

1. Start with Combined Movement Rocking from the coccyx and sacrum. Be aware of the sexual organs, bladder, large intestine, and lower limbs. Smile to the sexual organs and large intestine as you rock. Picture the nerves that extend from the coccyx and sacrum to these organs. You can also slightly contract the muscles around the anus, perineum, and lower abdomen.

2. Continue the rocking movement up to the lower lumbar region (L-5 to L-1). Be aware of the small intestine, kidneys, bladder, and sexual organs. Look at these organs in your anatomy book, close your eyes, and start to smile to them. Feel their connection to the spine. Continue rocking and gently contract the abdominal muscles to massage the organs, squeeze out any toxins, and create space for more life-force.

3. When you feel warm and comfortable, extend the movement up to the large intestine. Keep contracting the abdominal muscles gently.

4. Continue rocking and be aware of the kidneys as you extend the movements up to them. Feel them connect to the spine and picture them

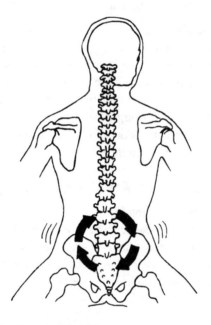

Figure A-26. Circular Rocking. Circle at the lower spine.

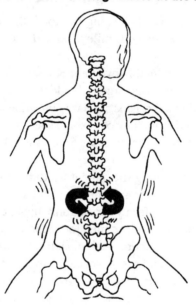

Figure A-27. Circular Rocking of the lumbar area

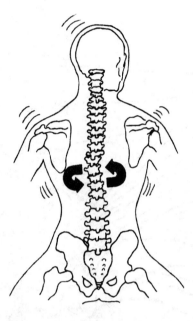

Figure A-28. Circular Rocking at the T-11 area

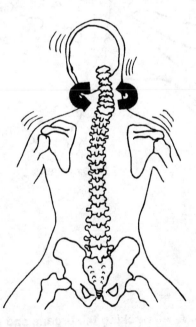

Figure A-29. Circular Rocking at C-7 and the neck

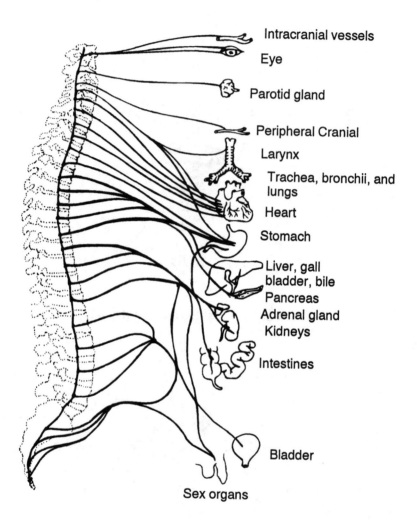

Figure A-30. Rocking the organs and glands

branching out from the spine. Slightly pull the abdomen in toward the kidneys.

5. Continue to extend the movement up to the middle back (T-12 to T-5). Be aware of the liver, gall bladder, spleen, pancreas, stomach, small intestine, and abdominal blood vessels. Feel their connection to the spine. Try to see and feel the organs as you rock, circle, twist, and squeeze them. Focus on each organ individually, then work on all of them together.

6. Extend the movements to the thoracic vertebrae (T-4 to T-1). Be aware of the lungs, heart, and thymus gland. Feel their connection to the spine. Twist, rock, and squeeze them separately, then together in one continuous movement.

7. Extend the rocking movements up to the cervical vertebrae (C-7 to C-1). Feel the neck loosen as Chi flows to the hands. Here the spine connects to the thyroid and parathyroid glands and the throat. Concentrate on this connection. Always smile to these areas as you extend the rocking movements into them.

8. Continue rocking up to the head, where many glands reside in the brain. Smile into these glands as you move through the region (Figure A-31). It is important to train your inner senses to see and feel the organs and glands and their connections to the spine through the nervous system.

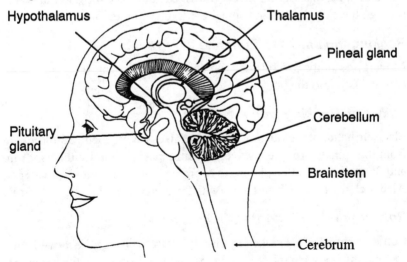

Figure A-31. Smile into the brain and the glands

9. Reverse directions by rocking downward until you reach the coccyx. You can do this 3 to 6 times.

10. Combine all the rocking movements into one continuous motion, traveling up and down the spine.

11. Rest, and smile down the length of the spine. Feel it become warm and relaxed. Feel the spine absorb Chi into the brain and marrow to increase the life-force in the bones. Men, practice 3, 6, or 9 times; women, practice 2, 4, or 6 times.

Advanced Practices (Optional)

In the beginning, some people do not feel much happening inside as they learn these exercises, but with continued practice, they eventually develop an internal awareness of the organs and nervous system.

External and Internal Rocking

This is an extension of the combination rocking exercise. Feel internal comfort and warmth surrounding the organs and glands and expanding to every cell in the body. Feel this warmth extend to the limbs, fingers, and toes, then radiate through the skin as you harmonize with the outer universe. Feel this warmth being drawn back in from the outer universe through the skin, limbs, and spinal cord, returning to the organs.

Rocking the Limbs to Enhance the Process

Moving the limbs as you rock the spine will help you feel and absorb external Chi into the body.

Silkworm Rocking with the Limbs

Place the hands at the sides and keep the knees slightly bent. Start rocking from the spinal cord like a wave, and simultaneously raise the hands up and down in a wavelike pattern to coordinate with the spinal movement. Also rock the feet back and forth with the spinal cord, hands, and knees.

Rocking Left and Right with the Limbs

Continue from the previous exercise, but start to change the movements, rocking the body from left to right. Simultaneously move the hands left and right, coordinating with the movements of the spinal cord. It is also important to rock the feet back and forth as you sway the body left and right. Feel the weight of the body shift from the heels to the balls of the feet as you alternate their positions against the left-and-right swaying of the body. This will help activate the energy of the earth, drawing it up the spine.

Rest, and smile down the length of the spine and limbs. Feel them become warm and relaxed. Feel the spine and limbs absorb Chi into the brain and bone marrow to increase the life-force in the bones.

Circular Rocking with the Limbs

Continue from the previous exercise, but start to change the movements by circling as you rock the spine. Circle as you rock from left to right, and simultaneously move the hands in front of the body, swaying them right and left. Also let the feet twist back and forth together with the movements of the spinal cord, hands, and knees. Some people may become dizzy. When this occurs, just change directions for a while, or stand still until the dizziness stops. Don't practice for too long if you don't feel well.

Combining the Motions While Absorbing the Cosmic Force

This exercise includes moving the limbs and internally massaging the organs and glands.

Practice using the combined rocking movements to relax the body as you smile inward to the organs and glands. Smile to the glands in the brain and down the face to the neck, then down to the parathyroid, thyroid, thymus, adrenal glands, to the heart, lungs, liver, pancreas, spleen, stomach, small and large intestines, and sexual organs (Figure A-32). Extend the limbs outward, relax the mid-eyebrow and perineum, and slightly contract the sexual organs and anus. Feel the cosmic energy being absorbed into the skin, spine, mid- eyebrow, perineum, and soles of the feet.

Continue the absorption process as you alternate between rocking the body and relaxing it. This harmonizes the inner and outer energies. Think of the alternating states of activity and rest as conditions of Yin and Yang. Rest, and smile down the length of the spine and limbs. Feel them become warm and loose. Feel the spine and limbs absorb Chi into the brain and bone marrow to increase the life-force in the bones. Practice 18 to 36 times.

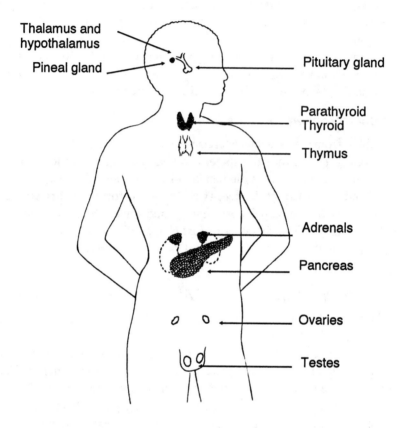

Figure A-32. Rock and smile inward to the glands

Finish from a seated position. Put the palms together and touch the edges of the thumbs against the heart center, which is located one inch up from the base of the sternum. This activates the heart's energy. Hold this position and practice the Inner Smile (Figure A-33).

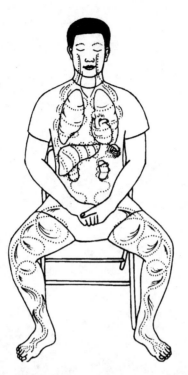

Figure A-33. Rock and smile inward to the organs.Finish in a sitting position and practice the Inner Smile.

BIBLIOGRAPHY

Becker, Robert. *The Body Electric.* New York: William Morrow, 1985.

Beinfield, Harriet, and Korngold, Efrem. *Between Heaven and Earth.* New York: Ballantine Books, 1991.

Bohm, David. *The Implicate Order.* London: Routledge & Kegan Paul, 1981.

Brennan, Barbara Ann. *Hands of Light.* New York: Bantam Books, 1987.

Chang, Jolan. *The Tao of Love and Sex.* New York: E.P. Dutton, 1977.

Chang, Jolan. *The Tao of the Loving Couple.* New York: E.P. Dutton, 1983.

Chia, Mantak. *Awaken Healing Energy Through the Tao.* New York: Aurora Press, 1983.

Chia, Mantak, and Michael Winn. *Taoist Secrets of Love: Cultivating Male Sexual Energy.* Santa Fe, NM: Aurora Press, 1984.

Chia, Mantak. *Chi Self Massage: The Taoist Way of Rejuvenation.* Huntington, NY: Healing Tao Books, 1985.

Chia, Mantak. *Taoist Ways to Transform Stress into Vitality.* Huntington, NY: Healing Tao Books, 1985.

Chia, Mantak and Maneewan. *Healing Love Through the Tao: Cultivating Female Sexual Energy.* Huntington, NY: Healing Tao Books, 1986.

Chia, Mantak and Maneewan. *Iron Shirt Chi Kung I.* Huntington, NY: Healing Tao Books, 1986.

Chia, Mantak and Maneewan. *Bone Marrow Nei Kung.* Huntington, NY: Healing Tao Books, 1989.

Chia, Mantak and Maneewan. *Fusion of the Five Elements I.* Huntington, NY: Healing Tao Books, 1989.

Chia, Mantak and Maneewan. *Chi Nei Tsang: Internal Organs Chi Massage.* Huntington, NY: Healing Tao Books, 1990.

Cleary, Thomas, trans. *The Inner Teachings of Taoism*, by Chang Po-Tuan. Boston: Shambhala, 1986.

Cleary, Thomas, trans. *The Taoist I Ching.* Boston: Shambhala, 1986.

Cleary, Thomas, ed. and trans. *The Book of Balance and Harmony.* San Francisco: North Point Press, 1989.

Cleary, Thomas, ed. and trans. *Immortal Sisters.* Boston: Shambhala, 1989.

Cleary, Thomas, trans. *The Secret of the Golden Flower*. San Francisco: HarperCollins, 1991.

Cleary, Thomas, ed. and trans. *Vitality, Energy, Spirit: A Taoist Sourcebook*. Boston: Shambhala, 1991.

Eisenberg, David. *Encounters with Qi*. New York: Viking Penguin, 1987.

Fung, Yu-lan. *The Spirit of Chinese Philosophy*. London: Kegan Paul, Trench, Trubner & Co., 1947.

Ho, Kwok Man, and O'Brien, Joanne, eds. and trans. *The Eight Immortals of Taoism*. New York: Penguin/Meridian, 1990.

Ishihara, A., and Levy, H.S. *The Tao of Sex*. New York: Harper & Row, 1968.

Kohn, Livia, ed. *Taoist Meditation and Longevity Exercises*. Ann Arbor, MI: Center for Chinese Studies, University of Michigan, 1989.

Lao Tzu. *Tao Te Ching*. Translated by Gia-fu Feng and Jane English. New York: Random House/Vintage, 1972.

Liberman, Jacob. *Light--Medicine of the Future: How We Can Use It to Heal Ourselves Now*. Santa Fe, NM: Bear & Co., 1991.

Maciocia, Giovanni. *The Foundations of Chinese Medicine*. New York: Churchill Livingstone, 1989.

Maspero, Henri. *Taoism and Chinese Religion*. Amherst: University of Massachusetts Press, 1981.

Ni, Hua-ching. *Tao: The Subtle Universal Law and the Integral Way of Life*. Los Angeles: Shrine of the Eternal Breath of Tao, College of Tao and Traditional Chinese Healing, 1979.

Ni, Hua-ching. *The Book of Changes and the Unchanging Truth*. Los Angeles: Shrine of the Eternal Breath of Tao, College of Tao and Traditional Chinese Healing, 1983.

Painter, John. *The Basic Premise: A Taoist Perspective of Existence*. Arlington, TX: Paper Lantern Publishing, 1982.

Porkert, Manfred. *The Theoretical Foundations of Chinese Medicine*. Cambridge, MA: MIT Press, 1974.

Reuben, David. *Everything You Always Wanted to Know About Sex (But Were Afraid to Ask)*. New York: Bantam, 1971.

Saso, Michael R. *Taoism and the Rite of Cosmic Renewal*. Pullman, WA: Washington State University Press, 1989.

Welch, Holmes, and Seidel, Anna, eds. *Facets of Taoism: Essays in Chinese Religion*. New Haven and London: Yale University Press, 1979.

Willhelm, Helmut. *Heaven, Earth and Man in the Book of Changes*. Seattle and London: University of Washington Press, 1977.

Yang, Jwing-ming. *The Root of Chinese Chi Kung*. Jamaica Plain, MA: Yang's Martial Arts Association, 1989.

Yu, Anthony C., ed. and trans. *The Journey to the West*, vol. I. Chicago and London: University of Chicago Press, 1977.

THE
INTERNATIONAL
HEALING TAO SYSTEM

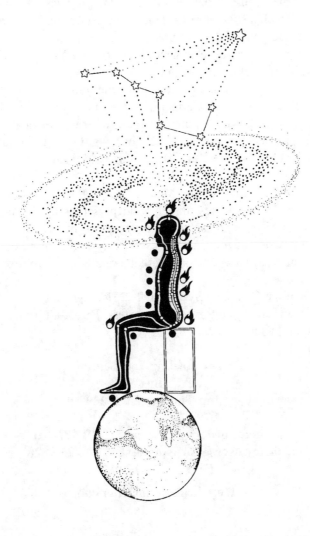

The Goal of the Taoist Practice

The Healing Tao is a practical system of self-development that enables the individual to complete the harmonious evolution of the physical, mental, and spiritual planes the achievement of spiritual independence.

Through a series of ancient Chinese meditative and internal energy exercises, the practitioner learns to increase physical energy, release tension, improve health, practice self-defense, and gain the ability to heal oneself and others. In the process of creating a solid foundation of health and well-being in the physical body, the basis for developing one's spiritual independence is also created. While learning to tap the natural energies of the Sun, Moon, Earth, and Stars, a level of awareness is attained in which a solid spiritual body is developed and nurtured.

The ultimate goal of the Tao practice is the transcendence of physical boundaries through the development of the soul and the spirit within man.

International Healing Tao Course Offerings

There are now many International Healing Tao centers in the United States, Canada, Bermuda, Germany, Netherlands, Switzerland, Austria, France, Spain, India, Japan, and Australia offering personal instruction in various practices including the Microcosmic Orbit, the Healing Love Meditation, Tai Chi Chi Kung, Iron Shirt Chi Kung, and the Fusion Meditations.

Healing Tao Warm Current Meditation, as these practices are also known, awakens, circulates, directs, and preserves the generative life-force called Chi through the major acupuncture meridians of the body. Dedicated practice of this ancient, esoteric system eliminates stress and nervous tension, massages the internal organs, and restores health to damaged tissues.

Outline of the Complete System of The Healing Tao

Courses are taught at our various centers. Direct all written inquiries to one central address or call:

The Healing Tao Center
P.O. Box 578
Jim Thorpe, PA 18229

To place orders please call: (800) 497-1017
Or for overseas customers: (570) 325-9820
Fax: (570) 325-9821

www.healingtaocenter.com

INTRODUCTORY LEVEL I: Awaken Your Healing Light

Course 1: (1) Opening of the Microcosmic Channel; (2) The Inner Smile; (3) The Six Healing Sounds; and (4) Tao Rejuvenation—Chi Self-Massage.

INTRODUCTORY LEVEL II: Development of Internal Power

Course 2: Healing Love: Seminal and Ovarian Kung Fu.

Course 3: Iron Shirt Chi Kung; Organs Exercise and Preliminary Rooting Principle. The Iron Shirt practice is divided into three workshops: Iron Shirt I, II, and III.

Course 4: Fusion of the Five Elements, Cleansing and Purifying the Organs, and Opening of the Six Special Channels. The Fusion practice is divided into three workshops: Fusion I, II, and III.

Course 5: Tai Chi Chi Kung; the Foundation of Tai Chi Chuan. The Tai Chi practice is divided into seven workshops: (1) Original Thirteen Movements' Form (five directions, eight movements); (2) Fast Form of Discharging Energy; (3) Long Form (108 movements); (4) Tai Chi Sword; (5) Tai Chi Knife; (6) Tai Chi Short and Long Stick; (7) Self-Defense Applications and Mat Work.

Course 6: Taoist Five Element Nutrition; Taoist Healing Diet.

INTRODUCTORY LEVEL III: The Way of Radiant Health

Course 7: Healing Hands Kung Fu; Awaken the Healing Hand—Five Finger Kung Fu.

Course 8: Chi Nei Tsang; Organ Chi Transformation Massage. This practice is divided into three levels: Chi Nei Tsang I, II, and III.

Course 9: Space Dynamics; The Taoist Art of Energy Placement.

INTERMEDIATE LEVEL: Foundations of Spiritual Practice

Course 10:
Lesser Enlightenment Kan and Li: Opening of the Twelve Channels; Raising the Soul, and Developing the Energy Body.

Course 11: Greater Enlightenment Kan and Li: Raising the Spirit and Developing the Spiritual Body.

Course 12: Greatest Enlightenment: Educating the Spirit and the Soul; Space Travel.

ADVANCED LEVEL: The Immortal Tao (The Realm of Soul and Spirit)

Course 13: Sealing of the Five Senses.
Course 14: Congress of Heaven and Earth.
Course 15: Reunion of Heaven and Man.

Course Descriptions of The Healing Tao System

INTRODUCTORY LEVEL I: Awaken Your Healing Light
Course 1:

A. The first level of the Healing Tao system involves opening the Microcosmic Orbit within yourself. An open Microcosmic Orbit enables you to expand outward to connect with the Universal, Cosmic Particle, and Earth Forces. Their combined forces are considered by Taoists as the Light of Warm Current Meditation.

Through unique relaxation and concentration techniques, this practice awakens, circulates, directs, and preserves the generative life-force, or Chi, through the first two major acupuncture channels (or meridians) of the body: the Functional Channel which runs down the chest, and the Governor Channel which ascends the middle of the back.

Dedicated practice of this ancient, esoteric method eliminates stress and nervous tension, massages the internal organs, restores health to damaged tissues, increases the consciousness of being alive, and establishes a sense of well-being. Master Chia and certified instructors will assist students in opening the Microcosmic Orbit by passing energy through their hands or eyes into the students' energy channels.

B. The Inner Smile is a powerful relaxation technique that utilizes the expanding energy of happiness as a language with which to communicate with the internal organs of the body. By learning to smile inwardly to the organs and glands, the whole body will feel loved and appreciated. Stress and tension will be counteracted, and the flow of Chi increased. One feels the energy descend down the entire length of the body like a waterfall. The Inner Smile will help the student to counteract stress, and help to direct and increase the flow of Chi.

C. The Six Healing Sounds is a basic relaxation technique utilizing simple arm movements and special sounds to produce a cooling effect

upon the internal organs. These special sounds vibrate specific organs, while the arm movements, combined with posture, guide heat and pressure out of the body. The results are improved digestion, reduced internal stress, reduced insomnia and headaches, and greater vitality as the Chi flow increases through the different organs.

The Six Healing Sounds method is beneficial to anyone practicing various forms of meditation, martial arts, or sports in which there is a tendency to build up excessive heat in the system.

D. Taoist Rejuvenation—Chi Self-Massage is a method of hands-on self-healing work using one's internal energy, or Chi, to strengthen and

rejuvenate the sense organs (eyes, ears, nose, tongue), teeth, skin, and inner organs. Using internal power (Chi) and gentle external stimulation, this simple, yet highly effective, self-massage technique enables one to dissolve some of the energy blocks and stress points responsible for disease and the aging process. Taoist Rejuvenation dates back 5000 years to the Yellow Emperor's classic text on Taoist internal medicine.

Completion of the Microcosmic Orbit, the Inner Smile, the Six Healing Sounds, and Tao Rejuvenation techniques are prerequisites for any student who intends to study Introductory Level II of the Healing Tao practice.

INTRODUCTORY LEVEL II: Development of Internal Power

Course 2: *Healing Love: Seminal and Ovarian Kung Fu; Transforming Sexual Energy to Higher Centers, and the Art of Harmonious Relationships*

For more than five thousand years of Chinese history, the "no-outlet method" of retaining the seminal fluid during sexual union has remained a well-guarded secret. At first it was practiced exclusively by the Emperor and his innermost circle. Then, it passed from father to chosen son alone, excluding all female family members. Seminal and Ovarian Kung Fu practices teach men and women how to transform and circulate sexual energy through the Microcosmic Orbit. Rather than eliminating sexual intercourse, ancient Taoist yogis learned how to utilize sexual energy as a means of enhancing their internal practice.

The conservation and transformation of sexual energy during intercourse acts as a revitalizing factor in the physical and spiritual development of both men and women. The turning back and circulating of the generative force from the sexual organs to the higher energy centers of the body invigorates and rejuvenates all the vital functions. Mastering this practice produces a deep sense of respect for all forms of life.

In ordinary sexual union, the partners usually experience a type of orgasm which is limited to the genital area. Through special Taoist techniques, men and women learn to experience a total body orgasm without indiscriminate loss of vital energy. The conservation and transformation of sexual energy is essential for the work required in advanced Taoist practice.

Seminal and Ovarian Kung Fu is one of the five main branches of Taoist Esoteric Yoga.

Course 3: *Iron Shirt Chi Kung;*
Organs Exercises and
Preliminary Rooting
Principle

The Iron Shirt practice is divided into three parts: Iron Shirt I, II, and III.

The physical integrity of the body is sustained and protected through the accumulation and circulation of internal power (Chi) in the vital organs. The Chi energy that began to circulate freely through the Microcosmic Orbit and later the Fusion practices can be stored in the fasciae as well as in the vital organs. Fasciae are layers of connective tissues covering, supporting, or connecting the organs and muscles.

The purpose of storing Chi in the organs and muscles is to create a protective layer of interior power that enables the body to withstand unexpected injuries. Iron Shirt training roots the body to the Earth, strengthens the vital organs, changes the tendons, cleanses the bone marrow, and creates a reserve of pure Chi energy.

Iron Shirt Chi Kung is one of the foundations of spiritual practices since it provides a firm rooting for the ascension of the spirit body. The higher the spirit goes, the more solid its rooting to the Earth must be.

Iron Shirt Chi Kung I—Connective Tissues' and Organs' Exercise: On the first level of Iron Shirt, by using certain standing postures, muscle locks, and Iron Shirt Chi Kung breathing techniques, one learns how to draw and circulate energy from the ground. The standing postures teach how to connect the internal structure (bones, muscles, tendons, and fasciae) with the ground so that rooting power is developed. Through breathing techniques, internal power is directed to the organs, the twelve tendon channels, and the fasciae.

Over time, Iron Shirt strengthens the vital organs as well as the tendons, muscles, bones, and marrow. As the internal structure is strengthened through layers of Chi energy, the problems of poor posture and circulation of energy are corrected. The practitioner learns the importance of being physically and psychologically rooted in the Earth, a vital factor in the more advanced stages of Taoist practice.

Iron Shirt Chi Kung II—Tendons' Exercise: In the second level of Iron Shirt, one learns how to combine the mind, heart, bone structure, and Chi flow into one moving unit. The static forms learned in the first level of Iron Shirt evolve at this level into moving postures. The goal of Iron Shirt II is to develop rooting power and the ability to absorb and discharge energy through the tendons. A series of exercises allow the student to change, grow, and strengthen the tendons, to stimulate the vital organs, and to integrate the fasciae, tendons, bones, and muscles into one piece. The student also learns methods for releasing accumulated toxins in the muscles and joints of the body. Once energy flows freely through the organs, accumulated poisons can be discharged out of the body very efficiently without resorting to extreme fasts or special dietary aids.

Iron Shirt Chi Kung I is a prerequisite for this course.

Bone Marrow Nei Kung (Iron Shirt Chi Kung III)—Cleansing the Marrow: In the third level of Iron Shirt, one learns how to cleanse and

grow the bone marrow, regenerate sexual hormones and store them in the fasciae, tendons, and marrow, as well as how to direct the internal power to the higher energy centers.

This level of Iron Shirt works directly on the organs, bones, and tendons in order to strengthen the entire system beyond its ordinary capacity. An extremely efficient method of vibrating the internal organs allows the practitioner to shake toxic deposits out of the inner structure of each organ by enhancing Chi circulation. This once highly secret method of advanced Iron Shirt, also known as the Golden Bell System, draws the energy produced in the sexual organs into the higher energy centers to carry out advanced Taoist practices.

Iron Shirt Chi Kung is one of the five essential branches of Taoist Esoteric Practice.

Prior study of Iron Shirt Chi Kung I and Healing Love are prerequisites for this course.

Course 4: *Fusion of the Five Elements,*
Cleansing of the Organs, and
Opening of the Six Special Channels

Fusion of the Five Elements and Cleansing of the Organs I, II, and III is the second formula of the Taoist Yoga Meditation of Internal Alchemy. At this level, one learns how the five elements (Earth, Metal, Fire, Wood,

and Water), and their corresponding organs (spleen, lungs, heart, liver, and kidneys) interact with one another in three distinct ways: producing, combining, and strengthening. The Fusion practice combines the energies of the five elements and their corresponding emotions into one harmonious whole.

Fusion of the Five Elements I: In this practice of internal alchemy, the student learns to transform the negative emotions of worry, sadness, cruelty, anger, and fear into pure energy. This process is accomplished by identifying the source of the negative emotions within the five organs of the body. After the excessive energy of the emotions is filtered out of the organs, the state of psycho/physical balance is restored to the body. Freed of negative emotions, the pure energy of the five organs is crystallized into a radiant pearl or crystal ball. The pearl is circulated in the body and attracts to it energy from external sources—Universal Energy, Cosmic Particle Energy, and Earth Energy. The pearl plays a central role in the development and nourishment of the soul or energy body. The energy body then is nourished with the pure (virtue) energy of the five organs.

Fusion of the Five Elements II: The second level of Fusion practice teaches additional methods of circulating the pure energy of the five organs once they are freed of negative emotions. When the five organs are cleansed, the positive emotions of kindness, gentleness, respect, fairness, justice, and compassion rise as a natural expression of internal balance. The practitioner is able to monitor his state of balance by observing the quality of emotions arising spontaneously within.

The energy of the positive emotions is used to open the three channels running from the perineum, at the base of the sexual organs, to the top of the head. These channels collectively are known as the Thrusting Channels or Routes. In addition, a series of nine levels called the Belt Channel is opened, encircling the nine major energy centers of the body.

Fusion of Five Elements III: The third level of Fusion practice completes the cleansing of the energy channels in the body by opening the positive and negative leg and arm channels. The opening of the Microcosmic Orbit, the Thrusting Channels, the Belt Channel, the Great Regulator, and Great Bridge Channels makes the body extremely permeable to the circulation of vital energy. The unhindered circulation of energy is the foundation of perfect physical and emotional health.

The Fusion practice is one of the greatest achievements of the ancient Taoist masters, as it gives the individual a way of freeing the body of negative emotions, and, at the same time, allows the pure virtues to shine forth.

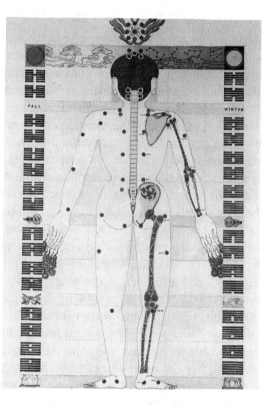

Course 5: *Tai Chi Chi Kung; The Foundation of Tai Chi Chuan*

The Tai Chi practice is divided into seven workshops: (1) the Original Thirteen Movements' Form (five directions, eight movements); (2) Fast Form of Discharging Energy; (3) Long Form (108 movements); (4) Tai Chi Sword; (5) Tai Chi Knife; (6) Tai Chi Short and Long Stick; (7) Self-Defense Applications and Mat Work.

Through Tai Chi Chuan the practitioner learns to move the body in one unit, utilizing Chi energy rather than muscle power. Without the circulation of Chi through the channels, muscles, and tendons, the Tai Chi Chuan movements are only physical exercises with little effect on the inner structure of the body. In the practice of Tai Chi Chi Kung, the increased energy flow developed through the Microcosmic Orbit, Fusion work, and Iron Shirt practice is integrated into ordinary movement, so that the body learns more efficient ways of utilizing energy in motion. Improper body movements restrict energy flow causing energy blockages, poor posture, and, in some cases, serious illness. Quite often, back problems are the result of improper posture, accumulated tension, weakened bone structure, and psychological stress.

Through Tai Chi one learns how to use one's own mass as a power to work along with the force of gravity rather than against it. A result of increased body awareness through movement is an increased awareness of one's environment and the potentials it contains. The Tai Chi practitioner may utilize the integrated movements of the body as a means of self-defense in negative situations. Since Tai Chi is a gentle way of exercising and keeping the body fit, it can be practiced well into advanced age because the movements do not strain one's physical capacity as some aerobic exercises do.

Before beginning to study the Tai Chi Chuan form, the student must complete: (1) Opening of the Microcosmic Orbit, (2) Seminal and Ovarian Kung Fu, (3) Iron Shirt Chi Kung I, and (4) Tai Chi Chi Kung.

Tai Chi Chi Kung is divided into seven levels.

Tai Chi Chi Kung I is comprised of four parts:

a. Mind: (1) How to use one's own mass together with the force of gravity; (2) how to use the bone structure to move the whole body with very little muscular effort; and (3) how to learn and master the thirteen movements so that the mind can concentrate on directing the Chi energy.

b. Mind and Chi: Use the mind to direct the Chi flow.

c. Mind, Chi, and Earth force: How to integrate the three forces into one unit moving unimpeded through the bone structure.

d. Learn applications of Tai Chi for self-defense.

Tai Chi Chi Kung II—Fast Form of Discharging Energy:

a. Learn how to move fast in the five directions.

b. Learn how to move the entire body structure as one piece.

c. Discharge the energy from the Earth through the body structure.

Tai Chi Chi Kung III—Long Form Tai Chi Chuan:

a. Learn the 108 movements form.

b. Learn how to bring Chi into each movement.

c. Learn the second level of self-defense.

d. Grow "Chi eyes."

Tai Chi Chi Kung IV—the Tai Chi Sword.
Tai Chi Chi Kung V—Tai Chi Knife.
Tai Chi Chi Kung VI—Tai Chi Short and Long Stick.
Tai Chi Chi Kung VII—Application of Self-Defense and Mat Work.
Tai Chi Chuan is one of the five essential branches of the Taoist practice.

Course 6: *Taoist Five Element Nutrition; Taoist Healing Diet*
Proper diet in tune with one's body needs, and an awareness of the seasons and the climate we live in are integral parts of the Healing Tao. It is not enough to eat healthy foods free of chemical pollutants to have good health. One has to learn the proper combination of foods according to the five tastes and the five element theory. By knowing one's predominant element, one can learn how to counteract imbalances inherent in one's nature. Also, as the seasons change, dietary needs vary. One must know how to adjust them to fit one's level of activity. Proper diet can become an instrument for maintaining health and cultivating increased levels of awareness.

INTRODUCTORY LEVEL III: The Way of Radiant Health

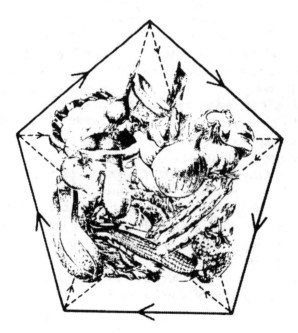

Course 7: *Healing Hands Kung Fu; Awaken the Healing Hand—Five Finger Kung Fu*

The ability to heal oneself and others is one of the five essential branches of the Healing Tao practice. Five Finger Kung Fu integrates both static and dynamic exercise forms in order to cultivate and nourish Chi which accumulates in the organs, penetrates the fasciae, tendons, and muscles, and is finally transferred out through the hands and fingers. Practitioners of body-centered therapies and various healing arts will benefit from this technique. Through the practice of Five Finger Kung Fu, you will learn how to expand your breathing capacity in order to further strengthen your internal organs, tone and stretch the lower back and abdominal muscles, regulate weight, and connect with Father Heaven and Mother Earth healing energy; and you will learn how to develop the ability to concentrate for self-healing.

Course 8: *Chi Nei Tsang; Organ Chi Transformation Massage*

The practice is divided into three levels: Chi Nei Tsang I, II, and III.

Chi Nei Tsang, or Organ Chi Transformation Massage, is an entire system of Chinese deep healing that works with the energy flow of the five major systems in the body: the vascular system, the lymphatic system, the nervous system, the tendon/muscle system, and the acupuncture meridian system.

In the Chi Nei Tsang practice, one is able to increase energy flow to specific organs through massaging a series of points in the navel area. In Taoist practice, it is believed that all the Chi energy and the organs, glands, brain, and nervous system are joined in the navel; therefore, energy blockages in the navel area often manifest as symptoms in other parts of the body. The abdominal cavity contains the large intestine, small intestine, liver, gall bladder, stomach, spleen, pancreas, bladder, and sex organs, as well as many lymph nodes. The aorta and vena cava divide into two branches at the navel area, descending into the legs.

Chi Nei Tsang works on the energy blockages in the navel and then follows the energy into the other parts of the body. Chi Nei Tsang is a very deep science of healing brought to the United States by Master Mantak Chia.

Course 9: *Space Dynamics; The Taoist Art of Placement*

Feng Shui has been used by Chinese people and emperors for five thousand years. It combines ancient Chinese Geomancy, Taoist Metaphysics, dynamic Psychology, and modern Geomagnetics to diagnose energy, power, and phenomena in nature, people, and buildings. The student will gain greater awareness of his own present situation, and see more choices for freedom and growth through the interaction of the Five Elements.

INTERMEDIATE LEVEL: Foundations of Spiritual Practice

Course 10: *Lesser Enlightenment (Kan and Li); Opening of the Twelve Channels; Raising the Soul andDeveloping theEnergy Body*

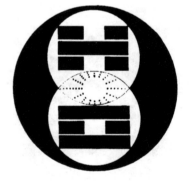

Lesser Enlightenment of Kan and Li (Yin and Yang Mixed): This formula is called *Siaow Kan Li* in Chinese, and involves a literal steaming of the sexual energy (Ching or creative) into life-force energy (Chi) in order to feed the soul or energy body. One might say that the transfer of the sexual energy power throughout the whole body and brain begins with the practice of Kan and Li. The crucial secret of this formula is to reverse the usual sites of Yin and Yang power, thereby provoking liberation of the sexual energy.

This formula includes the cultivation of the root (the Hui-Yin) and the heart center, and the transformation of sexual energy into pure Chi at the navel. This inversion places the heat of the bodily fire beneath the coolness of the bodily water. Unless this inversion takes place, the fire simply moves up and burns the body out. The water (the sexual fluid) has the tendency to flow downward and out. When it dries out, it is the end. This formula reverses normal wasting of energy by the highly advanced method of placing the water in a closed vessel (cauldron) in the body, and then cooking the sperm (sexual energy) with the fire beneath. If the water (sexual energy) is not sealed, it will flow directly into the fire and extinguish it or itself be consumed.

This formula preserves the integrity of both elements, thus allowing the steaming to go on for great periods of time. The essential formula is to never let the fire rise without having water to heat above it, and to never allow the water to spill into the fire. Thus, a warm, moist steam is produced containing tremendous energy and health benefits, to regrow all the glands, the nervous system, and the lymphatic system, and to increase pulsation.

The formula consists of:

1. Mixing the water (Yin) and fire (Yang), or male and female, to give birth to the soul;
2. Transforming the sexual power (creative force) into vital energy (Chi), gathering and purifying the Microcosmic outer alchemical agent;
3. Opening the twelve major channels;
4. Circulating the power in the solar orbit (cosmic orbit);
5. Turning back the flow of generative force to fortify the body and the brain, and restore it to its original condition before puberty;
6. Regrowing the thymus gland and lymphatic system;
7. Sublimation of the body and soul: self-intercourse. Giving birth to the immortal soul (energy body).

Course 11: *Greater Enlightenment (Kan and Li); Raising the Spirit and Developing the Spiritual Body*

This formula comprises the Taoist Dah Kan Li (Ta Kan Li) practice. It uses the same energy relationship of Yin and Yang inversion but increases to an extraordinary degree the amount of energy that may be

Catalog-18

drawn up into the body. At this stage, the mixing, transforming, and harmonizing of energy takes place in the solar plexus. The increasing amplitude of power is due to the fact that the formula not only draws Yin and Yang energy from within the body, but also draws the power directly from Heaven and Earth or ground (Yang and Yin, respectively), and adds the elemental powers to those of one's own body. In fact, power can be drawn from any energy source, such as the Moon, wood, Earth, flowers, animals, light, etc.

The formula consists of:

1. Moving the stove and changing the cauldron;
2. Greater water and fire mixture (self-intercourse);
3. Greater transformation of sexual power into the higher level;
4. Gathering the outer and inner alchemical agents to restore the generative force and invigorate the brain;
5. Cultivating the body and soul;
6. Beginning the refining of the sexual power (generative force, vital force, Ching Chi);
7. Absorbing Mother Earth (Yin) power and Father Heaven (Yang) power. Mixing with sperm and ovary power (body), and soul;
8. Raising the soul;
9. Retaining the positive generative force (creative) force, and keeping it from draining away;
10. Gradually doing away with food, and depending on self sufficiency and universal energy;
11. Giving birth to the spirit, transferring good virtues and Chi energy channels into the spiritual body;
12. Practicing to overcome death;
13. Opening the crown;
14. Space travelling.

Course 12: *Greatest Enlightenment (Kan and Li)*

This formula is Yin and Yang power mixed at a higher energy center. It helps to reverse the aging process by re-establishing the thymus glands and increasing natural immunity. This means that healing energy is radiated from a more powerful point in the body, providing greater benefits to the physical and ethereal bodies.

The formula consists of:

1. Moving the stove and changing the cauldron to the higher center;
2. Absorbing the Solar and Lunar power;
3. Greatest mixing, transforming, steaming, and purifying of sexual

power (generative force), soul, Mother Earth, Father Heaven, Solar and Lunar power for gathering the Microcosmic inner alchemical agent;

4. Mixing the visual power with the vital power;
5. Mixing (sublimating) the body, soul and spirit.

ADVANCED LEVEL: The Immortal Tao
The Realm of Soul and Spirit
Course 13: *Sealing of the Five Senses*

This very high formula effects a literal transmutation of the warm current or Chi into mental energy or energy of the soul. To do this, we must seal the five senses, for each one is an open gate of energy loss. In other words, power flows out from each of the sense organs unless there is an esoteric sealing of these doors of energy movement. They must release energy only when specifically called upon to convey information.

Abuse of the senses leads to far more energy loss and degradation than people ordinarily realize. Examples of misuse of the senses are as follows: if you look too much, the seminal fluid is harmed; listen too much, and the mind is harmed; speak too much, and the salivary glands are harmed; cry too much, and the blood is harmed; have sexual intercourse too often, and the marrow is harmed, etc.

Each of the elements has a corresponding sense through which its elemental force may be gathered or spent. The eye corresponds to fire; the tongue to water; the left ear to metal; the right ear to wood; the nose to Earth.

The fifth formula consists of:
1. Sealing the five thieves: ears, eyes, nose, tongue, and body;
2. Controlling the heart, and seven emotions (pleasure, anger, sorrow, joy, love, hate, and desire);
3. Uniting and transmuting the inner alchemical agent into life-preserving true vitality;
4. Purifying the spirit;
5. Raising and educating the spirit; stopping the spirit from wandering outside in quest of sense data;
6. Eliminating decayed food, depending on the undecayed food, the universal energy is the True Breatharian.

Course 14: *Congress of Heaven and Earth*

This formula is difficult to describe in words. It involves the incarnation of a male and a female entity within the body of the adept. These two entities have sexual intercourse within the body. It involves the mixing of the Yin and Yang powers on and about the crown of the head, being totally open to receive energy from above, and the regrowth of the pineal gland to its fullest use. When the pineal gland has developed to its fullest potential, it will serve as a compass to tell us in which direction our aspirations can be found. Taoist Esotericism is a method of mastering the spirit, as described in Taoist Yoga. Without the body, the Tao cannot be attained, but with the body, truth can never be realized. The practitioner of Taoism should preserve his physical body with the same care as he would a precious diamond, because it can be used as a medium to achieve immortality. If, however, you do not abandon it when you reach your destination, you will not realize the truth.

This formula consists of:
1. Mingling (uniting) the body, soul, spirit, and the universe (cosmic orbit);
2. Fully developing the positive to eradicate the negative completely;
3. Returning the spirit to nothingness.

Course 15: *Reunion of Heaven and Man*

We compare the body to a ship, and the soul to the engine and propeller of a ship. This ship carries a very precious and very large diamond which it is assigned to transport to a very distant shore. If your ship is damaged (a sick and ill body), no matter how good the engine is, you are not going to get very far and may even sink. Thus, we advise against spiritual training unless all of the channels in the body have been properly opened, and have been made ready to receive the 10,000 or 100,000 volts of super power which will pour down into them. The Taoist approach, which has been passed down to us for over five thousand years, consists of many thousands of methods. The formulae and practices we describe in these books are based on such secret knowledge and the author's own experience during over twenty years of study and of successively teaching thousands of students.

The main goal of Taoists:
1. This level—overcoming reincarnation, and the fear of death through enlightenment;
2. Higher level—the immortal spirit and life after death;
3. Highest level—the immortal spirit in an immortal body. This body functions like a mobile home to the spirit and soul as it moves through the subtle planes, allowing greater power of manifestation.

HOW TO ORDER

Prices and Taxes:
Subject to change without notice. New York State residents please add 8.25% sales tax.

Payment:
Send personal check, money order, certified check, or bank cashier's check to:

The Healing Tao Center
P.O. Box 578
Jim Thorpe, PA 18229
To place orders please call: (800) 497-1017
or for overseas customers: (570) 325-9820
Fax: (570) 325-9821
All foreign checks must be drawn on a U.S. bank. Mastercard
Visa, and American Express cards accepted.

Shipping
Domestic Shipping via UPS, requires a complete street address. Allow 3-4 weeks for delivery

✧ **Please call or write for additional information in your area** ✧

www.healingtaocenter.com

T.A.O. - Inc. (Transformational Assistance For Offenders)
James Cappellano, Executive Director
P.O. Box 471, Revere, MA 02151
E-mail: **taojching@msn.com**   Website: **www.tao-inc.org**

Teaching the Healing Tao to perpetrators of violence, many of who are drug and alcohol abusers, addresses the seed causes of crime and brutality. This invokes a deeper understanding of life resulting in personal transformation to a lifestyle of non-harming. It is an ideal self-help method to empower prisoners to help themselves within the confines of prison. Books and letters sent have an exponential effect with prisoners sharing the books and benefits of their practice with each other.

T.A.O. - Inc. is a non-profit organization and provides: an interactive newsletter for prisoners and instructors, a website pen-pal list, volunteer instructors and free books to inmates. The program is sustained through individual cash donations, office supplies and stamps (34¢, 55¢ & $1 are constantly needed). Contributions are tax-deductible. Please make checks payable to T.A.O., Inc. For a free copy of the newsletter please include a first-class stamp with your name and address.

NOTES

NOTES

NOTES

NOTES

NOTES

NOTES

NOTES

NOTES